PERVERSION

Psychoanalytic Perspectives/
Perspectives on Psychoanalysis

Edited by

Dany Nobus and Lisa Downing

First published in 2006 by
H. Karnac (Books) Ltd.
6 Pembroke Buildings, London NW10 6RE

Copyright © 2006 Dany Nobus and Lisa Downing to the edited collection and the individual authors to their contributions.

The right of the contributors to be identified as the authors of this work has been asserted in accordance with §§ 77 and 78 of the Copyright Design and Patents Act 1988.

All rights reserved. No part of this publication may be reproduced, stored in a retrieval system, or transmitted, in any form or by any means, electronic, mechanical, photocopying, recording, or otherwise, without the prior written permission of the publisher.

British Library Cataloguing in Publication Data

A C.I.P. for this book is available from the British Library

ISBN-10: 1 85575 917 9
ISBN-13: 978 1 85575 917 6

Edited, designed and produced by The Studio Publishing Services Ltd,
www.publishingservicesuk.co.uk
E-mail: studio@publishingservicesuk.co.uk

Printed in Great Britain by Biddles Ltd., King's Lynn, Norfolk

10 9 8 7 6 5 4 3 2

www.karnacbooks.com

PERVERSION

CONTENTS

ACKNOWLEDGEMENTS ix

CONTRIBUTORS xi

PART I: PSYCHOANALYTIC PERSPECTIVES 1

INTRODUCTION
Locating perversion, dislocating psychoanalysis 3
Dany Nobus

CHAPTER ONE
Perversion, perversity, and normality: diagnostic and
therapeutic considerations 19
Otto F. Kernberg

CHAPTER TWO
An overview of perverse behaviour 39
Arnold Goldberg

CHAPTER THREE
Perversion and charity: an ethical approach 59
Sergio Benvenuto

CHAPTER FOUR
The problem of inscription and its clinical meaning
in perversion 79
André Michels

CHAPTER FIVE
The perversion of pain, pleasure, and thought:
on the difference between "suffering" an experience
and the "construction" of a thing to be used 99
Nicola Abel-Hirsch

CHAPTER SIX
The structure of perversion: a Lacanian perspective 109
Serge André

CHAPTER SEVEN
Birth, death, orgasm, and perversion: a Reichian view 127
Nick Totton

PART II: PERSPECTIVES ON PSYCHOANALYSIS 147

INTRODUCTION
Perversion, historicity, ethics 149
Lisa Downing

CHAPTER EIGHT
Perversion and French *avant-garde* art 1912–1916 165
Claire Pajaczkowska

CHAPTER NINE
The perverse domination of the fascist and the Sadean master 187
Antonios Vadolas

CHAPTER TEN
The feminist ethics of lesbian sadomasochism 217
Mandy Merck

CHAPTER ELEVEN
Maternal fetishism 241
Emily Apter

CHAPTER TWELVE
Lacan meets queer theory 261
Tim Dean

CHAPTER THIRTEEN
On sexual perversion and transsensualism 323
Vernon A. Rosario

INDEX 343

ACKNOWLEDGEMENTS

"Perversion, perversity, and normality: diagnostic and therapeutic considerations", by Otto F. Kernberg, was originally published in *Psychoanalysis and Psychotherapy*, 1997, 14(1): 19–40. A slightly modified version appeared in Otto F. Kernberg, *Aggressivity, Narcissism, and Self-Destructiveness in the Psychotherapeutic Relationship: New Developments in the Psychopathology and Psychotherapy of Severe Personality Disorders* (Yale University Press, 2004). The text is reprinted here with the kind permission of the author.

"Perversion and charity: an ethical approach", by Sergio Benvenuto, is a revised version of a text that originally appeared as "On perversions" in *Journal for Lacanian Studies*, 2003, 1(2), 243–260.

"The problem of inscription and its clinical meaning in perversion", by André Michels, originally appeared as "Die Problematik der Einschreibung und ihre klinische Bedeutung, unter besonderer Berücksichtigung der Perversionen" in *Texte*, 1996, 53–71, and was translated by Dany Nobus and Lisa Downing for this volume, with the kind permission of the author.

"The structure of perversion: a Lacanian perspective", by Serge André, is the translated transcription of a lecture entitled "La structure de la perversion" presented at the University of Ghent

(Belgium) on 13 January 1990. Before his untimely death in 2003, Serge André looked over the edited transcription and agreed to it being translated into English and included in this collection. The text was translated by Dany Nobus and Lisa Downing for this volume.

"The feminist ethics of lesbian S/M", by Mandy Merck, is reprinted with the kind permission of the author and the Time Warner Book Group UK from Mandy Merck, *Perversions: Deviant Readings* (Virago Press, 1993, pp. 236–266 and pp. 289–293).

"Lacan meets queer theory", by Tim Dean, is reprinted from T. Dean, *Beyond Sexuality* (The University of Chicago Press, 2000, pp. 215–268), with the kind permission of the publisher.

"On sexual perversion and transsensualism", by Vernon A. Rosario, was originally delivered as part of a day-long colloquium at the École Lacanienne de Paris, on 21 October 2000. An earlier version of it was published in French as "Perversion sexuelle et transsensualisme. Historicité des théories, variations des pratiques cliniques", *L'Une-bévue*, 2002, 19, 91–104. The present essay was translated from the French and modified and expanded by the author for the purposes of this volume.

CONTRIBUTORS

Nicola Abel-Hirsch trained as a psychoanalyst at the British Institute of Psychoanalysis. She works in private practice and is the author of *Eros* (2001), and a number of papers on the work of Wilfred Bion.

Serge André (1948–2003) was a psychoanalyst in Brussels and a member of the Ecole de la Cause freudienne. He is the author of *L'imposture perverse* (1993); *What Does a Woman Want?* (1999); and *Flac: A Narrative* (2001). The publication of his annual seminars is under way, with two volumes already available: *Devenir psychanalyste . . . et le rester* (2003); *Le sens de l'holocauste. Jouissance et sacrifice* (2004).

Emily Apter is Professor of French and Comparative Literature at New York University. She is the author of *Feminizing the Fetish: Psychoanalysis and Narrative Obsession in Turn-of-the Century France* (1987); *Continental Drift: From National Characters to Virtual Subjects* (1999); and *The Translation Zone: A New Comparative Literature* (2005). She is co-editor with William Pietz of *Fetishism as Cultural Discourse* (1991).

Sergio Benvenuto is a psychoanalyst practising in Rome and a researcher in psychology and philosophy at the National Research Council (CNR) of Italy. His books include *La strategia freudiana* (1984); *La bottega dell'anima* (with Oscar Nicolaus) (1990); *Capire l'America* (1995); *Dicerie e pettegolezzi* (1999); *Un cannibale alla nostra mensa* (2000); and *Perversioni: Sessualità, Etica, Psicoanalisi* (2005). He is also the editor of *Journal of European Psychoanalysis*.

Tim Dean is Professor of English at the State University of New York, Buffalo, where he teaches queer theory, psychoanalytic theory, and poetics. He is the author of *Gary Snyder and the American Unconscious* (1991), and *Beyond Sexuality* (2000), as well as co-editor of *Homosexuality and Psychoanalysis* (2001). His forthcoming book, on bareback subculture, is titled *Unlimited Intimacy*.

Lisa Downing is Reader in French Discourses of Sexuality in the School of Modern Languages at Queen Mary, University of London. She is the author of *Desiring the Dead: Necrophilia and Nineteenth-Century French Literature* (2003); *Patrice Leconte* (2004); and of numerous articles and chapters on the intersection of sexuality and death in imaginative, psychoanalytic and scientific discourses.

Arnold Goldberg is the Cynthia Oudejeans Harris Professor of Psychiatry at Rush-Presbyterian–St. Luke's Medical Center in Chicago IL. He is a Training and Supervising Analyst at the Institute for Psychoanalysis, and also has a private practice in Chicago. He is the author of numerous papers and books, including *The Problem of Perversion: The View from Self Psychology* (1995); *Being of Two Minds: The Vertical Split in Psychoanalysis and Psychotherapy* (1999); *Errant Selves: A Casebook of Misbehavior* (2001); and, most recently, *Misunderstanding Freud* (2004).

Otto F. Kernberg is the Clinical Director of the Borderline Personality Disorder Research Center at New York-Presbyterian Hospital, Westchester Division. He is also Professor of Psychiatry at the Weill Medical College of Cornell University and a Training and Supervising Analyst at the Columbia University Center for Psychoanalytic Training and Research. He is the author, most recently, of *Contemporary Controversies in Psychoanalytic Theory, Technique and* *their Applications* (2004), and *Aggressivity, Narcissism and Self-Destructiveness in the Psychotherapeutic Relationship* (2004).

Mandy Merck is Professor of Media Arts at Royal Holloway, University of London. She is a former editor of the journal *Screen* and of the Channel 4 series *Out on Tuesday*. Her books include *Perversions: Deviant Readings* (1993); *In Your Face: Nine Sexual Studies* (2000); and *Coming Out of Feminism?* (1998), co-edited with Naomi Segal and Elizabeth Wright. Her next book is an edited collection on the constitution of "American-ness" in US cinema, tentatively titled: *America First: Naming the Nation in US Film*.

André Michels is a psychoanalyst in private practice in Luxemburg. He has published numerous papers on the theory and practice of psychoanalysis in French and German. He is also the editor of *Actualité de l'hystérie* (2001), and (with Peter Müller, Achim Perner, and Claus-Dieter Rath) of *Jahrbuch für Klinische Psychoanalyse*, six volumes of which have appeared since 1998.

Dany Nobus is Senior Lecturer in Psychology and Psychoanalysis at Brunel University, where he directs the MA Programme in Psychoanalysis and Contemporary Society. He is also an Adjunct Professor of Sociology at the University of Massachusetts, Boston and a Visiting Professor of Psychiatry at Creighton University Medical School in Omaha, Nebraska. He is the author of *Jacques Lacan and the Freudian Practice of Psychoanalysis* (2000), and *Knowing Nothing, Staying Stupid: Elements for a Psychoanalytic Epistemology* (with Malcolm Quinn) (2005). He is also the editor of *Key Concepts of Lacanian Psychoanalysis* (1997) and *Journal for Lacanian Studies*.

Claire Pajaczkowska is Reader in Psychoanalysis and Visual Culture, in the Department of Film and Visual Culture, School of Arts, Middlesex University. She is the author of numerous works on feminism, cultural studies and psychoanalysis, including *Perversion* (2000), in the Ideas in Psychoanalysis series published by Icon Books.

Vernon A. Rosario is an Assistant Clinical Professor in the Neuropsychiatric Institute at the University of California, Los Angeles and a child psychiatrist in private practice in Los Angeles. He is the author of *The Erotic Imagination: French Histories of Perversity* (1997), and *Homosexuality and Science: A Guide to the Debates* (2002). He is also co-editor with Paula Bennett of *Solitary Pleasures: The Historical, Literary, and Artistic Discourses of Autoeroticism* (1995) and the editor of *Science and Homosexualities* (1997). His current clinical research is on sexuality and gender identity in transgendered and intersexed children and adults.

Nick Totton is a psychotherapist and trainer in private practice. He is the author of several books, including *The Water in the Glass: Mind and Body in Psychoanalysis* (1998), *Psychotherapy and Politics* (2000) and *Body Psychotherapy: An Introduction* (2003). He is also the editor of *Psychotherapy and Politics International*.

Antonios Vadolas is a PhD student in the School of Social Sciences and Law at Brunel University. His thesis comprises a Lacanian critique of the discursive links between fascism and types of perversion, identified in texts of cinema and social theory.

PART I
PSYCHOANALYTIC PERSPECTIVES

INTRODUCTION

Locating perversion, dislocating psychoanalysis

Dany Nobus

When a happily married man and woman take advantage of the romantic atmosphere of Valentine's day to spice up their sex-life with the help of a tantalizingly ticklish plumed feather, they might feel a touch embarrassed at first by the daringness of their act, yet no one is likely to dispute that they are creatively pursuing the joys of eroticism. Yet, if the same couple were to build sexual confidence as a result of their deeply satisfying experience with the added sensation and subsequently decide to exchange the feather for an entire bird, they might feel less embarrassed about the act, yet there is no doubt that it would be invariably perceived as perverse. Why is using a plumed feather for sexual purposes regarded as "healthy", "normal" and "erotic", whereas employing a whole bird is unequivocally considered "sick", "bizarre", "abnormal", "deviant" and "pathological"? When does the erotic become kinky? How far can our couple extrapolate, quantitatively or qualitatively, on their single feather before entering the realm of perversion? And where shall we situate the bird's cut-off point? Where lies the object's boundary that separates the pleasurable play of normal eroticism from the painful pathology of abnormal perversion? A wing? A drumstick, perhaps?

When an attractive young woman in her mid-twenties decides to enter into a sexual relationship with a poor, stupid, and ugly octogenarian, she is unlikely to attract the envious gaze of her female peer group, but might instead very well attract the sexological label of gerontophilia, authoritatively defined in John Money's book as "a paraphilia of the stigmatic/eligibilic type in which the partner must be parental or grandparental in age (from Greek, *geras*, old age + -philia)" (Money, 1988, p. 202). The best way for the woman to avoid the stigma of pathology would be for the community to believe, or for she herself to create the impression, that the man may very well be stupid and ugly, but definitely not poor, in which case the opprobrium of the "gerontophiliac" will presumably give way to the equally dismissive, yet slightly more socially acceptable category of the "gold-digger". The man, however, will definitely attract the envious gaze of his male peer group, but will simultaneously escape the sexological classifications of paraphilia, if only because there is no proper designation for the reciprocal paraphilic condition of gerontophilia. Money suggests that the opposite of gerontophilia is "paraphilic gerontalism", "in which a younger person must impersonate a parent or grandparent" (*ibid*., p. 202), yet the actual reciprocal condition would of course be "a paraphilia of the stigmatic/eligibilic type in which the adult partner must be so young that s/he could be the person's (grand-)son or (grand-)daughter". Instead of being labelled a pervert, the poor, stupid, and ugly octogenarian may be called "a dirty old man" by those protecting the moral high-ground, but in the eyes of the majority of the male population he will probably just be deemed "lucky". What makes the difference, in this case, between a happy, healthy, male "normophiliac" and a perhaps equally happy, yet distinctly unhealthy female "paraphiliac"? Why is it perverse for a beautiful young woman to enjoy sex with an ugly old man, yet quite normal for the ugly old man to enjoy sex with his beautiful young girlfriend? Is it because the woman in question *actively* pursues an *unusual, counter-(re)productive* and therefore potentially *unnatural* desire, while the man just *passively* accepts his good fortune? Or is it because the old men who have traditionally constructed the pathologizing discourses of perversion do not want to see their own kind being stigmatized in the pages of their sexological handbooks?

However silly the two vignettes described above may be, they capture the gist of the endless (and largely unresolved) debates surrounding the nature and status of perversion that have pervaded psychiatry, sexology, and psychoanalysis since the late nineteenth century. For one, the two examples demonstrate how "perversion"—or what psychiatrists and sexologists, following a suggestion by Stekel (1923, p. 156) now choose to dub "paraphilia"—concerns an issue of human sexuality. Virtually all contemporary mental health care professionals, regardless of their training, expertise, and epistemological stance, agree that a "pervert" is a (predominantly male) human being whose sexuality is problematic (if not for himself at least for his environment), unusual, bizarre, deviant and (in many cases) transgressive and illegal. As such, "perversion" has come to signify those specific modalities of human sexuality that are fully functional (as opposed to the sexual dysfunctions of impotence and orgasmic disorder, for example), yet fundamentally abnormal (in the statistical as well as the medical sense), and which generally affect some or all psycho-social aspects of sexual life; that is to say, involving the components of sexual identity, sexual orientation, sexual fantasy, and sexual behaviour.

As a synonym for "human sexual abnormality", the contemporary notion of "perversion" still largely reflects the way in which the term was appropriated by the medico–legal discourse on sexuality during the late nineteenth century (Lantéri-Laura, 1979), a process which occurred in two consecutive stages. First, the term was transferred from its original socio-religious context, in which "to pervert" (from the Latin *pervertere*) meant "to turn around", "to turn upside down", into the general medical sphere, where "perversion" became a synonym for the fourth, pathological modification of a human function—the others being "diminution", "augmentation", and "abolition". The function of hearing, for example, was considered "perverted" in patients suffering from acoustic hallucinations: it is not that the patient has partial or complete hearing loss, or that his hearing has become sharper, but that he is hearing "bad" instead of "good" things. Likewise, if the function is appetite, it can be considered "perverted" when the patient is neither excessively hungry nor excessively aversive to food, but insists on eating things that are not "normally" part of the human diet, such as worms, insects, or excrement. Following its implantation in the medical domain, "perversion" was then applied by French and German medico–legal experts to the budding research field of human sexuality. Arnold Davidson (2001) has argued that the scientific extension of the term "perversion" into the sexual realm, which occurred around the same time in France and Germany, took place against the background of a medico–philosophical conception of the human sexual instinct as the essential function of reproduction, responsible for the preservation of the species. Davidson has recognized this perspective in the medico–psychological texts of Paul Moreau de Tours (1844–1908), whose book *Des aberrations du sens génésique* (Moreau de Tours, 1877) was not only the first psychiatric textbook on perversion but also the main source of inspiration for Krafft-Ebing's seminal *Psychopathia Sexualis*, the first edition of which appeared in 1886. Yet it can be traced further back to the work of Pierre Cabanis (1757–1808), whose distinction between the conservative instincts (for self-preservation) and the sexual instincts (for reproduction) influenced a plethora of French and German scholars, including Freud, throughout the nineteenth and early twentieth century (Bercherie, 1991, pp. 167–169; Cabanis, 1843; Valas, 1986, pp. 10–11). Once the human sexual instinct was identified as the reproductive function, the known types of physio-pathological modification were applied to human sexuality, which gave rise to Krafft-Ebing's notorious four-fold classification of the "anomalies of the sexual instinct": sexual anaesthesia (a diminution of the sexual function to the point of it being completely abolished; a lack of sexual interest altogether), hyperaesthesia (the increase of the sexual function, as in nymphomania), paradoxia (the sexual instinct expressing itself outside the period of its normal occurrence, as in the case of our "dirty old man" above, or in the case of over-sexed children) and paraesthesia (when the sexual instinct does not seek satisfaction in a reproductive act, i.e., when it defies the intrinsic purpose of its function) (Krafft-Ebing, 1886). The last category included the perversions proper and showed the greatest phenomenological variety of all, as Krafft-Ebing (and other specialists) would prove in a steady stream of ever-expanding descriptions of perverse sexual acts (Oosterhuis, 2000).

This definition of perversion as an aberration of the sexual instinct, in which the reproductive purpose of the human sexual function is literally perverted, posed an unexpected problem when applied to actual instances of human sexual behaviour. Indeed, psychiatrists recognized that their definition might be too encompassing and insufficiently distinctive, in so far as "mild" instances of non-reproductive sexual behaviours were acknowledged as a regular feature of the sexual menu of most "normal" human beings. In order to address this issue, Krafft-Ebing and his fellow sexologists introduced a further distinction between a "true-blue" pervert (*appellation contrôlée*), whose sexual instinct is radically and permanently diverted from the normal procreative act and who, therefore, enjoys only non-reproductive activities, and a recreational pervert, who is not a real pervert at all, but someone who indulges in "perversities" merely to increase the pleasure and satisfaction of coitus-orientated sexual behaviour. This conceptual and clinical separation between the "abnormal pervert" and the "normal pervert" (Karpman, 1954, pp. 416–457) continued to inform scientific accounts of perversion until well into the twentieth century, and I am quite confident that it still lurks in many regions of contemporary scholarship, even those whose mast-head clearly says "progressive", "liberal-minded" and "cutting-edge".

The nineteenth-century definition of the human sexual instinct as the reproductive function, and the associated description of perversion as a "permanent", "exclusive" and "fixated" deviation from the normal procreative aim of sexuality, also provided Freud with the necessary backdrop for his first essay, on "the sexual aberrations", of his *Three Essays on the Theory of Sexuality* (Freud, 1905d). Freud admitted that the "normal sexual aim is regarded as being the union of the genitals in the act known as copulation" (*ibid.*, p. 149), yet he also conceded that "even in the most normal sexual process we may detect rudiments which, if they had developed, would have led to the deviations described as "perversions" (*ibid.*). As a result of this, he, too, adopted the sexological distinction between "pathological perversion" and "perverse variations of the normal function":

> In the majority of instances the pathological character in a perversion is found to lie not in the *content* of the new sexual aim but in its relation to the normal. If a perversion, instead of appearing merely *alongside* the normal sexual aim and object, and only when

circumstances are unfavourable to *them* and favourable to *it*—if, instead of this, it ousts them completely and takes their place in *all* circumstances—if, in short, a perversion has the characteristics of exclusiveness and fixation—then we shall usually be justified in regarding it as a pathological symptom. [*ibid.*, p. 161]

The reader of these lines cannot fail to note the tentativeness of Freud's tone and his ostensible hesitancy in making general statements: "in the *majority* of instances", "we shall *usually* be justified" ... Like his contemporaries, Freud knew very well that there are instances in which the pathological character *does* lie in the content of the new sexual aim, *even* when *it* appears merely *alongside* the normal sexual aim and object. Freud would have felt hard-pressed to entertain the idea that there are cases of paedophilia that are not pathologically perverse. And most of us today would still feel uncomfortable disputing that our aforementioned bird-lovers, even when they eventually opt for normal, genital intercourse, have definitely crossed the line of subsidiary or preliminary sexual experimentation and sailed straight towards the land of the sick.

What we are encountering here is the intervention of a sociocultural standard of ethico-legal acceptability, which has (often implicitly) confounded all of the purportedly value-free taxonomies of sexual perversion, whether sexological, psychiatric, or psychoanalytic. No matter how hard scholars have tried to avoid discussing perversion with reference to moral principles, they have generally failed to live up to the expectations of an "objective" and "neutral" science. Of course, it may be noted, here, that the nineteenth-century alignment of the human sexual instinct and the reproductive function was already predicated upon a restrictive moral–theological code that distinguishes between "natural", "evolutionarily advantageous", "divinely sanctioned" and therefore "acceptable" sexuality (a genital act between two consenting partners belonging to the opposite sex), and "counter-natural", "evolutionary disadvantageous", "devilish" and therefore "unacceptable" sexuality (everything else). And so the medico–legal fathers of sexology perhaps forfeited *a priori* the possibility of ever arriving at an objective scientific theory of perversion. Yet, when Freud argued, against the sexologists, that the human sexual instinct is neither unified nor intrinsically geared towards genital copulation and reproduction, but is a fundamentally partial drive functioning on the precepts of a polymorphously perverse disposition (*ibid.*, p. 191), he none the less maintained a belief in "the normal sexual aim of copulation". With the notion of a constitutional polymorphous perversity that presides over the sexual disposition of every human being, Freud would not seem to need a concept of sexual normality in order to describe and explain perversion. For, if we accept Freud's idea, perversion is simply synonymous with the permanent and unrestrained expression of the human sexual instinct. Perversion is no longer a deviation from normality, here. Rather, normality (if such a thing exists) is always a deviation from perversion! If we take Freud seriously, perversion does not require much explanation, since it is part and parcel of each individual's original sexual make-up. Instead, the real Freudian question would be "Why and how does anyone ever become sexually normal?". Of course, Freud and his followers (as most papers in the first part of this book show) have never really been satisfied with the idea that the "pervert", rather than "becoming" one, has always been one and simply stayed that way. And so the radical psychoanalytic question as to why and how someone would develop into a normal sexual being shifted again to the (much less radical) issue of why and how a pervert remains entrenched in the original mechanisms of polymorphous perversity.

Why did Freud re-introduce the criterion of "sexual normality" as a measure for diagnosing sexual perversion, and as a benchmark for distinguishing between real, professional perverts and fake amateurs? The question shall remain unanswered, here, but I do want to point out that Freud's unnecessary recourse to a concept of normality, and all its associated moral–theological meanings, seems to indicate, yet again, the difficulty (impossibility, perhaps) of formulating a perspective on perversion without embracing a set of social, moral, and legal values. Some theorists, such as Money, make explicit reference to a socio-culturally endorsed value system in order to distinguish the normal from the abnormal. Paraphilia, for Money, is

> a condition occurring in men and women of being compulsively responsive to and obligatively dependent on an *unusual and personally or socially unacceptable stimulus*, perceived or in the ideation and imagery of fantasy, for optimal initiation and maintenance of erotosexual arousal and the facilitation of orgasm. [Money, 1988, p. 216, italics added]

Paraphilia is explicitly set against "normophilia", which is defined as "a condition of being erotosexually in conformity with the standard as dictated by customary, religious, or legal authority" (*ibid.*, p. 214). The paraphiliac, in other words, is someone whose sexuality is disturbingly non-conformist, defiantly recalcitrant, intolerably dissident. Ironically, the American Psychiatric Association decided to substitute "paraphilia" for "perversion" from the *DSM-III* onwards because the latter was believed to have too many pejorative moral connotations (American Psychiatric Association, 1980).

Non-conformist progressive psychoanalysts such as Robert Stoller and Joyce McDougall have gone out of their way to expose the flaws and fallacies of theories of perversion that take their lead from a socio-moral concept of sexual normality, yet they themselves have often surreptitiously re-imported such a concept through the backdoor. Here is Stoller at his most polemical:

> *Normal* has no meaning ... Where is that normal person or aspect? No analyst has ever recorded such a case, met one as a patient, known one in oneself, one's loves, one's relatives, one's friends, one's colleagues. I need not elaborate this point; it is obvious, universally known, and usually denied, especially by psychoanalytic theorists of perversion. [Stoller, 1991, pp. 41–42]

Since Stoller is a psychoanalytic theorist of perversion himself, but one of the few who has not denied the uselessness of the notion of "normality", he reminds his readers of his own, earlier definition of perversion:

> *Perversion*, the erotic form of hatred, is a fantasy, usually acted out but occasionally restricted to a daydream ... It is a habitual, preferred *aberration* necessary for one's full satisfaction, primarily motivated by hostility ... To create the greatest excitement, the perversion must also portray itself as an act of risk taking. [*ibid.*, p. 37, italics added]

Immediately following this self-quotation, Stoller sums up his definition of perversion in one sentence: "In other words, [perversion is] *sin*" (*ibid.*)

Since the 1960s, Joyce McDougall has similarly criticized people in her own profession for uncritically espousing moral criteria in their theories of perversion. Instead of "perversion", McDougall has favoured the allegedly less pejorative term "neo-sexuality", thereby emphasizing the creative potential of the condition: "To emphasize the innovative character and intensity of the investments involved, I refer to deviant heterosexualities and deviant homosexualities as "neosexualities" (McDougall, 1995, p. 174). It should be noted, here, that the adjective "deviant" is not a remnant of a previous discourse, but a central component of McDougall's own theorizing . . .

If "perversion" is inseparable from a regulatory discursive system of normality, then it could be argued that those theorizing and diagnosing the condition merely pathologize, as authoritative extensions of the ruling ideology, those behaviours that threaten the sustainability of the system, with a view to their segregation and eradication. Such an outlook might throw into doubt the actual existence of the pervert, as an incarnated entity or structure, outside the institutionalized, hegemonic procedures of truth-production, but it would not by definition exclude the possibility of perversion *per se*, as a dissident, revolutionary sexual power. This is what Jonathan Dollimore has rendered as the "insurrectionary nature of the perversions":

> [P]erversion is a refusal or attempted subversion of those organizing principles of culture which are secured psychosexually, principles which include sexual difference, the law of the father, and heterosexuality. This perspective usually assumes that these struggles are contained, or at least can be explained, *by and within* psychoanalysis. However, another line of enquiry finds in the insurrectionary nature of the perversions a challenge not only to the Oedipal law, but to the entire Oedipal drama as a theory: perversion comes to challenge the integrity of the psychoanalytic project itself. [Dollimore, 1991, p. 198)

Although Dollimore's claim, here, that perversion epitomizes a subversive challenge to psychoanalysis (and, we may add, to psychiatry and sexology) has been criticized by De Lauretis (1994) and others for its lack of persuasive argumentation, I believe that the idea is worth pursuing, if only because of the way in which most psychoanalysts have simultaneously maintained a concept of perversion and expressed a certain disappointment with the inadequacy of their theories.

Although my discussion until now has already highlighted various contentious issues with regard to our understanding of sexual perversion, I have only scratched the surface of the muddy waters into which sexologists, psychiatrists, and psychoanalysts have often put themselves. Indeed, I have thus far only broached the difficulty of delineating perversion and separating it from what is non-perverse. A much more challenging assignment concerns the explanation of perversion and the definition of the principles and goals of its treatment. Needless to say, treatment principles often follow aetiological considerations, yet in many cases the perceived urgency of a therapeutic intervention has overruled the absence of clear-cut explanations, and in some cases the hypothesis of an acquired developmental trauma (a "vandalized love-map", in Money's terminology) has not excluded the "policing" of perversion (Tsang, 1995) via the administration of anti-androgens (Money and Lamacz, 1989). Given the fact that the pervert is sometimes also a "sex-offender", psychotherapists often find themselves torn between confidentiality and disclosure (if the patient has not been apprehended) or between the role of a health care professional and that of a law-enforcer (when working in a prison setting or for the probation services) (Schorsch, Galedary, Haag, Hauch, & Lohse, 1996). And in light of the lingering definition of perversion as "sexual deviance", therapists are also inevitably confronted with the ethical dilemma of working on behalf of the patient (making him better equipped to cope with his sexuality, despite the social stigmas and the pathologizing discourses) or on behalf of society (helping him to redirect his sexuality towards the existing standards of normality and thus making him conform to the socio-cultural and legal norm).

As far as explanations are concerned, most contemporary psychoanalysts rely on one (or both) of the two basic paradigms of perversion in Freud's work, on the one hand that of the partial drives (the polymorphously perverse disposition) and their vicissitudes (Freud, 1915c) and on the other hand that of castration anxiety (the mechanism of disavowal and fetishism) (Freud, 1927e; Rey-Flaud, 1994). Although the paradigms are not mutually exclusive, they have often proved difficult to reconcile (if reconciliation is needed), and they were also relativized by Freud himself as distinctive explanatory frameworks for perversion. In addition, the difficulty with the drive-paradigm is that it potentially makes every human being into a pervert, whereas the fetishism-paradigm excludes one half of the population from the joys and sorrows of perversion, merely by virtue of their not having a penis. Since the day Freud barred women from fetishism (not from sadism and masochism, it must be noted), feminists have of course redressed the balance (see Gamman & Makinen, 1994) and overturned psychoanalytic phallocentrism. Some authors have also explored the possibility of an entirely separate strand of female perversions (Kaplan, 1991) and others have even invented a completely new, specifically female, perverse psychic conflict that is played out between the woman-*cum*-mother and her child (Beier, 1994; Kelly, 1993). The most contentious point of much contemporary theorizing about women and perversion seems to be the question, first raised by Helene Deutsch (1930), although as a postulate rather than a debatable idea, whether women are masochistic, and perhaps more "naturally" so than men (Caplan, 1993).

From the following chapters in this book, in which authors draw out the implications of Freud's work, but also of various other traditions in the history of psychoanalysis (Kleinian, object-relations, self-psychology, Lacanian, Reichian), in order to formulate their own explanations of perversion, the reader will be able to gauge the diversity of opinion and the extent to which contemporary psychoanalytic views have developed since Freud. Personally, I do not believe in the possibility (nor in the necessity, for that matter) of these divergent opinions being combined into a comprehensive, unified psychoanalytic theory of perversion. Apart from the fact that each of the authors in this section substantiates Dollimore's point that the perversions constitute a subversive challenge for psychoanalysis, "disrupting that from which they derive, that which is invoked to explain them" and proving "the undoing of the theory which contains" them (Dollimore, 1991, p. 197), the variety of different perspectives, much like Freud's own complex and inconsistent explanations of male homosexuality (Lewes, 1988), may also show that perversion is not one, but a multitude of structures, behaviours, fantasies, identities, and orientations—and perhaps an eternally shifting, yet none the less determined structural attempt at dislocating any type of sexual structuration.

Over and beyond the particular challenges posed by perversion to the theoretical and clinical doctrine of psychoanalysis, perhaps psychoanalysts are also challenged in their explanatory power because thoroughbred perverts, assuming that they actually exist, rarely come to their attention. Indeed, Freud's own cardinal "Contribution to the study of the origin of sexual perversions" (Freud, 1919e) was, by his own account, "based on the exhaustive study of six cases (four female and two male)": "two ... cases of obsessional neurosis", "a third case which at all events exhibited clearly marked individual traits of obsessional neurosis", a fourth case "of straightforward hysteria", and a fifth patient "who had come to be analysed merely on account of indecisiveness in life" and who "would not have been classified at all by coarse clinical diagnosis, or would have been dismissed as 'psychasthenic'" (ibid., pp. 182–183). As Strachey noted, Freud seemed to have forgotten about the sixth case, but we can reasonably assume that he would probably have told his reader if the patient in question was a genuine pervert. What Freud reported, here, without reluctance or disappointment, seems to echo many a psychoanalyst's personal experience: "real" perverts do not seek the help of mental health professionals, whether psychoanalytically or otherwise disposed. Indeed, the rule is so commonly accepted by the psychoanalytic community that whenever a member claims to have a huge clientele of genuine perverts, he himself is regarded as a strange, possibly perverse exception. Moreover, psychoanalysts have come up with good reasons why perverts do not seek out their company. For as long as they manage to cope with the marginalizing and stigmatizing finger of their social environment, and for as long as they keep themselves out of the hands of the law, they are generally happy, satisfied people. Why would our "pseudo-avisodomic" couple above, assuming that they are true perverts, decide to ask for help if they achieve full sexual satisfaction in the company of their bird? And if they do fall victim to social, moral, or legal repression, would they really feel that a psychoanalyst might be able to do anything to lift the burden, without taking away the satisfaction that they perhaps barely feel to possess?

In the face of poor clinical materials, the erotic literary imagination has always provided a welcome source of relief. This is not only true for psychoanalysts, but for all theorists of perversion since the dawn of sexology at the end of the nineteenth century. Rather than relying on his own patient population, Krafft-Ebing constructed his two central perversions of sadism and masochism with reference to the literary works of de Sade and von Sacher-Masoch. In similar fashion, psychoanalysts throughout the twentieth century have elaborated and illustrated their theories of perversion in constant allegiance to the great (and sometimes minor) works of literature, thereby wilfully exchanging their clinical research laboratory for the museums of artistic representation. The psychoanalytic literature on perversion is no longer satisfied with references to Sade and Masoch, but has explored the works of Flaubert, Baudelaire, Huysmans, Zola, Gide, Klossowski, and Jouhandeau (to name but the French contingent) in search of the central coordinates of perversion, or in search of critical evidence to demonstrate that psychoanalytic theories of perversion have been formulated in allegiance to the stylistic and narrative procedures of a particular literary period (Apter, 1991; Castanet, 1999; Downing, 2003; Jadin, 1995; Rosario, 1997). In this way, too, perversion can be seen to dislocate psychoanalysis, in so far as it has driven practitioners outside the familiar setting of their consultation room into the province of the artistic creation, with more methodological difficulties and epistemological pitfalls that any psychoanalyst is usually willing to risk.

All of this shows that perversion (as the name for a certain type of human sexual pathology and its underlying structure) challenges the doctrine of psychoanalysis at three separate levels: clinically, perversion highlights the moral basis of the diagnostic enterprise, thus raising important issues about the ethics of diagnosis in general, and it also defies the purportedly value-free principles governing the direction of the psychoanalytic treatment; theoretically, perversion exposes the limits of the central explanatory paradigms of psychoanalysis, most notably the Oedipus- and castration complexes, the dualistic models of the drives, and the fundamental principles of psychic functioning (the reality principle, the pleasure principle, and that which lies beyond); epistemologically, perversion is the touchstone for the logic of psychoanalytic discovery, since it rarely seems to enter the clinical laboratory, thus forcing the psychoanalyst to consider alternative, "applied" methodologies for probing its source and origin within the confines of artistic representation. Since psychoanalysis is one of the few, perhaps the only contemporary clinical discourse that insists on maintaining the name "perversion" (as the papers in Part I of this book make clear)—despite its pejorative connotations and despite the fact that it has been abandoned by psychiatry and sexology—psychoanalysts are perhaps in a privileged position to acknowledge and confront its "insurrectionary nature", not with a view to taming it but with the purpose of measuring the intellectual significance of insurrection as such. And the fact that psychoanalysts have decided to maintain the term "perversion" is perhaps in itself a sufficient indication that they are also prepared to "be challenged" and "be dislocated", at each of the three levels of their disciplinary practice.

References

American Psychiatric Association (ed.) (1980). *Diagnostic and Statistical Manual of Mental Disorders* (3rd edn). Washington, DC: American Psychiatric Association.

Apter, E. (1991). *Feminizing the Fetish: Psychoanalysis and Narrative Obsession in Turn-of-the-Century France*. Ithaca, NY: Cornell University Press.

Beier, K. M. (1994). *Weiblichkeit und Perversion. Von der Reproduktion zu Reproversion*. Stuttgart: Gustav Fischer.

Bercherie, P. (1991)[1983]. *Genèse des concepts freudiens. Les fondements de la clinique 2*. Paris: Editions Universitaires.

Cabanis, P. J. G. (1843)[1802]. *Rapports du physique et du moral chez l'homme*. Paris: Fortin-Masson.

Caplan, P. J. (1993)[1985]. *The Myth of Women's Masochism*. Toronto: University of Toronto Press.

Castanet, H. (1999). *La perversion*. Paris: Anthropos.

Davidson, A. (2001)[1987]. How to do the history of psychoanalysis: A reading of Freud's *Three Essays on the Theory of Sexuality*. In: *The Emergence of Sexuality: Historical Epistemology and the Formation of Concepts* (pp. 66–92). Cambridge, MA: Harvard University Press.

De Lauretis, T. (1994). *The Practice of Love: Lesbian Sexuality and Perverse Desire*. Bloomington, IN: Indiana University Press.

Deutsch, H. (1930). The significance of masochism in the mental life of women (Part 1: "Feminine" masochism and its relation to frigidity). *International Journal of Psycho-Analysis*, 11: 48–61.

Dollimore, J. (1991). *Sexual Dissidence: Augustine to Wilde, Freud to Foucault.* Oxford: Clarendon Press.
Downing, L. (2003). *Desiring the Dead: Necrophilia and Nineteenth-Century French Literature.* Oxford: Legenda.
Freud, S. (1905d). Three Essays on the Theory of Sexuality. *S.E.,* 7: 123–243.
Freud, S. (1915c). Instincts and their vicissitudes. *S.E.,* 14: 109–140.
Freud, S. (1919e). "A child is being beaten": A contribution to the study of the origin of sexual perversions. *S.E.,* 17: 175–204.
Freud, S. (1927e). Fetishism. *S.E.,* 21: 149–157.
Gamman, L., & Makinen, M. (1994). *Female Fetishism: A New Look.* London: Lawrence and Wishart.
Jadin, J.-M. (1995). *André Gide et sa perversion.* Strasbourg: Arcanes.
Kaplan, L. J. (1991). *Female Perversions: The Temptations of Emma Bovary.* New York: Doubleday.
Karpman, B. (1954). *The Sexual Offender and His Offenses: Etiology, Pathology, Psychodynamics and Treatment.* New York: Julian Press.
Kelly, M. (1993). The smell of money: Mary Kelly in conversation with Emily Apter. In: E. Apter and W. Pietz (Eds.), *Fetishism as Cultural Discourse* (pp. 352–362). Ithaca, NY: Cornell University Press.
Krafft-Ebing, R. von (1886). *Psychopathia sexualis. Eine klinisch-forensische Studie.* Stuttgart: Ferdinand Enke.
Lantéri-Laura, G. (1979). *Lecture des perversions. Histoire de leur appropriation médicale.* Paris: Masson.
Lewes, K. (1988). *The Psychoanalytic Theory of Male Homosexuality.* New York: Simon & Schuster.
McDougall, J. (1995). *The Many Faces of Eros: A Psychoanalytic Exploration of Human Sexuality.* London: Free Association.
Money, J. (1988). *Gay, Straight, and In-Between: The Sexology of Erotic Orientation.* New York: Oxford University Press.
Money, J., & Lamacz, M. (1989). *Vandalized Lovemaps: Paraphilic Outcome of Seven Cases in Pediatric Sexology.* Buffalo, NY: Prometheus Books.
Moreau de Tours, P. (1877). *Des aberrations du sens génésique.* Paris: J. B. Baillière & Fils.
Oosterhuis, H. (2000). *Stepchildren of Nature: Krafft-Ebing, Psychiatry and the Making of Sexual Identity.* Chicago, IL: The University of Chicago Press.
Rey-Flaud, H. (1994). *Comment Freud inventa le fétichisme ... et réinventa la psychanalyse.* Paris: Payot.
Rosario, V. A. (1997). *The Erotic Imagination: French Histories of Perversity.* New York: Oxford University Press.

Schorsch, E., Galedary, G., Haag, A., Hauch, M., & Lohse, H. (1996). *Perversion als Straftat. Dynamik und Psychotherapie.* 2., unveränderte Auflage. Stuttgart: Ferdinand Enke Verlag.

Stekel, W. (1923)[1908]. *Störungen des Trieb- und Affektlebens. Vol. 1: Nervöse Angstzustände und ihre Behandlung* (vierte vermehrte und verbesserte Auflage). Berlin-Wien: Urban & Schwarzenberg.

Stoller, R. J. (1991). The Term Perversion. In: G. I. Fogel & W. A. Myers (Eds.), *Perversions and Near-Perversions in Clinical Practice: New Psychoanalytic Perspectives* (pp. 36–56). New Haven, CT: Yale University Press.

Tsang, D. C. (1995). Policing "Perversions": Depo-Provera and John Money's new sexual order. *Journal of Homosexuality, 28*(3/4): 397–426.

Valas, P. (1986). Freud et la perversion I. *Ornicar?, 39*: 9–50.

CHAPTER ONE

Perversion, perversity, and normality: diagnostic and therapeutic considerations

Otto F. Kernberg

What follows is an overview of my current efforts to develop a classification of the broad spectrum of disorders traditionally grouped under the heading of sexual perversions, and now referred to as paraphilias. I hope to provide a diagnostic frame helpful both in establishing prognosis and in developing guidelines for treatment of these patients. Because of space limitations, I must present my views in brief, and, at times, categorical ways, in spite of which I hope to convey my conviction that this field is still wide open in terms of our contemporary knowledge and therapeutic approaches.

The problem of "normality" in the sexual realm

It is practically unavoidable that culturally determined value judgements and ideological cross-currents influence our evaluation of human sexual life. When the concept of "normality" is considered to be equivalent to average or predominant patterns of behaviour, treatment may become a matter of promoting "adjustment", and we lose the usefulness of normality as a standard of health. On the other hand, if the concept of normality refers to an ideal pattern of behaviour, we run the risk of imposing ideologically motivated measures. If, in ideologically motivated opposition to conventional notions, we proclaim the equivalent nature of any and all manifestations of human sexuality, we may miss significant, even crippling, limitations of sexual enjoyment and of the integration of eroticism and emotional intimacy. An "objective", "scientific" view would appear as ideal, if the human sciences were not, in turn, contaminated by cultural biases and conventionality.

I believe that psychoanalysis, with all its limitations as an instrument for the evaluation of human behaviour, provides an optimal combination of non-conventional exploration of the intimate life of the individual, with an evaluation of how sexual patterns enrich, modify, or restrict the potential for enjoyment, autonomy, adaptation, and effectiveness. The unavoidable ideological and cultural biases imbedded in psychoanalytic theory have been challenged, and have tended to self-correct over time. It is sobering, however, to recall that only a hundred years ago psychoanalysis was at one with a scientific community that regarded masturbation as a dangerous form of pathology, that our literature lumped homosexuality and sexual perversions together for many years without a focus on their significantly differentiating features, and that scarcely any psychoanalytic studies of the affective nature of sexual excitement have been undertaken since Freud's pathbreaking discoveries (Freud, 1905d).

Clinical and psychoanalytic criteria of normality

I would propose as the most general criteria for normality, the capacity to enjoy a broad range of sexual fantasy and activity, to integrate such a broad range of sexual involvement with the capacity for a tender, loving relationship within which the mutuality of sexual pleasure, of the emotional relationship, and of idealization of that relationship reinforce each other (Kernberg, 1995). By implication, these criteria imply control over the aggressive components of sexual behaviour to the extent of eliminating from this spectrum hostile, dangerous, exploitive intentions and behaviour expressed in the sexual encounter. These criteria do not exclude autoerotic sexual activity that is neither dangerous nor actively self-destructive.

From a psychoanalytic viewpoint, normality implies the integration of early, pregenital fantasy and activity with genital fantasy and activity, the capacity to achieve sexual excitement and orgasm in intercourse, and the capacity to integrate into sexual fantasy, play, and activity aspects of the sadistic, masochistic, voyeuristic, exhibitionistic, and fetishistic components of polymorphous perverse infantile sexuality. In fact, from a psychoanalytic viewpoint, the integration of polymorphous perverse infantile sexuality into a tender and loving relationship within which mutual emotional gratification and idealization reinforce and are reinforced by the sexual encounter, reflects an optimum of psychological freedom and normality.

At a deeper level, the capacity for full sexual enjoyment implies the integration of preoedipal and archaic oedipal object relations into the advanced oedipal relationship enacted in a sublimatory way. In every love relationship, an unconscious fantasy life is activated that maintains the idealization of sexual excitement, and gratification in both polymorphous perverse infantile play and fantasy and in sexual intercourse. An aggressive element is an essential component of normal sexual excitement, and, in fact, contributes crucially to the full development of eroticism (Stoller, 1979; Kernberg, 1991).

What these proposed criteria for normality leave out is the question of the exclusiveness, the duration of the relationship with, and the gender of, the sexual object; and it is in this area that a scientific approach is particularly vulnerable to contamination by ideological and cultural bias. There are good theoretical reasons for considering a stable heterosexual relationship to be a normal outcome of the oedipal conflicts and their sublimatory resolution in adulthood. However, biological determinants and a primary intrapsychic bisexuality may powerfully influence object choice and, under the influence of cultural factors, co-determine different paths to object choice in both genders (Kernberg, 1992).

Definition and psychodynamics of perversion

Clinically, perversions can be defined as stable, chronic, rigid restrictions of sexual behaviour characterized by the expression of one of the polymorphous perverse infantile partial drives as an obligatory, indispensable precondition for the achievement of sexual excitement and orgasm (Kernberg, 1989b, 1991; Stoller, 1975). All sexual perversions combine severe inhibition of sexual freedom and flexibility with idealization of the sexual scenario derived from the particular polymorphous perverse infantile drive that is dominant. The diagnosis of sexual sadism, masochism, voyeurism, exhibitionism, fetishism, and transvestism is not difficult if one keeps this definition in mind. It also applies to cases of episodic perversion in which dissociative phenomena permit the expression of perversion alternating with and completely split off from conventional, though somewhat impoverished, sexual behaviour.

From a descriptive viewpoint, perversions can be classified along a continuum of severity, according to the degree to which aggression dominates a particular perversion and dangerous, even life-threatening behaviour invades the potential object relationship within which the perversion becomes manifest. In addition to the potentially dangerous manifestations of the severe cases of the various perversions already mentioned, such aggressive infiltration is particularly marked in the cases of paedophilia, and the rarer perversions of zoophilia, coprophilia, urophilia, and, of course, necrophilia.

From a psychodynamic viewpoint, a consensus has been evolving in the psychoanalytic literature dividing the perversions into two major groups according to the level of severity of the illness. Here the work of André Lussier (1982) on fetishism, I believe, has become a standard reference. Both levels of pathology have in common the rigidity of the perverse pattern, the development of an idiosyncratic "scenario" linked to the particular perversion, and a remarkable inhibition of sexual fantasy and exploration outside the realm of this scenario. An important common feature of perverse scenarios at the higher or less severe level is the containment of aggression; in fact, the recruitment of aggression at the service of love and eroticism. This containment provides a sense of safety as well as an intense erotic experience within which a fusion with the object in sexual excitement and orgasm is reinforced by the sadomasochistic fusion, the internal identification as perpetrator and victim. This higher level of the psychodynamic structure of perversions is best described by the classical constellation originally conceptualized by

Freud (1905d, 1919e, 1927e, 1940e). Here, the fixation at a partial drive serves the purpose of denial of castration anxiety by means of the enactment of a pregenital sexual scenario as a defence against oedipal genital conflicts. Genital sexuality is feared as a realization of oedipal wishes; there is severe castration anxiety linked to powerful aggressive components of the positive oedipal complex; all sexual interaction becomes a symbolic enactment of the primal scene; and whatever regression has occurred to preoedipal levels of development has a clearly defensive nature. Preoedipal aggression is not a major component of the aggressive aspects of the oedipal conflict in these patients. Clinically, perversions at this level appear typically in the context of neurotic personality organization, that is, in patients with obsessive-compulsive, depressive-masochistic, and hysterical personality disorders (Kernberg, 1996).

The second, more severely pathological level of organization of perversion, described in more recent psychoanalytic literature (Chasseguet-Smirgel, 1984; Lussier, 1982), has a typical two-layer defensive organization, with oedipal conflicts condensed with severe preoedipal conflicts whose aggressive aspects dominate the clinical picture. These perversions are typically found in patients with borderline personality organization. In fact, the characteristic psychodynamics of borderline personality organization I had described on the basis of the experience of the psychotherapy research project of the Menninger Foundation (Kernberg, 1975) turned out to overlap dramatically with the dynamics of the severe level of perversion described by André Lussier (1982) in his study on fetishism.

This severe level of perversion appears in two major personality organizations: first, the ordinary borderline personality organization with dominant reliance upon splitting mechanisms affecting ego and superego, and a combination of sadistic and masochistic features both in sexual behaviour and in the general character structure, reflecting the abnormal "metabolism" of aggression; second, the narcissistic personality structure, in which the perverse scenario is infiltrated by the aggressive aspects of the condensed oedipal and preoedipal conflicts. In the case of the syndrome of malignant narcissism, the aggressive drive derivatives are integrated into the grandiose pathological self with consequent dangerous sadistic deterioration of the perversion (Kernberg, 1989a).

In the psychoanalytic literature on perversion, narcissistic features have been suggested as a general characteristic. From a clinical perspective, however, it is extremely important to differentiate patients with "narcissistic conflicts" in a non-specific sense from those whose specific narcissistic character structure has particular implications for prognosis and treatment. The anal and oral regression at this severe level of perversion is reflected in "zonal confusion" (Meltzer, 1977). Zonal confusion refers to the symbolic equivalence of all protruding or invaginated sexual areas of both genders, with corresponding condensation of oral, anal, and genital strivings. Unconscious anal fantasies dominate the sexual life of these patients, with "faecalization" of genital organs and genital intercourse. The anal-sadistic regression of these patients involves an attack on, and destruction of, object relations, while the oral regression is reflected in the oral-sadistic expression of envy and destructive greed.

The most dramatic combination of all these dynamics can be found in the perversions of narcissistic personalities where the specific dynamics described by Chasseguet-Smirgel (1984) are dominant: the unconscious fantasy of a faecal penis and a faecal vagina, the unconscious equalization of genders and ages, a primitive idealization of the perversion linked with the denial of castration, and the tendency to universal equalization of all object relations and all sexual activities that, in the process, become "spoiled", "digested", and "expelled" as faeces. Here, the perverse scenario may succeed in containing the aggression, but the aggressive impulses overshadow the libidinal ones, threatening to neutralize erotic excitement and to corrode or destroy the object relation. The defensive idealization of the perversion may express itself in a stress on aesthetic qualities of both the sexual object and the sexual scenario, reflecting both the defence against, and the expression of, the image of faecalized sexual organs, and an illusory surface adaptation in the form of "as if" relationships.

From a psychostructural viewpoint, the pathology of perversion may be classified into six major groups, that I shall briefly describe from least to most severe, in terms of the pathology of object relations and the sexual life of these patients, as well as their prognosis for psychoanalytic treatment (Kernberg, 1992). First, perversions in the context of neurotic personality organization: all these cases have excellent prognosis with psychoanalytic treatment. The presenting obligatory "scenarios" vary from patient to patient, but are typically clearly defined. As in all perversions, they are an indispensable precondition for the gratification of the patient's sexual needs and the achievement of orgasm. The idealization of the perversion goes hand in hand with sexual inhibition in other areas. The patient's capacity for object relatedness is deep and solid, and oedipal conflicts clearly predominate in the transference.

Second, perversions at the level of borderline personality organization: here we find typically the condensed preoedipal–oedipal conflicts with dominance of preoedipal aggression. Specific perversions at this level usually are combined with a pathology of object relations that makes the scenario of these perversions less clearly circumscribed or differentiated, and rather blending with the general character pathology of these patients. It is important to differentiate a generalized polymorphous perverse infantile sexuality in these cases, that is, a chaotic combination of many infantile perverse trends, from the consolidation of a typical perversion. Paradoxically, the chaotic combination of polymorphous perverse impulses significantly improves the prognosis for borderline patients treated with psychoanalytic psychotherapy or psychoanalysis. By contrast, a subgroup of borderline patients with severe inhibition of all eroticism carries a poor prognosis because, as the borderline personality organization is resolved in treatment, the sexual inhibition tends to become more intense. A specific perversion in these cases is prognostically favourable, although the treatment is, of course, more complex than in the case of neurotic personality organization.

Third, a perversion combined with a narcissistic personality disorder: these cases are particularly difficult to treat because the idealization of the perversion is condensed with the idealization of the pathological grandiose self in a defensive structure that is often difficult to dismantle.

As in the borderline cases, it is important to differentiate generalized, polymorphous, perverse infantile behaviour from a specific perversion. Such polymorphous, perverse behaviour in narcissistic patients may reflect a replacement of object relations by the compulsive use of sexual behaviour to relieve anxiety.

Fourth, perversion in cases of malignant narcissism: here ego syntonic aggression may infiltrate the particular perversion, and transform it into a sadomasochistic pattern that may objectively endanger both patient and partner. In fact, it is because the syndrome of malignant narcissism is at the very limit of treatability that it deserves to be classified as a fourth group. Here, we encounter the more severe and dangerous forms of sadism, masochism, paedophilia, and anally regressed perversions such as coprophilia.

A fifth group is constituted by the antisocial personality disorder in a strict sense, as originally described by Cleckley (1941), and currently studied by Robert Hare (Hare & Hart, 1995; Hare, Hart, & Harpur, 1991), Michael Stone (1980), and myself (1992). These cases [not accurately conceptualized, in my view, in the *DSM-IV* classification (APA, 1994)] represent the most severe type of narcissistic character disorder, in which superego development has failed entirely. A consolidated perversion in an antisocial personality always has to be considered as extremely dangerous until proven otherwise: here we find sexual murderers and serial killers, in whom the remnants of eroticism are totally overshadowed by extreme forms of primitive aggression. The prognosis of any presently known treatment for the antisocial personality proper is practically zero.

Finally, in a sixth group are perversions as part of psychotic personality organization, in schizophrenic illness, and, particularly, pseudopsychopathic schizophrenia (Kernberg, 1996). A perversion in a schizophrenic illness might be psychopharmacologically controlled if the schizophrenic illness itself responds to such treatment.

Perversion and perversity

The syndrome of perversity in the transference consists, in essence, in the recruitment of eroticism and love at the service of aggression. The fact that this important and severe form of negative therapeutic reaction should have been equated with perversion as a specific sexual pathology is due to a semantic confusion to which, unfortunately, psychoanalytic literature has contributed. In fact, some of the most important contributors to the study of both perversion and perversity, such as Herbert Rosenfeld (1987), Donald Meltzer (1977), and Wilfred Bion (1968, 1970), tend to use the terms *perversion* and *perversity* in the transference as equivalent, or, at least, do not differentiate sufficiently clearly between them. In addition, in both British and French psychoanalytic literature one finds the term *perverse structure*, that implies a particular and unique personality organization or psychodynamic constellation characteristic of perversion that, as we have seen, does not do justice to the broad spectrum of personality organizations in which perversion appears.

At the same time, the same authors I just referred to have given the most specific description of the syndrome of perversity in the transference. This may occur in patients who suffer from a perversion, but it occurs as well in patients without a sexual perversion, such as, characteristically, patients with narcissistic personality disorder or the syndrome of malignant narcissism.

I have pointed in earlier work to some patients' efforts to extract goodness, concern, and love from the analyst precisely to destroy them, in an envious feast that goes beyond the need to demonstrate the analyst's incompetence and impotence, and instead expresses the wish to destroy the sources of the analyst's equanimity and creativity. Because the syndrome of perversity appears particularly in patients with severe narcissistic personality structure who, at the same time, may present a perversion in a narrow sense, both syndromes may go together.

The diagnostic evaluation of patients with sexual perversions

What follows summarizes briefly the diagnostic questions derived from what has been said so far. First, in all cases it is important to evaluate completely the patient's sexual life, activities, fantasies, daydreams, dreams, and masturbatory fantasies, as well as the fantasies linked with actual sexual interactions. The patient's sexual preferences and their continuity or discontinuity, and the entire spectrum of his or her sexual responses need to be evaluated. Second, the basic aspects of core sexual identity, dominant object choice, gender role identity, and intensity of sexual desire should be evaluated, as these four features jointly define the patient's sexual identity

(Kernberg, 1995). Third, it is important to evaluate the linkage between the patients' tender and loving capabilities and their sexual life: does he or she have the capacity to fall in love? Is there a capacity to integrate love and eroticism, or are they usually or always dissociated from each other? Are sexual inhibitions present, and, if so, what type and severity? Fourth, what is the predominant personality constellation, the level of severity of personality pathology? The presence or absence of pathological narcissism and the syndrome of malignant narcissism, the quality of object relations, the presence of antisocial features, the degree to which the expression of aggression is pathological and egosyntonic, should all be assessed.

And fifth, we are interested in the evaluation of the couple, in cases where marital or couple conflicts are an essential aspect of the presenting symptom. Under particularly complex circumstances, a combined team of a specialist in personality disorders, a couples' or family therapist, and a sex therapist may jointly make a strategic analysis of diagnosis and treatment, a methodology that I have found very helpful in especially difficult cases.

From all these data flow the essential considerations that will determine prognosis and treatment: the level of personality organization and predominant personality disorder, the quality of object relations, the presence or absence of pathological narcissism, the severity of the disturbance of expressed aggression, the organization and level of superego functioning, the degree of sexual freedom, and the particular prognostic implications for the relationship of a couple, as elaborated by Henry Dicks (1967).

Psychoanalysis and psychoanalytic psychotherapy

Psychoanalysis is the treatment of choice for sexual perversions in patients with a neurotic personality organization, and for patients with a narcissistic personality disorder who have sufficient capacities for anxiety tolerance, impulse control, and sublimatory functioning, and who are able to maintain reasonable stability with regard to work, social adaptation, and some degree of emotional intimacy.

Psychoanalysis proper is usually contra-indicated for patients with the syndrome of malignant narcissism, but there are exceptions to this rule. Patients with a combined hysterical–histrionic personality disorder also may respond to psychoanalytic treatment, as do some patients with paranoid and schizoid personalities, although the large majority of patients with borderline personality organization should be treated by psychoanalytic psychotherapy rather than by standard psychoanalysis.

The overall prognosis is strongly influenced by the extent to which antisocial features are present (i.e., the relative integrity of the superego) as well as by the capacity for maintaining object relations in depth over a period of time, neurotic as they may be, as long as they are not purely parasitic or exploitive (Kernberg, 1992).

The most essential aspect of the treatment of perversion, in my experience, is the focus on the activation or enactment of the underlying unconscious fantasies in the transference. The patient may attempt to draw the analyst into being a spectator of the patient's relationship with the external object of his perverse scenario, thus fulfilling aspects of the perverse fantasy itself as it involves the analyst. It is, of course, important to explore the unconscious fantasies experienced by the patient in the course of enactment of the perverse scenario, as long as the analyst remains aware that this is only a preliminary exploration of what eventually will become a transference enactment.

For example, a patient was impotent with his wife, while fully potent in sexual engagements with other women, who had to submit to him in a masochistic scenario. He would tie them up and have them carry out self-demeaning acts that symbolically represented their humiliation and his total control over them. In contrast, he behaved like a shy little boy with his wife. With me he displayed almost a caricature of submissiveness: he became interested in psychoanalytic ideas, sought out my published papers, and, in an overblown identification with me, used the ideas he found there to argue with his friends and colleagues about alternative psychological theories.

In the course of the treatment, as the image of a violent father who was sexually promiscuous and a tyrant at home came into focus, the patient gradually became aware of his inhibited behaviour as a fear of rebelling against such a violent father, and of the fantasy that the only way to rebel against him would be a violent, bloody overthrow. An underlying fantasy slowly emerged in which he would sexually submit to powerful father representatives and thus solve the conflict with the father by becoming his sexual love object.

What made the analysis of the transference particularly difficult was the surface, "as if" submission of the patient that protected him against an underlying wish for a dependent, sexual relation with me. The analysis of that underlying wish was interfered with by the patient's "guessing" my thoughts, and immediately accepting what he thought were my theories, fully endorsing them in intellectual speculations that raised serious doubts in my mind whether all this had any emotional meaning. It dawned upon me after a period of time that I had become the bound-up victim of the patient's sadistic control in the transference; his ready acceptance of what he thought was my train of thought, his way of disorganizing my thinking had led to a temporary paralysis of all work in the sessions. The analysis of that "as if" quality in his relationship with me eventually induced a sense of confusion and intense anxiety in the patient, and the emergence of fear of me as a threatening father who wanted to keep him in the role of a little child, and stood ready to castrate him if he were to penetrate his wife, who represented unconsciously the oedipal mother.

This case illustrates the "as if" quality of perversion in the transference even under conditions of neurotic personality organization. The patient presented a typical sadistic scenario in the context of an overall psychological functioning that was remarkably normal in terms of the emotional relationship with his wife as well as his capacity for effective and mature object relations in his work and social life. He had initiated the treatment with a hidden idealization of his perversion that he only gradually dared to express in the sessions.

The following case, in contrast, presented a sadistic perversion in the context of a borderline personality organization, a narcissistic personality structure, and polymorphous perverse infantile features strongly reflected in conscious anal sadistic fantasies and behaviours that infiltrated the patient's entire life. He was obese as a result of overeating, abused multiple drugs, and, while he was very effective in his business, the chaotic style of his business management created continual problems with associates and subordinates.

This patient was able to have intercourse with his wife only if he subjected her to physical abuse. Her willingness to undergo significant pain was a precondition for his achieving orgasm. What brought him to treatment was that she became unwilling to continue this situation, not because of the nature of their sexual interaction *per se*, but because of aspects of his behaviour that she considered disgusting, such as not cleaning himself appropriately after defecating, to the extent that small segments of faeces would be found in their bedclothes. He would almost never flush the toilet, and as he used hand towels for cleaning his genitals and anal region, his wife felt obliged to hide the towels that she herself would use.

In the course of his analysis, the patient talked in an apparently free way about present reality and fantasy, childhood memories, and emotional reactions to the analyst and his office, in what might be described as an almost "perfect" style of free association, speculating about deep motivations of his behaviour, and dramatically displaying affects that shifted from moment to moment. What was striking was his "throwing out" ideas and feelings without assuming any responsibility for them, in what impressed me as a thoughtless spreading of chaotic material for me to pick up and make sense of.

It may already become apparent to the reader that it was as if little pieces of excrement were being thrown around, in a general devaluation and equalization of all thoughts, feelings, and behaviours that, unconsciously, were the equivalent of covering the analyst and his office with excrement while the patient maintained an illusional superiority as the producer of this digested material. Any interest I expressed in any particular material would lead to immediate ironic speculations of the patient regarding what I now had in mind, and a derogatory attack on my capacity to understand him. Implicit in these enactments was the fantasy that the analyst would make sense of the faecal chaos, and in so doing bolster the patient's belief in his own superiority. These developments could eventually be understood as the symbolic equivalents of the sadistic attacks on his wife as an essential requirement for orgasmic climax.

Only the systematic interpretation and working through of this massive defence expressed in the patient's non-verbal communications and my countertransference led to the underlying hatred of the oedipal couple, his effort to deny the possibility of a sexual relation that could be mutually gratifying and creative, and from which he felt excluded forever. He, in contrast, identified with a sadistic and mutually destructive couple, and replicated this relationship in the transference.

It is essential in the psychoanalytic treatment of perversion, I believe, to focus on the areas of significant inhibition in the patient's sexual life. The patient's efforts to draw the analyst into an excited, voyeuristic countertransference engagement may permit a subtle acting out of the transference rather than leading to further understanding. The perverse scenario, with its tightly knit construction and defensive idealization, may successfully resist the analysis of the repressed, dissociated, or projected fears and fantasies against which the perverse scenario serves as a defence. In contrast, the areas of sexual inhibition that perverse patients strenuously attempt to avoid exploring may provide a direct link to the repressed conflicts around castration anxiety and preoedipal aggression that are condensed with archaic oedipal material.

For example, a patient with a masochistic perversion was able to achieve sexual excitement and orgasm only when he was controlled by two women who would force him into a subservient position while showing their excitement and desire for him when he was physically immobilized and sexually stimulated. This man experienced a total lack of sexual interest in the woman whom he loved and with whom he lived without any sexual intimacy over several years.

At one point I began to focus our work upon the almost bizarre splitting between his intense sexual life with any pairs of women he could induce to participate in his particular scenario, and the total lack of sexual desire for the woman who loved him and was willing to live with him in spite of his avoidance of sexual engagement with her. My efforts to explore what he felt in the relation with his girlfriend, whom he described as objectively attractive and who, in the distant past, had been one of a pair of women engaged in the masochistic scenario with him, at first created intense anxiety and perplexity in the patient. Any effort to explore his thoughts or feelings when she would undress in his presence would lead him to an expression of boredom, to the extent of falling asleep in the sessions when that subject was mentioned. It gradually emerged that he did not dare to depend on his girlfriend because of the unconscious conviction that all women would try to sadistically control and attempt to "brainwash" him if he became dependent on them. Therefore, only intense sexual encounters orchestrated by him with women for whom he had no feelings permitted him any sexual gratification. Fantasies of swimming underwater and being approached by a huge fish that wanted to swallow him up, memories of humiliating experiences with his mother taking him to doctors because she thought his penis was distorted toward one side, alternated with the patient's attempt to talk about the relationship with his girlfriend while, in fact, he could only describe her behaviour towards him. He was completely oblivious of any feeling that he might have in relation to her, or what her internal life might be: the patient described himself as feeling as if a glass wall separated him from her.

The emergence of this strange combination of frightening fantasies of oral castration interspersed with total repression of thoughts and feelings about his girlfriend, and the patient's irresistible somnolence in the analytic hours, permitted me to become aware that some parallel development was occurring in his relationship with me. His empty talk about the actual interchanges with his girlfriend produced a somnolence in me that at various points made me struggle with the temptation to fall asleep. I observed that the patient's attitude on the couch was one of growing tension, and his associations became more and more strenuous efforts to carry out the task of understanding what happened in the relationship with his girlfriend. It was as if he were in some kind of cognitive–behavioural therapy, carrying out concrete tasks of fantasy formation rather than simply letting himself depend on his relationship with me.

In short, powerful narcissistic defences against dependency on a maternal object (because such dependency would mean a dangerous sexualization leading to castration) were the gradual discoveries in the transference that led to the understanding of the idealized masochistic perversion. In that masochistic scenario his erect penis emerged as a most desirable object in the context of humiliation and physical restraint. He allayed his deep fears of castration by arranging for the dependent position to be forced upon him while eliminating any emotional involvement with his paired partners.

He did not dare to depend on his girlfriend, because of his oedipal prohibition condensed with the fear of an invasive, castrating, preoedipal mother, and he did not dare to depend on me, replicating the same relationship. To depend on me would imply a sexual submission to the oedipal father, and to be castrated by an invasive mother at the same time. This case, I believe, illustrates the indirect road to understanding the perversion by focusing on the patient's inhibitions as the corresponding conflicts become activated in the transference. In my somnolence, I was identifying with the patient's masochistic submission to, and avoidance of, a dangerous mother, while his intellectualized speculations implied his identification with an omnipotent and castrating mother.

Patients with borderline personality organization and narcissistic personality structure invariably stir up countertransference responses that are not easy to use effectively. But the analyst's skill in the therapeutic use of his countertransference disposition will be put to serious test in the analysis of all patients with perversions, including those with neurotic personality organization where the idealization of the perverse scenario may be particularly effective. The analyst may either be seduced by fascination with the perverse scenario, or so unable to identify with it that the patient seems strange and robotlike. Countertransference defences against a threatened identification with the protagonist of a perverse scenario interfere with the appropriate subtlety in empathizing with both the patient's and his object's emotional experiences.

The analyst's access to his or her own polymorphous perverse infantile erotic fantasies and memories is as important in these cases as is the ability in general to identify with both homosexual and heterosexual impulses of patients of both genders. Obviously, when the main purpose of the perverse scenario is a destructive attack on the object, such an identification with the patient's aggressive impulses may be particularly anxiety producing in the analyst. It is important, when the patient actually fantasizes or potentially enacts dangerous perverse behaviours, to apply the general principles for limit setting that are useful in life-threatening situations of borderline patients (Kernberg, Selzer, Koenigsberg, Carr, & Appelbaum, 1989). Concretely, if the patient's sexual behaviour would create a life endangering situation for himself or his object, or threaten the patient or his object with severe social and legal consequences of that behaviour, it is necessary to make it a precondition for analysis that the patient refrain from such behaviours.

For example, one female patient who would walk at night into a dangerous part of town with the wish to prostitute herself as an enactment of masochistic submission to sadistic men, objectively created potential dangers for herself that required limit setting to that behaviour before analysing its unconscious meanings. As I pointed out in earlier work (1993), such limit setting is not only perfectly compatible with analytic work but may, in fact, be an essential precondition for it, if the meaning attached to the analyst's limit-setting behaviour is immediately taken up in the analysis of the transference.

The combination of such limit setting and an analytic approach to its implications in the sessions may provide not only the necessary space to resolve the particular symptomatology, but also the freedom for the analyst to engage in an exploration of his countertransference, where either excitement or disgust with the particular behaviour of the patient may provide important clues to its meanings. For example, one adult male patient's paedophilic perversion, his sexual seduction of little girls, could be analysed only after prohibiting the enactment of the perversion. Limit setting created a safe countertransferential space that permitted the analyst to identify with the patient's excitement with the hairless genitals of little girls that reassured him against the frightening aspect of adult women's genitals, while their submission to him powerfully confirmed there was no danger of castration involved with being faced with a split genital on the body's surface.

The issue of technical neutrality is important in the analytic treatment of patients with sexual perversion because the patient's defiant assertion of the perversion as being much superior to ordinary sexual encounters may provoke the analyst into a countertransference defence of "normal" sex. As mentioned earlier, when discussing normality, it is unavoidable that the analyst's general value system regarding the protection of life, the opposition to destructiveness and self-destructiveness, and the affirmation of enjoyment and mutuality in a sexual experience be considered basic values that might rightly, I believe, limit technical neutrality. Within the context of such broad values, it seems important to me that the analyst honestly tolerate very different ways and solutions to a patient's dilemma of how to deal with love and the erotic dimension of life. If a patient is happy with a perversion that provides a safe island of ecstasy within a reasonably gratifying and effective context of love and work, there is no reason why the analyst should urge, even implicitly, a different sexual pattern on the patient. If patients seek treatment for their perversion, it is because there are aspects of the perverse solution that are eminently unsatisfactory to them, that limit them both in their erotic experience and love life, and that they intuitively sense as a restrictive imprisonment.

The counterpart of perversion is the deadening of the erotic, a frequent and insufficiently recognized pathology of daily life. That erotic ecstasy, together with the ecstasy stimulated by works of art and religious experiences constitute, as Georges Bataille (1957) has suggested, a fundamental counterbalance to ordinary life focused on work and conventional social existence, would seem an important contribution of psychoanalysis that tends quite often to be neglected.

While the various types of ecstasy all derive, as Freud suggested, from erotic sources, the psychoanalyst's personal experience confirming that erotic dimension of life would seem an important precondition for treating all sexual inhibitions, including the perversions. I would not have found it necessary to say this, had clinical experience not shown how often the antierotic aspects of conventional culture influence psychoanalytic perspectives. The capacity for an object relation in depth is a fundamental precondition for a full erotic capability: this is a contribution from psychoanalysis that, while originally presented in a theoretical frame by Freud, has found an important confirmation in our knowledge regarding the deterioration of the erotic capability under conditions of severe destruction of internalized object relations in severe narcissistic personality structures. The recovery of both normal object relations and the capacity for a synthesis of love and the erotic is a crucial treatment goal with borderline patients. It is also a realistic goal in the treatment of the perversions.

References

American Psychiatric Association (1994). *Diagnostic and Statistical Manual of Mental Disorders* (4th edn). Washington, DC: American Psychiatric Association.

Bataille, G. (1957). *L'Erotisme*. Paris: Minuit.
Bion, W. R. (1968). *Second Thoughts: Selected Papers on Psychoanalysis*. New York: Basic Books.
Bion, W. R. (1970). *Attention and Interpretation*. London: Heinemann.
Chasseguet-Smirgel, J. (1984). *Creativity and Perversion*. New York: Norton.
Cleckley, H. (1941). *The Mask of Sanity*. St. Louis, MO: Mosby.
Dicks, H. V. (1967). *Marital Tensions*. New York: Basic Books.
Freud, S. (1905d). Three Essays on the Theory of Sexuality. *S.E., 7*: 123–243. London: Hogarth.
Freud, S. (1919e). "A child is being beaten": A contribution to the study of the origin of sexual perversions. *S.E., 17*: 175–204. London: Hogarth.
Freud, S. (1927e). Fetishism. *S. E., 21*: 149–157. London: Hogarth.
Freud, S. (1940e). Splitting of the ego in the process of defence. *S.E., 23*: 271–278. London: Hogarth.
Hare, R., & Hart, S. (1995). Commentary on antisocial personality disorder. In: J. Livesley (Ed.), *The DSM-IV Personality Disorders* (pp. 127–134). New York: Guilford Press.
Hare, R., Hart, S., & Harpur, T. (1991). Psychopathy and the *DSM-IV* criteria for antisocial personality disorder. *Journal of Abnormal Psychology, 100*: 391–398.
Kernberg, O. F. (1975). *Borderline Conditions and Pathological Narcissism*. New York: Jason Aronson.
Kernberg, O. F. (1989a). The narcissistic personality disorder and the differential diagnosis of antisocial behavior. *Psychiatric Clinics of North America: Narcissistic Personality Disorder, 12*: 553–570.
Kernberg, O. F. (1989b). A theoretical frame for the study of sexual perversions. In: H. P. Blum, E. M. Weinshel, & F. R. Rodman (Eds.), *The Psychoanalytic Core: Festschrift in Honor of Dr. Leo Rangell* (pp. 243–263). New York: International Universities Press.
Kernberg, O. F. (1991). Sadomasochism, sexual excitement, and perversion. *Journal of the American Psychoanalytic Association, 39*: 333–362.
Kernberg, O. F. (1992). *Aggression in Personality Disorders and Perversion*. New Haven, CT: Yale University Press.
Kernberg, O. F. (1993). The psychotherapeutic treatment of borderline patients. In: J. Paris (Ed.), *Borderline Personality Disorder: Etiology and Treatment* (pp. 261–284). Washington, DC: American Psychiatric Press.
Kernberg, O. F. (1995). *Love Relations: Normality and Pathology*. New Haven, CT: Yale University Press.

Kernberg, O. F. (1996). A psychoanalytic theory of personality disorders. In: J. F. Clarkin & M. F. Lenzenweger (Eds.), *Major Theories of Personality Disorders* (pp. 106–140). New York: Guilford Press.

Kernberg, O. F., Selzer, M. A., Koenigsberg, H. W., Carr, A. C., & Appelbaum, A. H. (1989). *Psychodynamic Psychotherapy of Borderline Patients*. New York: Basic Books.

Lussier, A. (1982). *Les Déviations du désir: Etude sur le fétichisme*. Paris: Presses Universitaires de France.

Meltzer, D. (1977). *Sexual States of Mind*. Strath Tay, Perthshire: Clunie Press.

Rosenfeld, H. (1987). *Impasse and Interpretation*. London: Tavistock.

Stoller, R. J. (1975). *Perversion: The Erotic Form of Hatred*. Washington, DC: American Psychiatric Press.

Stoller, R. J. (1979). *Sexual Excitement*. New York: Pantheon.

Stone, M. H. (1980). *The Borderline Syndromes*. New York: McGraw-Hill.

CHAPTER TWO

An overview of perverse behaviour

Arnold Goldberg

Introduction

The nature of perverse behaviour becomes an issue both because of its moral position in society as well as because of its personal relevance to psychopathology. In the latest viewpoint of American psychiatry, perversions no longer exist (American Psychiatric Association, 1994). They have been replaced by a less offensive set of words: the paraphilias. These are defined as preferences for, or addictions to, a specific sexual practice, and so this redefinition removes the moral component that is usually understood to be necessarily connected to perversion. I feel that psychoanalysis needs to define the perversions primarily on the basis of the data of psychoanalysis, and so it should try not to mimic the descriptive efforts of psychiatry.

Psychiatry has surely bypassed psychoanalysis in its efforts to reorganize and classify psychopathology. The manuals of diagnosis up to and including *DSM-IV* are careful collections of descriptive categories that aim to carve out fairly distinct entities that conform, for the most part, to observables and reports. The present state of psychiatric nomenclature is one of description or, perhaps more felicitously, that of phenomenology. Such a choice for categorization is, of course, dictated by a lack of a more clear-cut set of causal determinants of illness. And the accepted classification of infectious diseases is an ideal counter example, wherein the descriptive efforts are all secondary to the specific agents leading to specific maladies. The hope in psychiatry seems to lie more or less in the direction of concentrating upon neuro-anatomical and/or biochemical foci of disease and thereby ultimately to better delineate categories that will go beyond mere behaviour and unreliable subjective experiences.

Psychoanalysis has a different database. It should, thereupon, have a different form of classification. However, the disease entities that reign in analytic texts are ordinarily either descendants from categories passed on from the writings of Sigmund Freud or else are newer ones borrowed from textbooks of psychiatry. Among the first that we list as examples are the hysterias, and, among the second, the borderline states. Each of such efforts to capture disease entities strains to encompass both the descriptions of psychiatry, along with some special contributions of psychoanalysis. A good example of the resultant lack of congeniality in diagnostic categorization between psychiatry and psychoanalysis is that of the familiar "anxiety disorder", which is handled in one manner in *DSM-IV* and quite differently in the book of *Psychoanalytic Terms and Concepts* of the American Psychoanalytic Association (Moore & Fine, 1990, pp. 25–26). The latter struggles with its allegiance to Freud's "anxiety hysteria", a term that is fairly widely ignored outside of this glossary. As a counter example, one effort that nicely illustrates the analytic struggle to bridge the gap between pure description and so-called "structural" considerations is exemplified by Otto Kernberg (1989), who himself, and with others, offers a range of descriptive criteria, along with or coupled to psychodynamic formulations, meant to encompass the diagnosis of narcissistic personality disorders (Kernberg, 1989, pp. xiii–xiv). This last categorization is, however, stretched to include behavioural disorders that include antisocial behaviour even to the point of murder (*ibid.*, p. 643). The mix is one of folk psychology, social issues, and theoretical jargon, without a clear boundary and a clear guiding principle.

Thus, we see an attempt at diagnosis that employs the descriptive categories of psychiatry and then joins them with one or the other psychoanalytic model to effect a marriage of two disciplines. For a start, a particular category may be described in one manner, such as overt behaviour. This is then elaborated in terms of (say) a psychic apparatus configured in one way, or else in a developmental path traversed in some special manner, or by way of any other vehicle of psychoanalytic conceptual thinking. The result fails to be unified. Although there is an ease of entry to descriptions such as "fixed, repetitive, obligatory behaviours required to obtain sexual gratification", this is clearly only the first step to an understanding of perverse behaviour, and it is only by way of a careful delineation of specific transference configurations that a psychoanalytic perspective allows such behaviour a standing that goes beyond the descriptive as well as the moral dimensions. Therefore, the ideal presentation of perverse behaviour for psychoanalysis comes from the psychoanalytic treatment of patients who both conform to the behavioural descriptions and also demonstrate a fairly clear clinical picture that can be generalized to encompass an improved definition. We have gathered together a number of such cases and propose a three-step requirement for a comprehensive definition.

Definition

The first component of our three-step definition of perversion has to do with the phenomenon of sexualization. This, of course, derives from Freud's original description of the capturing of a non-sexual function by sexual activity. It has been elaborated by Hartmann in terms of his thoughts about instinctualization, and by others who describe it as a defence. I propose to consider it as a manifestation of a structural deficit. The movement from sexualization to desexualization is therefore one of filling in such a structural need. This is seen to occur somewhat readily in most well-conducted psychoanalytic treatments of cases of sexual perversion. What clearly becomes apparent in treatment is the particular function of sexualization, the existence of which usually represents an inability to experience and manage otherwise painful affective states; the sexualization obliterates these negative feelings. If we posit psychic structure as a broad set of capacities or enduring functions, then we can visualize what composes defects or deficiencies in such a conceptualization of structure, and we can also see how the analyst can serve to fill in for, or temporarily substitute for, the missing structure. Thus, all of our cases of perverse sexual activity are seen as individuals with faulty structure, in whom sexualization is a manifestation of that fragile or insufficient structure. The initial aim in the treatment of these patients is that of desexualizing the aberrant behaviour.

What we have found in the study of a significant number of cases (Goldberg, 1995) is that the supposed pleasure, which is said by other investigators to be of an intense and special experience, is more often directed to the alleviation of anxiety than anything else. Without in any way discounting the anecdotal tales of exquisite pleasure, we more often find that it is in the pursuit of relief from anxiety and agitation that most perverse activity takes place. Here is an example of the desexualization.

The patient was loath to tell of one part of his masturbatory fantasy, wherein he performed fellatio on an older man. This man would instruct the patient as to just what to do and how to do it—much as a tutor—but then as the patient reached his ejaculation the imagined man would ask of the patient the thing that disgusted the patient the most and that he had so long withheld from telling the analyst, i.e., the man wished to ejaculate into the patient's mouth and have him swallow the semen. When this was rephrased into the patient feeling that he had to do more for the other person than for himself, that he had to passively endure a discomfort for another's happiness, he recalled the events of his childhood that seemed best to highlight the scenario. Whenever he would do something with his father, it had to be what his father wanted or else he could see the irritation on his father's face. Once the father took his son, the patient, skateboarding, but he was so miserable watching his son that the boy could not stand it. The events they both enjoyed, from shooting to sailing, were *primarily* those of the father and only *secondarily* for the son. In the sexual scenario, the patient represented this in his being asked (or forced) to swallow the ejaculate. In the transference this occurred prior to a vacation of the analyst's. The desexualizations enable us to see the clarity of the father–child relationship.

A common feeling that follows a patient's participation in a wide variety of sexual behaviours is that of shame or guilt. This highlights the second key element in the study of all behaviour disorders and especially those having to do with sexual behaviour or misbehaviour. This is the existence of the vertical split (Goldberg, 1999). First described by Freud in his elaboration of the mechanism of disavowal in fetishism (Freud, 1927e; 1940a), a wide range of psychological varieties of splitting have been popularized in discussions, particularly of borderline personality disorders, in terms of good and bad objects. The split in the psyche that is characteristic of the disorders discussed, here, has to do with the "side-by-side existence of disparate personality attitudes in depth; those with different pleasure aims, different moral and aesthetic values" (Kohut, 1971, p. 183). The vertical split is an extensive demonstration of disavowal, in which one part of the personality, that which is realistic and subscribes to the usual moral values, looks askance at the other part with an attitude that ranges from disbelief to condemnation.

An example of this can be seen in a physician patient with a perversion of having fellatio performed on him by his pet dogs. Following one incident that occurred after he had had to be rescued from a surgical mishap during an operation by his assistant, who then successfully completed the surgery, the patient acted out with his pet and recounted his experience with this animal with shame and disgust. He felt that it was very much as if another person had committed the sexual act, and he was convinced that he would never again indulge in this sort of "pleasurable" behaviour. Our patients, for the most part, show a range of responses to their aberrant behaviour, but it is ordinarily ego-dystonic and split off from what they claim is the "real me". Such vertical splits of disavowal are to be distinguished from the horizontal splits of repression in that the former remain conscious and fully accessible, but are denied complete ownership by the person. To the degree that there is a good deal of negative affect, usually in the form of shame, there is the greatest promise for effective analytic intervention. Indeed, the first goal of all such treatments is the recognition, and resolution, of this vertical split. In line with the above-mentioned concept of structural insufficiency, this, then, is another form of a defect, in that the patient's personality is unintegrated and requires a structural repair.

The integration of such splits is best seen in analytic treatment wherein the perverse behaviour becomes an active participant in the analysis. Here is a clinical example. A physician patient had a routine perversion of having female patients who were undergoing a physical examination perform fellatio on him. For the most part these women were unknown to him before these routine physicals and remained so afterwards. During his analytic treatment the incidence of this activity diminished and seemed to disappear, until one day he reported a recurrence. He told of this with a great deal of shame and remorse. In the analytic session he associated to a wish to ask for a substitute appointment, a wish that he had decided not to allow to surface. He said that he felt that he did not want to trouble or upset me by making a request for a schedule change so he had squelched his desire. As a young boy this patient had suffered from a severe, undiagnosed osteomyelitis, which caused him extreme pain and distress. He often cried out at night to his parents, who took him to a number of physicians, none of whom could diagnose this malady. Finally, one of the doctors had told him to stop complaining and thereby to just live with his pain. Not surprisingly, this advice was superimposed upon a family setting of suffering in silence and not sharing one's feelings with others. Stoicism became the familial mark of correct behaviour and no one ever complained or even asked for very much. In the particular act of fellatio performed by this man it was necessary that the anonymous woman remain completely silent, just as did my patient. Only when his wish to ask me, as the ungiving mother, for a response of care and understanding (i.e., the changed appointment) was admitted was he able to realize his wish in the treatment. Thus, the previously split-off act of perversion became joined or integrated into the analysis.

A further complication is introduced into our understanding of the vertical split, in that to say the split-off sector is readily available to consciousness is not quite true, since it seems in some individuals to remain periodically concealed and so is perhaps better called descriptively unconscious. It may appear, at times, literally to burst into consciousness after a period of quiescence, and we see this especially in certain forms of perversion that enjoy long periods of absence. Thus, we see that a rather complicated set of relations exists between these two sectors of the ego or the self, and the so-called split is maintained only under certain conditions and at a certain psychological expense. The connection between these sectors is therefore functionally unconscious, the appearance or emergence of the split-off sector, which may be termed unreal or primitive, is not under the control of the reality self, and the reality sector experiences a wide variety of reactions to this sometimes alien presence. Thus, the fundamental feature of these disorders is the condition of non-integration. This is what allows us to claim such behaviour disorders as those of the self, or as narcissistic; i.e., the persistent lack of a consolidated or cohesive self. All of our further concerns about the proper treatment of these conditions, as well as the problem of delineating the essential transferences involved, ultimately refer back to the fundamental failure of the establishment of an integrated self that is evidenced periodically but is present, albeit hidden from view, persistently.

The third element that is crucial to the understanding and treatment of sexual perversion has to do with what has heretofore been the somewhat singular interest of most psychoanalytic investigators: that of the individual dynamics of the patient, more often than not some variation on the theme of the oedipal conflict. I think that most analysts who have worked with these sorts of disorders have found that a very wide variety of psychodynamics are seen, that they include both oedipal and pre-oedipal problems and, perhaps most significantly, usually show profound narcissistic disturbances. An individual analyst's preferred use of one way of seeing clinical material over another will ordinarily shape the particular story or narrative that emerges in describing a patient, but our own experience has been rather telling. It is, essentially, that these patients have multiple problems with no unitary set of dynamics specific to any particular manifestation of pathology. Some exhibitionists, for example, show more early problems with their mother, as do most cross-dressers. But one should be very cautious in making any generalizations. The transferences that occur are rarely of one stable form, and one is well advised to follow Stoller (1975), whose list of "specific indicators" leads us to conclude that one can readily fashion any story to explain some perversions, but the story will equally explain other disorders, too, and will not explain many perversions that seem to defy neat categorizations.

The study of sexual perversions can be seen as a part of a larger group of behaviour disorders that includes delinquent and addictive behaviour as well. Contrary to some authors, our experience in the treatment of these patients reveals that some do shift from one sort of behaviour to another, both within the sexual sphere and outside it. No doubt there are patients with a single, devoted type of sexual perversion, but there also exist others who move between thievery, drug abuse, and sexual misbehaviour. I think it very important to recognize that the caseload of any single analyst is often not capable of generalization, and our own group of a dozen psychoanalysts who share their experiences seems much more revealing in terms of the analytic treatment of this group.

In light of the above, our diagnostic category takes on the definition of all of those behavioural aberrations that exist in a parallel sector of the self. The person with a narcissistic behaviour disorder, in particular a perversion, has a vertical split involving a side-by-side personality configuration with different ambitions, goals, and values. This parallel sector appears either occasionally or persistently, and is met by a variety of critical reactions from the non-participating sector. Thus, a conforming and seemingly well-adjusted married man who has episodes of bizarre sexual behaviour is a prototype of an individual split into sectors of adaptation and misbehaviour, with the one viewing the other with emotions ranging from puzzlement to fear. All of our cases of perverse behaviour have this psychic structure, and so all satisfy the triad of unacceptable, split-off action. They vary in terms of (1) the dominance, or extent, of the split-off sector, (2) the particulars of the behaviour, and (3) the reaction of the reality sector to its parallel companion.

The split-off sector

In certain forms of narcissistic behaviour disorders or perversions, the reality self is almost without a voice. Perhaps best seen in cases of severe substance abuse, we often find that the appeal to reason seems futile, and all of our therapeutic efforts are geared to handling the wayward behaviour, usually by a variety of suppressive techniques. As we move towards a midline from this extreme of misbehaviour, we find a mix of reason and pathology that exemplifies the peculiar state of co-existing persons who can seemingly both agree to behave and simultaneously to misbehave. It is only in those individuals who seem to display a narrow and infrequent display of behaviour disorder that we ordinarily consider psychotherapeutic or psychoanalytic efforts. For the most part, this depends upon an appeal to reality; i.e., we speak to the realistic sector about the misbehaviour. In the case of an episodic perversion, the interpretation becomes directed to the division of the person that is both curious and critical about his or her waywardness. In the case of an eating disorder we join forces with the segment of the personality that looks upon the anorexia or bulimia with disdain and disgust.

As essential as this may seem as a therapeutic manoeuvre, by itself it has a rather regular failing in its effectiveness, except as a short-lived measure or as a device that seems to require a continuing or sustained emphasis. Thus, much of our therapeutic effort is without effect, either because the misbehaviour so dominates the psyche that the periods of its absence are too infrequent to be reliable enough for treatment, or else because during its absence it seems not to attend to our interpretive efforts.

To better comprehend the dilemma in our understanding of these narcissistic behaviour disorders, it is necessary to have an altered view of the nature of the transference in these conditions. And, accordingly, the transference is of a different configuration than in those disorders that are singular or integrated. In the behaviour disorders with a vertical split, the transference is also a duality.

The dual transference

It is usually best to begin a discussion of transference with the disclaimer that it is a word with many definitions and much disagreement about those meanings. However, in the usual sense of the term it refers to unconscious ideations, either fantasy or drive derivatives (or whatever else one assigns to the unconscious), which become somehow lifted into the preconscious and thereby assigned to the person of some individual. Since transference is ubiquitous and universal, this assignment may be to a casual acquaintance as well as to a therapist or analyst, but it is upon the latter that we ordinarily focus for our therapeutic work. Thus, the transference to the analyst (say) is a manifestation of a distorted or contaminated vision of that person, although certainly we now know that a kernel of justified perception seems to accompany each and every supposed misperception. With such a minimal agreement upon the use of the word, we can turn to examine how we meet and deal with transference.

In the usual and sometimes caricatured case of the interpretation of the transference, there is an unpacking of the mistaken (or deviant or wrongful) attribution of a trait or perception to the analyst or therapist. This recognition by the patient of seeing the therapist as a figure from the past is followed happily by insight, and there ensues a new and better vision of reality. Putting aside for the moment all the many qualifications of this scenario, there does seem to be some agreement that the unconscious ingredients of the transference become reorganized into a more conscious (and therefore better understood and controlled) perception and consideration of the therapist. He or she becomes more of what they really are rather than what the patient hoped them to be. The clarification that results resides in one person.

It is not the same in the narcissistic behaviour disorders, in that the split does indeed involve two sets of transferences that, although they may derive from some unified unconscious material, play out in distinctly separate fashion. It is also different in the sense of these transferences more properly being considered self object transferences or partial aspects of the self. These are self disorders, and so the usual problem is a failure of structuralization leading to action and/or disintegration. In perversions, the failed structuralization gives rise to a sexualization, and so most of the activity or misbehaviour of the split-off sector is a manifestation in one form or another of this sort of structural deficit. But the deficit lies not only in the sector of behaviour. It is most telling in the very existence of the split, which itself can be seen as a defect in need of filling in or of healing.

The side-by-side existence of "cohesive personality attitudes with different goal structures, different pleasure aims, different moral and aesthetic values" (Kohut, 1971, p. 183) results in a person living in two different worlds and so necessarily manifesting two different transference configurations in treatment. There is never a singular or unitary transference to the analyst. We do not mean this in the sense of a change over time, but rather in the simultaneous existence of a dual transference: one to the reality sector and one to the sector of action. That the analyst may not be aware of this dual presence is but one problem. The other is the periodic absence of the one or the other sector, which is regularly hidden from view. Thus, we encounter treatments that consist of discussions about the errant behavioural manifestations that are regularly taking place outside of the treatment. A more unfortunate variation of this is the behaviour continuing its course without its being discussed in treatment. Both situations are examples of a failure to engage the duality of the transference.

One common example is that of eating disorders, in which there is an endless discussion about the specifics of the behaviour that often extends to group participation and a variety of other supportive methods. To the extent that such interventions, either in individual or group therapy, are effective, they are often primarily efforts to suppress the wayward behaviour by strengthening the alliance with the reality sector, which surely "knows better" and so will try harder. If a more careful analytic effort is attempted, but still one restricted to the one sector, we find a resulting person who is truly only half-cured. If the patient joins one of the many programmes modelled on AA, we see the major thrust certainly being toward education and suppression of the symptoms but, in certain cases, the other personality organization likewise emerges and participates, albeit without interpretation and so, once again, without lasting benefit.

This, then, is the second form of transference deployment (the first being complete non-recognition) that we see in narcissistic behaviour disorders and especially in perverse behaviour: one in which one sector is more actively engaged and interpreted while the other remains alive but unaddressed. Indeed, it seems that some of this must occur in every treatment, but the *conditio sine qua non* for the definitive co-existence of the dual transference in treatment is the gradual diminution and disappearance of the wayward behaviour. Short of that, we find evidence of alterations in the outward manifestations of the behaviour that are based most probably upon unrecognized and unacknowledged transference enactments.

One sometimes hears of a patient whose treatment was devoted to educational and instructional efforts aimed to alter or modify aberrant behaviour by coercion and suppression. Not surprisingly, this sort of rationalized acting-out by a therapist is ameliorative, and much of this is due not to the correcting action of the therapist but to the silent engagement of a transference that remains unnoticed and uninterpreted, and results in a rapid recurrence of the behaviour when the treatment stops. This is also, most probably, the explanation for the never-ending need of the above-noted support groups with their high rate of recidivism.

Sole recognition of the narcissistic or self object transference occasioned by the split-off aberrant sector of behaviour is subject to the same problematic issue of a lack of an integrative approach. One way to view the behaviour is to see it as an effort, usually successful, to obliterate painful affects along with unbearable self concepts. When able to fully experience the associated thoughts and feelings, these patients may dream of themselves as hideous animals, or deformed individuals, or in a variety of distasteful and disgusting presentations. Although we may feel that the split-off sector originates from a more basic megalomaniacal fantasy, it is often the case that personal conceptualizations of one's self are imbued with horror and distaste, because of the manner in which childhood fantasies and performance were greeted. Thus, the convenience of pleasurable action, which also serves to annihilate unpleasant thoughts, is a wonderful solution. Viewed in this manner, one can see the split-off behaviour as an absolutely essential and life-preserving solution, which is not and cannot easily be disabused.

The vigour of self-hate experienced by these patients is often matched by the intensity of their acts. A concerted empathic stance that aims to connect with, let us say, the reason for a particular form of perverse behaviour, will often lead to a cessation of the behaviour but, tragically, will also fail to include that sector in a connection to the more realistic part of the personality. The same sort of problem will ensue as noted in suppressive therapy, in that the behaviour, now understood, is still not under the control of an integrated and unified self. In this way we see the plight of the poor soul who, indeed, seems to know the why of the behaviour disorder, but remains at a loss as to its eradication or diminution. Each approach is unilateral, and each fails.

Treatment

In this chapter I can only point to a few salient characteristics in the psychoanalytic treatment of patients who both engage in sexually perverse activity and feel them ego-dystonically enough to consider doing without such behaviour. It is highly unusual to find a happy and successful person with a sexual perversion, such as a shoe fetishist, who is equally happy and successful in his or her psychoanalysis. On the other hand, it is not at all unusual to find analytic success in a patient, such as the previously mentioned surgeon, who suffers mightily because of his or her sexual behaviour. It is also not unusual to find a perversion revealed during the course of an analysis that was initiated for other problems. However, for the most part the presentation of a patient with perverse sexual pathology calls for an immediate reaction from the analyst, the nature of which can often be a decisive factor in the long-term success of the treatment.

To put it in the briefest way possible, the analyst must respond to the patient's presentation of his or her unwelcome parallel personality with a recognition that it is both necessary for the patient, as well as something to be removed or at least diminished. The vertical split of the patient must meet a corresponding split in the analyst; one of condemnation and condonement. If one or the other is absent, the analysis will probably not be a profitable one.

The sexually perverse behaviour that takes place outside of the analysis is ordinarily seen to subside and disappear as the analysis proceeds, only to reappear as one begins the working through of the emergent transference configurations. We have a host of reports of psychotherapy that seems to aid perverse activity, but only for a specified period of time, with no lasting results. Our feeling is that in these cases the therapist has temporarily filled in the structural defect, but without analytic work the cure is evanescent. The existence of the overt sexual behaviour outside of the analysis, as seen during weekend breaks, vacations, and failed empathic connections in the treatment, becomes a barometer of the progress of the treatment, in as much as the split-off part of the personality must inevitably join in the conversation with the analyst. Only when both parts of the personality become recognized in the engagement with the analyst as parallel but distinct transference phenomena does the analysis proceed to a lasting successful conclusion. I have no doubt that this happens in many treatments without it being recognized, but the major need for its recognition and monitoring arises from the countertransference reactions evoked by this dual transference.

Sharing analytic experience with a number of trained analysts who treat sexually perverse behaviour has allowed me to recognize a particular constellation of factors that seem quite characteristic of these treatments. In the analysis of such patients I have regularly noted a tendency to act out by the analyst, along with a particular set of countertransference reactions, both of which seem to relate to the particular form of misbehaviour evidenced by the patient. For example, in the psychoanalytic treatment of cross-dressers there is a range of negative responses to the symptoms, with a regular appearance of the symptom in the treatment either in the form of photos or subtle personal appearance changes. The analyst is always being asked to respond actively to the appearance of the symptom. Our thieves seem to provoke dishonesty in some analysts; our stalkers often provoke quite a range of contradictory responses. It is vitally important that one be alert to the pull of enactment with these patients, but it seems equally important to recognize that an effective treatment makes a demand upon the analyst to somehow share the patient's experience. Since no one of us is without sin, it seems fair to say that the successful treatment of the sexual perversions requires an analyst who is capable of knowing and being with the patient. Unless and until we can get in touch with our own myriad perverse wishes, we will be at a loss in getting in touch with those of our patients.

Case illustrations

Here are some illustrations of the particular countertransference reactions. A cross-dressing male in analysis reports an experience of intense depression at the onset of his analyst's brief vacation. He feels this is especially significant, since he connected the feeling to one he had had earlier and forgotten, when his mother left him to stay with a relative, and he attended a new school, when he was around eight years of age. But the newly rediscovered feeling was even more significant in as much as it was followed by an episode of cross-dressing that the patient now attributed to this recalled and re-experienced painful memory and affect. The analyst joined in acknowledging the connection and further noted to the patient how he had turned a passive experience of being left into an active one of cross-dressing. This interpretation was readily accepted by the patient but was followed that night by an unpleasant dream in which the patient was being scrutinized and examined by a strange doctor who probed him with a sharp instrument. The analyst was puzzled as to why a seemingly correct and even effective interpretation would be the stimulus for a dream that to him clearly reflected an image of a misunderstanding and an unempathic treater.

This is an example of a split transference in which the analyst speaks (correctly) to the reality sector about the misbehaviour of the split-off part. But that one-sided division of recognition also needs an acknowledgment of the parallel struggle with the coldness and emptiness of being left. Speaking only to reality makes for a split-off sector that is essentially more estranged, since it is unacknowledged. And so comes the dream of mistreatment. If, alternatively, he had recognized the depression without making the connection, the analyst would allay the negative affect but this would, in itself, not connect the misbehaviour to the parallel sector and so would not achieve the desired integration. The latter interpretation, about the difficulty of enduring the painful emptiness of depression, does indeed connect in recognition with the sector of the self involved in cross-dressing, but it still stands alone as an indicator of a symptom handling a problem. The mastery of that problem can be achieved only by the analyst's directing the patient's attention to the how and why of the symptom. The transference is split: one side needing an empathic acknowledgment of its pained state, another needing an affirming acknowledgment of the cause of the symptom by way of behaviour. Of course, each sector has its own developmental history; i.e., that of turning passive into active and that of dressing like a woman to handle depression. It may seem unnecessary to insist upon a connecting statement, until we recognize that the disavowal that operates does indeed allow the misbehaviour to exist in a seemingly separate manner. The behaviour has, up to this point, effectively obliterated the emotions, and once these are allowed to re-emerge they need a linkage to the sector of the self that has a realistic connection to the analyst.

I think it fair to consider both aspects of connecting to the analyst as transference; the first as a mirror to the patient as a woman covering over the depressed affect; the second as a mirror responding to the growing dominance of the patient over his reversal of passive to active. In an integrated self a single interpretation would suffice. In a split self the parallel interpretations must also be joined. In an integrated self the interpretation of the reversal made by the analyst allows for insight along with the emotional impact, but in a behaviour disorder the affect is unavailable for it to become part of the ensuing insight. However, this is not the split of affect isolated from ideation, but rather one of two separately operating personality configurations that, in turn, divide the analyst into a corresponding duality.

A clinical illustration of the split transference characteristics of a perverse behaviour disorder comes from the case of a male voyeur who visited athletic clubs in order to view the genitals of middle-aged men, whose image he retained until there was an opportunity to masturbate with fantasies of these men. This patient had entered analysis with a fearful conviction of being a homosexual, in as much as he felt aroused only by certain kinds of men with certain very specific physical characteristics. He had never gone so far as to become physically intimate with any man (or any woman), but confined his sexual life to magazines, television, and locker room stimuli, all of which lent themselves to fantasies of fellatio, or variations on a theme of sexual involvement with these men who fulfilled his very specific requirements of age and physique. For the most part he felt disgusted by his voyeuristic life.

In the analysis of this patient, much of the material dealt with his relationship with his father, who came alive as a preoccupied and distracted individual given to periodic angry tantrums. The transference that developed was one of idealization, and, once established, the patient initiated heterosexual relations with a co-worker. This progressed into a deepening relationship with another woman who seemed fairly sexually lively and even aggressive. The patient improved in every area of his life, but his voyeuristic activity—which I considered a behaviour disorder—was ever-present in the background and periodically came to the fore. The outbreaks of his masturbatory activity were regularly connected to an analytic disruption, but there seemed to be an added component of resistance in its persistence.

One day the patient announced that he had masturbated after seeing a specimen of his yearned-for masculine ideal in a locker room of the gym, and he went on to say that this would very likely diminish his sexual appetite and performance with his girlfriend that night. I asked a question, something like how he felt about that. The exact words are lost in time, but it may well have been that they carried along a charge of disapproval of the masturbatory activity and a more favourable consideration of heterosexual intercourse. The patient was furious. He went on to say that at no time had I ever indicated to him that he was to control, or limit, or certainly not to eliminate, his masturbation, and now it sounded as if I was instructing him in some sort of proper form of behaviour. I held my tongue as he explained to me that he had assumed that he could and would have both, i.e., a sexual pleasure looking at middle-aged men and a parallel one with a chosen female. He certainly had never considered having to consciously choose to stop looking and masturbating. To be perfectly honest, he did now and again think that one day the homosexual feelings might simply disappear as a result of his analysis, but he hardly felt that he would have, or need, to do much about them. I found myself preparing a careful rebuttal to this position by way of an analogy of someone eating candy all day and so ruining his or her appetite for regular, wholesome meals, when the patient's rage shifted to a plea for me to be more clear as to just what he was to do and what I expected of him. Thus, he changed from a combatant to an apprentice, and the following analytic hours took on a different form.

It had always been clear to the patient and myself that missing hours were extremely disruptive for him, and often led to his acting out. He had always reported his voyeuristic behaviour with deep regret and shame, together with a wish to get rid of it. It should be clear that he was indeed "of two minds" about his voyeuristic behaviour. In the hours after the sudden and (for him) painful recognition of his now conscious need to curb his acting-out behaviour, his yearning for me seemed to reach an epiphany. He would do anything to get me to talk, he felt at times as though he were delivering a monologue to a black hole, he wanted to hold me, he had a fantasy of my arms around him. Interestingly, for him there was nothing sexual whatsoever in the longing, and he also clearly connected it to an anticipated missing of several days. He next reported that he had been tempted on several occasions to resume his voyeuristic and masturbatory behaviour, but had not done so.

He mentioned a dream of reporting to a doctor who had casually said something that embarrassed the patient, who soon thereafter became angry with this unfeeling physician.

I saw this transference as manifesting two parallel and distinct forms. In the one there is the wish for a close relationship with the father, which had heretofore been sexualized. As this was interpreted and worked through in the analysis, it started to join with a parallel one of a mentor who prescribed and directed proper behaviour. This seems to indicate a dual transference: one directed to the reality sector, which aims (in his words) to see himself as a normal, heterosexual man, and another that yearns for a more infantile, and likewise a periodically sexualized, connection to a man. This is the nature of the vertical split, and this is the arena for analytic work that aims for integration. I think this vision of a dual transference of simultaneity is not a psychodynamic (i.e., a clashing of forces) or a descriptive categorization, but is more honestly seen as diagnosis by way of transference. I, of course, have no argument or doubt that other formulations are possible, but I offer this as a way of seeing (i.e., diagnosing) and so treating narcissistic behaviour disorders, and also as illustrative of the reciprocal countertransference issues which are divided into parallel views of reality alongside more infantile (and narcissistic) needs. The special way of handling this phenomenon of the dual transference will not be addressed here, except to emphasize that this does qualify the category of narcissistic behaviour disorders for diagnosis by way of specifically recognized transference configurations.

Having noted the variation of the dominance of one split aspect versus the other, and the particulars of the behaviour of one part versus the other, we now turn to the relationship between the one part and the other. This becomes a crucial factor in the evaluation of such patients for the variety of interventions that are considered for behaviour disorders: interventions that range from incarceration to support groups, to psychoanalytic psychotherapy and to psychoanalysis. The delineation of the group, and the careful assessment of the aforementioned structural considerations, allow one to make educated assumptions about recommended approaches to treatment.

One side looks at the other side

The ideal constellation of factors for treatment in a narcissistic behaviour disorder is one in which the reality sector greets the misbehaviour and its parallel sector with a predominantly negative affect, reinforced by an equally negative reaction of the environment. Negative, in this case, need not mean hostile and/or primitive, since that can often be a component of a perverse disorder. Rather, I mean that a connection to a satisfying self object, i.e., one that can gratify the disordered sector, cannot be obtained or retained, and the reality sector does not readily accommodate the needs of the split-off sector for such a connection. This negative, or alien, approach to the behaviour may occur after a treatment has begun.

In a seemingly contradictory way, this distancing stance allows for the emergence of the wayward behaviours' transference needs within the treatment, and so makes for the awareness of the split. If a patient claims a happy acceptance of his or her misbehaviour, as initially seen in some perverse disorders, it may be the case that deeper shameful feelings emerge only after an effective therapeutic engagement takes place. I take it as a rule that claims of greater pleasure in, or resigned contentment with, misbehaviour are always evidence of a significant and, at times, unhealable split, but it is this gap that makes possible the denial of a more genuine affect. It is never a genuine contentment.

In summary, I believe there is a new frontier open in the psychoanalytic treatment of the sexual perversions. They are complex structural disorders that cannot be seen as simple oedipal disasters. They demand a new perspective on psychic structure, a reconsideration of the vertical split and the concomitant formation of a split transference, and a more careful scrutiny of particular countertransference reactions that match the misbehaviour of the patient. With a combined effort in our work on this new frontier, perhaps a reawakened enthusiasm for psychoanalysis will be our reward.

References

American Psychiatric Association (1994). *Diagnostic and Statistical Manual of Mental Disorders* 4th edn). Washington, DC: American Psychiatric Association.

Freud, S. (1927e). Fetishism. *S.E., 21*: 149–157. London: Hogarth.
Freud, S. (1940a). An outline of psycho-analysis. *S.E., 23*: 139–207. London: Hogarth.
Goldberg, A. (1995). *The Problem of Perversion: The View from Self Psychology*. New Haven, CT: Yale University Press.
Goldberg, A. (1999). *Being of Two Minds: The Vertical Split in Psychoanalysis and Psychotherapy*. New York: Analytic Press.
Kernberg, O. F. (1989). Narcissistic personality disorder. *Psychiatric Clinics of North America, 12*(3): 553–570.
Kohut, H. (1971). *The Analysis of the Self*. New York: International Universities Press.
Moore, B. E., & Fine, B. D. (1990). *Psychoanalytic Terms and Concepts*. New Haven, CT: Yale University Press.
Stoller, R. J. (1975). *Perversion: The Erotic Form of Hatred*. New York: Pantheon.

CHAPTER THREE

Perversion and charity: an ethical approach

Sergio Benvenuto

Moral psychopathology

Today, simply using the word "perversion" is not considered politically correct, and rouses suspicions—above all in the USA. "What is perverse and what is not?", people ask perplexedly. "Perversion", it is often said, "is basically a moral category, which varies according to the customs of each epoch." The American sexologist John Money no longer speaks of perversion but of "paraphilia", as distinct from "normophilia". The latter is defined as "a condition of being heterosexually in conformity with the standard as dictated by customary, religious, or legal authorities" (Money, 1988, p. 214). Thus, paraphilia is still defined as sexual behaviour that deviates from the norm.

Nineteenth-century positivist sexology, which produced the term "perversion" for a type of sexuality, gave itself the ethico-legal mission of distinguishing the "pervert" from the "libertine" (Lantéri-Laura, 1979). The former is a sort of sick person, while the latter is a normal subject to be judged according to moral criteria. Today, the distinction between pervert and libertine has been abandoned, and replaced with the distinction between "sexuality according to the average standard" and "sexuality deviating from the average standard". Thus, perversion tends to be considered less and less as a disorder and more as a variation in sexual phenomenology.

In Freud's time, any act was labelled as perverse if it deviated from "orthodox", procreative, heterosexual intercourse: anal penetration of the woman, homosexual coitus, observation of others' copulation, "swinging", and so on. Nowadays, these "perversions" are either performed by the majority of the population, or at least widely accepted as legitimate sexual practices. The Civil Rights movements in the West have actually forbidden psychiatry from dealing with homosexuality as either a pathology or a perversion. It is virtually impossible to find articles about "homosexual perversion". Analysts have had to conform—often unwillingly—to the prevailing point of view.

In his early theory of perversion, Freud defined neuroses as "the negative of perversions" (Freud, 1905d, p. 166; 1908d, p. 191). In a certain sense, perversion appeared here as a "natural" and undeveloped state of sexuality, which is later converted into its negative by repression. Perversion appeared at that time as a *positive* sexuality, a sexuality in its pure state that invests partial objects, a primary childish sexuality not subjected to the refined demands of love for others, reproduction, and responsibility. Yet, Freud himself subsequently corrected this thesis, which was still very much bound to the beliefs of his time (perversion as a "primal" sexuality). After all, what can be "natural" or "authentic" in a fetishist who is able to penetrate a woman only if she wears shoes of a certain shape? There is some sophistication, a "negative" aspect in the above sense, even in perverted eroticism.

Undoubtedly, "perversion" is an ethical concept and the term is commonly used as a moral reproach. But this does not mean that psychoanalysis should reject it. On the contrary, it belongs to psychoanalysis *precisely because of* its moral connotation. Even neurosis is, in the end, an "ethical illness". This does not mean that neurosis and perversion are moral failures, but rather that the barrier separating the objective analysis of psychic processes from the moral evaluation of the acts should be lifted. What we call "neurosis" and "perversion" are in fact specific ways of *being-in-the-world*, as some phenomenological philosophers would say, whereby affective dynamics, moral positions, and aesthetic preferences intertwine. The classic position of analysts is to look at neurosis and perversion *objectively*, as scientists, without expressing any moral judgment. By doing so, they find that in neurosis and perversion *moral conflicts* are (in part) at play. In other words, classical psychoanalysis sees "a-morally" neurotic and perverse subjects as "moral objects". It is the merit of hermeneutical and deconstructive thought to have raised serious doubts about this division: on the one hand, the "objective" gaze of the analyst is more moralistic than the classical analyst assumes; on the other hand, the problem of neurotics and perverts, which seems purely moral, concerns objectivity to a much greater degree than analysts believed until now.

Psychoanalysis has in fact weakened—even if unbeknown to analysts themselves—the dichotomy which haunts modern thought, and according to which facts lie on one side (for example, certain "mechanisms" of the human mind) and values lie on the other (certain acts are judged to be good or bad, ugly or beautiful). In what sense can we say that a behaviour is perverse because it is inherently ethical? To answer this, we must abandon the behavioural criterion of perversion. *What* one does erotically and *with whom* or *with what* no longer counts. Instead, what for me is relevant is the question *if and how the other (with whom one does it) exists in that which is done*. Psychoanalysts should thereby consider "perverse" any mode of sexual pleasure in which the other subject appears only as *a tool* or *a means* of pleasure, that is, where his/her (especially sexual) pleasure is not an aim.

In so-called "normal", irreproachable intercourse (whether hetero- or homosexual), the other is also *an end*, in so far as I aim to give him/her pleasure as well: what gives me pleasure is not only the sensual pleasure I take from the other, or even my pride in my power of giving him/her sensual pleasure, but the simple fact that s/he experiences sensual (and other) pleasure with me. From this point of view, even an apparently very normal heterosexual act—for example, coitus with a prostitute—should be considered as perverse, or at least at the limit of perversion, since, presumably, no one goes to see a prostitute in order to give her sexual pleasure. Conversely, a homosexual act is not perverse, in so far as the two same-sex partners take a mutual pleasure not only from each other, but from each other's pleasure.

But the reader must not misunderstand me: I am not saying that perversion consists simply in considering the other as a mere object. This is the prevailing view in psychoanalysis, according to which perversion is the use of others as things rather than persons, as objects of envy and desire rather than love, and for the purpose of implementing an act rather than establishing a real relation between persons (Khan, 1965; Stoller, 1975). Yet this is a rather contradictory position: how can one experience desire and envy with respect to things? Instead, perversion is not about using the other *as an object*, but about *using the other as a subject*. In fact, as we shall see, the subjectivity of the other is very often an essential component in the perverse act. For example, the exhibitionist requires the gaze, admiring or surprised, of the woman to whom he exhibits his penis; the subjectivity of the other then comes into play. But perversion is the exploitation of the other's subjectivity as a means for one's own pleasure.

Lack of charity

It is normal for a man to like women's legs, Gosselin and Wilson (1980, p. 43) write, but a man is a fetishist "if he prefers to come *on* the legs of his partner rather than *between* her legs". But what makes this difference so decisive? The difference only becomes important because the latter is usually something a woman also enjoys, while the former usually does not take into account what she enjoys. It is not the desired anatomical object that makes the perversion, but rather the presence or lack of *care for the other as a libidinal subject*.

In short, *the non-perverse sexual act is one in which there is charity for the other*. In the Middle Ages, *caritas* did not imply giving alms to the needy: it meant love as distinct from *amor*, intended as sensual love. *Caritas* was love for God, for the church, for one's neighbour—and even for one's wife, because with her *amor* does not suffice. Of course, a decent act of intercourse requires both *amor* and *caritas*. Charity is to feel com-passion for the other's desire, to feel concern for the need and attraction the other has for us, and then to go to his/her aid. Coitus, as compassionate charity, is an ethical act *par excellence*. It is no mere coincidence that the Catholic church made a sacrament out of coitus: when done in the requisite manner, it is called matrimony. To call coitus an act of compassionate charity risks ridicule. But if we remove our behaviourist blinkers, we soon realize that without compassionate charity any sexual act—even the most apparently normal kind of heterosexual intercourse—is perversion: the use of the other subject (or of the other's subjectivity) not as an end but as an instrument of pleasure.

Intercourse is com-passion because each partner enjoys giving to the other what the other lacks. This enjoyment certainly implies a narcissistic pride in one's power to satisfy the other, but it is not just that: it also entails joining one's satisfaction to the filling of the other's void. This filling of the void is resolved in the excess of orgasm, in which the two opposites seem to be united: the *delicium* (delight/crime) of becoming absent to oneself and the pleasure of finally giving this absence to the other.

It is against this ethical background of sexual intercourse that perverse fantasies and modes of behaviour should be analysed. Perversions are complex ways of being-in-the-world.

Perversion shuns jealousy

My thesis here is the following: perversion is a way of warding off the devastating emotions of jealousy and delusion, brought out when the beloved other has sexual relations with another. Classical psychoanalysis has usually dealt with envy and its by-products. But perverse sexuality has its original root and most powerful trigger in jealousy (and not only in envy), all of which should sound obvious to many Freudians. By placing the Oedipus complex at the core, Freud placed jealousy at the heart of the psyche—in fact, the Oedipus complex is not only the inadmissible desire of a child for an adult, but also and above all the jealousy of the fact that the beloved (whom he cannot satisfy) is enjoyed by another, and that the beloved enjoys the other. But I think that even such a common feeling as jealousy needs to be clarified.

Orthodox analysts usually see jealousy as essentially the fear of losing the beloved object (what matters is the relationship between a subject and its objects of love and hate). From this perspective, I am jealous of my wife only because I am afraid that, by falling in love with another, she might leave me; my ambivalence towards her, or my sadistic fantasies and consequent guilt feelings are all considered as stemming from this. But we all know that this fear of losing the beloved object is only one aspect, and perhaps not the essential one, of the theme of jealousy.

Take that most famous jealous man, Othello. We cannot say that his torment lies in his fear of losing Desdemona to Cassio, or in his feeling less loved by her. In fact, we know his jealousy is unjustified and we think that Desdemona loves Othello as much as before—thus we know that the fulcrum of his jealousy cannot be any cooling of passion on Desdemona's part (in fact, Othello never refers to that in the text). Othello's suffering is instead caused by his imaginary scene, in which Desdemona is enjoying sex with Cassio. No one can console him by saying, for example, "But why do you care what Desdemona does when you are not there and whether she has sex with Cassio or not? What matters is that you enjoy her, and that she enjoys you, the rest is her business". This wise discourse does not make sense for the jealous person, who is in his own way even too hetero-centric: foremost in his thoughts is whether and with whom the beloved gets pleasure when he is absent. In short, jealousy is a *realistic passion*: it is suffering for the truth, and not at all an abandonment to the self-sufficient world of fantasies.

This is why all of the dominant psychoanalytic theories—focusing on what the others signify for a subject, without taking into consideration this reality-in-itself that others are for us—miss the core of the oedipal drama. I am, of course, referring to the *significant others* for each of us. It goes beyond recognizing the importance, for our psychic life, of what significant others (first of all, our mothers) do to us, or of how our psychic life is conditioned by the image we build up of significant others (again, first of all, our mothers). What matters most is that I recognize that my psychic life is focused by the often enigmatic reality of significant others as subjects, and catalysed by what these others think, enjoy, and suffer. This tropism toward the other as a real being is something that Freudian and post-Freudian "psychological" theories tend to repress.

As Othello says clearly to Iago: "[When I did not suspect Desdemona], I found not Cassio's kisses on her lips". Othello is a gentleman and uses chaste language. We think, more crudely, that "Cassio's kisses" is a euphemism for Cassio's penis, which Othello implacably "finds" inside Desdemona. We can describe masculine jealousy as the atrocious doubt that the beloved woman's cavity is "inhabited" by an other's phallus; in short, that having sex with one's own woman is reduced to a kind of homosexual encounter with the other's phallus. So, there is some Freudian paranoia in every form of jealousy, even in the most normal and justifiable kind. By this, I do not mean to say that every jealous person is a paranoiac, but that paranoiac persons are more "normal" than we generally think.

However this may be, the jealous person prefers to destroy the loved object, to kill Desdemona, rather than to accept that s/he might have sexual enjoyment without him. This fact is enough to refute the idea that reduces jealousy to anguish for the loss of the other as object: the jealous person prefers to lose the object rather than recognize its right to enjoy with others (he is anguished not so much by the loss of the object, but rather by his exclusion from the other's sexual enjoyment). Jealousy is *heterocentric* in so far as it is a suffering for being excluded from the jouissance of the beloved other. Jealousy, which is at the centre of the Oedipus complex, is pain over one's own exile from the other who enjoys sex. And this elementary truth is at the heart of the perverse "choice". As we will see, the perverse masterpiece (Stoller, 1975) consists in transforming the trauma of jealousy into an exclusive sexual enjoyment.

This brings us to an aspect that analysts have sometimes highlighted regarding perversion: perverse acts usually betray an anxiety in the face of a *mystery*. It is not anxiety in the face of danger (as in the case of castration), but in front of something mysterious, often linked to sexual difference itself. But why does sexuality continue to appear to be something so enigmatic, puzzling, and mysterious, much more so, for example, than the difference between races, cultures, the young and the old, or the past and the present? This mystery is probably what haunts every jealous person: *what is the other and what does s/he really feel, especially when having sex with another?* The mystery is the other's subjectivity (and thus his/her suffering and pleasure), something from which we are all, in the end, excluded. The anxiety over the mystery of sexual difference is thus the anxiety over being excluded from what the other is and feels.

Exhibitionism and voyeurism

In a well-known joke a sadist and a masochist meet. The kneeling masochist pleads with the sadist and cries, "Beat me, please! Punch me!" To which the smirking sadist replies: "No! Never!" Gilles Deleuze (1971) remarked that this is an absurd story, because in effect a sadist and a masochist never meet. They belong to two completely separate perverse universes. This is true not only of masochists and sadists, but of all kinds of perverts. In general, we never find complementarity between perversions; moreover, this lack of complementarity constitutes the essence of perversion itself.

Even the exhibitionist and the voyeur are never complementary. Take, first, the exhibitionist, a man who, usually in a public space, abruptly shows his penis—either limp or erect—to an unknown woman. The aim of the exhibitionist is never the seduction of the woman: his pleasure derives from the act itself. So, if a woman were to play along and say to the exhibitionist, "Shall we go to my place? Do you want to give it to me then?", the exhibitionist would most probably turn on his heels and run a mile, confused and disappointed. Exhibitionism is a perversion in so far as it does not inaugurate, but substitutes for, a shared sexual action (Christoffel, 1956).

In fact, as an exhibitionist, I choose as a "victim" a woman who apparently is not seeking an erotic experience: I am interested in capturing her gaze in order to make her see something that should be delightful for her (the exhibitionist generally hopes to excite his victim). But it is not a "charitable" act, as can be the case even in a pornographic show, where voyeurism and exhibitionism are not perverse, because we suppose that both the couple performing the sexual acts and the viewing public derive pleasure from the show (even when the pleasure of the actors consists only in making money). In a porno-show there is in any case an agreement, a conjunction of desires.

Nothing similar happens in perverse exhibitionism, where instead the woman usually reacts by being disgusted, upset, or scared by the performance. What matters for me, an exhibitionist, is to fix the woman's gaze so that she cannot remain indifferent and be free to seek what interests her. I force her gaze to not ignore my penis. A woman's gaze—like anybody else's—is like a void trying to be filled by stimulating and delightful objects, but certainly neither I nor my genitals are included among these objects. This woman is not looking for me, she does not desire me, yet she carries her void around with her—a void in which I put, not my penis, but its perception. As an exhibitionist, I wish to "expose" the woman's desire, what she is supposedly seeking by her wandering gaze, but I do not fulfil it. By imposing the view of my penis on this woman, I unsettle her: what she had excluded (my penis) is imposed upon her. In short, I, as exhibitionist, expose my exclusion from the woman's sexual enjoyment, while getting pleasure from this exclusion by imposing my penis upon her, from which—prior to the perverse act—she was free.

Such exposure of the subject's exclusion is more evident in voyeurism. For us, the voyeur is a pervert in so far as he enjoys lustily watching people engaged in sex or in some intimate activity—without being watched in turn. A voyeur is someone who observes the sexual act of a person who does not desire to be observed. So, what the voyeur really enjoys is not the act of intercourse, but *his exclusion from that intercourse*. This distinction is fundamental. The two lovers do not want to include me at all, not even as an observer, which rather ought to prompt my anger at being excluded. Instead, in the end, it is sometimes the two actors who suffer, when they realize that they have been "included" in the gaze of an unknown observer. I, the voyeur, transform the suffering resulting from my own exclusion into lustful pleasure, because I have become an active player who overcomes their activity: the two actors, who take pleasure without paying any attention to me, are reduced to simple objects of my enjoying gaze. Unbeknown to them, I, the voyeur, "possess" them precisely because I have transformed my exclusion into a secret relationship wherein I now include in my gaze the two who excluded me. Thus, I, the voyeur, not only vindicate myself against that which my father and mother had imposed upon me—my not participating in their intercourse—but in a devious way I invert the relationship of mastery: now it is the lovers who are excluded from a gaze that "captures" them, and hence from the vision of what they are doing.

Masochism and sadism

In masochism, the transformation of exclusion into enjoyment is effectuated in a spectacular way. I, the masochist, do not demand that the woman love, desire, or appreciate me; on the contrary, I wish to be beaten and humiliated, neither desired nor loved by her. The woman's contempt is the masochist's enjoyment. But why this need for such severity?

The masochist very often answers in a spiritual tone: "Through humiliation and pain I am uplifted". The masochist's erotic pleasure apes the soul's elevation through mortification—as is explicitly proclaimed in Pauline Réage's novel *Histoire d'O*, which is almost a manifesto of female masochism (Réage, 1972). It is no coincidence that Italian prostitutes advertise in newspapers their availability for masochist clients by offering "education". Education raises the spirit, gives access to a superior enjoyment that comes from sacrifice and humiliation. The important point is that the masochist does not offer himself as the complement of a genuine feminine desire to punish and humiliate: the woman here is only an instrument, she has only to pretend to be severe. The woman's rejection thus becomes a show, of which the masochist is the director. The scene of the most painful rejection is played out by the masochist as his pleasurable object.

It is true that the masochist has to make do with prostitutes, but deep down he dreams of a woman who really wants to punish him, a woman who would be truly severe with him. But even if the masochist succeeded in finding this woman—one who would really be angry with him—in this case the charitable complementarity that would cancel the perverse strategy of the act might not take place. In fact, a woman who is really angry with the subject would not have any particular pleasure in being so: after all, what is pleasurable in being indignant at another's behaviour? The masochist desires a severe woman, but he does not desire to satisfy her desires: the feelings of his longed-for partner are not an end for him (in the sense that he would have the end of satisfying them), but a means towards obtaining pleasure for himself. In making himself the object of the severity of a woman, he does not aim towards satisfying her desire to be strict, but aims only at egoistically intercepting the effects of this severity. When, for example, the masochist declares himself to be the "slave" of his "mistress", he does not enjoy satisfying the desire of the woman to be the mistress of slaves: he only enjoys his feeling of being her slave.

In a Woody Allen movie, *Take the Money and Run* (1969), Woody lives as a child in a violent and run-down American slum. Skinny and with oversized glasses, he is often, rightly or wrongly, punished by adults, who tear off his glasses, throw them on the ground, and crush them underfoot. After so many repetitions of this treatment, the grown-up Woody introduces a variation: just when he feels that the usual attack is coming, he himself tears off his glasses and crushes them on the ground. He self-administers this violence of which, until then, he had been a passive victim. This gag illustrates a process Freud had already described when he tackled the mystery of neurotics, who appear to inflict upon themselves pain and sorrow without any (even unconscious) plausible reason. Ultimately, he elaborated his notion of the death drive as a way to account for this mystery (Freud, 1920g). But the introduction of the death drive is more a reformulation of the mystery than its solution. Before reaching this conclusion, Freud had hypothesized that the many ways of self-inflicting pain none the less obey the pleasure principle (*Lustprinzip*), even if indirectly: by transforming himself from a passive victim into an active agent of suffering, the subject consoles himself by re-establishing a certain mastery. Just like Woody Allen, in as much as he cannot avoid being the target of violence, he prefers to inflict it upon himself and, in doing so, he derives some pride from it. We might suppose that Woody takes a certain pleasure from his "masochism": he participates in the sadistic pleasure of the persons who punish him, hitting himself as if he were his own sadistic object.

As with every perversion, even masochism is a strategy for deriving pleasure from something initially very unpleasant. Masochism is sublime in the Kantian sense: as a displeasure that pleases, or as a pleasure that displeases. This contrivance transforms my masochistic painful exclusion from the other's enjoyment into a scene, an object, and subsequently into my own enjoyment, from which the other is then excluded (this shows again why perversion is a lack of charity for the other). Freud, however, did not exactly say this in relation to perversion; rather, he spoke about the *Urszene*, or "primal scene" (Freud, 1918b). Many human beings would find it traumatic to witness the coitus of others, or, maybe, even to imagine it. The reasons for which a child's observation of adult coitus can be traumatic are varied. But certainly it is very painful for the child who thinks: "Adults get a mutually intense, dramatic, happy experience from which I am totally excluded". The primal scene is first of all a scene of primal exclusion—the subject is outside it. In more formal terms: "I am not the object of my beloved other's desire or enjoyment". This betrayal of the other is the matrix of perversion.

As regards sadism, it, too, has often appeared to analysts as an expression of a primary aggressiveness, a natural reactive impulse that is fundamentally non-problematic. They see it as a sort of zero degree on the perversion scale: the most inadmissible perversion of all would also be the most original, to the extent that we all desire to revenge ourselves against anyone who has made us suffer. But when the primary sadism we all possess becomes sexualized, things get complicated. I, the sadist, get enjoyment from beating a woman in order to punish "The Woman" for her original "betrayal", i.e., for her having experienced pleasure with another, and not with me. Sadistic rape is thus in its own particular way an application of the law of retaliation: I (the excluded child) now make "my" original woman pay for the pleasure she took from another man, or from another child, by forcing intercourse on a woman representing the original one. In a French film entitled *Code Unknown* (dir. Haneke, 2000) there is a scene on the Paris metro in which a couple of young Arabs are insistently harassing an attractive white girl, who does not respond to the provocation. After a while, one of the two youths spits in her face. The act of sexual refusal on the part of the woman is turned on its head by the physical action of spitting, the oral inverse of the kiss—a very simple dynamic, implicit in every sadistic sexual experience.

The same sadism happens in wars: soldiers of an invading army rape the women of the enemy nation, usually in front of their husbands or fathers, who are reduced to a state of impotence. The woman of the enemy must be "punished" because she has enjoyed the enemy. In France and Yugoslavia, the women who had love affairs with German soldiers during the Nazi Occupation had their hair shorn—a softer variation of the gang rape of a woman who has enjoyed the "other man".

Fetishism

The analysis of fetishism has occupied an eminent place in psychoanalytic theory, if perhaps for no other reason than that Freud (1927e, 1940e) dealt with it in order to elaborate his very important theory of *Ichspaltung*, the splitting of the Ego. According to Freud, the fetishist lives in a dual world: in the adult one, he knows that women do not have a penis, and in the other (infantile) world, he does not believe they lack a penis. The fetish of the pervert is, in fact, a detachable part of the woman—comparable to a penis—which he desires. This is often why fetishists say they feel like homosexuals, even if in fact they are not particularly attracted to men. Yet, for them, the woman is desirable only in so far as she has a penis, and the fetish is its metaphorical substitute.

But analysts often ask themselves why shoes and socks are the most common fetishes. Where does this preference for shoes and, secondarily, for feminine feet come from? Lacan (1994, p. 42) wondered how fetishists behaved in ancient times, when few shoes existed. Of course, in so far as the shoe is something detachable, it has a phallic connotation. But the shoe, the sock, and the corset are also *containers*: they connote the vagina. The fetish has a double face, which makes it so indispensable: as a detachable object, it is the phallus marking the woman; as a container, it is the vagina or the anus that might finally be "given". Freud, charmed by the phallic metaphor, saw only one side of the coin.

The fetishist, thus, views the putting on and taking off of shoes as an *analogon* of sexual intercourse. The fetish evokes the inseparable unity of the male and female in an act of intercourse from which the subject is excluded. In so far as the woman puts on and takes off her shoes, she realizes in herself a copulative completeness: in putting on and taking off her shoes, she integrates both sexes. She is the container and the contained, but this integration renders the fetishist subject superfluous. In fact, it is precisely this completeness that the woman lacks: she lacks the penis and coitus, and the fetishist is unable to adequately give them to her. At the root of any fetishist conversion there is probably an unsatisfied mother, desiring an intercourse that does not arrive. But this woman does not seek what she lacks in her son and even less in his penis—a severe mother, who does not know what to do about her son's masculinity.

Perverse femininity

How can one explain the fact that perversions are usually male, and almost never female? For the early psychoanalysts, the woman is almost never perverse simply because she *is* so by her very psychic constitution. Freud (1924c) spoke of *feminine masochism*: *qua* female, the woman is a masochist. Although this thesis has always infuriated feminists, it was a woman, Helene Deutsch (1930, 1944–1945), who most developed this idea of the supposedly "masochist core" of women. The thesis sounds exaggerated to us today, but this should not prevent us from trying to understand its core of truth: just like every pervert, every woman also has to transform humiliation into pleasure. That is, she has to move past the discomfort of being penetrated, invaded by the other, towards pleasure. It suffices to observe children of both sexes in order to realize that being penetrated, in whichever orifice it may be—for example when enemas are administered—arouses much repulsion in them: they feel dispossessed of their own bodies. Masturbation among pre-adolescent girls is generally clitoral (when a small girl penetrates herself, we actually have to suspect some psychic disturbance). Every woman must therefore turn this childhood offence into her triumph and re-elaborate the intrusion of herself as a body by turning it into a source of non-clitoral enjoyment. The bizarre pleasure that strikes us in the case of the (male) pervert, is, in this sense, similar to the bizarre (vaginal) pleasure of every woman. Paradoxically, clitoral sexuality is "normal", while vaginal sexuality is "perverse", even though our culture (as well as Freud's) actually considers the latter to be healthy and normal.

The hysterical subject, described by Freud as an imaginary pervert, is in many ways a woman who does not resign herself to female masochism: she does not accept "suffering" from penetration and thus identifies with the central void of her own bodily being. Indeed, she does everything in order to protect this void. Analogously, the anorexic rejects both food and the penis as intolerable intrusions that are damaging to the glorious autarchy of her own body. The hysteric and the anorexic, by renouncing femininity as a perversion, renounce femininity *tout court*: they dream of themselves as virgin and mother, like the Madonna. They idealize themselves as women; they abhor themselves as females.

The success of the Marian cults certainly does not mean that all Catholics, for two millennia, have been hysterical. The point is that both the cult of Mary and hysteria try to provide an answer to a difficult problem of femininity: how can a woman accept being invaded, penetrated, "shafted", while turning all this into her own *sublime* pleasure (in the Kantian sense)? How can she offer her own emptiness to the other, while preventing its being filled, cancelling the *female power*, her capacity for production and reproduction? But if it is true that hysteria is a female "weakness", while perversion is a male "weakness", there is still no lack of perverse women. We often do not classify these women as being perverse, probably because women, until a short time ago, had less sexual initiative and therefore their "perversion" emerged more rarely.

Take the case of some women who obtain real pleasure from sexual intercourse only if they imagine that the man who is penetrating them is, in turn, anally penetrated by another man. When the woman convinces her partner to let himself be penetrated, for example by a vibrator that she herself manipulates, this is an example of female perversion, because the partner is reduced to a means rather than an end of pleasure: whether or not her companion likes it, the woman enjoys sex only if she sees him being "sodomized". At the root of this fantasy or act lies the woman's experience of coitus as something humiliating; she can therefore concede her own pleasure to a man only if he, in turn, symmetrically suffers this humiliation. This, then, is the erotic flipside of the law of tit-for-tat—not "an eye for an eye" but "a shafting for a shafting". With the man reduced in his turn to a female role, the rancour towards the possessor of a violent phallus is attenuated: coitus thus becomes a gay retaliation "between equals". A complex affective knot emerges here (so complex that it explains the relative rarity of perverse behaviour in women): on the one hand, envy of the male for his power to give the woman pleasure; and on the other, the woman's inability to enjoy coitus "normally" because of her humiliation and the forced entry into what is hers. Hence, her getting back at the intrusive male by imagining (or effecting) his anal penetration.

Perhaps cases of this kind can give us an idea of why women are less inclined towards sexual perversion, and instead more inclined towards hysteria. Just as the pervert obtains pleasure from reliving obliquely a traumatic experience of betrayal, so does every woman in her own sexual experience, which is labelled as normal. It is as if the little girl experienced a triple trauma: her mother "betrays" her with a man; her beloved father "betrays" her with a woman; and she suffers the "insult" of coitus passively. It is as if behind every real act of coitus the woman risks reliving this triple defeat, while succeeding in making it into an opportunity for pleasure just as in the case of perversion.

But precisely because for every woman her own partner is a substitute, a *pis-aller*, a surrogate for the ideal Man, in the end she opens herself to the care of this "poor man", who desires her and sometimes loves her, dedicating to him that charitable cult destined for the Man, who for her will always be lacking.

But do others exist?

All that we have said about perversion until now involves compromising the subjectivity of the other as something real that we take into account. But today there is considerable confusion regarding the way of conceiving the other and his/her subjectivity.

Our mentality leads us to believe that when we treat others well we are, *ipso facto*, looking after their subjectivity, but psychoanalysis should lead us to distrust this overly hasty equation. For example, one often hears it being said that "the Nazis treated the Jews not as subjects but as objects, and that for this reason they exterminated them". In reality, if the Nazis had treated the Jews as objects, i.e., as instruments for their own advantage, they would instead have given them a good wage to make them work in their factories and industries. Above all, they would have treated exceptionally well the Jewish scientists who could have built the atomic bomb for them. Unfortunately, the Nazis treated Jews as subjects: they enjoyed humiliating them and making them feel to the core that they were sub- or non-human. But if I enjoy making another human being feel like a beast for slaughter, it is precisely his humiliated subjectivity that causes my enjoyment. For this reason, the Nazis put into effect sadistic perversion on a political scale. The sadist, as we have seen, does not treat his victim at all as if he were an inanimate object; he does not simply express his own rage and aggression. Rather he enjoys the other's suffering; he exploits the other's pain in order to reach jouissance, that is, in order to overcome his own pain. Even when the sadist limits himself to inflicting pain on animals, it is the other's pain that he needs, that capacity for suffering that makes animals so similar to us.

This is why many view modern society—which tries to guarantee the others' welfare and civil rights—as alienating, since it is a society that has realized that only by treating others well is it possible to get the best out of them. It has long been known that a free, well-paid worker does a better job for us than a slave. But the logic is the same: whether he be a slave or a free man, the important thing is that the other should be an instrument of production to be optimized. Paradoxically, it is precisely perversion that leads us to understand in what sense the subjectivity of the other regards us, and how it is connected to the edification of our own subjectivity.

It is true that certain psychoanalytical schools, some of which enjoy great popularity today, have overcome the theoretical solipsism of classical metapsychology and have explicitly developed themes of the reality of the other as something that regards subjective development. This is the case in particular of Winnicott, Lacan and analysts of a hermeneutic tendency. Winnicott, by distinguishing the mother who is "good enough" from the one who is not, turned the real mother (and not only the mother imagined or hallucinated by the subject) into the protagonist of psychic development. For this reason, he emphasized the mother's ability to "fantasize" and to understand the true desires of her child. Lacan, by saying that "man's desire is the desire of the Other" (Lacan, 1988, pp. 235–247), introduced the central dimension of the Other: every subject is constituted, not as "a celibate machine" (as Duchamp would have expressed it), by means of one's own fantasies and internal imaginary processes, but in relation to the desire and enjoyment of the Other. Every subject does not simply want to satisfy his own drives or fantasies, but also wishes to satisfy the Other (first of all the mother), whose desires he is able to detect (Verhaeghe, 2001). The hermeneutic trends dissolve the unity of the subject in the relations between subjects: the phenomenology of the single subject is brought back to intersubjective relations, which are described as constituting every personal individuation. *Dasein* (the human being in its singularity) is identified with *Mit-sein*, being-with. From this stems the phenomenologists' insistence on the "relationship", the "field", the "system of relations". And yet, despite these steps forward, I believe that even now psychoanalysis has not really succeeded in focusing upon the reality of the other as a constitutive factor of subjectivity.

For Winnicott, our psychic destiny depends on our mother, but only in so far as she is *our* mother, something for us and in relation to us, not in so far as she is a woman who is and does many other things apart from being our mother. What our mother does and thinks is relevant only as far as her doing and thinking pass through her relationship with us, her children. The reality of both the subject and the other is reduced to their being in relation to each other, to their reciprocal presence or absence, and this reality does not go beyond what each one is *for the* other.

For Lacan, the reality of the Other is confiscated by language: the Other counts, in the final analysis, not in as much as he is a subject different from myself, but in as much as he embodies the instance of the symbolic. The Other blends into the "treasure of the signifiers", in which it basically consists, in the Objective Mind of Hegel. True otherness is no longer one's mother, father, siblings, and friends in flesh and bone, but the signifier which determines us. If in Winnicott the Other blends into the "mother who is more or less good for me", in Lacan it blends into the symbolic Mind that commands its action.

For phenomenology, instead, the subject is freed *d'emblée* from his solitude, and appears determined within the irreducible play of his being-with-others and being-for-others. But, in fact, phenomenology axiomatically assumes as resolved a problem that instead remains: our being-with-the-other is not an immediate, primary, total, and unanalysable reality. Moreover, not all others count for us, and those others who remain only matter under certain conditions. Even hermeneutic phenomenology tends to dissolve the reality of the subject and of the other, that which is on this and on the other side of their ontological interdependence. In this way, the great Freudian discovery—the *force* of drives and biological tensions—is almost cancelled out in a sort of disembodied interpsychism. The neurotics' problem, as lack of care for others in their reality becomes instead in phenomenology an absolute datum from which to begin: every one of us is a *cure for others*. If only it were so! In other words, others condition us not only because they have the power to make us do or not do the things we want, but also because what they feel, think, and know about us concerns us to the utmost degree. We live in large part in order to please and gratify others. We are never autonomous or alone.

The experience of perversion ultimately teaches us that some subjects have no concern for the other. They have no compassionate charity for the other's sexuality, precisely because they have experienced an early trauma: *they have discovered that the other lives a reality that excludes them*. Realizing that the other is not a function of us, *the right object for us*, but a thing-in-itself-and-for-itself, is highly traumatic for many people. The subject suffers from his exclusion from the other, and, in the end, from his *limitation* as a (spatially, temporally, and erotically) finite being. The pervert is nostalgic for "a true life", in which he would enjoy the other as if he himself were the other, and to whom he has never had access. And yet, he is able to transform his exclusion into his sexual pleasure. On the other hand, this exclusion haunts the neurotic, despite his will to go beyond the trauma and become included in the life of others.

References

Christoffel, H. (1956). Male genital exhibitionism. In: S. Lorand & M. Balint (Eds.), *Perversions: Psychodynamics and Therapy* (pp. 243–264). New York: Gramercy.

Deleuze, G. (1971)[1967]. *Masochism: An Interpretation of Coldness and Cruelty*. J. McNeil (Trans.). New York: George Braziller.

Deutsch, H. (1930). Der feminine Masochismus und seine Beziehung zur Frigidität. *Internationale Zeitschrift für Psychoanalyse, 16*(2): 172–184.

Deutsch, H. (1944–1945). *The Psychology of Women* (Vols 1 and 2). New York: Grune & Stratton.

Freud, S. (1905d). Three Essays on the Theory of Sexuality. *S.E., 7*: 125–245. London: Hogarth.

Freud, S. (1908d). "Civilized" sexual morality and modern nervous illness. *S.E., 9*: 177–204. London: Hogarth.

Freud, S. (1918b). From the history of an infantile neurosis. *S.E., 17*: 1–123. London: Hogarth.

Freud, S. (1920g). Beyond the pleasure principle. *S.E., 18*: 3–66. London: Hogarth.

Freud, S. (1924c). The economic problem of masochism. *S.E., 19*: 159–170. London: Hogarth.

Freud, S. (1927e). Fetishism. *S.E., 21*: 152–157. London: Hogarth.
Freud, S. (1940e). Splitting of the ego in the process of defence. *S.E., 23*: 275–279. London: Hogarth.
Gosselin, C., & Wilson, G. (1980). *Sexual Variations: Fetishism, Sadomasochism and Transvestism*. London: Faber & Faber.
Khan, M. M. R. (1965). Foreskin fetishism and its relation to ego pathology in a male homosexual. *International Journal of Psycho-Analysis, 46*: 64–80.
Lacan, J. (1988)[1954–1955]. *The Seminar. Book 2: The Ego in Freud's Theory and in the Technique of Psychoanalysis*. J.-A. Miller (Ed.), S. Tomaselli (Trans.). Cambridge: Cambridge University Press.
Lacan, J. (1994)[1956–1957]. *Le Séminaire, Livre IV: La relation d'objet*, texte établi par J.-A. Miller, Paris: du Seuil.
Lantéri-Laura, G. (1979). *Lecture des perversions. Histoire de leur appropriation médicale*. Paris: Masson.
Money, J. (1988). *Gay, Straight and In-between: The Sexology of Erotic Orientation*. New York: Oxford University Press.
Réage, P. (1972)[1954]. *Story of O*. S. D'Estree (Trans.). London: Corgi Adult.
Stoller, R. J. (1975). *Perversion: The Erotic Form of Hatred*. New York: Pantheon.
Verhaeghe, P. (2001). Perversion I: Perverse traits. *The Letter, 21*: 59–74.

CHAPTER FOUR

The problem of inscription and its clinical meaning in perversion

André Michels

Freud recommends the study of fetishism to anyone who wants to understand the enigma of the castration complex: "An investigation of fetishism is strongly recommended to anyone who still doubts the existence of the castration complex or who can still believe that fright at the sight of the female genital has some other ground . . ." (Freud, 1927e, p. 155). Because repression fails, at least partially, the fetishist has recourse to another defence mechanism, which differs from the neurotic one, and which allows him to replace the missing phallus with another organ (such as the foot) or with a lifeless object. In this way the fetishist finds it easier to come to terms with what is missing, castration being simultaneously acknowledged and denied.

This paper is concerned with the problem of inscription in terms of sexual differentiation, and the way in which it is conditioned by castration. Perversion is inextricably linked to this problem and therefore has a different meaning for men and women. Perversion also affects the generational process and therefore the fundamental differences on which the symbolic order and mental life are based.

In so far as it challenges the core processes of becoming a subject and becoming human, perversion is of great relevance today, in an era that is indelibly marked by the Nazi catastrophe, radical breaks with tradition and the failure of traditional discourses. Nobody is able to gauge the terrible consequences of "biological and scientific" racism. Much like all the other discourses, science produces its own form of perversion. It was incapable of erecting a barrier against barbarism and it failed to derive ethical criteria from its own structure. These criteria always rely on singularity, the particularity of a subject, for which there is no place in science. As a result, the danger of biologism and eugenics becoming leading discourses has not completely disappeared, especially at a time when the genome can be deciphered and genetics are a central aspect of research. The only thing we are left with at the moment is memory, but we also know to what extent it can be falsified. Time and again we encounter people who have seen certain things, yet who claim at the same time that what they have seen is not there and could never have existed.

Memory and writing

In a short paper from 1925 on the "mystic writing-pad", Freud relates the necessity of writing to a distrust of our capacity to remember: "If I distrust my memory ... I am able to supplement and guarantee its working by making a note in writing" (Freud, 1925a, p. 227). Through writing it is possible to overcome the distortions of memory, i.e., of censorship. Yet, this is only partially successful, since writing is no less subjected to censorship. This is something an analysand may ascertain quite easily when he tries to write down his dreams in order not to forget them. What happens in this process is generally not much more than a displacement of censorship. It is not because the analysand is holding his dream on paper that it will become more transparent to him. We therefore have to take account of this close relationship between censorship and writing.

To this, Freud adds another idea, which is extremely valuable for our clinical and theoretical understanding. Depending on the surface and the instrument of writing, traces can be transient, erasable or permanent. Freud is especially interested in the "writing-surface", which, like a chalk-board, "retains its receptive capacity for an unlimited time and the notes upon which can be destroyed . . ., without any need for throwing away the writing-surface itself" (*ibid.*, p. 227). In this case it is impossible to leave a permanent trace, since I need to erase what I have written if I wish to make a new note. This is not the case when I use ink and a sheet of paper, yet in this case the receptive capacity of the writing-surface is again limited and, if necessary, I need to use another blank sheet.

> Thus an unlimited receptive capacity and a retention of permanent traces seem to be mutually exclusive properties in the apparatus which we use as substitutes for our memory: either the receptive surface must be destroyed or the note must be renewed. [*ibid.*, pp. 227–228]

Our psychic apparatus includes both types of inscription: "[I]t has an unlimited receptive capacity for new perceptions and nevertheless lays down permanent—even though not unalterable—memory-traces of them" (*ibid.*, p. 228). After indicating what he had already elaborated in *The Interpretation of Dreams* (Freud, 1900a) and "Beyond the pleasure principle" (Freud, 1920g), Freud believes he has found a model for this in the "mystic writing-pad" that has recently fallen into his hands. It concerns a small contrivance that allows for both functions: unlimited receptive capacity and permanence of the traces. Even if we did not completely agree with Freud's topological conception here, which emanates from his first topography and the system Pcpt–Cs, it none the less raises an extremely important question: *How does writing relate to time?*

From the start Freud relates the status of the unconscious to the status of memory-traces and therefore to that which can be written down. Thereby, he cannot avoid probing deeper into the question of writing, formulating some hypotheses on inscription and time. At the end of his paper on the mystic writing-pad he points out the "discontinuity" in the psychic apparatus's adopted way of writing, which he derives from "the periodic non-excitability of the perceptual system" (Freud, 1925a, p. 231). Yet it is more likely for this discontinuity to be the *work of censorship*, which may exercise a more or less pervasive function of cutting with regard to the unconscious as well as with regard to time. Perhaps one might say that it is not the "discontinuous method of functioning of the system Pcpt-Cs", which "lies at the bottom of the origin of the concept of time" (*ibid.*,

p. 231), as Freud assumes, but the discontinuous registration as a result of censorship.

In this day and age Freud would definitely have referred to the computer, which, in a way completely different from the mystic writing-pad, also has an "unlimited receptive capacity" and the capacity to store permanently what has been written down. The electronic age does not seem to know the traditional limitations of space and time. None the less, another type of limitation lies in the binary writing system, which generates a form of censorship whose proportions we can only guess but which seems to be much more authoritarian than all the forms of censorship we have known until now. It is almost comforting when Freud talks in his example about "a return to the ancient method of writing on tablets of clay or wax" (*ibid.*, p. 229).

Time erases traces, whether they have been written in sand or stone, wax or clay, papyrus or parchment. The documents that have survived of the pre-history or the early history of writing are like the exceptions that confirm the rule. Only that which has the capacity to be retranscribed, with all the associated distortions, is capable of being inscribed permanently in time. The erasure of traces is therefore an essential aspect of their recording (*Inschrift*). Perhaps we can also conclude from this that the importance of the writing-surface is almost negligible. Yet in the search for a model, all analogies will always already be set within very strict limits.

In the process of psychoanalysis we pay attention to the material of the signifier. Yet what has been inscribed is already the result of a retranscription, for which censorship is responsible. Perhaps we can say that every type of inscription only comes about by means of the *auctoritas* (the authorship and the authority) of censorship. This is why a written text is neither accessible nor revealing as such, but always requires interpretation. What we eventually arrive at is a specific reading or a certain version of the text. The letter itself, however, escapes us and our understanding. It belongs to another dimension, which we can approximate, but never join.

On this basis we can talk (also with reference to clinical work) about the *transcendental text*, which consists of multifarious interpretive layers. However far the analyst may go back in time, the only thing she will be able to find is one or the other variant of this text, the original being forever lost. Only the fantasy is capable of covering up this hole in the symbolic, which is why the subject loves to engage himself with its imaginary contents. And the analyst needs to take account of this fantasmatic structure as well. In this respect, Lacan has tried to render the fantasy with an algebraic formula, in order to preserve the place from which speech retreats and in which the subject is dissolved, yet which is extremely important for the subject's libidinal economy (Lacan, 2001[1960–1961], p. 398). For some subjects the fantasy even functions as a proper name, with which they try to compensate for an inadequate anchoring in the symbolic order. This may help us to understand why many perverts define themselves, or create a new identity for themselves, in accordance with a peculiarity of their fantasy.

The clinical relevance of inscription

The study of the other clinical structures (neurosis and psychosis) is very useful for developing our understanding of perversion. The structures differ with regard to the subject's engagement with the fantasy, which can of course only be accessed via interpretation, much like other clinical materials.

As far as the fantasy is concerned, the neurotic stumbles over his attempts at interpretation and suffers from their idleness. The neurotic prefers to eradicate, i.e., repress, what he cannot undo, with the result that the traces of the past continue to exist as erased traces, and are actually maintained precisely because they have been erased. In paradoxical fashion, the traces have been preserved and accentuated by virtue of the fact that they have been wiped out. This process also conditions the way in which the neurotic deals with his subjective truth, which he can often approach only via a lie. This in turn leads to the subversion of his discourse, with the implication that something else is always speaking in everything he says. This is recognizable in the neurotic's symptoms, dreams, and other formations of the unconscious.

The main difference between neurosis and psychosis is that the psychotic rarely lies. When he reaches the limits of what can be said, that is to say, when he arrives at the boundaries of his discursive possibilities, the psychotic can only have recourse to his delusion (instead of using a metaphor). Accordingly, every change in his professional or family life that has a symbolic value for him and that touches upon his name constitutes a danger. He then tries to inscribe these events upon himself in an acute phase of his psychosis, like a form of self-mutilation. The psychosis is an attempt at reconstructing the symbolic anchoring at the level of the unconscious body-image, which offers (and also represents) a kind of "writing-surface".

Similar questions appear in each of the clinical structures. Wherein lies the originality of the perverse answer? The pervert attempts to approach the inadequacy of inscription via the visualization of traces—like flagellation, which demonstrates a close connection between the rod, the instrument of writing, and the marked body as a place of inscription (Lacan, 1991[1969–1970], p. 55)—that cannot be effaced. This can also lead to a fetishization of the letter, which gives the place of enjoyment its indication and translation, and draws it into the centre of the perverse scenario as its means and end. Is this why so many perverts are writers? This dynamic is by no means unrelated to the visualization of marks on the body that is so popular in contemporary culture. For some people it is tempting to leave behind definitive traces, which are supposed to be eternal, and which turn out to be morbid because they are opposed to time and therefore to life. The way in which the pervert deals with truth is also significant. In order to keep the truth pure, the pervert would like to eradicate the lie completely, yet in order to deal with it better, he turns the lie into a system. The pervert is capable of letting truth and falsity exist simultaneously without either being too threatened by its counterpart, similar to how he manages to give castration both a positive and a negative content. Freud explains this with reference to "the divided attitude of fetishists to the question of the castration of women": "In very subtle instances both the disavowal and the affirmation of the castration have found their way into the construction of the fetish itself" (Freud, 1927e, p. 156).

The inscription, which is subjected to a very strict necessity and stems from a certain engagement with castration, also conditions the way in which a subject inhabits his body. The mutual influence of psyche and soma demands an interpretation, because the question of what holds our body and soul together can only be answered in the singular. Yet the point where both intersect is conditioned by the deictic (*nennende*) function of the name, which is the line of continuity that runs through our lives. The name is what binds the sexes and the generations. Both the small and the large family histories affecting every human being unfold and are shaped by the name. These histories give most people a form of support and content, but they can also make people suffer and sometimes even drive someone to despair.

The purpose of interpretation, which often involves thinking around corners, is to provide a reading of this function of the name. The problem of neurosis represents a variant of this, because it is already the product of an interpretation of the paternal signifiers. This is not the case for the psychotic, who cannot but obey the paternal discourse in its entirety. It is as if the discourse has enslaved him, and every attempt at breaking out can be life threatening. In order to create an opening in this compact discourse, the psychotic can eventually go so far as to kill a family member or himself. In this way he tries to inscribe the lack, which the neurotic encounters in the Symbolic, in the Real, even if he has to pay the price of a life.

Between the generations the pervert occupies the role of a plaything or a waste product. The pervert is like someone who does not acknowledge his debt and who is not prepared to take responsibility for it. He may also abdicate every involvement in generational and genealogical links or, at least, prefer not to have to justify these. His attitude towards others is conditioned by his flight into anonymity, as if he expects to be able to shed the *burden of the name*. In some circumstances, this may lead to a chaotic, unrestricted sexuality or, alternatively, to the abandonment of sexuality altogether. Yet, behind this façade a completely different drama is being played out: confused, the pervert tries to liberate himself from a nameless and therefore ungraspable sense of guilt. In as much as nobody ever took responsibility for it, this guilt is difficult to symbolize and therefore hardly possible to pay off.

When the pervert gives the impression that he is not tied to the *deictic function of the name*, then this is only because he has not encountered anyone in that place—he has not met anyone who occupied this function, even temporarily. By means of his scenario, which we designate as perverse, the pervert tries to recreate the scene of inscription, a kind of primal scene on whose horizon stands the figure of death as the sole and unique point of temporal reference. When the pervert often gives the impression of being without guilt, then this is founded upon nothing less than a presumably very severe and inflexible Superego, which is incapable of structuring enjoyment and elicits a potentially lethal practice of enjoyment-seeking.

Traces and their erasure

One of Freud's letters to Fließ (the letter of 6 December 1896, sometimes also designated as "Letter 52") provides us with some very valuable indications for elaborating the problem of inscription. Freud reminds his friend of his working hypothesis: "[O]ur psychic mechanism has come into being by a process of stratification: the material present in the form of memory traces being subjected from time to time to a *rearrangement* in accordance with fresh circumstances—to a *retranscription*" (Masson, 1985, p. 207). The memory traces that are accessible to us are thus already the product of time, which has rearranged and retranscribed them. Yet, the question remains: where does this scansion and punctuation stem from? We also hear from Freud that various stages (at least three) are necessary for an inscription to come about:

> Thus what is essentially new about my theory is the thesis that memory is present not once but several times over, that is laid down in various kinds of indications . . . I do not know how many of these registrations there are—at least three, probably more. [*ibid.*, p. 207]

So how is a trace being formed and how is it inscribed? The assumption of various retranscriptions, coinciding with various periods of time, provides us with a valuable starting-point. The traces undergo changes, although they are at once endowed with a high degree of stability. They become the carriers of subjective memory, which follows a certain code and proceeds in a very selective way. All the essential features of a real event can disappear, so that only something completely trivial remains behind as a trace. Yet this trace only acquires a subjectifying function when it is in turn either erased or forged. Only in this case, in specific circumstances, is it possible for the discourse of the subject to be ignited by metaphor.

Freud notices something similar with regard to dreams. Nothing is apparently less variable and less reliable than the narrative of a dream, which we either forget instantly when we wake up or are only able to recount inadequately. Freud observes: "It is true that we distort dreams in attempting to reproduce them . . . But this distortion is itself no more than a part of the revision to which the dream-thoughts are regularly subjected as a result of the dream-censorship" (Freud, 1900a, p. 514). The dream-account is not the only distorting and falsifying process: the manifest dream itself is already the product of a much more fundamental distortion: "[W]e know that a much more far-reaching process of distortion, though a less obvious one, has already developed the dream out of the hidden dream-thoughts" (*ibid.*, p. 514). And Freud continues by pointing out that it would be a mistake to underestimate, as most pre-analytic authors have done, "the extent to which psychical events are determined. There is nothing arbitrary about them" (*ibid.*, p. 514).

The analysis of speechlessness (mutism) in the psychotic patient demonstrates that he is incapable, often for a long period of time, of uttering a single word because he is afraid he will betray his own thoughts, since he can only ever present part of them. In this way, the psychotic patient expresses, in his own way, that a subject is always lying, which is quite unbearable for him, and that lies appear as soon as a subject opens his mouth because it is impossible to say the whole truth and nothing but the truth. The truth is always bisected, which is something a child experiences when it learns to speak and sometimes with reference to its own body. This experience becomes all the more important when the child approaches the "nucleus of its being", that is to say, the processes of sexuation and symbolic anchoring.

Only a forged trace is able to yield a subject. The successive retranscriptions of traces coincide with successive life-periods. Freud talks about "epochs of life":

At the boundary between two such epochs a translation of the psychic material must take place. I explain the peculiarities of the psychoneuroses by supposing that this translation has not taken place in the case of some of the material, which has certain consequences ... If a later transcript is lacking, the excitation is dealt with in accordance with the psychological laws in force in the earlier psychic period and along the paths open at that time. Thus an anachronism persists: in a particular province, *fueros* are still in force; we are in the presence of "survivals" [Masson, 1985, p. 208]

The term "transcript" (*Überschrift*) is a conflation of "translation" (*Übersetzung*) and "transcription" (*Umschrift*), which are synonymous here. It is worth noting Freud's reference to writing, i.e., to a text, here, which has existed in many different versions for a long time, yet which is only accessible in translation. The versions consist of unequal and incomplete layers of translation, each of which coincides with a particular degree of interpretation of a law. An important consequence of this is that entire regions of our psychic life and our enjoyment are still controlled by anachronistic laws, which have long since been overtaken by others. The editor of Freud's correspondence with Fließ notes that the Spanish word *fuero* refers to "an ancient Spanish law still in effect in some particular city or province, guaranteeing that region's immemorial privileges" (*ibid.*, p. 215). "Survivals" thus refers to remnants of ancient privileges, that is to say, to an old form of enjoyment that has not completely disappeared. Freud's letter contains a small essay, here, on the relationship between writing and time, law and enjoyment.

However, the most trenchant idea appears in the following paragraph of the letter:

> A failure of translation—this is what is known clinically as "repression". The motive for it is always a release of the unpleasure that would be generated by a translation; it is as though this unpleasure provokes a disturbance of thought that does not permit the work of translation. [*ibid.*, p. 208]

In *Studies on Hysteria*, which appeared more than one year before this letter was written, Freud had claimed that "the primary factor is defence. But I can say nothing about this" (Freud & Breuer, 1895d, p. 286). In the letter to Fließ, defence does not appear as the primary phenomenon. Instead, defence is seen as originating in something more archaic, a translation that coincides with the transcription of an unknown text. This process also creates a temporal differentiation, on which all of psychic life is based. In addition, defence remains unproblematic when it occurs within one and the same phase:

> Within one and the same psychic phase, and among registrations of the same kind, a *normal* defence makes itself felt owing to a generation of unpleasure. But *pathological* defence occurs only against a memory trace from an earlier phase that has not yet been translated. [*ibid.*, p. 208–209]

Pathological means disproportionate or ineffective here. Over time, this disproportion may harden and turn into a psychic characteristic for the neurotic. The neurotic is reminded time and again that time does not essentially change anything and definitely does not heal his wounds, but rather constantly reopens them.

Repression thus induces a more or less encompassing temporal confusion. But what is it able to preserve? The aforementioned traces are remnants of a bygone suffering and enjoyment. Indeed, the two often go together and they exercise a compulsion that the subject finds hard to escape. The traces are "survivals" of a pre-temporal Other, which cannot be emulated by anything afterwards, yet which has never had a real existence. The latter is linked to the traces of enjoyment of this mythical Other, in which both Freud's theory of the "primal father" and Lacan's theory of the "Other enjoyment" have their roots. In this way it becomes easier to understand why the subject likes to preserve these traces and what they transmit, even if this entails a high degree of suffering. In any case, repression opposes the erasure of traces, sometimes through devious means, so that time appears to be excluded.

Repression can thus be situated at a symbolic boundary, at the threshold of the unconscious, we may say. Repression enables the subject at once to forget and to preserve a signifier, and in this way it creates a link between two different registers, from which some kind of ideal present results—a present without a past. The subjective representation of time requires the translation of memory traces, which can hardly take place without a potentially very painful loss. Yet the one who is unable to lose or forget becomes incapable of living and sometimes delusional. It is also necessary to accept that the symbolic has a hole, which could only have come into existence on the basis of a radical primordial loss, for an interpretation to be altogether possible and for a new meaning to emerge.

Untranslated and untranslatable memory traces hold on to a certain enjoyment, which resists interpretation (metaphor). Interpretation, on the other hand, effectuates a renunciation of the drive (*Triebverzicht*), which first of all concerns the object of primordial enjoyment, so that the subject can be inscribed in a symbolic order. The latter will only be fundamentally acknowledged through repression, as opposed to other defence mechanisms, although repression is of course problematic in its own right. Yet, before I develop this point further, I wish to discuss briefly a clinical vignette.

The example of passionate love gives us some idea of the compulsion that can result from untranslated memory traces. When the trace emerges in the Real, it may awaken an old, long "forgotten" enjoyment, which the subject in most cases does not remember or does not want to know anything about. A mechanism can be triggered, then, that is difficult to control and that can drive someone to madness and even to death. Even the less extreme cases rarely occur without drama. For example, a young woman cannot resist a certain intonation of the voice and a certain movement or posture of the body, which remind her of her first love. The affair remains unconsummated and rapidly leads to a suicide attempt. Afterwards, nothing is resolved or worked through. Some time later, she finds herself in another situation that is diametrically opposed to the previous one, and on to which her earlier problem has been displaced. She claims that she wants to stay with a man, and even wants to marry him, in order to avoid that he has to go through the same event she went through a couple of years before. The situation stays like this for a while, until she refuses to have sex with him and decides to take a lover, whom she does not really love but in whose company she feels like a woman for the first time. It does not stop her from pursuing the wedding plans with her fiancé. One week before the wedding she tries to commit suicide again, but she recovers just in time to stick to the agreed time-plan. A suicide attempt is for her the only way to create a discontinuity and to oppose the compulsion associated with the realization of a certain trait, which operates as if it has been inscribed on both sides of a single sheet. However, the compulsory nature of the entire process is still somehow maintained.

A hypothesis concerning inscription

In keeping with what we have said until now, inscription may be situated alongside the problem of primal repression. Inscription is directly related to what cannot be represented, to the hole that the subject encounters in the place of the Other. The trace is what remains of that which is irrecoverably lost, although the trace (as a remnant) may not have anything in common with what has been lost, because the inscription is made elsewhere. In so far as the original object has been forever lost, that which has been inscribed of this object exists in a different place—it has been displaced. The oldest inscription is therefore not a faithful testimonial of what once was, but already the product of a distortion, which requires interpretation.

If the hole in the Symbolic coincides with a radical non-knowing, then its letter becomes the carrier of a completely different type of knowledge, which we call the unconscious. The subject is thus confronted with the failure of any guarantee at a central place, against which he constantly has to adopt a position. In this context, it is worth mentioning that the Western world has developed two fundamentally different answers to this problem. First, mathematics and science, two distinct modalities of writing, have tried to erect a dam against this bottomless insecurity. The dam was held firmly in place until it was put into perspective by the arrival of the new mathematics of infinity and the transfinite. The second answer comes from so-called *Holy Writ* and the oral (Talmudic) transmission with which it is connected. In both cases, access to the writing system is so severely hindered by technical difficulties that it remains for most people completely beyond their reach, like the Law in Kafka's story. We are confronted here with a certain protective measure against the abyssal depth of nothingness, which is revealed to anyone who is preoccupied with the interpretation of the letter. Psychoanalysis is concerned with exactly the same thing.

The letter is like a last vestige at the edge of a ravine. It is inscribed at the edge of an erogenous zone, such as an opening in the body. The necessary condition for this inscription is that an opening in the body offer itself, or that a locus of the body let itself be negativized, which cannot be represented in any representational system. This process elicits a division and hierarchization of the erogenous zones. It is thus necessary for a point to be established through which the symbolic can be inscribed on the body, and the body itself can be inscribed. We are concerned, here, with a point of articulation between the letter and the unconscious image of the body, which contributes to both its fragmentation and its unity. This topological model outlines the condition of hysteria and elevates it to the rank of a paradigm for the other clinical structures. At least so much can be inferred from the work of psychoanalysis, which can deservedly be conceived as a hystericization of discourse.

Hystericization may also be understood as a process of feminization, which the paranoiac desperately tries to keep at bay. The paranoiac singles out dispersed statements about femininity, feminization, and homosexuality in the discourse of the Other as assertions concerning himself. Heterosexual relationships constitute a massive danger for the paranoiac because they carry the meaning of a real castration and thus question the unity of his body. The paranoiac often tries to conjure this situation, alleviating the anxiety it brings about, by doing something to himself. In each case he tries to restore the lost unity, for example in the mirror, which becomes the imaginary carrier of that which has not found a solid foundation in the Symbolic. Some paranoiacs succeed in circumventing this boundary condition by radically avoiding all contact with the other sex. Yet, love can also lead to this kind of reaction, because it mobilizes the name, i.e., the inscription in the Symbolic. Instead of the negativity of the letter, the paranoiac encounters the complete fullness of an inerasable trace that carries too much meaning. And he experiences this trace as a threat coming from the outside—as in a persecutory delusion—which can turn into a threat coming from the inside; for example, in the form of self-reproaches. Hence, there is a significant structural similarity between paranoia and melancholia, and they have both found a common somatic denominator in the term hypochondria.

A somatic illness may contribute to the improvement of a psychotic condition, because it situates the negativization in the real of the body. This brings us to a renewed examination of the interaction between psyche and soma, and of the meaning of the so-called psychosomatic phenomena. These phenomena correspond to a striving for autonomy in a certain locus of the body, which tries to break free from the very strict libidinal or erotic control either by freeing itself from the libidinal net or by stretching out over a part of the body. In both cases the limitation of the original zone disappears, as a result of which the zone cannot be clearly delineated any more and thus is no longer inscribed. Somatic illnesses oppose this process because they leave behind permanent traces, which give content to an overwhelming expression of the drives. Somatic phenomena thus have the paradoxical meaning of healing attempts, and, in general, they follow a subject's refusal to accept the *primacy of the phallus*. It is, then, as if this point needs to be placed elsewhere, temporally as well as spatially. The sick part of the body succeeds, in the best of cases only temporarily, to hold the sceptre and to subjugate entire parts of the bodily realm in order to impose upon them another libidinal economy. In this case we might refer to a tyranny of the illness, in so far as it attempts to impose its own law and to transcend the symbolic order. Of course, it is impossible to decide what was first, the erogenous reorganization or the somatic illness, because both manifest and inscribe themselves simultaneously at two different levels, without a translation of one into the other. The classic law of cause and effect is therefore made inoperative. And in this lies, no doubt, the greatest difficulty for our understanding of the so-called psychosomatic phenomena. Only with hindsight does it become possible, by means of an interpretation, to introduce a temporal discontinuity, which also enables the re-introduction of the law of cause and effect.

Let us return to the issue of hysteria. Here, too, it might be the case that an erogenous zone breaks free from the others, i.e., extracts itself from the primacy of the phallus. Yet the neurotic can rely on a fairly large *somatic plasticity*. The symbolic inscription remains solid, here, so that the isolation of a locus of the body, however much it may lead to bodily fragmentation, always maintains bodily unity. We only start discovering this paradox when we succeed in elucidating the relationship between writing and narcissism. For narcissism not only concerns that which is conspicuous, but also that which remains hidden and which cannot be recognized in the mirror, and which involves recognition by a third party. For the neurotic, the letter occupies the place of what cannot be represented, and on this basis his symbolic inscription becomes possible. Yet, inscription requires, on the other hand, also metaphor, which at different moments or on certain occasions gives rise to a translation or a different version. Metaphor is essentially metaphor of the body, and it regulates the subject's sexual behaviour. In the case of an inadequate translation, a *residual enjoyment* stemming from an earlier psychic phase remains operative, which may also have deleterious effects for the neurotic. It represents a *point of fixation* in his life, which may excessively control his abilities and which may lead to a form of paralysis. None the less, the neurotic rarely agrees to get rid of this fixation, because it also gives him a kind of certainty.

In the case of perversion, this fixation acquires another meaning and another outlook, because it makes up the foundation of the pervert's scenario; that is to say, of his enjoyment. The pervert desperately tries to eradicate loss and transient life. In particular, he does not want to relinquish an earlier, infantile enjoyment, despite the *oedipal sanction*. Only in so far as the pervert has observed this sanction is he also able to *disavow* it. The pervert does not retreat into a pre-oedipal position; instead he reacts to the primacy of the phallus with an attitude of *obnoxiousness* and *provocation*. Both are characteristic of the pervert's behaviour and they are all the more persistent as the primacy of the phallus is insecure and has not been safely anchored. It is as if the pervert believes he needs to provoke something in order to drive it out. Yet, because he can never be sure of its effect, he starts a search for a solid or fixed point of departure, which he ultimately believes to find in death. Death provides the pervert with a central outlook, which gives him the hope of fulfilling an *absolute measure of time*. In Mishima's work, this issue gradually acquires more significance, so much so that, from a certain point onwards, he concentrates almost exclusively on the preparation of a unique, unreplicatable scenario. Mishima wants to erect a monument for inscription through the enactment of a spectacular suicidal scenario. However, it is not an exaggeration to talk in this context about a *lethal metaphor*. This also applies to the perverse scenario in general, which singles out death as the most appropriate temporal framework, whether or not this is explicitly formulated.

On the basis of this constellation, and with a view to preserving and consolidating some traditional values—like country and family, *throne* and *altar*—the pervert may orchestrate a widely cast social provocation and thereby end up in circumstances that lead to his death. Yet he might equally well use these values or agencies as excuses for his dissident and revolutionary behaviours, especially when his plans are supported by a collective movement. In this way he realizes a scenario that has been transferred on to the social or political level, which stands in the service of his lethal enjoyment and which explains it as generally in accordance with the law. This is precisely what Sade (1990) demands in his seminal text "Français, encore un effort, si vous voulez être républicains", included in *Philosophy in the Bedroom*. The same issue has also been adumbrated by Jean Genet. After having spent most of his life challenging every possible agency and authority, he manages to re-connect with the crucial issue of the existence of the state of Israel during the last phase of his life. In this way, he also provides the key to an understanding of his political commitment: his challenge is primarily directed against what the name Israel represents, that is to say the law, the Torah. This example demonstrates that the provocation is essentially part of the mechanism of disavowal, as its positive aspect, because it seeks to bring forward that which it simultaneously disavows.

Freud mentions *throne* and *altar* in his paper on fetishism, and uses both terms with reference to the boy's reaction to the woman's castration:

> No, that could not be true: for if a woman had been castrated, then his own possession of a penis was in danger; and against that there rose in rebellion the portion of his narcissism which Nature has, as a precaution, attached to that particular organ. In later life a grown man may perhaps experience a similar panic when the cry goes up that Throne and Altar are in danger, and similar illogical consequences will ensue. [Freud, 1927e, p. 153]

On the basis of what we have experienced concerning narcissism in cases of neurosis, we can now understand how one of the main functions of the fetish consists in rescuing the imaginary unity of the body. Freud forges a fundamental link between narcissism and the castration of the mother (of women). Yet what is maintained at the level of the imaginary is therefore not inscribed symbolically. The fragmentation of the body is unbearable for the fetishist to the extent that he remains excluded from the inadequacy, the splitting of the Other, at the level of the symbolic. His relationship with the body and with everything related to it is therefore governed by relentless and innumerable attempts at restoration. The search for a perfect body offers him an escape, yet he is only intermittently concerned with it. The confrontation with Otherness and strangeness represents a major threat to him, which in some circumstances may provide his xenophobia with a welcome justification and a rich source of nourishment.

The fetishist's enjoyment is devoted to the fulfilment of the Other, to whose completion he is keen to contribute. It is not difficult to see how the structure of numerous religious practices is conditioned by this principle. The fetish takes the place of inscription, with the result that the letter becomes fetishized in itself. As we pointed out earlier, this process may prompt the fetishist to become a writer, which is likely to give him an excess of enjoyment. Yet the fetishist prefers the body of the Other as a writing-surface, on which he leaves a visible mark in order to increase its libidinal value. In his scenario he tries to bring forward, in a positive way, as a *stigma indelebile*, that which remains invisible for the neurotic (Freud, 1927e, p. 154). In another context, Freud argued that "neuroses are, so to say, the negative of perversions" (Freud, 1905d, p. 165). We can, therefore, also regard tattooing (and many other visible markings of the body) as part of the fetishism of writing in a broad sense.

The pervert seems compelled to repeat what is problematic about inscription, in order to transcribe it into another register. As already mentioned, his scenario has the meaning of a primal scene in which he needs to act out the "nucleus of his being", which remains radically unconscious for him. The pervert, strictly speaking, does not exceed "anatomical boundaries", as is often assumed, because the latter do not really exist for him. In *transgressing* boundaries, the pervert gives them first of all *consistency*, and in this way he also consolidates the body that carries these boundaries. The latter must then take the place of an inconsistent, untrustworthy Other. Yet the inscription of the traces that have been left behind there can only convince the pervert on the basis of the anxiety, horror, and pain he reads in the eyes of the other. Indeed, he seems mainly concerned with triggering this kind of reaction, because he believes it is the only indication capable of validating the inscribed trace in an *authentic* way. In order to achieve this, the pervert is sometimes capable or compelled to go very far, too far, in the hope of obtaining some kind of guarantee.

The pervert is, more than anyone else, confronted with the fact that there is nobody beyond the Other who can provide him with a guarantee for the Symbolic and the law. The pervert's problem is similar to that of every modern person who observes with anxiety that the place from which the law has derived its legitimacy until now is actually empty and has always been like that. Yet this observation is completely unbearable for the pervert and he tries to formulate a specific answer to it. In so far as he himself becomes the object of the Other's enjoyment, he belongs to those few contemporaries who are able to give to the Other a long lost state of completion.

References

Freud, S. (1900a). *The Interpretation of Dreams. S.E.*, 4/5.
Freud, S. (1905d). *Three Essays on the Theory of Sexuality. S.E.*, 7: 123–245.
Freud, S. (1920g). Beyond the pleasure principle. *S.E.*, 18: 1–64.
Freud, S. (1925a). A note upon the "mystic writing-pad". *S.E.*, 19: 225–232.
Freud, S. (1927e). Fetishism. *S.E.*, 21: 149–157.
Freud, S. and Breuer, J. (1895d). *Studies on Hysteria. S.E.*, 2.
Lacan, J. (1991[1969–1970]). *Le Séminaire, Livre XVII: L'envers de la psychanalyse*, texte établi par J.-A. Miller, Paris: du Seuil.
Lacan, J. (2001[1960–1961]). *Le Séminaire, Livre VIII: Le transfert*, 2ième édition corrigée, texte établi par J.-A. Miller, Paris: du Seuil.
Masson, J. M. (Ed.) (1985). *The Complete Letters of Sigmund Freud to Wilhelm Fließ, 1887–1904*. J. M. Masson (Trans.). Cambridge, MA: The Belknap Press of Harvard University Press.
Sade, D. A. F. de (1990)[1796]. *Justine, Philsophy in the Bedroom and Other Writings*. A. Wainhouse (Trans.). London: Grove Press.

CHAPTER FIVE

The perversion of pain, pleasure, and thought: on the difference between "suffering" an experience and the "construction" of a thing to be used

Nicola Abel-Hirsch[1]

It is widely recognized today that perversion is not limited to a person's sexual behaviour, but may influence all of an individual's experiences, relations, and attitudes to reality. This raises the question of whether the perverse relations in these different spheres share a similar structure. This chapter explores the issue in relation to pain, pleasure, and thought, and suggests that the perverse relations in each case are "constructed", in contrast to experiences that are "suffered" and "discovered" to arise within the self.

A key question asked throughout the history of debates about sado-masochism is why a person would derive pleasure from pain. In these discussions the nature of pleasure and pain has, on the whole, been taken for granted as a "known", and the question asked only of the relation between them, i.e., why pleasure from pain? I think, however, largely due to the work of Wilfred Bion and its development by Betty Joseph, that the nature of the pain and pleasure themselves, and not just the relation between them, can now be better explored.

Bion wrote little directly on perversion. However, his work introduces the possibility of distinguishing between what he describes as pain "suffered" and pain "felt". This difference is not to do with whether the experience comes from inside or outside, but with how it is received by the person. His distinction has not been developed in a widespread or explicit way and this may well be because of his use of the term "suffer". At least at first sight the term is confusing because it carries the connotation of pain inflicted. However it does have another meaning, which can be seen in the following Biblical quotation:

> 13. Then were there brought unto him little children, that he should put his hands on them, and pray: and the disciples rebuked them.
> 14. But Jesus said, Suffer little children, and forbid them not, to come unto me: for of such is the kingdom of heaven [Matthew 19, 905]

Here we get more sense of a meaning of "suffer" that is also contained in its dictionary definition, of enduring a change and bearing or allowing something to happen. This is the meaning I think Bion has in mind in the following:

> There are patients whose contact with reality presents most difficulty when that reality is their own mental state. For example, a baby discovers its hand; it might as well have discovered its stomach-ache, or its feeling of dread or anxiety, or mental pain. In most ordinary personalities this is true, but people exist who are so intolerant of pain or frustration (or in whom pain or frustration is so intolerable) that they feel the pain but will not suffer it and so cannot be said to discover it. *What* it is that they will not suffer or discover we have to conjecture from what we learn from patients who *do* allow themselves to suffer. The patient who will not suffer pain fails to "suffer" pleasure and this denies the patient the encouragement he might otherwise receive from accidental or intrinsic relief. [Bion, 1993, p. 9]

Bion suggests that a difference between "suffering" pain and "feeling" pain is that the former is a discovery made in contact with reality (internal and external reality). By "discover" he conveys a sense of finding the pain within oneself, as an experience of what it is to be oneself. The psychoanalyst David Bell put it as follows: "There is not an 'I' which discovers certain states, thoughts, feelings within itself, but more than that, it is in the act of the discovering, in that moment, that the 'I' is itself" (personal communication).

In contrast to this, pain felt but not suffered may be believed to carry information only about the "torturer" and hold no meaning for the self. If we take two patients and consider how they might experience pain in relation to their analyst (in connection with Bion's distinction), we could suggest that in the first case of suffering pain, the patient discovers that he or she is someone who misses, who can feel excluded, and can be jealous. Britton uses the term "suffer" to describe such a situation: "The suffering is felt to arise within the self as a consequence of something missing" (Britton, 1998, p. 111). By contrast, in the second case of feeling pain but not suffering it, the patient takes personally, for example, the analyst's going. The patient feels pain, not as his or her own experience of loss, but as pain purposefully inflicted on him or her by the analyst.

Pain felt as a "thing" inflicted rather than suffered can also be inflicted by a person on him or herself; for example, in a young child's head banging. Such pain is a constructed event rather than a discovery. The pain is a thing that is felt, rather than an experience that is found, and as a thing it can be used or manipulated. Joseph has illustrated the difference she finds between pain *used* in a masochistic or sadistic way and pain suffered by the person (Joseph uses the term "real"): "At the same time the analyst will sense that there is real misery and anxiety around and this will have to be sorted out and differentiated from the masochistic use and exploitation of misery" (Joseph, 1989, p. 128)

The differentiation of pain as a felt thing that is used and pain that is suffered and thence discovered by the person is consistent with a parallel development of thought on perversion that looks at the way disavowal or misrepresentation can be used to obscure an unwanted discovery of reality. The misuse of pain and the misrepresentation of reality can both be regarded as constructions rather than discoveries.

Disavowal and misrepresentation in a perverse relation to reality

In his discussion of perversion in *Psychic Retreats*, Steiner begins with Freud's work on fetishism (Freud, 1927e). Freud argues that the little boy believes the mother to have a penis and, when faced with the reality that this is not the case, maintains his belief, and an acknowledgement of reality, by believing the fetish, for example, a shoe, to be the penis. The recognition of reality is experienced as a threat (in this case in relation to castration anxiety) and this is avoided by a simultaneous acknowledgement and disavowal of reality. Steiner states: "I believe that these misrepresentations are central to an understanding of perversions and that they arise from a quite specific mechanism in which contradictory versions of reality are allowed to coexist simultaneously" (Steiner, 1995, p. 90).

Bion refers to the same phenomena in his discussion of the "lie"—the structure of a lie being such that the truth is known and at the same time misrepresented. In his portrayal of the liar, Bion describes how the lie needs repeated action to keep the "belief" in the lie going:

> Some [liars], knowing full well the risks they ran, nevertheless laid down their lives in affirmations of lies so that the weak and doubtful would be convinced by the ardour of their conviction of the truth of even the most preposterous statements. [Bion, 1993, p. 100]

While a true state of affairs does not require constant restatement, the "thinker is of no consequence to the truth, but the truth is logically necessary to the thinker. His significance depends on whether or not he will entertain the thought" (*ibid.*, p. 103). In terms of artistic creativity, I think Hodgkin was trying to get at the same thing in the following comment:

> My pictures are finished when the subject comes back. I start out with the subject and naturally I have to remember first of all what it looked like, but it would also perhaps contain a great deal of feeling and sentiment. All of that has got to be somehow transmuted, transformed or made into a physical object, and when that happens, when that's finally been done, when the last physical marks have been put on and the subject comes back—which, after all, is usually the moment when the painting is at long last a coherent physical object—well, then the picture's finished and there is no question of doing any more to it. My pictures really finish themselves. [quoted in Graham-Dixon, 1994, p. 178]

The subject is not repetitively insisted on, but is there and is found anew in a transformed state. Hodgkin also conveys the sense that the painting has a "true life" or life of its own; when "thought" (painted) exists separately from the painter, the painter becomes redundant.

The "discovered" state of affairs is not dependent on our knowing about it at any particular moment. The construction of a misrepresentation or lie by contrast has to be kept going. As will be seen in the example below, this is a complicated and convoluted business. Not only is the unwanted reality known and not known at the same time, but the fact that there is a disavowal or lie may be equally known and not known at the same time. The patient described below, for example, knew there was a lie, but attributed by projection the lying to the analyst.

Example

The patient is in analysis five times a week and uses the couch. The patient, whom I will call B, had a number of dreams in which she had sex with a series of strangers, while another woman was "free to go". In one dream, for example, the other woman drove her to a house. She was imprisoned in a dark room and a succession of men arrived to have sex with her. She conveyed that this was horrendous, but also a service she had to perform.

At the time it was difficult to understand the dreams. Over the following months we slowly came to clarify her view of hatred. B had a belief that she contained other people's hateful feelings. This left the other people, including me, her analyst, free of their own hate. This was a horrific task for her, but one she also felt she had a special strength to perform. B believed that I lied to her and myself about the existence of my own hatred and that I secretly used her as a vehicle for it. It occurred to me then that the above dreams might refer to the same view about sex, i.e., all (taboo) sex was to be with her. B agreed and told me about a time when she had sex, as a young woman, with her cousin's father. B consciously believed she had a superior knowledge in which she knew what the father and daughter could not admit to themselves, namely that they wanted to have sex with each other. B saw her sexual relations with her uncle as being at the limits of the acceptable. It was, she said, the only place where a father and daughter could have sex, i.e., a place where a father both was and was not a father at the same time and a daughter both was and was not a daughter at the same time. B had a fantasy of the daughter (B's cousin) walking in on them (B and the cousin's father) and being excited by the realization (put into practice by the patient) that she, the daughter, wanted sex with her father. B was enacting, she believed, the other young woman's phantasy.

If there had been a complete split B may, for example, have had sex with her cousin's father with no conscious awareness of his being a "father" or of her being a "daughter". However, B is aware that his position of father is significant and that a daughter can want exciting and possessive relations with her father. B takes up a position of disavowal in which, as she says, she both is and at the same time is not a daughter.

The concreteness of the oedipal enactment is significant, as is the fact that B did not feel sexual pleasure herself in the affair. Through our exploration of the material about her cousin we could see more clearly her belief that I was in a disavowing state of mind in which I pretended to do analysis, while secretly wanting her masochistically to fulfil phantasies I could not be honest about to myself. As with her cousin, B believed herself to be where my secret phantasies lay. My impression is that this is a perverse compromise, in which she is neither the same as me (with the fears of annihilation this would bring) nor different from me. It is also a position in which she feels powerful and exciting/excited, which leads to the question of the nature of the gratification involved in constructed perverse relations. In the next part of this chapter, I talk about the difference between perverse pleasure, which is constructed and inflicted on the self, and pleasure that is suffered, in the sense of discovered as arising within the self.

On the suffering of pleasure

In her paper "Addiction to near-death", Joseph comments:

> [W]e are still left with a major problem as to why this type of masochistic self-destruction is so self perpetuating ... One reason ...—the sheer unequalled sexual delight of the grim masochism—is undeniable, yet it is usually very difficult for a long time for such patients to see that they are suffering from an addiction, that they are "hooked" to this kind of self destruction. [Joseph, 1989, p. 136]

A number of analysts, including Joseph, here, refer to the pleasure involved in perversion as an *addiction*. If we return to Bion's notion of suffering, we can ask: what of the "suffering" of pleasure? An addiction does not have the same quality as the discovery of pleasure. In an analogous way to the inflicted pain discussed at the beginning of the chapter, an addiction does not add anything to the personality. As we can see with drug-induced pleasure, the pleasure is inflicted on the self and, like a lie, has to be kept going; that is to say, it has to be inflicted in a repetitive way. The excitement in perverse pleasure, while felt, remains essentially undiscovered by the person. This would seem right for the patient referred to above, who believed herself to be in my phantasy life, rather than discovering herself as a person who could have sexual phantasies of her own.

Bion concludes his discussion of suffering, quoted at the beginning, with the following comment: "The patient who will not suffer pain fails to 'suffer' pleasure and this denies the patient the encouragement he might otherwise receive from accidental or intrinsic relief" (Bion, 1993, p. 9). What does Bion mean by "accidental or intrinsic relief"? The "suffering of pleasure", I would suggest, is an experience of passion or joy that arises internally and is "to the point", i.e., it is directly and meaningfully connected with one's internal and external world. Such pleasure can be differentiated from pleasure used as an avoidance of reality. Blackpool Pleasure Beach has a sign saying "Enter here and leave all your problems behind". There is a difference between "accidental or intrinsic relief" arising from an engagement with reality (internal and external), and "constructed" pleasure used to avoid it.

In the Pleasure Beach we have externally inflicted events. Interestingly, these events may simulate internal experience. A further point of difference between the two kinds of pleasure is that the inflicted events of the Pleasure Beach can be switched on and off as one enters and leaves. If, by contrast, pleasure arises within the self, the consequences of the experience cannot be switched off in the same way. One might feel delight, for example, in something different from the way one's life is being led.

Suffering pleasure: an example

A nine-year-old girl had the following dream. She was with her friend in the girl's toilet at school. Each was in a neighbouring cubicle and each had the door open. Two boys from their class came in. The girl quickly closed her door. She reassured herself about her worries of being seen with the thought that the other girl's door was still open and she would certainly have been seen. Then the girl was in the seaside resort she visited every year with her family. She was out in deep water waiting for a wave to surf on. She could not see them, but knew her family were around her in the sea. She was then picked up by a wave and flung through the water. It was, she said on telling the dream, like flying.

In the first part of the dream the child experiences conflicting feelings, in the second part she has a pleasurable release. The family around her in the sea probably act as a container for her experience. This experience, like adult orgasm, falling in love, or feeling an idea come to life, has in it a moment of considerable mobility and it is possible that mobility is as, if not more important, in suffered pleasure than the element of relief is.

The suffering of pleasure involves an openness to be affected. It is the uncertain outcome of an intercourse. A person may not have access to pleasure "which arises within the self" because their avoidance of pain and frustration has as a consequence the loss of experiences of pleasure. It may also be that the suffering of pleasure is avoided in its own right because it can be disruptive and unsettling as well as a relief. Pleasure is not generated by the aspect of the self one feels in control of; there is something essentially uncontrolled about it—as there is about creativity.

Conclusion

I have suggested that the work of Bion and Joseph enables a differentiation to be made between experience that is suffered (in the sense of endured or allowed) and thence discovered to be meaningful; and pain or pleasure that is felt, but not experienced as being of the self. The same differentiation holds between the suffering and discovery of reality and the construction of a lie. In perverse organization, pain, pleasure, or lies are not suffered, but felt as things to be used. Drug addiction and Pleasure Parks are examples of pleasure inflicted on the self. Two examples have been given. The first of a young woman who believed she knew about phantasies about which other people lied to themselves. The second example is of the suffering of pleasure in a young girl's dream, in which an orgasmic experience of being flung by a wave brings "accidental and intrinsic relief" to rather anxious and conflicting feelings about her nascent sexuality.

Note

1. My thanks to my patients. I would also like to express my gratitude to Eric Hirsch, Betty Joseph, Elizabeth Bott Spillius, and Penny Woolcock. My gratitude also to Ron Britton and the other members of the postqualification seminar—Orna Hadary, Mary Heller, Ken Robinson, Edgar Sanchez, and Mary Target.

References

Bion, W. R. (1993)[1970]. *Attention and Interpretation*. London: Karnac.
Britton, R. (1998). *Belief and Imagination*. London: Routledge.
Freud, S. (1927e). Fetishism. *S.E.*, 21: 149–157.
Graham-Dixon, A. (1994). *Howard Hodgkin*. London: Thames and Hudson.
Joseph, B. (1989)[1982]. Addiction to near-death. In: *Psychic Equilibrium and Psychic Change* (pp. 127–139). London: Routledge.
Steiner, J. (1995)[1993]. *Psychic Retreats*. London: Routledge.

CHAPTER SIX

The structure of perversion: a Lacanian perspective

Serge André

Freud's work only provides us with a very basic idea of the structure of perversion. He explains the mechanism that he calls *Verleugnung*, translated into English as "disavowal", in his 1927 paper "Fetishism" (Freud, 1927e) and subsequently in his 1938 paper "Splitting of the ego in the process of defence" (Freud, 1940e), yet Freud's explanations in these texts merely constitute a beginning, a way in to the issue of perversion as structure. For example, in "Fetishism", Freud leaves us completely in the dark concerning the actual turning point of the perverse orientation:

> Probably no male human being is spared the fright of castration at the sight of a female genital. Why some people become homosexual as a consequence of that impression, while others fend it off by creating a fetish, and the great majority surmount it, we are frankly not able to explain. It is possible that, among all the factors at work, we do not yet know those which are decisive for the rare pathological results. [Freud, 1927e, p. 154]

This turning point is not clarified any better in 1938, in the paper on the splitting of the ego. Between the third and the fourth moment in the model for the genesis of fetishism that Freud proposes here—between the moment when the threat of castration elicits fear in the child and leads to the "normal" solution of the abandonment of masturbation, and the moment when a fetish is erected in order to disavow castration and authorize the pursuit of masturbation— there remains a major hiatus in Freud's explanation. Why and how do certain subjects, at that moment, have recourse to a fetish and treat castration via the mechanism of disavowal? It is clear that between those two moments something else needs to happen, which might explain the subject's turn towards perversion. This additional element, which Freud fails to recognize, must be found in a particular oedipal configuration, which the psychoanalytic treatment of perversion regularly allows us to identify in perverse subjects.

The perverse Oedipus does not unfold in the same way as the neurotic Oedipus and its particularity enables us to account for the fact that the threat of castration, however well it may have been integrated by the subject (for it is not being rejected altogether, foreclosed, as in psychosis), none the less remains ineffective. In Freudian terms, the threat of castration does not make the Oedipus complex of the pervert dissolve, but rather consolidates it in a definitive way. The oedipal triangle in which the pervert needs to find a place—the place from which the pervert needs to be able to interrogate the desire of the Other—differs from the oedipal triangle of the neurotic. It differs because of the special place accorded to the phallus as a symbol and an imaginary representation, which proposes to the subject an ideal on which narcissism can be based. Within this configuration, the father is not foreclosed symbolically as is the case in psychosis, but the father is nonetheless discarded in a particular way, namely as a real father. In other words, the gap between the symbolic and the real function of the father, which is negated in neurosis through the figure of the imaginary father (castrating tyrant or impotent father, depending on the case), is never so strongly emphasized as in the structure of perversion.

In the structure of perversion, the father is recognized symbolically as Name-of-the-Father, but he is only recognized in this way in so far as he is rejected in the real as a man who only has the task of representing symbolically the function he has attained. Whether owing to his physical absence or his real inconsistency, or because of the kind of interior exile in which he is placed within the bosom of the family, the father of the pervert becomes a derisory personality, a purely fictional character. In this way, the father of the pervert disavows the status of symbolic father, depository of the law and authority, despite the fact that this status is often highly prized and recognized within the family. This type of father is comparable to an actor who has been awarded, by unanimous vote, the leading part in the play, but who never gets to appear on the stage, or who only gets to appear on the stage in order to say nothing, no lines having been given to him.

The paradox of this paternal position does not so much take its bearings from the father's personal behaviour of abstention or resignation, but rather from the way in which the mother's discourse designates his place. The mother of the perverse subject constitutes the source from which the disavowal is formulated, and around which the perverse structure will take form. Although she demonstrates a superficial recognition of the symbolic authority of the father, the mother subsequently turns this symbolic authority into derision by reducing it, in the discourse she addresses to her son or daughter, to a façade that needs to be preserved for the outside world, a simple convention that one should only respect in order to keep up appearances.

When the perverse subject deciphers the discourse of the Other and, for example, like the children in Freud's description of infantile sexual theories (Freud, 1908c), wonders about the role of the father, it is only to discover that fatherhood is for the mother but a part in a play of which the actor is unaware. And she believes it is better not to shatter this illusion in order to preserve her control behind the scenes. Better still, this mother is not content to keep the reality of the father at a distance only for herself; rather she invites her son or daughter to participate also in the process of exiling the father. First, she makes her child witness the paternal comedy by revealing its artifices; subsequently, she summons the child as an accomplice to the father's submission to her; finally, she makes the father into the depository of the reality that this theatre allows to exist, completely intact, beyond the stage, where one only plays in order to laugh. The result is that the paternal law does exist within the perverse oedipal configuration, and is recognized there in its symbolic value, but *only* in its symbolic value. The very notion of "symbol" thereby loses its seriousness. The law of the father is recognized, but at the same time it is considered a law without consequence; for example, because all its statutory orders will always depend on the good will of the mother. The result is also that the universe of the family (and, by extension, of the rest of the world) is constituted as a scene in which everything is in a permanent state of comedy, deception, cheating. In fact, the world of the pervert involves the creation of two scenes: a public scene (of society, of external appearances) where the law, the authority, and the prohibitions of the father rule, and a private scene where the mother and the child exempt themselves together from this law, which thus only has value for the outside world.

As a result, the entire tragedy of desire and its relationship with *jouissance* become false for the subject. This can be observed when one measures the deviation of the phallic function that is brought about by this type of oedipal configuration, at the level of desire as well as the level of *jouissance*. It is appropriate, here, to rethink the notion of the phallus with what Lacan has taught us, and to detach this notion from the status it has been given in Freud's research: that of representation. If Freud took a decisive step when he conceived the castration complex as not being aimed at the penis (the masculine genital as present) but at the phallus (the masculine genital in so far as it can lack), this step still does not sufficiently detach the function of the phallus from the organ of the penis, which seems to offer the phallus an imaginary support in the real. It is important to grasp that the man's penis is but a sign of the Other's object of desire, which cannot be confused with the object that this desire actually indicates. Nothing whatsoever, no organ, no real object, can incarnate in a definitive way this object of the Other's desire. The object of desire is never a real presence. It is by definition lost, the equivalent of a lack to which nothing but an other desire can correspond. As Lacan put it in the early 1950s: "man's desire is the desire of the Other" (Lacan, 1988, pp. 235–247).

The only object to which desire relates is an immaterial, unreal object, such as an Other desire. In other words, the phallus is not the signifier of the penis, but the signifier of desire, of the lack that is constitutive for the object of desire, starting with the Other's desire. When Freud talks about the traumatic discovery of the experience of castration, and regards this as the absence of the phallus in the mother, we must not understand this as the absence of a penis in the mother, but as the absence of a signifier—beyond this discovery of the absence of a penis, which the subject discovers at a moment when the Other does not possess the object that could satisfy his desire. This is what Lacan wants to say when, in his *Seminar IV* on object-relations, he proposes a schema of the original triangle of desire in which the phallus is placed as a third term between the mother and the child (Lacan, 1994, p. 29). When Lacan writes this triangle, it already presupposes that the symbolic agency of the father, the Name-of-the-Father, is present, because the fact that the mother's object of desire is symbolized as a lack, in a signifier (as opposed to as a signified, in a real object), depends upon this symbolic agency. This triangle also shows that for Lacan the original situation of the child, when it is called upon to subjectivize the Other's desire, is already triangular. It is not, as it has been argued by Mahler and others, fusional or dual (Mahler, Pine, & Bergman, 1975). The fusion between the mother and the child is a myth because in the beginning there are always three rather than two, or one. The place of the phallus (the signifier of lack) as a third term within this primordial triangle means that in the beginning neither the mother nor the child is complete. Each lacks something, which the Other may have the power to represent, but which is always situated elsewhere, outside of the Other. The mother is not the object of the child's desire, nor is the child the object of the mother's desire. In each case, desire is the desire of the Other. At this level, the phallus represents that which the mother lacks in order for her to be fulfilled by the mere presence and existence of her child. Since the phallus also represents that which the child lacks in order for it to be fulfilled by the mere presence of the mother, this lack only seems to be concealed through the misunderstandings of speech or the imaginary complicity of their narcissism, which is exactly what can be found in perversion.

In order to grasp why the object of desire is structurally equivalent to the phallus here, it suffices to re-read Lacan's 1958 paper "The signification of the phallus" (Lacan, 2002a). In distinguishing between the three levels of need, demand, and desire, Lacan shows that in the process which transforms the exigency of the need into a demand for "a proof of love" (*ibid.*, p. 276) something disappears that has the singular quality of the object of the initial need. None the less, this singularity is simultaneously dissolved by the totality of the presence of the Other, which constitutes the object of the demand for love. It is this lost particularity, this aspect of the object that cannot be substituted for, which resurfaces as an absolutely claimable residue at the next stage, in the passage from demand to desire. What has not been possible to articulate in the demand because it radically defies articulation in the signifier, what has therefore been impossible to fulfil in the reply to the demand (the proof of love does not count as satisfaction for the drive), is what reappears as eliciting, causing desire. In Lacan's words:

> For the unconditionality of demand, desire substitutes the "absolute" condition: this condition in fact dissolves the element in the proof of love that rebels against the satisfaction of need. This is why desire is neither the appetite for satisfaction nor the demand for love, but the difference that results from the subtraction of the first from the second, the very phenomenon of their splitting (*Spaltung*). [*ibid.*, p. 276]

Where is the phallus to be situated in this three-tiered process? Precisely in what is lost in each transition—from need to demand and from demand to desire—only to re-emerge at the end as the constitutive lack of desire. On the one hand, the symbolic phallus is lost in the transition from need to demand, because a bodily exigency is alienated in the signifiers of the Other. On the other hand, it is lost in the transition from demand to desire, because of the inadequacy of the proof of love with regard to the particularity of satisfaction. Thus, the phallus is the signifier of the central loss that structures desire as the beyond of demand and the beyond of need. The phallus is the signifier of this loss, but it is simultaneously the signifier that covers up the loss, because it gives desire the aim of satisfying itself by gaining access to the desire of the Other. In brief, the phallus turns the desire of the Other into the veil that covers up the real object of the loss, i.e. Lacan's famous "object *a*", which causes desire instead of satisfying it. Lacan writes:

> The fact that the phallus is a signifier requires that it be in the place of the Other that the subject have access to it. But since this signifier is there only as veiled and as ratio [*raison*] of the Other's desire, it is the Other's desire as such that the subject is required to recognize—in other words, the other insofar as he himself is a subject divided by the signifying *Spaltung*. [*ibid.*, p. 278]

The phallus therefore envelops the object *a*, similar to the Socratic *agalma*, and accentuates in this way the separation between the subject and this object—separation that the fantasy will try to repair by reconnecting the subject and the object through an imaginary *mise-en-scène*.

In the original triangle "mother–child–phallus", the child finds the keys to its own desire by constituting this desire as a desire for the Other's desire, whereby its object, its goal, is symbolized by the phallus, that is to say by "the signifier that is destined to designate meaning effects as a whole" (*ibid.*, p. 275). The phallus is the signifier indicating that the object that it seems to designate is never more than an effect of signification that always falls short of the real object, because the latter is never accessible as such. The phallic signifier somehow guarantees that no desired object will ever be the pure, ultimate Object of desire but will always fail. This connection of the child's desire to the Other's desire, notably to the mother's desire, is conditioned by the mother's desire itself, or at least by what she is able to perceive about it as its interpreter. The mother's position with regard to the phallus—the signifier that takes the place of the object of desire, which veils it and provides it with a simulacrum—will orientate the way in which the child will constitute itself as desiring. Within this connection of the phallus to the Other's desire, and the connection of the Other's desire to the child's desire, the child's neurotic or perverse fixation will be decided. The decisive moment takes place when the phallus acquires meaning in the Other's desire (that is to say, in the child's deciphering of the Other's desire) and is thus transformed from a signifier into a signified, moving from the rank of a pure symbol to that of an imaginary representation. It is also at this turning point that the intervention of the paternal function is called for, no longer merely as a symbolic agency but also as a real agency, in order to support the phallus's value as a signifier against its imaginary consistency.

In "The signification of the phallus", Lacan at one point talks about "the test [*l'épreuve*] constituted by the Other's desire" (*ibid.*, p. 278). Indeed, in connecting need, demand, and desire, the child has to forge its path as a subject, and it has to experience the Other's desire as well as putting it to the test.[1] The child has to experience the Other's desire in so far as it has to undergo it and be subjected to it, yet it also has to put it to the test in order to decipher its enigma. Lacan claims that this test constituted by the Other's desire "is decisive, not in the sense that the subject learns by it whether or not he has a real phallus, but in the sense that he learns that his mother does not have one" (ibid., pp. 278–279). If we want to avoid reducing the notion of the phallus to the image of the penis again, which would portray the mother's castration as a lack of organ, it is necessary to interpret this passage as indicating that the child needs to learn, in the test constituted by the Other's desire, that its mother also lacks the object that might satisfy her beyond her demand for love, and that she needs to find this object somewhere else, in another desire. This also implies that this object of the Other's desire cannot be conflated with the real child, as is the case in psychosis, but that it is situated outside the pure presence of the child, although the latter would only ever be its imaginary representation. If the mother's desire is for the phallus, the child wants to be the phallus in order to satisfy her. This entails the imagination of the phallus and of the subject itself. For the child who wishes to be the phallus, in order to satisfy the mother, wants to be something it is not, by virtue of its mere presence. In this mechanism, a being (être) envelops itself with a semblance, a seeming (paraître) of comedy, which masks a fundamental want-to-be (manque-à-être).

At the point where the phallus is imagined and transforms itself from a pure symbol into an imaginary representation, the law introduced by the real father will decide over the child's future. The law introduced by the father, the fourth term already implied in the original triangle, is exercised within the oedipal complex along two axes: an axis of symbolization and an axis of realization. On the axis of symbolization, it is the function of the Name-of-the-Father, i.e., a symbolic function, which introduces the law in the primordial Other by providing the mother's desire with a symbol that represents it—the identity of this symbol does not matter. The father's intervention points to the fact that the mother's desire is fundamentally a lack. She lacks something that the real presence of the child cannot fulfil. This is the minimal condition, without which it is impossible to conceive of the function of the phallus within the relationship between the mother and the child.

If this symbolic function of the Name-of-the-Father protects the subject against psychosis, it does not orientate the subject towards neurosis or perversion. For this, the paternal function also has to manifest itself as a real function. This means that with regard to the phallus, conceived as "the ratio [*raison*] of desire" (*ibid.*, p. 278) of the mother, it is necessary for the real father (the man who, in the family, adopts and supports the paternal function, without necessarily being the biological father) to appear to represent the place where the phallus is given to the mother, as signifier of her desire. In other words, lest the subject orientates itself in the direction of perversion, the real father needs to intervene in order to cut short the child's wish to be the representative of the phallus for the mother's desire, a wish which might be shared with the mother. The father in this way imposes himself and is also recognized as the authentic holder of that which can satisfy the mother's desire. The law introduced by the father thus fulfils a dual mission with regard to the phallus: on the one hand, as symbolic function, it supports the existence of the phallus as signifier of the Other's desire; on the other hand, as real function, it deposes the phallus as the imaginary representation that the child tries hard to be, or that it believes to incarnate for the mother's desire. This real intervention of the paternal agency fails in the perverse Oedipus complex. This does not mean that the paternal function does not count in it, as is the case in psychosis, but that it is reduced to a mere role, without any real consequence for the triangle "mother–child–phallus".

In this case, a mechanism is at work that pushes the father outside of the triangle constituted around the imaginary representation of the phallus. From this moment, the subject is given over to the "test constituted by the Other's desire" without any other horizon and any other support than the imaginary phallus, whose representation maintains the belief in the consistency of the object of the Other's desire, in the consistency of an object that is really capable of fulfilling the Other's desire. And, thus, the subject is led to believe that it is possible to incarnate this representation of the object that satisfies the Other's desire. In pretending to be capable of representing that which essentially belongs to the register of lack, the imaginary phallus realizes the fundamental operation of the perverse structure. The imaginary phallus makes it possible for something that is by definition "less" to appear as "more".

This is what allowed Henri de Montherlant to justify his paedophilic desire for prepubescent boys. In *Tous feux éteints*, he writes that paedophilia is the love of femininity in male children and adolescents, that is to say "it is heterosexuality with a small difference" (Montherlant, 1975, p. 116). This statement implies that the small difference in question is, for Montherlant, actually positivized. What is a "minus" for the girl is only recognized by the paedophile in as much as he encounters it as a "plus" in the body of the young boy who is not a man yet. The role of the imaginary phallus in perversion seems to be that of a veil that is eventually placed over the very nature of the phallus as signifier, a veil that masks the phallus as signifier of lack. In this way we can also understand how, in certain perversions, the penis is accorded the role of a pre-eminent support of this veil, in so far as the penis can operate (as prototypical fetish, to recall one of Freud's explanations) as an imaginary representation, as the sign which indicates that something does not lack and thus as a disavowal of the phallus as signifier. Cases of perversion show that the importance of the penis lies in its power to represent an antithesis to the phallus. It offers an imaginary representation of the phallus, which disavows the fact that the phallus is a lack, something that cannot be there, not even as a representation. In the test constituted by the Other's desire, this condemns the pervert to endlessly interrogate the Other's desire in order to ensure that what is structurally a "less", a "minus", appears as a "more", a "plus".

This process also explains why perverse subjects often become virtuosos of discourse, handling contradictions and paradoxes with a remarkable talent for persuasion, only affirming in order to say that they are denying or denying in order to say that they are affirming, because they have to maintain at all cost the fiction of an Other who does not lack anything, whether it concerns the Other of desire, the Other of *jouissance*, or the Other of language. As a consequence, the perverse subject is constantly obliged to furnish this Other with the imaginary supplement that masks the lack (the fissure that structurally affects the Other). The belief in the imaginary phallus as positivization of the phallus, this belief that the absence of the real father leaves intact in the pervert, thus serves to constitute the Other as a complete Other, who possesses the object of desire, or who is endowed with the intrinsic power to represent the object and to satisfy desire.

At this point, we need to consider the Other along two distinct lines. On the one hand, we must consider the symbolic Other, as the place from which the discourse is produced and where the subject needs to find its place by deciphering the code and the message that designate it, according to a certain unconscious desire. On the other hand, we have the real Other, the being who incarnates this place of discourse and who confronts the subject with the enigma of desire and *jouissance*. The disavowal of castration and the function of the imaginary phallus, common to perversion, function along these two lines. Indeed, in both cases the perverse subject is committed to offering the Other something that can mask the Other's defects. On the side of the subject, the imaginary phallus can attain the function of fetish, whether in discourse or in the sexual act. At the level of the relationship with the Other of language, the pervert will be committed to fulfilling the structural lack that founds the possibility of the phallic signifier in the unconscious. In his famous graph of "The subversion of the subject and the dialectic of desire in the Freudian unconscious", Lacan represents this structural lack as an "impossible to say" with the matheme S(Ø), the signifier for the lack in the Other (Lacan, 2002b, p. 302). Before acquiring meaning in the unconscious, within the dialectic of desire and *jouissance*, S(Ø) simply means that there is no metalanguage, that language cannot accurately say what language is, and equally cannot say what the absence of language is. As a result, it is impossible to say everything, and this opens the endless possibilities of discourse. Language assigns to discourse its limits whilst at the same time opening it up to infinity. It is no doubt possible to pronounce "being", "death", "*jouissance*", "hole", "infinity", as signifiers, yet by this very fact they are being put out of reach in terms of their essence. Language can say everything apart from non-language. It is precisely against these limits that the pervert protests, by upholding in many instances, be it only in the peculiar relationship entertained with the fantasy, the challenge of saying everything.

This challenge of saying everything is a constant factor, for example, in the works of de Sade and Céline, and it also explains the frequency of the manic symptom among many perverts. It is in this challenge, which the perverse disavowal addresses at the S(Ø), that we may also find the reason for Sade's virulent atheism. The negation of God in Sade's work operates as a negation of the limits of reason. This point has been argued brilliantly by Annie Le Brun in *Sade: A Sudden Abyss*. Le Brun writes:

Such a God inhibits thinking, since he causes thought to revolve around the notion of primordial cause; like a conjuror he also whisks away infinity, the better to squash man into the prisons of finitude. If Sade never forfeits an occasion to deny him, it's because the vigor of his own thought is at stake, this new type of thought which he is busy training to confront that absolute uncovered by God's absence. [Le Brun, 1990, p. 42]

According to Le Brun, Sade sees in the notion of God a revolting lack of being (*manque d'être*) that generates an even more revolting "deficiency of human being", a genuine "want-to-be" [*manque à être*] (*ibid.*, p. 136). In his relationship to language, the type of speech that Sade proposes in order to replace this lack of being plays exactly the same role as the imaginary phallus with regard to the mother's castration. Sade responds with a proliferation of blasphemy to the gaping hole that God, as signifier, leaves in reason. The profanation of religious beliefs played an important part in the scandals Sade provoked during his life and also in the circumstances of his imprisonment. It is not so much because he had flogged or tortured, or even because he had sodomized, his valet or certain prostitutes (although sodomy was at the time still considered a crime punishable by death) that Sade was imprisoned for such a long time. Rather, it is because he had committed these acts on Easter day, while demanding that his prostitute partners invoke the name of God and desecrate the Holy Wafer. If we take this type of blasphemy to the letter, psychoanalysts will not have any difficulty in recognizing how Sade substitutes for the gaping emptiness of language the perfectly representable and represented material hole by which he incessantly expressed, in his life as well as his works, his horror for the mother's genital. It is worth recalling, here, a couple of lines from his poem *La vérité* (Truth) in which he addresses himself to God in the following terms:

> As for me, I admit, so strongly do I hate,
> My horror is at once so just, and so great,
> That with pleasure, vile Deity, and in tranquillity,
> I would masturbate upon your divinity,
> Or even bugger you, if your tenuous existence
> Could present a bum to my incontinence.
>   (quoted in Le Brun, 1990, p. 136)

Within this logic, excess takes the place of lack and regulates the life and, above all, the discourse of the Sadean hero. As Le Brun puts it: "[F]or Sade, excess is itself a metaphor for the momentum of desire" (*ibid.*, p. 181). Excess, rather than lack, organizes desire. The beyond of satisfaction, which the Sadean master turns into the maxim governing his relationship to desire is, in this way, first of all an excess of language, and only subsequently a sexual excess. That the challenge of saying everything is doomed to fail is beyond doubt and this is perfectly illustrated by the end of *The 120 Days of Sodom*, where one can see the fall-out of the manic symptom (Sade, 1990).

One element of the pervert's discourse acquires particular significance in the context of this ineluctable impossibility of the challenge to construct a complete, faultless Other. From the beginning of his 1958 paper "Jeunesse de Gide ou la lettre et le désir", Lacan draws his readers' attention to the perverse style as fetish, as an artifice designed to mask the impossibility of saying everything. Lacan emphasizes that the essential problem raised by Gide concerns "the relationship between man and the letter", which subsequently prompts him to change Buffon's famous aphorism "Style is the Man Himself" into "Style is the Object" (Lacan, 1966, pp. 739–740). The lengthy development of Lacan's argument concerning Gide's style culminates when he deciphers the crucial importance of Gide's letters to his wife Madeleine and attributes to these letters the status of fetish (*ibid.*, p. 763). For Lacan, this explains why Madeleine, when she decided to burn them, managed to open in her husband the hole that these letters were supposed to cover up in his relationships to women. One could also compare the vengeful bonfire to which Madeleine surrendered her husband's letters to the *auto-da-fe* during which Marcel Jouhandeau, one night in February 1914, destroyed everything he had written until then, in an attempt to expiate the grave mistake he had just committed and for which he believed he could only exonerate himself through fire. For Jouhandeau, this destruction constituted a rebirth, as if during that night of February 1914 he had crossed the limit of death—for which someone like Mishima never found a solution. It should be noted, however, that Jouhandeau made sure that one item was saved from the fire: the letters which his mother had sent him on a daily basis over the past thirty-eight years.[2]

The same function of the fetishism of style appears in the work of Céline. The famous ellipses that he introduces everywhere have exactly the opposite function to a temporal scansion. These three small dots aim to materialize in the writing the trace of what cannot be said; they aim to represent the unrepresentable. It is this same idea of style as a fetish-representation that Le Brun emphasizes, although without realizing it, when she pays just attention to Sade's way of thinking, which she analyses as an attempt to make the movement of thought identical to the physical movement of the universe (Le Brun, 1990, p. 41). For Sade, the logic of reason has to merge with the endless agitation of nature; that is to say, with a force that nothing can stop. This implies that everything should be represented, or at least representable; everything should be conceivable, which, of course, denies that there can be a lack of reason or a lack of representation and thus a scission between language and being.

The perverse subject's refusal of the impossibility of saying everything—the subject's refusal to acknowledge that there is something that cannot be said—leads to the assertion that everything should be said and represented in the relation with the Other of language. This affects, in turn, the relationship with the real Other (of which the mother has evidently been the first representative) and, more specifically, it affects the relationship with the Other's desire and *jouissance*. With regard to this desire and *jouissance*, the perverse subject will depose the phallus as signifier of lack, in order to replace it with the imaginary phallus, an imaginary representation that positivizes the phallus. In this way, the perverse subject confirms the belief in an Other who does not lack an object that can satisfy desire. The Other constituted by the pervert therefore can escape the hiatus that separates desire and *jouissance* in the neurotic. In providing the Other's desire with a positive object, by means of the imaginary representation, the pervert can create a continuum between desire and *jouissance* in the Other. In the structure of perversion, the imaginary phallus therefore has both the value of a positivization of the phallus and a representation of the object *a*. This is why one can say that the pervert recuperates, in an imaginary way, the loss that re-emerges at each level of the transition from need to demand, from demand to desire, and from desire to *jouissance*. In perversion, the object that was lost initially, the singular object that was drowned in the demand for a proof of love, is refound and reinstalled in the place of the object at which desire is aimed. Hence, there is a confusion between the object cause of desire and the object aim of desire. The pervert lets the object *a* operate as a positivized phallus, in this way disavowing the lack that constitutes the symbolic phallus as distinct from the object *a*. The logic of the father's desire is thus separated from the dialectic of the want-to-be, which, in neurosis, opens up an abyss between desire and *jouissance*, and which the fantasy, operating in the imaginary, is supposed to plug. For the pervert, by contrast, it is a question of being and phallicizing being, so that the subject of desire and the object of *jouissance* can be reunited in a single representation.

This process can also be gauged from the schema of the Sadean fantasy that Lacan includes in "Kant with Sade" (Lacan, 1989, p. 62). The schema shows how the pervert's desire impels him to put himself in the position of *a*, in order to address his partner in the name of a will to *jouissance* and with the purpose of dividing his partner as subject. He does this with a view to letting emerge, at the end of the line, a non-divided subject, which Lacan calls a "raw subject of pleasure" (*sujet brut de plaisir*), a subject which would only have pleasure in enjoying (*ibid.*, p. 63). This is the assembly of the perverse fantasy, which aims to reunite the subject and the object of desire with *jouissance*. The perverse subject's refusal of the castration of the Other thus means that he makes himself the supplier of the Other, someone who provides the Other with the representation of its lack and in this way ensures the Other's *jouissance*.

This elision of the disjunction between the desire and the *jouissance* of the Other will inevitably have consequences for the way in which the subject relates to the fantasy. The fantasy does not allow us to distinguish between perversion and neurosis, in so far as the fantasies of perverts are exactly the same as those of neurotics. The fantasy is perverse by definition. What distinguishes the pervert from the neurotic is not the content of the fantasy, but the subject's position with regard to the fantasy. Whereas the neurotic remains silent about the fantasy, or only "confesses" to it with a high degree of reticence, in this way bearing witness to the division he experiences between his position as a subject and the position he tends to occupy in the fantasy, the pervert pronounces his fantasy, claims the right to it, even forces the Other to listen to it when he does not succeed in convincing him through so-called perverse behaviours alone.

In reality, even if the pervert is the one who gives us the most information about the fantasy, at least about the content of the fantasy, he does not really know what a fantasy is, because the pervert does not really need a fantasy in order to create a continuum between the desire and the *jouissance* of the Other—his belief in the imaginary phallus suffices to maintain this continuity. This does not mean that the pervert is a subject without fantasy; it simply means that he makes a different use of it. The way in which the pervert uses his fantasy is characterized, at least amongst those "confirmed" perverts who have come to recognize their perversion and who have engaged with it, by the fact that he does not so much use it for private purposes, as the neurotic does, but with the aim of including an Other into it. Whereas the fantasy is a private matter for the neurotic, for the pervert it serves to attract an Other, either to persuade this Other that this fantasy is also his, or to corrupt him in such a way that he is willing to act out the fantasy with him. Hence, in his relationship with his fantasy, the pervert is not alone. Of course, it is true that originally it was through complicity, even seduction by the Other (the mother), that the pervert established his belief in the imaginary phallus, so perhaps in this way he also inherited, through obscure means and without knowing it, the fantasy of an Other.

Notes

1. [The French verb *éprouver* means "to test' as well as "to experience']
2. A selection of these letters has since been published as *Lettres d'une mère à son fils*. See Jouhandeau (1971).

References

Freud, S. (1908c). On the sexual theories of children. S.E., 9: 205–226. London: Hogarth.
Freud, S. (1927e). Fetishism. S.E., 21: 149–157. London: Hogarth.

Freud, S. (1940e). Splitting of the ego in the process of defence. *S.E., 23*: 271–278. London: Hogarth.

Jouhandeau, M. (1971). *Lettres d'une mère à son fils*. Paris: Gallimard.

Lacan, J. (1966[1958]). Jeunesse de Gide ou la lettre et le désir. In: *Ecrits* (pp. 739–764). Paris: du Seuil.

Lacan, J. (1988)[1954–55]. *The Seminar. Book 2: The Ego in Freud's Theory and in the Technique of Psychoanalysis*. J.-A. Miller, (Ed.), S. Tomaselli (Trans.). Cambridge: Cambridge University Press.

Lacan, J. (1989)[1962]. Kant with Sade. J. B. Swenson, Jr. (Trans.). *October*, 51: 55–75.

Lacan, J. (1994)[1956–1957]. *Le Séminaire, Livre IV: La relation d'objet*, texte établi par J.-A. Miller, Paris: du Seuil.

Lacan, J. (2002a)[1958]. The signification of the phallus. In: B. Fink (Trans.), *Ecrits: A Selection* (pp. 271–280). New York: W. W. Norton.

Lacan, J. (2002b)[1960]. The subversion of the subject and the dialectic of desire in the Freudian unconscious. In: B. Fink (Trans.), *Ecrits: A Selection* (pp. 281–312). New York: W. W. Norton.

Le Brun, A. (1990)[1986]. *Sade: A Sudden Abyss*. C. Naish (Trans.). San Francisco, CA: City Lights.

Mahler, M. S., Pine, F., & Bergman, A. (1975). *The Psychological Birth of the Human Infant: Symbiosis and Individuation*. New York: Basic Books.

Montherlant, H. de (1975). *Tous feux éteints—Carnets 1965, 1966, 1967, Carnets sans dates et 1972*. Paris: Gallimard.

Sade, D. A. F. de (1990)[1785]. *The 120 Days of Sodom and Other Writings*. A. Wainhouse & R. Seaver (Trans.). London: Arrow.

CHAPTER SEVEN

Birth, death, orgasm, and perversion: a Reichian view

Nick Totton

"Why do you have to talk like that?" she asks me. "Talk like what?" I respond. "Speak to them, for them," she answers. I have fielded this question many times. This time I try to keep it simple: "I am one of them," I answer. Unsatisfied, she retorts, "But why must your language be so theoretical, so inaccessible?" Finally, I arrive at the answer I should have made long ago: "I like theory," I tell her, "it is a kind of fetish for me; it turns me on." [Hart, 1998, p. 13]

A term to get rid of?

There is no getting around it: the word "perversion", by etymology and usage, is clearly both *normative*, implying that there is a straight path to which this crooked one is opposed, and *punitive*, a stamp of disapproval upon those perceived as bad and/or inadequate. What is more, there is not even any agreed and solid definition of "perversion" in psychoanalytic terms. The word can be, and is, used in very different ways, and some of the definitions on offer beg the question of aetiology completely. For example, Stoller (1975) chooses to *define* perversion as sexually aberrant behaviour based on hatred, thus eliminating all possibility of counter-examples to his hypothesis that this is in fact what perversion signifies.

Trying to define or discuss perversion involves complex distinctions between, for example, perverse phantasy and perverse sexual activity. Other uses of the term include *conscious* perverse fantasy (with an "f") as a component of "normal" sex; "perverse" sexual behaviour that everyone regards as normal, for example, kissing, whether or not as a component of "normal" sex; and perverse character structure.[1] The term also includes sublimated perversion, which, according to Freud, covers most human cultural activity: "The forces that can be employed for cultural activities are thus to a great extent obtained through the suppression of what are known as the *perverse* elements of sexual excitation" (Freud, 1908d, p. 189).

Perversion, then, is an unhelpful term both for its broad vagueness of usage and for its moralistic/pathologizing overtones. But to substitute "paraphilia", or some equivalent term, merely papers over the cracks in our thinking, pretending to a value-neutrality that is neither earned nor authentic. Is it possible that "perversion" is actually a *usefully* indigestible term, one that forces us to become aware of the tensions held within the concept, the political differences it sparks? Perhaps by leaving the term undefined, but exploring the space it points to, we can trace out the contours of something we do not yet know. Among other goals, I hope in what follows, by using the term "perversion" thoroughly, as it were, to test it to destruction.

Two Reichian theories

An account of the Reichian theory of perversion must consist of two parts. There is the official, explicit Reichian view, which has little to commend it, and also an implicit, underground theory, which, once articulated, seems to me a great deal stronger than the other. This split between the "two Reichs" is, I think, a characteristic of his work as a whole (Totton, 1998, pp. 98ff.). On the one hand there is Reich the positivist mind-doctor, "smashing" resistances and establishing (or imposing) "natural" genitality, but on the other hand we encounter Reich the gentle, process-orientated therapist who supports whatever psychic structure he encounters and celebrates defences as successful survival strategies.

The explicit Reichian theory of perversion, which was clearly the theory consciously held by Reich himself, belongs very much to the first of these two Reichs. Like the great majority of other analysts and therapists, Reich regards perversion as, so to speak, *perverted*: a failure or distortion of sexual function, which needs cure, needs to be put straight:

> Now, when the *natural* streaming of the bioenergy is dammed up, it also spills over, resulting in irrationality, perversions, neuroses, and so on. What do you have to do to correct this? You must get the stream back into its *normal* bed and let it flow *naturally* again. [Reich, 1967, pp. 43–44, italics added]

If perversion is abnormal, then clearly something else must be contrastingly normal, and "Reich One" has no difficulty in deciding what that is. "Reich One" is a genital supremacist, who writes beautiful, univocal descriptions of heterosexual penetrative intercourse as *the* way to do sex. Homosexuality, for example, he sees as mostly a response to sexual privation, which will automatically fade away when the opportunity for heterosexual intercourse arises. Thus, he militantly opposes antihomosexual legislation, but on the grounds that "homosexuality is . . . the result of a very early inhibition of sexual love" (Reich, 1969, p. 209) and therefore an inevitable side-effect of life in an anti-sexual society. Homosexuals should be helped, not punished. Reich's position on all this is, in fact, rather similar to Freud's, but as we shall see, Reich's theoretical work, also like Freud's, subverts his own personal morality.

Reich's heirs in orgonomy and bioenergetics have generally preserved his attitude, so that, paradoxically, body psychotherapy tends to be perhaps more reactionary in this area than therapy as a whole: what was progressive in the 1920s was deeply conservative by the 1960s, when the prominent orgonomist Elsworth Baker announced: "[T]he basic cause of homosexuality is fear of heterosexuality. Extensive therapy is usually required to cure this condition" (Baker, 1980, p. 89). The founder of bioenergetics, Alexander Lowen, similarly combines a strongly affirmative attitude towards "normal" heterosexual activity with an equally strong pathologization of homosexuality: "Despite the protestations of some confirmed homosexuals that homosexuality is a 'normal' way of life, the average invert is aware that his propensity amounts to an emotional illness" (Lowen, 1965, p. 74). Contemporary body psychotherapists may (one hopes) no longer think like this about homosexuals, but—in line with the general anti-theoretical bias of their field—they have not yet produced a new account of homosexuality or perversion.

Reich and his heirs, then, unashamedly and uncritically base their thinking on the concept of normality. In their gloss on "perversion", Laplanche and Pontalis (1988, pp. 306–309) emphasize that the ground for a definition of "normality" has been radically undercut by Freud's work, which presents *every* feature of human sexuality as constructed and in need of explanation: "[T]he exclusive sexual interest felt by men for women", for example, "is also a problem that needs elucidating and is not a self-evident fact" (Freud, 1905d, p. 144, n.). Yet, as Laplanche and Pontalis point out, some notion of normality, and hence of perversion, is endemic to psychoanalysis (and certainly no less so to psychotherapy as a whole). "[T]he fact remains that Freud and all psychoanalysts do talk of 'normal' sexuality" (Laplanche and Pontalis, 1988, p. 308),[2] which is perhaps simply to say that as there are (at least) two Reichs there are also two (many) psychoanalyses. And while "Psychoanalysis One" speaks of "normality" and "perversion", some of the others certainly do not. By studying the alternative Reich, I hope also to elucidate some of the alternative positions available to psychoanalysis as a whole. Freud's theory of sex, after all, also reminds us that sexuality demands *explanation*, not just description. Yet explanation becomes an approachable goal only if we can unbolt it from any relationship to normality.

Character

Looking at what Reich has to say about perversion, which is largely in asides and by implication, it soon becomes obvious that he does not make a primary distinction between perversion and neurosis. In fact, he makes no radical break between either of these two categories and those of psychosis or character. This is in contrast to some analytic schools that found their clinical approach on such distinctions. For Reich, however, each of these categories represents rather a degree of intensity, of extremity, in what is essentially a continuum of possible positions.

Schizophrenia, for example, is an extreme response to an extreme problem, but it is the *same* problem in a milder version that another individual tries to solve through a "schizoid" character structure, which is certainly far from psychotic or, indeed, in a different variation, through voyeurism, or mediumship, or intellectuality.[3] From a Reichian viewpoint ("viewpoint" itself being a visual metaphor), all of these strategies draw on a relationship with the world that privileges *sight* and *thinking* over other modes of experience: a relationship that Reich links to very early stages of infancy, when the baby is seeking a contact with her carer that can be represented as a *gaze*.[4] In Reich's schematization, the developmental phase corresponds with a particular erogenous zone (in this case, the eyes, which Reich firmly identifies as erogenous); with a set of needs and issues which come together into a particular character structure; and with a body type which reflects that character structure (Reich, 1972, pp. 358ff).

Thus, in each case (schizophrenia, schizoid structure, voyeurism, etc.), a fundamentally similar response is being made to a fundamentally similar problem. In a sense, the response (an array of cognitive/perceptual attempts to control and distance reality) *is* in fact the problem, arises out of the problem, out of the baby's experience of being cognitively/perceptually flooded or deprived (*ibid.*, pp. 437ff.). Which precise response emerges will depend on an array of other factors, including the degree of support available in the baby's environment, and what happens at later developmental thresholds—what ensemble of further character attitudes, therefore, blends in with and colours this initial one. This is only one example of a general approach, which we can clarify by looking at Reich's discussion of what he terms the "phallic–narcissistic character":

> Almost all forms of active male and female homosexuality, most cases of so-called moral insanity, paranoia, and the related forms of schizophrenia, and, moreover, many cases of erythrophobia and manifestly sadistic male perverts, belong to the phallic–narcissistic character type. Productive women very often fall under this category. [*ibid.*, p. 219]

At first this list may look like an extraordinarily bizarre, almost Borgesian, collection of incommensurate categories, jumbling the normal, neurotic, perverse, and psychotic. We can only make sense of it if we understand that Reich is working outwards, as it were, from the unitary, *bodily developmental* viewpoint I have outlined above. What he calls the "phallic–narcissistic character" (in my own work I would call it the "thrusting character") is primarily defined by a fixation in the phallic stage of development, "that phase of childhood development in which the anal–sadistic position has just been left, while the genital object–libidinal position has not been fully attained, and is, therefore, governed by the proud, self-confident concentration on one's own penis" (*ibid.*, p. 220) or, of course, one's own clitoris. Reich argues that fixation at the phallic stage comes about through "disappointment ... in the heterosexual objects" (*ibid.*, p. 220), that is, the boy's mother, the girl's father, at just this crucial moment. As a consequence of this disappointment, pride mutates into aggression, the search for phallic revenge, and at the same time tends to crystallize into a compulsive symbolic and bodily "erectness" as a defence against feared collapse into passive anality (which would also constitute a developmental retreat). This defence, "in the form of phallic sadism and exhibitionism" (*ibid.*, p. 221), is what structures the phallic–narcissistic character: "the character is determined not by what it wards off but by the way in which it does it" (*ibid.*, p. 222). Now we can see how the various categories listed by Reich unfurl from the phallic–narcissistic stem:

> In cases of moral insanity, active homosexuality, and phallic sadism, as well as in sublimated forms of these types, e.g., professional athletes ... the warded off tendencies of passive and anal homosexuality are merely expressed in certain exaggerations. In cases of paranoia, on the other hand, the warded-off tendencies break through in the form of delusions. ... A patient suffering from erythrophobia falls victim to a symptomatic breakthrough of the warded off passive and anal homosexuality inasmuch as he gives up masturbation because of acute castration anxiety ... [*ibid.*, p. 222]

And so on. It is apparent that what is essentially the same character structure can find expression in "normal", sublimated forms (athletes, "productive women"), in neurosis (erythrophobia), in psychosis (paranoia), and in perversion (homosexuality, phallic sadism, exhibitionism). Character is the more fundamental concept here and character is of the body, is specifically a *quality of embodiment* (Totton, 1998, p. 193), which functions

> as a means of avoiding what is unpleasant (*Unlust*), of establishing and preserving a psychic (even if neurotic) balance, and finally, of consuming repressed quantities of drive energy and/or quantities which have eluded repression. The binding of free-floating anxiety ... is one of the cardinal functions of character. [Reich, 1972, pp. 52–53]

Masochism

Character, for Reich, is also structured like a symptom: it embodies (literally) both desire and its repression. A person's character conserves and at the same time wards off the function of certain childhood situations (Reich, 1973, p. 305). These situations are, of course, primarily sexual ones, in the broad Freudian sense of "sexual": they tend to fixate both desire and anxiety around the same theme. The example that Reich treats in most depth, and that also brings out very clearly the relationship between character and perversion, is that of masochism, where, in line with what we have already said, he proceeds "not—as is usual—from the masochistic perversion, but from *its reaction basis in the character*" (Reich, 1972, p. 236, italics added). As Reich says, "very few masochistic characters develop a masochistic perversion" (*ibid.*, p. 237), but that perversion, when it does develop, arises out of the character structure, as its expression in sexual life.

In his work on "the masochistic character", one of Reich's chief concerns is to demonstrate, against Freud, that "[m]asochism is not a biologically-determined drive; rather, it is ... the result of a repression of natural sexual mechanisms ... There is no biological striving for unpleasure; hence, there is no death instinct" (*ibid.*, p. 224). Cleaving to Freud's earlier formulations on anxiety and the drives, Reich argues that the general perception of masochism is back to front. Masochists do not, in fact, take pleasure in pain; rather, they experience pleasure itself as painful:

> [T]he masochist's specific mechanism of pleasure consisted precisely in that, while he [*sic*] strives after pleasure like any other

person, a disturbing mechanism causes this striving to miscarry ... The masochist, far from striving after *unpleasure*, demonstrates *a strong intolerance of psychic tensions* and suffers from a quantitative *overproduction of unpleasure* ... [ibid., p. 236]

Reich starts out from his basic definition of the two functions of character, "defense and the binding of anxiety", that is, guarding the ego against the outer world and the drives on the one hand, and "the consumption of the surplus sexual energy produced by the sexual stasis" on the other. In other words, character structure provides a home base, as it were, for libido that is not permitted direct satisfaction, and hence binds the anxiety associated with sexual frustration (*ibid.*, p. 237). He takes up what he defines as the basic traits of the "masochistic character" (which contemporary theorists also call an "anal character", a "holding character", etc.): "a chronic subjective feeling of *suffering* which ... stands out as a *tendency to complain*... tendencies *to inflict pain upon and to debase oneself* ... and an intense passion for tormenting others ... *an awkward, ataxic behavior*" (*ibid.*, pp. 237–238).

Through a case history, Reich derives all of these character traits from what he calls "a *deep disappointment in love*" (*ibid.*, p. 243) at the heart of the character structure, which equally corresponds to an "inordinate demand for love" (*ibid.*, p. 245). "Thus, the feeling of suffering corresponds to ... the continual high-pitched inner excitement and predisposition to anxiety" (*ibid.*, p. 245). The demand for love derives from "a *fear of being left alone* which was very intensely experienced in early childhood" (*ibid.*, p. 246). As a result, the masochistic character "seeks to bind the inner tension ... by an inadequate method, namely by *courting love through provocation and defiance*" (*ibid.*, p. 246).

We can readily see how these traits of the masochistic *character* are also expressed in the masochistic *perversion*. What needs further explanation is the desire for punishment, together with the special role of skin eroticism. Reich argues that what is sought is not pain as such, but the sensation of *warmth in the skin*, which represents the longed-for contact: "[T]he special combination of skin eroticism, anality, and the fear of being left alone which seeks resolution through bodily contact is specifically characteristic of masochism" (*ibid.*, p. 249). However, "[t]he masochistic character is more than a disposition to anal or skin eroticism; rather, it is the result of a specific combination of external influences exercised upon the erogenic susceptibility of the skin and upon the entire erotic apparatus" (*ibid.*, p. 249). Reich proceeds to map out this "specific combination": a "very peculiar spastic attitude" that "immediately inhibits every strong sensation of pleasure and transforms it into unpleasure" (*ibid.*, p. 256). The masochistic character, as soon as it begins to open up to pleasurable sensation, locks down and tightens up on both the bodily and the psychological levels. Reich derives this from harsh and premature toilet training, and from a *fear* of punishment that in his view precedes and ultimately creates the *desire* for punishment.

We can now begin to appreciate how, in the example of masochism, "[a] person's character conserves and at the same time wards off the function of certain childhood situations" (Reich, 1973, p. 305). Seeking to break through the impasse of their fear of pleasure, the spastic, contractive reaction to sensations of melting and sweetness in the body that is caused by their terror of punishment, the masochist imagines release through *piercing* and *bursting*, through being hurt by someone else, so that they themselves are not responsible for the forbidden orgasm: "Beat me so that, without making myself guilty, I can release myself!" (Reich, 1972, p. 265). The original trauma of punishment is taken up into the form of the satisfaction. This operates in a double way: organismically as a way of breaking through the muscular spasm that is a conditioned response to excitement, and psychically as a way of exorcizing the overwhelming guilt that accompanies it.

I have summarized a complex argument of more than forty pages, but I hope that the essential logic of Reich's presentation will be clear. Every point in it has been confirmed for me through clinical work time and time again. In fact, each time I go back to Reich's account, I find more details that I recognize from my own clients.

Orgasm

Masochism as a sexual perversion, then, is a dramatized acting-out of the basic scenario of the masochistic *character*: an intensified and explicit version of issues that, for most of these individuals, are expressed in subtle symbolic forms:

> Since I first came to recognise this deepest function of the passive beating fantasies, I have observed the above mechanism in a number of other patients who have not developed any manifest perversion but, rather, had been able to hold the masochistic tendency in a latent stage through character changes in the ego ... In this category we also have the masochistic sexual attitude of neurotic women, which is regarded by some analysts as normal female behavior. [Reich, 1972, pp. 265–266]

This is Reich's view of the general structure of perversions, and of their relationship to character. He acknowledges implicitly Freud's distinction between neurosis and perversion: neurotics repress their desire while perverts act upon it (e.g., Freud, 1905d, pp.165ff.). However, he takes up strongly the further implication of Freud's formulation itself: that it is *the same desire* which the pervert acts upon and the neurotic represses. Reich addresses directly the question of what makes it possible for the perverse structure to overcome the repression of desire. It is *by incorporating the trauma into the pleasure* that perversion is able to bypass the block placed upon pleasure by traumatic experience.

This fact illuminates the hatred and aggression aimed at perverse practices, not only in the general culture but also in clinical and theoretical accounts by analysts who cover over their hostility with a thin veneer of sympathy (e.g., Limentani, 1996; Socarides, 1996). Why is it, for example, that so many writers assume that a perverse structure is incompatible with analytic training (so that the argument about homosexual analysts focuses on whether or not homosexuality is perverse)? Why do so many analytic writings on perversion emphasize its deathliness, its alienation, its unreality? Well, for the neurotic, even the normal neurotic, the pervert *has escaped*: in other words, is capable of sexual satisfaction, which for the neurotic structure is never complete. The pervert *shows neurotics what they want*, but cannot allow themselves to have. It is not surprising that the internal persecutory mechanisms of neurosis are turned outwards against perversion.[5]

When I talk about orgasm, here, I am using the word in Reich's very specific sense, as something much bigger than ejaculation or even simple climax: "Orgastic potency is the capacity to surrender to the flow of biological energy free of any inhibitions; the capacity to discharge freely the dammed-up sexual excitation through involuntary, pleasurable convulsions of the body" (Reich, 1973, p. 102). As is well known, Reich argued that orgasm in this full sense is actually rather rare: any form of neurosis entails some degree of blocking against complete surrender, and it is this blocking, and the sexual frustration that follows, which both creates and maintains the specific neurotic symptoms. In his experience, "all patients, without exception, are severely disturbed in their genital function" (*ibid*., p. 100), although many of those individuals would not be consciously aware of any disturbance, and would believe themselves to have normal sexual functioning.

In the light of what I have been saying so far, perversion is an attempt to defend orgastic potency against traumatic attack. As Stoller says, one of the functions of perversion is the preservation of pleasure (Stoller, 1975, p. 215). The perverse strategy is limited, though, in two senses. First, at the same time that it defends sexuality, it tends to abandon love. Reichians and post-Reichians would generally argue that sexual climax without loving feelings towards the partner—orgasm involving the pelvis but not the heart—cannot be considered full orgasm in Reich's sense.[6] And it is very apparent that perverse sexual behaviour frequently entails an instrumental attitude towards the sexual partner, sometimes no more than a sexual *victim*, that precludes the possibility of love.

However, the same is very frequently also true of "normal", penetrative heterosexual behaviour. We seem to have two choices. We can argue that behaviours like heterosexual rape, use of pornography, or promiscuity are in fact perverse (which is what Stoller tends to do). Or we can separate the question of love from that of perversion. This need not be a total separation—we can recognize an *association* between perversion and "heartlessness", just as there is an association between neurosis and "sexlessness". But the association is a tendency rather than a law: partners in perversion can also be deeply loving (and partners in neurosis can, of course, be deeply unloving). There is probably a necessary element of using and objectification, even of destruction, in every satisfying sexual encounter, much as in every satisfying breast feed; to claim otherwise is a sort of neurotic idealism that serves primarily to fend off actual sex. As so often, the key question is how far this objectifying element can be treated *playfully*, rather than acted out with a literalism that, in the extreme case, can be deadly in more ways than one.

Death

The second problem with the perverse strategy, however, is right at its core: the very fact that it takes up trauma and installs it within the sphere of pleasure. It is clear from Reich's description of masochism as I have summarized it above, for instance, that there is a great deal of suffering and frustration involved in the masochist's crabwise, surreptitious pursuit of satisfaction. So cunning is the masochist in exploiting the minute spaces between desire and punishment that he may conceal his pleasure even from himself, never letting his left hand know what his right hand is doing.

Inevitably, then, there is a tremendous price to pay for perverse sexual satisfaction. Perversion is not without its "foreign body". No one survives into adulthood with their original polymorphous sexuality intact: what we discover is always a *reconstruction*, a facsimile, having passed through and been reshaped by the traumatic encounter between "the language of tenderness and the language of passion", which has been so well described by Ferenczi: "The perversions, for instance, are perhaps only infantile as far as they remain on the level of tenderness; if they become passionate and loaded with guilt, they are perhaps already the result of exogenous stimulation, of secondary, neurotic exaggeration' (Ferenczi, 1949, pp. 229–230).[7] Ferenczi suggests, in fact, that orgasm itself carries an intrinsically "violent" quality.

None shall escape: perverse satisfaction is always bound up with retraumatisation, either experienced directly as in masochism, or projected onto the other as in sadism. It is precisely traumatised dissociation which appears so clearly in the trance-like, repetitive automatism of fetishism and some elaborate perverse scenarios, just as traumatised hyperactivity appears in other forms of perversion.[8] Perversion, which aims to enlarge the range of sexual activity, can often end up actually restricting and stereotyping it. Whatever its limitations and contradictions, however, perversion does constitute a radical *insistence on sexual satisfaction*, even at a terrible cost (and occasionally that cost is someone else's).

All this relates directly to Reich's reinterpretation of the "death drive" as orgasm anxiety. Reich regards Freud's death drive theory as a mystical substitution of metaphor for concrete explanation: "Like every metaphysical view, the hypothesis of the death drive probably contains a rational core, but getting at this . . . is difficult because its mysticism has created erroneous trains of thought" (Reich, 1972, p. 332). By a "rational core" he means an account grounded in the material body, and one that is not based on inherent conflict and anxiety. For Reich, conflict is primarily between inner and outer realities, and anxiety is the product of the sexual repression that this conflict creates.

Reich's alternative to the death drive is based on the fact that, although he did indeed find in his patients "strivings after disintegration, unconsciousness, non-being, dissolution, and similar longings . . . which seemed to confirm the existence of an actual original striving after death", these mainly arose at the *end* of the treatment; that is, when the patients were faced, in Reich's terms, with the problem of overcoming their "orgasm anxiety", their resistance to bodily surrender (*ibid.*, pp. 333–334). And these anxieties, he stresses, arose mainly not in masochistic characters, but in those "whose masochistic mechanisms were hardly developed":

> [W]hy should patients who were on the verge of recovery, whose masochistic mechanisms were hardly developed, and who had not demonstrated any negative therapeutic reactions . . .—why should precisely these patients have allowed the "silent" death drive to have such a strong effect? [*ibid.*, p. 334]

The reason is that for these patients, death represents *orgasm*. "The striving after non-existence, nirvana, death, is identical with the striving after orgastic release" (*ibid.*, p. 336): both orgasm and death are simultaneously sought and fended off. As Reich puts it elsewhere:

> The patient's fear of death could always be traced back to a fear of catastrophes and this fear, in turn, could be traced back to genital anxiety. Moreover analysts who accepted the theory of the death

drive frequently confused anxiety and drive. It was not until eight years later that the matter became clear to me: *fear of death and dying is identical with unconscious orgasm anxiety, and the alleged death drive, the longing for disintegration, for nothingness, is the unconscious longing for the orgastic resolution of tension.* [Reich, 1973, p. 155]

For Reich, the ego (that illusory impression of a continuous, self-monitoring awareness which, if we are lucky, temporarily ceases in orgasm) carries within itself the desire for its own dissolution, for resolution of the state of continuous psychic and bodily tension that constitutes its being. At the same time, the ego (being, among other things, the distorted psychic expression of the organismic imperative of survival) profoundly *fears* its own "death", and hence resists orgasm in the heart of the act.

However, while it will always be *difficult* for the ego to surrender to orgasm, this only becomes *impossible* through traumatic childhood experiences that reinforce the sense that surrender is a threat to survival. Masochism is one response to this impossibility: "conserving and warding off", taking up the trauma within the sexual act, bundling together punishment, death, and orgasm.[9] This is why masochists do not actively express the fear of death, which is instead bound silently into their whole character structure. Unlike Freud, Reich radically separates from these ambivalent attitudes to death the whole question of aggression, which he sees as a natural human function, "the life expression of the musculature, of the system of movement" (*ibid.*, p. 156).

From Reich's perspective, Freud's theory of the death drive is a false synthesis of several disparate phenomena into a supposed cellular drive to "restore an earlier state of things" (Freud, 1920g, p. 36). Freud's revised theory of anxiety, which treats it no longer as a direct transformation of repressed sexual libido, but rather as a "signal" of the (perceived) danger that leads to that repression—essentially, the threat of castration—is for Reich yet another abandonment of the "actual neurosis", the direct relationship between sexual frustration and emotional disturbance. Reich tends to see castration anxiety as itself a transformation of orgasm anxiety. He stresses "a functional antithesis between sexuality and anxiety" (Reich, 1973, p. 263), a single bodily energy that turns from one to the other depending on the degree of frustration present. Freud's revision of this view meant that "there is no longer any psychoanalytic theory of anxiety that satisfies the clinical needs" (*ibid.*, p. 137).

Freud's "nirvana principle" (Freud, 1920g, p. 47) is close to Reich's theory. But Reich strips away the metaphysical speculations to focus on the *loss of muscular tension and of conscious awareness and thought* that orgasm hopefully brings—what Reich calls the "ultimate surrender to the involuntary" (Reich, 1973, p. 108). Without bodily and psychic tension, the skewed perspective that we call the ego cannot exist. This is how "the pleasure principle seems actually to serve the death drives" (Freud, 1920g, p. 63): it is the surrender of orgasm that melts the ego into its "little death". The concept of binding, which Freud develops in the 'Project' (Freud, 1950, p. 308) and returns to in "Beyond the pleasure principle" (Freud, 1920g), underlies a good deal of Reich's thinking, and supports his image of the almost literal binding of repressed impulses into muscular armouring.

Birth

Several times in writing the above, I found myself wanting to refer to perversion as an *heroic* psychological strategy. This struck me as a surprising choice of terminology. Perversion, whether on the level of phantasy or of action, certainly emerges as a *cunning* response to circumstance, a skilful manipulation of the balance between drive and repression, desire and trauma. In many ways it can be admired; but surely not characterized as heroic? After all, perversion frequently, though not intrinsically, takes on the role of the monster rather than that of the hero or heroine. Once I examined this "heroic" formulation, though, I was able to understand what underlay it. It is the same connection that Rank makes in *The Trauma of Birth* (Rank, 1993): heroism is a quality specifically relating to birth, and birth trauma.

Rank argues that the hero's story is "the reaction to a specially severe birth trauma, which has to be mastered by over-compensatory achievements, among which the most prominent is the regaining of the mother" (*ibid.*, p. 106). But these "achievements" are simply a re-enactment of the epic struggle of birth itself, where the mother who has been lost as containing womb and nurturing placenta is "regained" in a transformed sense as object when the baby transcends death and emerges into the world. I suspect that very often, if perhaps not always, the themes of a perverse scenario can be related to elements of birth trauma, as Rank indeed suggests (*ibid.*, pp. 32–36), although for Rank this is perhaps simply part of his general principle that everything can be related to birth.

For example, asphyxiation, slipperiness, immobilization, and piercing or crushing (these last two being effects of medical intervention) all feature prominently in perverse menus. Stanislaf Grof (1975) specifically noted a link between sadomasochistic and rape fantasies, and what he calls "Basic Perinatal Matrix III", the stage at which the baby is propelled through the birth canal, which seems to be experienced, at any rate via *nachträglichkeit*, as an encounter with death. This complex of imagery and ideation also involves intense sexual and scatological elements, as well as titanic death and rebirth struggles. The equation of perversion, I have suggested, is that if "orgasm = death", then "death = orgasm." Perhaps also "both = birth".

Conclusion

So what are we to make of all this? To begin with, I think that (as is frequently true for him) Reich's views on perversion are a lot more coherent and tightly argued than at first they appear. Reich has a repeated tendency noisily to assert some unimportant and often untenable thesis, while quietly articulating something else of great importance and originality. In this case, the latter would be the view that perversion is a complex and courageous response to traumatic sexual inhibition, which attempts to escape that inhibition by subsuming the trauma into the sexual excitement itself.[10] The further step, which Reich was prevented from taking by his insistence on heterosexual genital supremacy, is to generalize this thesis, and identify the "perverse" component in all satisfying sexual experience.

To summarize my argument: the human sexual economy is organized around one fact, the enormous difficulty we have in surrendering to extreme pleasure, which throws the ego "off guard" and appears to threaten our bodily and psychic integrity. Learning to welcome deeply exciting sexual experience is thus a complex and gradual process, bound up with the whole process of maturation, the development of a sense of security that is internal rather than external, and the ability to tolerate a degree of physical and psychic violence. At the same time, though, orgastic surrender is, in reality, as important to our well-being as, say, surrender to sleep (although in both cases, some individuals can find alternative means of relaxation). Also, of course, as Woody Allen might say, pleasure is pleasurable, even when it is painful!

(Almost) everyone, therefore, seeks to be overwhelmed sexually, yet with equal urgency (almost) everyone tries to avoid it. Every variety of sexual behaviour can be understood in relation to this double effort—to embrace and to ward off overwhelming excitement, to bind anxiety, in the process binding our identity, and to discharge it, in the process releasing our identity.[11] The complexities of human desire can be explicated as an almost infinite range of personal strategies around this hard dialectic of binding and unbinding, on both bodily and psychic levels.

All of the usual psychic mechanisms are employed in our struggle with this central problematic: how can the ego trust that the life it protects will go on if it lets itself be thrown off guard? A frequent strategy is to rely on outside forces to overwhelm our resistance, to put ourselves in the way of rape, torture, *force majeure* of one sort or another. Instead of surrendering directly to our own bodily sensations, we surrender to someone else: because, we pretend, we have no choice. This generally also has the function, as I have already described, of re-enacting the traumatic material that obstructs us from surrendering. A different strategy is to project outwards, not the overwhelming power, but the *surrender*: we take on the role of torturer or rapist while secretly identifying with the surrendering victim. It is to be hoped that all this will happen on a symbolic, play-acting, or sublimated level rather than as literal reality.

Although perversion and neurosis do point in opposite directions around the theme of sexual satisfaction, it is plain that perverse and neurotic elements coexist in the individual character structure, just as psychotic and neurotic elements do. The logical conclusion of my argument, after all, is that *all* successful sexual activity—successful in the sense that it leads to orgasm—is perverse. It is nonsensical to draw an arbitrary line and say that what happens on *this* side of it, although structured identically to perversion, is magically defined as "normal" through a fortunate concentration of approved aims and objects. Everything in Freud's theory of sexuality militates against such a view, even if he occasionally allows his personal petit-bourgeois attitudes to express themselves.

It follows that we must ditch the liberal argument that homosexuals are, after all, not *that* perverse and so can be regarded as adequately normal—able, for instance, to train as analysts (maybe toe-suckers could slip under the wire too . . .?). Perversity is an indigestible presence at the core of all of our sexualities. It is also a major element in culture: psychoanalysis has talked frequently of civilization as *neurotic*, but not sufficiently of its *perverse* nature, its structuring as a response to massive collective trauma. There is really no way out: if we want to have orgasms, if we want to experience satisfaction on any level, then we must, in some way or other, embrace perversity; which, perhaps, is a very good reason for thinking of a new name for it.

Notes

1. What is included in the category of "perverse" sexual behaviour visibly shifts over time—fellatio and cunnilingus can now be discussed on prime time TV.
2. In the context of this chapter I cannot properly consider the reasons for this, but on the level of theory, the concept of "normality" seems to be tied to *reproduction*. See, for example, Freud (1908d, p. 189).
3. The schizoid character structure is also termed "ocular", "boundary", etc.
4. This contact can also be represented as *touch* and *holding*, which is equally crucial terrain for such characters.
5. Reich would look at this process in terms of the "emotional plague", which is his diagnosis of sexual vigilantes of all kinds. He sees "plague characters" as having high sexual energy that is blocked from direct expression. See Reich (1972, pp. 504ff.).
6. I think that in this they rather underestimate the potential power of the "perverse orgasm".
7. As is clear from this passage, Ferenczi is another theorist who does not distinguish rigorously between neurosis and perversion.

8. Dissociation and hyperarousal are currently widely regarded as the two common responses to childhood trauma. See Perry, Pollard, Blakley, Baker, & Vigilante (1995).
9. Although Reich does not comment on this, fetishism would be another such strategy, with its denial/affirmation of castration.
10. Stoller actually comes very close to this formulation, though in a much more critical tone:

> a perversion is the reliving of actual historical sexual trauma aimed precisely at one's sex (anatomical state) or gender identity (masculinity or femininity), and ... in the perverse act the past is rubbed out. This time, trauma is turned into pleasure, orgasm, victory. [Stoller, 1975, p. 6]

11. Warding off overwhelming excitement is especially clear, perhaps, in relation to perversion, where the "warding off" can sometimes be far more prominent than the "undergoing".

References

Baker, E. F. (1980)[1967]. *Man In The Trap: The Causes of Blocked Sexual Energy*. New York: Collier.
Ferenczi, S. (1949)[1933]. Confusion of tongues between the adult and the child (The language of tenderness and of passion). *International Journal of Psycho-Analysis*, 30: 225–230.
Freud, S. (1905d). Three Essays on the Theory of Sexuality. S.E., 7: 125–245. London: Hogarth.
Freud, S. (1908d). "Civilized" sexual morality and modern nervous illness. S.E., 9: 177–204. London: Hogarth.
Freud, S. (1920g). Beyond the pleasure principle. S.E., 18: 3–66. London: Hogarth.
Freud, S. (1950). A project for a scientific psychology. S.E., 1: 281–398. London: Hogarth.
Grof, S. (1975). *Realms of the Human Unconscious*. London: Souvenir.
Hart, L. (1998). *Between the Body and the Flesh: Performing Sadomasochism*. New York: Columbia University Press.
Laplanche, J., & Pontalis, J. B. (1988)[1967]. *The Language of Psycho-Analysis*, D. Nicholson-Smith (Trans.). London: Karnac.
Limentani, A. (1996). Clinical types of homosexuality. In: I. Rosen (Ed.), *Sexual Deviation* (3rd edn) (pp. 216–226). Oxford: Oxford University Press.

Lowen, A. (1965). *Love and Orgasm: A Revolutionary Guide to Sexual Fulfilment*. London: Collier Macmillan.

Perry, B. D., Pollard, R. A., Blakley, T. L., Baker, W. L., & Vigilante, D. (1995). Childhood trauma, the neurobiology of adaptation and use-dependent development of the brain: how states become traits. *Infant Mental Health Journal*, 16(4): 271–291.

Rank, O. (1993)[1929]. *The Trauma of Birth*. New York: Dover.

Reich, W. (1967). *Reich Speaks of Freud*. London: Condor.

Reich, W. (1969)[1949]. *The Sexual Revolution*. London: Vision.

Reich, W. (1972)[1945]. *Character Analysis*. New York: Touchstone.

Reich, W. (1973)[1942]. *The Function of the Orgasm*. London: Souvenir.

Socarides, C. W. (1996). Major advances in the psychoanalytic theory and therapy of male homosexuality. In: I. Rosen (Ed.), *Sexual Deviation* (3rd edn) (pp. 252–278). Oxford: Oxford University Press.

Stoller, R. (1975). *Perversion: The Erotic Form of Hatred*. New York: Pantheon.

Totton, N. (1998). *The Water in the Glass: Body and Mind in Psychoanalysis*. London: Rebus.

PART II
PERSPECTIVES ON PSYCHOANALYSIS

INTRODUCTION

Perversion, historicity, ethics

Lisa Downing

As has been pointed out by several of the authors whose contributions form the first section of this book, the notion of perversion is an increasingly controversial one. Sergio Benvenuto makes the comment that "today . . . the word 'perversion' is not considered politically correct". Nick Totton asserts that it "is both *normative* . . . and *punitive*" and may therefore be "an unhelpful term both for its broad vagueness of usage and for its moralistic/pathologizing overtones". This awareness has led in recent years to a change of emphasis from viewing perversions as moral deviations to seeing them as variations on a *statistical* sexual norm. However, while to differing degrees acknowledging that the meaning of perversion is dependent on historically and culturally contingent mores and morals, the writers in Part 1 unanimously state that the modes of human sexual fantasy and behaviour known as perversion, and the types of psychical organization they imply, continue to constitute a significant and *fruitful* problematic; one with which psychoanalysis cannot dispense.

We have seen that, within different psychoanalytic models and clinical methods, and according to the value systems and attitudes of individual clinical practitioners, the status accorded to perversion—or the contemporary and supposedly less pejorative synonym "paraphilia"—and the recommendation for "treatment" or other accommodation, varies considerably. Thus, any commentary on, or objection to, the psychoanalytic view of perversion must always be careful to bear in mind that this view is not a unified one. This said, most psychoanalytic thinkers and clinicians, following Freud's own description and understanding of perversion, in the first of the *Three Essays on the Theory of Sexuality* (1905d), draw a distinction between perverse elements of behaviour or fantasy that may occur in any subject alongside more "normal" or socially acceptable sexual behaviours, and a perverse *structure*, implying a fixed, sclerotic rigidity of psychical organization. Authors of canonical studies of perversion, Robert Stoller (1986), M. Masud R. Khan (1979), and Janine Chasseguet-Smirgel (1985) have argued, respectively, that elements of hatred, aggression and intimacy-inhibiting alienation underlie the perverse structure, leading the pervert inevitably to find difficulty in many relationships and areas of social functioning, not only those immediately related to their sexuality. This draws attention to one of the most troubling aspects of much psychoanalytic writing on perversion: the extent to which the diagnosis of perverse sexuality leads to the analysand inevitably being associated with a broader pathology. "Being a pervert" means so much more than a description of what one does in bed.

For Stoller, for example, it implies a whole personality structure equated with the Winnicottian false-self. Believing himself the author of his own perversion, the pervert appears as a delusional would-be Cartesian subject. He is a fraudster who has endlessly "connived, pandered and dissimulated" (Stoller, 1986, p. 95) in order to believe and enact his alternative sexual "reality". His whole being is in the service of maintaining and repeating the lie that is his perverse identity. This rhetoric of inauthenticity is taken up by Chasseguet-Smirgel, who writes: "fetishism and perversion are concerned with sham, counterfeit, forgery, fraudulence, deceit, cheating, trickery, and so on—in short with the world of semblance" (Chasseguet-Smirgel, 1985, p. 81). The notion that the heterosexual, genitally-fixated "normophile" has somehow attained "authenticity" merely by obediently assuming the societally approved outcome of sexuality, while the pervert needs to be convinced of his delusion by the "good enough" analyst (Stoller, 1986, p. 95) is a piece of reasoning whose normative cultural–political implications cannot be ignored.

Moreover, in making such assertions, clinicians such as Stoller deviate considerably from Freud's original perspective on the wider psychological and ontological implications of perversion. Freud writes: "people whose behaviour is in other respects normal can, under the domination of the most unruly of all the instincts, put themselves in the category of sick persons in the single sphere of sexual life" (Freud, 1905d, p. 161). The first of Freud's *Three Essays* represented an innovative and progressive departure from the logic of the nineteenth-century sexologists, such as Richard von Krafft-Ebing, for whom perverse sexual behaviour was evidence of a degenerate constitution and of systemic physiological and psychological pathology. Writing of two of the most "repulsive" perversions, coprophilia and necrophilia, Freud wrote: "[they] are so far removed from the normal in their content that we cannot avoid pronouncing them 'pathological'" (Freud, 1905d, p. 161). This is an almost direct echo of Krafft-Ebing's assertion regarding necrophilia that: "this horrible kind of sexual indulgence is so monstrous that the presumption of a psychotic state is, under all circumstances, justified" (Krafft-Ebing, 1901, p. 580). However, while the tone of the two statements is similar, there is an important difference in the way in which Freud and Krafft-Ebing construct the pathology of the perversion. For Krafft-Ebing, this behaviour is an indicator of the essential psychological (and moral) status of the person carrying it out: he who is a pervert is *inevitably* otherwise psychologically and morally sick. For Freud, the perversion—necrophilia in this case—is a piece of abnormal, even pathological, sexual behaviour that nevertheless does not guarantee that the subject "will necessarily turn out to be insane or subject to grave abnormalities of other kinds" (Freud 1905d, p. 161). In extending his assessment of the pervert's capacity for healthy functioning in other spheres of life to practitioners of the most apparently extreme and abnormal perverse practices, Freud struck a rhetorical blow for the decoupling of sexuality from pathology. Stoller seems to have rather regressively returned to the nineteenth-century pre-psychoanalytic model, seen in his assumption that "perverse" desire involves an otherwise antisocial and morally tainted psychology.

One of the major contradictions inherent to psychoanalytic writing on perversion is the tendency, on the one hand, to deny the authenticity of the "pervert's" self-designation and identity while, on the other hand, reifying him as a type, a clinical entity. The idea that sexology and psychoanalysis created the pervert and invert as a "class" of person, that they engineered an epistemological shift from a focus on the meaning of behaviour to the ascription of an identity, has been extremely influential since the publication of Michel Foucault's *Histoire de la sexualité* (1998). Certain strands of cultural studies and political theory, influenced by Foucault's historiographical writing, problematize the ongoing sexological and psychoanalytic practices of referring to, diagnosing, and treating perversion. Homosexuality, as a cornerstone of early sexological and psychoanalytic perversion theory, enjoys a special status with regard to the shift from pathology to identity. Discussions in psychiatric circles during the 1970s, leading to the removal of homosexuality from the American Psychiatric Association's *Diagnostic and Statistical Manual of Mental Disorders*, signalled the changing climate with regard to the question of homosexual legitimacy (See Stoller et al., 1973). Since then, a few psychoanalytic accounts of healthy, "functional" homosexuality (see especially McDougall, 1992), have offered an account of gay and lesbian sexuality freed from the once inevitable association with inauthenticity and pathology. However, such accounts rest on the understanding that a sexual object-choice or practice escapes the label "perversion" only if it is "actively chosen and consciously assumed", rather than enacted as a result of compulsion or fixation (*ibid.*, p. 139).

Certain politicized accounts of non-normative sexuality see the de-pathologization of sexual practices, and the formation instead of political identities based on allegiance to those practices, as wholly progressive social developments. Gayle Rubin, arguing in favour of "s/m liberation", on the model of "gay rights", proclaims somewhat triumphantly, "sexualities keep marching out of the *Diagnostic and Statistical Manual* and onto the pages of social history" (Rubin, 1984, p. 287). Yet, despite some concessions towards the "healthy" homosexual in psychoanalytic writing, the tendency to pathologize gay sexuality has not disappeared. Writing in 1995, five years after McDougall's plea for abnormality (in moderation), psychoanalyst Charles Socarides dubbed homosexuality "a freedom too far" in his politically reactionary account of the impact of gay liberation on American Society (Socarides, 1995). For the most part, the discursive substance of psychoanalysis and that of liberal politics pull in opposite directions, as the category of perversion retains the status of an illness to be treated in most psychoanalytic frameworks, while in the containing culture alternative lifestyles and "kinky" practices acquire a certain chic. Thus, while psychoanalysis in Freud's *fin-de-siècle* Vienna found itself in opposition to the sensibilities of the moral majority because of its willingness to accept the reality of, and to openly discuss, the manifold presence and influence of the sexual (it faced criticisms for being too progressive), psychoanalysis today, in the wake of Foucault, may, in contrast, find itself having to field accusations of a normative politics regarding the legitimacy of certain types of sexual subjectivity.

Yet, one may ask whether the liberal agenda of the acquisition of "rights" is the most appropriate strategic approach for those seeking an alternative discourse to that of pathology for marginalized sexualities. Perversion has been linked by numerous theoretical commentators with the idea of social transgression and the destabilization of hierarchy, with a radical rather than a liberal politics. Perversion, in certain quarters, is associated with a revolutionary impulse, as seen in those accounts that focus on the historical coincidence of periods of great social unrest and a predominance of perverse sexual behaviour. Chasseguet-Smirgel writes,

> we may recall ... that perversion and perverse behaviour are particularly present at those times in the history of mankind which precede or accompany major social and political upheavals: the Fall of the Roman Empire, as we know, coincided with a widespread decadence of behaviour. [Chasseguet-Smirgel, 1985, p. 1]

The historical simultaneity of the activities and writings of the Marquis de Sade and the bloodshed of the French revolution also provides a commonly cited example of perversion's capacity both to reflect and produce primarily social meanings.

Two perceptions of perversion persist and coexist uncomfortably, then, in much psychoanalytic writing. On the one hand, there is the tendency to see perversion as a transgressive, disruptive, dangerous force, a metonymy for the human desire and capacity to break down the social hierarchy and overturn meanings. (The traditional Freudian figure of the little boy disavowing his mother's "castration" is a creative rebel for whom the established order of things is not sufficient, and who will go on to behave as if it were otherwise.) On the other hand, there is the tendency to see perversion as conservative, rigid, and fixated, a mentality or practice not concerned with subversion, renovation, and re-creation but with endless unchanging repetition of a "script" carefully constructed in advance. The tendency then, is towards a polarized view of perversion that labels it either an ultra-conservative phenomenon or else a dangerously transgressive one. It may be that these mutually contradictory perceptions say more about cultural fears, projections and desires on to and for the marginal, than they do about the ways in which individual analysands, subjects, and communities experience their diverse sexualities. It is, perhaps, in response to such stigmatizing views on perversion that Foucault advocated the formulation of an understanding of "sex without the law" (Foucault, 1998, p. 91) as an alternative model of non-normative sexuality to that imbricated in the logic of transgression. In a Freudian model, the pervert is the subject always fleeing the truth of the law. Foucault's reformulation of "sex without the law, and power without the king" (*ibid.*) imagine alternative possibilities in which the epistemologies of perversion—created by the special relationship between power and knowledge in Western culture—can give way to the multiple expressions of "bodies and pleasures" (*ibid.*, p. 157) that fall outside of extant structures of knowledge.

Theorizing perversion in psychoanalytic terms, then, can too easily be seen as a reactionary or conservative political and intellectual project, or as an outmoded one. This criticism, ironically, obtains from the incompatible but dual contemporary perspectives of the prevalent neo-liberal discourse of "choice" and "individuality" on the one hand, and on the other, those deconstructive queer theories which question the status of ontology and the liberal concept of individuality, and which seek to undermine assumptions about the naturalness or inevitability of heterosexuality and the binary organization of gender. The rhetoric of some queer theory urges that any tarrying with the term perversion, or with the psychoanalytic discourse that borrowed it from the lexicons of religion and sexology and embraced it as part of its clinical repertoire, is not only wrongheaded, but politically dangerous. Others adopt the label of "pervert" as a celebratory, counter-discursive self-designation, liberating it from the ideological underpinnings of its conditions of construction. Psychoanalysis, in continuing to work theoretically and clinically with a notion of "perversion", may then find itself squarely at odds with the Zeitgeist. Yet, at the same time, cultural and political critics continue to refer incessantly to psychoanalysis, whether to question, borrow, or "pervert" its central controversial concepts of sexuality.

* * *

The essays collected together in the following chapters do not adopt straightforwardly counter-psychoanalytic arguments. Rather, they constitute attempts to dialogue with psychoanalysis from various other disciplinary viewpoints, in order to relativize, nuance, or put into perspective its theories of perversion. While some essays reflect upon and evaluate the usefulness of psychoanalytic models of perversion for understanding works of visual culture (Pajaczkowska, Apter) or political phenomena such as fascism and totalitarianism (Vadolas); others adopt a psychoanalytically-informed theoretical framework critically, in order to dismantle some common assumptions *within* psychoanalytic perversion theory. These include explorations of the vexed question of female perversion (Merck, Apter); revelations of the surprising "queerness" of Lacanian theory (Dean); and an assessment of the ways in which historical models of perverse pathology continue to influence and impact upon contemporary diagnosis and clinical practice (Rosario).

The psychoanalytic definition and theorization of perversion are not just of relevance to the clinical setting that produced them, but have taken on broader cultural applications, particularly within the fields of cultural and art criticism. The extent to which perversion has become a ubiquitous critical tool is perhaps best illustrated by the case of academic cinema studies. Laura Mulvey's gaze theory, which reads the perversions of scopophilia and fetishism not as "minority tastes" but as the entire mechanism by which cinema spectatorship operates, and in thrall to which narrative cinema is constructed (Mulvey, 1975), continues to be a dominant paradigm for theorists of gender and desire in the cinema, and her article is ubiquitously quoted in any discussion of these issues. Other writers have nuanced the relationship somewhat, asking not only what models psychoanalysis may offer for cultural criticism, but also what lessons psychoanalysis may learn about its key concepts from other disciplines and from the arts. In her chapter in this collection, Claire Pajaczkowska turns a critical lens upon pictorial art and its capacity to embody perverse energies, understood as social currents. Pajaczkowska literalizes Phyllis Greenacre's observation that "fetishism is a picturesque symptom" and issues an invitation to those for whom perversion is principally a clinical matter: anyone wishing to examine the implications of fetishism fully, she suggests, would benefit from a study of art and an engagement with theories of art criticism. French *avant-garde* art of the early twentieth century emerges in this essay as the locus of a particularly perverse political and artistic sensibility, characterized by a "pushing at boundaries", seen literally in the escape of the image beyond the picture frame.

Much current post-Lacanian theory, particularly by Slavoj Žižek and his followers, is engaged in exploring the applicability of psychoanalytic concepts to the analysis of political situations, conditions and dynamics. Examples are Žižek's edited selection of Lenin's writings (2002a) and his essays on September 11 (2002b). Relatively little work has been done, however, on the specific links between the concept of perversion and political structures. Notable exceptions are Joel Whitebook's study (1995), which argues that the impulses of perversion and Utopia have in common a striving to unsettle the reality principle that ordains the social status quo; and a recent edited collection on *Perversion and the Social Relation* (Rothenberg, Foster, & Žižek, 2003), which points up both the universality and the limitations of perversion as a structure underlying social organization. The editors of that collection use the concept of perversion as it is understood within Freudian/Lacanian frameworks, as a "specific relation to the paternal function" (Rothenberg & Foster, 2003, p. 4), characterized by disavowal of the father's Law and the attempt to create an alternative law. As Octave Mannoni has argued, disavowal is the mechanism by which any ideology may operate, such that "I see now that X was not true, but all the same, it is true in a way" (*ibid.*, p. 10). Thus, the fetishist and the subject of ideology find themselves relating to "reality" through a similarly disingenuous lens. Readings such as these dislocate perversion from its association with minority sexual orientation and pathology, and thereby de-stigmatize it. Yet, this strategy risks reducing "perversion" to a catch-all term for the mechanism of disavowal and ignoring the conditions of its production as a specifically sexual phenomenon. By universalizing the operation of perversion in this way, one is faced with a historical erasure, and the attribution to it of ideological implications that it may not properly bear.

Antonios Vadolas's original and timely chapter in the current collection is influenced by such investigations as the ones described above, yet works hard to avoid this reduction. It explores the apparent similarities between totalitarianism and perversion via a creative exploration of Lacanian discourse theory. Perversion has often been linked to totalitarian fantasies of holocaust-haunted mass destruction, as suggested by films such as Pasolini's *Salo* and Cavani's *The Night Porter* and by those psychoanalytic theorists who insist on the presence of destructive phantasies underlying all perversion. Chasseguet-Smirgel, for example, argues that the pervert operates in an undifferentiated phantasy universe that routinely obliterates the boundaries between generations, sexes, even life and death: "the pleasure connected with transgression is sustained by the fantasy that [the pervert] has destroyed reality, thereby recreating a new one, that of the anal universe where all differences are abolished" (Chasseguet-Smirgel, 1985, p. 3). Lacanian theory is used expertly by Vadolas to examine this equation. Minutely disentangling the position of the pervert *vis-à-vis* the Other's *jouissance* from that of the fascist, Vadolas's contribution submits to rigorous scrutiny the knee-jerk association of perversion with fascism, suggesting perhaps that Chasseguet-Smirgel's formulations may cast more light on fascism than they do on perversion.

The political implications of "perverse" female sexuality are explored in Mandy Merck's chapter on "The feminist ethics of lesbian s/m". This chapter, which was originally published in 1993, consists of a critical survey of erotic and theoretical texts produced by and about the lesbian s/m movement in the 1980s. The essay engages with, and challenges, traditional psychoanalytic notions of perversion in so far as it re-poses the question raised by Parveen Adams of whether it is possible to imagine a female sexuality that is not "oedipally organized", and whether lesbian s/m might be it.

However, it also explores the extent to which a feminist politics should accept and embrace the "perverse" as a part of its code of ethics. Taking issue with Freud's controversial assertion that women are less capable of morality than men, Merck shows how the 1980s feminist "sex wars" constituted an all-female moral battleground on which the right to enjoy s/m became an object of conflict. She concludes with an observation of the difficulty—and danger—of separating off apparently incompatible, but intimately proximate, "political and sexual imaginaries".

In a related vein, Apter's chapter on the fetishism of motherhood takes as its starting point the shortage of psychoanalytic theorization of perversion in the feminine. Existing work in this under-theorized domain includes Louise Kaplan's influential book-length account of this problem (Kaplan, 1993). As Apter does not deal with Kaplan's work in her article, it may be useful for the reader if I discuss briefly here the points on which the two writers diverge. Kaplan's central argument is that such constructed perverse scenarios as fetishism and sadism—which over-emphasize masculine techniques of objectification to compensate for the threat of loss (castration)—are properly "male" perversions. Aberrant feminine sexuality, on the other hand, is visible in such compulsive strategies as kleptomania and self-mutilation, behaviours that emphasize the very degraded, masochistic nature of the castrated femininity that is (partially) rejected. Thus, for Kaplan, perversion is a distorted exaggeration of the socially prescribed gender characteristics thought proper to each sex. Kaplan follows Stoller in insisting on the immensely limiting rigidity of the perverse solution, rather than on its transgressive or utopian qualities: "What distinguishes perversion is its quality of desperation and fixity. A perversion is performed by a person who ... would otherwise be overwhelmed by anxieties or depression or psychosis" (Kaplan, 1993, pp. 9–10).

She claims that, although perversion does not mean the same thing for men and women, in both cases it is a reaction to, and against, sexual difference and gender division. Apter, on the other hand, takes psychoanalysis's denial of female perverse capacity and its purported tendency to negate the female body as two symptoms of the same underlying problem: the gynophobia of psychoanalysis. In contradistinction to Kaplan's claim that fetishism would be nonsensical as a female perversion, Apter proposes that culturally denied maternal sexuality may equate to the unthinkable formula: "the mother's objectification of the child". Thus, she argues strategically for a provisional theory of maternal fetishism in order to redress the gender-biased understanding according to which "the sexuality of Christ upstages the question of what Mary wants". Female perversion appears in Apter's account as something that has first to be avowed and theorized before it can be critiqued, problematized and redefined.

In "Lacan and queer theory", Tim Dean invites the reader to see Lacan as he has seldom been seen: through the lens of queer. Dean claims that, far from being a conservative discourse which schematizes, diagnoses, and regulates "normal" and "perverse" desire, Lacanian psychoanalysis *is* "a queer theory". Arguing for the radical depersonalization of desire implicit in Lacan's theory of the object *a*, Dean persuasively shows that by including the category of the real in his formulation of sexuality, Lacan alone among modern thinkers decouples desire from an inevitable relationship with either gender or act. Dean opens his chapter with Lacan's opaque sound bite *"quand on aime, il ne s'agit pas de sexe"* (when one loves, it does not concern sex) and explores some of its far-reaching consequences via an "imagined dialogue" with queer thinkers Foucault, Deleuze, and Butler. Recast through Dean's argument, Lacan emerges as "radical" rather than "liberal" on the question of sexuality.

Vernon Rosario's piece, the last in the collection, is also an engaged exploration of the potential for queer thinking in a psychoanalytically informed setting. It interrogates the ethics of diagnosis in contemporary psychodynamic and psychiatric practice, advocating taking account of the ideological history of perversion in sexology and psychoanalysis, in order to illuminate the kinds of discourses applied by contemporary clinicians working with transgendered patients. Rosario argues powerfully against clinical work that is overly influenced by an unreconstructed sexological or Freudian model of the perverse, in favour of a reconceptualization of our sexed and gendered identities as characterized by "trans-sensualism"—a sliding scale of identities, desires and identifications orientated flexibly rather than fixedly. The rhetorical strategy of Rosario's intervention is one familiar to queer theorists.

Discussing the ways in which homosexuality is represented, Eve Kosofsky Sedgwick has described two strategies which she dubs "minoritizing" and "majoritizing" (Sedgwick, 1990). In the first case, the gay-positive theorist might argue that homosexuality is a matter only of concern to gays, members of a marginalized group who construct their identity against the hegemonic norm, hence the justification for separatist politics. The alternative strategy relies on the argument that being gay is a matter of concern for everyone—that we are all implicated in gay identity, we are all "a little bit gay". Freud's theory of primary bisexuality has been recuperated and adopted by some gay and lesbian theorists for this very reason. Rosario's article presents a convincing and original account of the majoritizing argument as applied to the whole "polymorphously perverse" sphere of gendered and sexual identities and practices.

* * *

If I were to seek to identify a common thread, a strand drawing together the essays on perversion collected together in the second half of this book, it would—perhaps surprisingly—be their shared concern with the ethical. Writing of the erotic and the ethical in the context of lesbian feminism, Mandy Merck has pointed out that these are "apparently contradictory, yet closely related, drives". This may be true in the context of psychoanalysis, too. Both erotic life and psychoanalysis are fields fraught with ethical challenges. Engaging in either of them involves an assumption of responsibility for the other; the dangers (and potential pleasures) of objectification; the necessity to tarry with one's own, and the other's, ambivalent and unconscious desires and fears. These underlie, and are stimulated by, both sets of practices. And both types of "practice", analytic and sexual, are characterized by the sheer range of their expression and the differences between them. From Reichian bodywork, through a Lacanian conception of the subject as constituted by and in language, to the Kleinian emphasis on infantile aggression and primary narcissism, psychoanalysis has developed many faces. Similarly, "vanilla" heterosexual intercourse, the controlled, rule-bound rituals of lesbian s/m, and the life-risking, autoerotic thrills of asphyxiophiliac practices demonstrate the endlessly multivalent faces of Eros. Types of psychoanalysis and types of sexual pleasure may differ to such an extent that one may be forgiven for the observation that they appear not to belong to the same category of phenomenon as each other at all. And this observation may perhaps lead us back to Foucault, who pointed out that sexual science constructed disparate bodily and desiring practices as taxonomical categories and constituted sexuality as a "knowable" field of enquiry in the first place. Yet, just as we must understand that "sexuality" was artificially constructed as a unified field, as a result of a particular configuration of certain historical forces, so "sexual science" must not be stigmatized as a monolithic, authoritarian discipline producing only one meaning, but as a complex network of influences, viewpoints, and strategies, offering sometimes competing, sometimes complementary perspectives.

This is precisely why writing about perverse sexuality and writing about psychoanalysis—just like practising sexuality and practising psychoanalysis—requires a careful commitment to the ethics of specificity. Ethics can never simply be about admitting of the universality, rather than the aberration, of perversion (which does not mean that it is invalid to make politically strategic "majoritizing" claims for polymorphous perverse potential). Nor is ethics just about a liberal, all-embracing, empathic "understanding" (though a liberal approach to difference may have a significant therapeutic and social value). The point is rather that many of the rhetorical strategies that are marshalled around perversion, even if they differ from each other, are characterized by a reductive tendency. Making monolithic claims about the "nature" of "the pervert" reifies experience into a category of being and denies specificity; universalizing perversion as a common condition of humanity risks ignoring the particularity of individual desire and experience; while designating the marginal as just an extravagant or elaborate annexe of the mainstream risks an annihilation of the conditions of difference. At stake in these cases, then, are both an ethical danger and an epistemological fallacy, which centre on reduction. This is because all of these strategies assume that "perversion" can be understood as the other to "the norm" in a neat dialectic.

French philosopher of ethics Emmanuel Levinas upsets such dialectical thinking when he shows that our historical conception of "the same" and "the other", privileged phenomenological terms, are not separate and equal, embodying difference, but that they coexist in a relation of totality: "if the same would establish its identity by simple *opposition to the other*, it would already be part of a totality encompassing the same and the other". (Levinas, 1969, p. 38). It is in reaction to this "totalizing" tendency to understand the other in relation to the same that Levinas strategically adopts the meta-category of infinity. By envisaging the plural narratives of diverse sexualities encountered in clinical practice as "perversion" in the singular, as the binaristic counterpart of "normal" or "healthy" sexuality, one commits an indiscretion in logic and in ethics. As an "optics" (*ibid.*, p. 29), to borrow Levinas's term, that allows both for specificity of difference and for an infinite plurality of possibility, ethics is, perhaps, always in tension with, if not in direct opposition to, diagnosis, categorization and definition.

As Vernon Rosario puts it in the conclusion of his contribution to this book, the "most productive approach to sexual diversity (as opposed to sexual perversity)" may only be realized if we resist the historically ingrained temptation to "[erect] sturdier walls between the varieties of gender and sexuality—separating the normal from the perverse". A commitment precisely to dismantling the sturdy walls that shore up our assumptions about the "normal" and the "perverse", coupled with an intellectual openness to interdisciplinarity, dialogue, and exchange, are the unifying quality and hallmark of the six, very different, perspectives presented below.

References

Chasseguet-Smirgel, J. (1985). *Creativity and Perversion*. London: Free Association.
Foucault, M. (1998)[1976]. *The History of Sexuality. Vol 1: An Introduction*, R. Hurley (Trans.). Harmondsworth: Penguin.
Freud, S. (1905d). *Three Essays on the Theory of Sexuality*. S.E., 7: 135–243. London: Hogarth.
Kaplan, L. J. (1993)[1991]. *Female Perversions: The Temptations of Madame Bovary*. Harmondsworth: Penguin.
Khan, M. M. R. (1979). *Alienation in Perversions*. London: Hogarth Press
Krafft-Ebing, R. von. (1901)[1886]. *Psychopathia Sexualis*. Translation of 10th German edn., F. J. Rebman (Trans.). London: Rebman.
Levinas, E. (1969)[1961]. *Totality and Infinity: An Essay on Exteriority*. A. Lingis (Trans.). Pittsburgh, PA: Duquesne University Press.

McDougall, J. (1992)[1978]. *Plea for a Measure of Abnormality*. Revised edn. New York: Brunner/Mazel.

Mulvey, L. (1975). Visual pleasure and narrative cinema. *Screen*, 16(3): 6–18.

Rothenberg, M. A., & Foster, D. A. (2003). Introduction. Beneath the skin: perversion and social analysis. In: M. A. Rothenberg, D. A. Foster, & S. Žižek (Eds.), *Perversion and the Social Relation* (pp. 1–14). Durham, NC: Duke University Press.

Rothenberg, M. A., Foster, D. A., & Žižek, S. (Eds.) (2003). *Perversion and the Social Relation*. Durham, NC: Duke University Press.

Rubin, G. (1984). Thinking sex: Notes for a radical theory of the politics of sexuality. In: C. S. Vance (Ed.), *Pleasure and Danger* (pp. 267–319). Boston: Routledge and Kegan Paul.

Sedgwick, E. K. (1990). *Epistemology of the Closet*. Berkeley, CA: University of California Press.

Socarides, C. (1995). *Homosexuality: A Freedom Too Far: A Psychoanalyst Answers 1000 Questions About Causes and Cure and The Impact of the Gay Rights Movement on American Society*. Phoenix, AZ: Adam Margrave.

Stoller, R., Marmor, J., Bieber, I., Gold, R., Socarides, C. W., Green, R., & Spitzer, R. L. (1973). A symposium: should homosexuality be in the APA nomenclature? *American Journal of Psychiatry*, 130(11): 1207–1216.

Stoller, R. (1986)[1975]. *Perversion: The Erotic Form of Hatred*. London: Karnac.

Whitebook, J. (1995). *Perversion and Utopia: A Study of Psychoanalysis and Critical Theory*. Cambridge, MA: MIT Press.

Žižek, S. (Ed.) (2002a). *Revolution at the Gates: A Selection of Writings from February to October 1917: V. I. Lenin*. London: Verso.

Žižek, S. (2002b). *Welcome to the Desert of the Real! Five Essays on September 11 and Related Dates*. London: Verso.

CHAPTER EIGHT

Perversion and French *avant-garde* art 1912–1916

Claire Pajaczkowska

"Man has always endeavoured to go beyond the narrow limits of his condition. I consider that perversion is one of the essential ways and means he applies in order to push forward the frontiers of what is possible and to unsettle reality"

(Chasseguet-Smirgel, 1985, p. 61)

"Fetishism is a picturesque symptom"

(Greenacre, 1953, p. 79)

The relation between perversion, transgression and creativity is profound and complex, expressing as it does a confrontation with, and simultaneous retreat from, the rule-governed and law-bound practices of "normal" sexual and social life.[1] Each of the three elements feeds off and stimulates the others. The transgressive element of perversion is well documented. Law-breaking itself may embody sexual fantasy. In a lecture given at the British Psychoanalytic Society in 1985, Arthur Hyatt Williams gave a lucid description of the structure of perversion as it is expressed in a range of criminal activities. (See also Hyatt Williams, 1998.) One example he offered was of a burglar who was completely unaware of the causes of his repetitive housebreaking. Analysis revealed that the conscious idea of stealing valuable goods was a rationalization of a less rational and unconscious fantasy. According to Hyatt Williams, the burglary was the enactment of a fantasy of entering a forbidden place, which had a sexual significance. The crime of burglary, then, was a form of a perverse fantasy that connected sexual excitement and aggression. From this psychoanalytic perspective we begin to define perversion as something that may be unconscious and that fuses sexual and aggressive ideas in a fantasy of transgressing or damaging law and order.

To move on to a consideration of creativity, we might bring to mind how the link between perversion and art can be understood by reference to the relation between perversion and sublimation. This equivalence works in so far as base elements of bodily energy can be transformed into cultural texts. Art can be sublime, or it can be ridiculous, and there are moments when the *avant garde* has fused both into acts of transgressive and creative innovation. A consideration of the French Dada movement may afford particularly rich insight into the ways that the interplay between transgressive and perverse structures of fantasy inform creative production.

Freudian theory holds that all perverse fantasy is based in preoedipal component drives, which are often directed at objects that are not fully differentiated in terms of gender or generation. Yet, the transgression we find in the art of Duchamp, Picasso, and Oppenheim expresses a fantasy that is more about the law of the father than the body of the mother. One motive for the urge to transgress comes from the need to deny the difference between infantile and adult subjectivity and to assert the superiority of the infantile. That this is both a sexual and an aggressive fantasy is something that only psychoanalytic theories are able to explain. In this chapter I use psychoanalytic ideas to consider the emotional and intellectual structures of perversion (particularly fetishism) and to show how they are embodied in the stylistic and formal components of the modernist art of the Parisian *avant garde* in the early twentieth century. I explore the transformation of meaning that enabled the pictorial frame to be "pushed" through abstraction to dematerialization, and suggest that this process fuses aggression and desire in a form that corresponds to the structure of perversion (Chasseguet-Smirgel, 1985, p. 12). The significance of this perverse dimension of French modernist art has been little recognized by art historians, who have generally investigated its meaning either in formalist or socio-historical terms.[2] By presenting the problem from the perspective of a theory that uses psychoanalytic concepts as an integral part of its method, I hope to invite art historians to consider new approaches to their discipline and to invite psychoanalysts to think beyond the couch.

Four psychoanalytic theories of perversion are particularly influential in guiding my thinking in this essay. The first is Sigmund Freud's concept of perversion, defined in the *Three Essays on the Theory of Sexuality* (1905d), which understands adult sexuality as comprising unconscious, repressed, infantile fantasy that has its own sexual logic, organized around the pre-genital component drives of oral, anal, and phallic libido. For Freud, the perverse, infantile drives form the basis, or "raw materials" of the process of sublimation, a process that displaces the aim and object of a drive in order to direct libidinal energy away from bodily aims towards cultural, social, and Symbolic goals. For Freud, perverse component drives and infantile fantasies are psychologically universal, are ubiquitous in culture, and their traces can be found throughout visual culture. It could also be argued that perverse symptoms in adults are a "mechanism of defence" in the classic Freudian sense of a defence created by the ego to avoid the experience of anxiety and the painful affects of hopelessness, helplessness, powerlessness, frustration, longing, and loss. In this chapter I refer to traces of the component drives of exhibitionism, urethral eroticism, phallic narcissism, and voyeurism as possible unconscious components of artistic production. I also refer to the defensive structure of fetishism, classified by Freud as a form of perversion, though one that seems to be a universal feature of human sexual life (Freud, 1927e). In relation to visual culture, I shall argue that the mechanisms of fetishism are relevant for a consideration of the formal dynamic between the centre and edge of an image, and the stylistic and conceptual presence of the pictorial frame. The fetishistic element of *avant-garde* art is thus found in its dynamic of pushing at boundaries, especially at the frame as a conceptual boundary demarcating different realities. The frame in art traditionally acts as a marker of the transition or split for the spectator from one kind of attention or state of mind to another. It marks the difference between the way we look, instrumentally, at material reality and the way we look, searching for meaning, at representational reality. Similarly, and not coincidentally, Freud speaks of a "splitting of the ego" in relation to fetishism (Freud, 1940e). It will be argued that the frame takes on the significance of a fetish for these artists and presents them with the interplay between safety and threat that is signified by all fetishes. This may seem a long way from infantile sexuality, in which component drives and part objects are features of universal fantasies of perversion, yet defences such as fetishism are the organization of those drives, objects, relations, and fantasies into a specific structure of the ego: a frame.

The second psychoanalyst whose concept of perversion is particularly fruitful here is Robert Stoller, who describes perversion as the "erotic form of hatred" (Stoller, 1975). His formula emphasizes the way in which perverse acts are vehicles for revenge fantasies in which aggression is fused with infantile fantasies to create narratives of omnipotence, reversing the infantile predicament of helplessness. In this respect we can see that the artists' use of the military metaphor of being an *avant garde* allowed them a potent fantasy, attributing the significance and power of war to their artistic activities and casting them as vanguard troops sent ahead to clear the terrain for the rest of the army or *arrière garde*. The combination of pioneering courage and straightforward, manly, authorized aggression, created through the metaphor of military organization, proved flattering to artists, who seized upon the concept and adopted it as an identity. Stoller's work casts light on the aggressive components of perversion, and we will find the subtle fusion of naked aggression, wit, and flamboyant exhibitionism in Duchamp's pioneering work at the New York Armoury show of 1916.

The third psychoanalyst whose work has been influential on my thinking here is Janine Chasseguet-Smirgel, a French clinician who stresses the extent to which perversion is a mechanism for denying, sometimes even violently obliterating, the psychic reality of difference. This extends Freud's original formula, according to which perversion is the vestigial remains of pre-oedipal sexuality within the adult. Chasseguet-Smirgel emphasized the strength of the denial of difference as a defence against symbolic castration, the loss of infantile omnipotence, a denial that is based on the denial of the knowledge of the absence of the maternal penis. Differences she identifies are the sexual difference of adult genitality, the difference between adult and infantile realities, the difference between subject and object, and differences between individual objects, which are denied through a fantasy of undifferentiated infantile sameness. Crucially, the difference between the generations is violently denied, leading to a psychic annihilation of the axis of History. This fantasy, which Chasseguet-Smirgel calls the perverse "universe", is also characterized as an "anal universe" in which infantile fantasies of control, possession, contemptuous denigration of difference, and even torture are enacted as triumphant assertions of the omnipotence of the pre-oedipal. We shall explore some of the traces of excremental fantasies that underlie the *avant garde*'s attack on the idealizations of traditional art. We will also demonstrate the differences between the masculine and feminine forms of the French *avant garde*, contrasting the phallic comedy of transgression with the receptive wit of ambivalence.

The fourth relevant concept is that developed by Joel Whitebook, who pursues the Frankfurt School's project of bringing psychoanalysis to bear on culture through the method of Critical Theory in order to demonstrate the social manifestations of the unconscious (Whitebook, 1995). It is Whitebook's development of the concept of sublimation that I find most useful, as he sees symbol formation in the ego as a process of reuniting severed relations between subject and object. The relation is severed when the fulfilment of infantile and oedipal fantasy is finally accepted as impossible, and the capacity for fulfilment is refound in symbolic form in the cultural processes of making meaning. This complex and sophisticated understanding of sublimation as an effect of symbolic castration enables us to identify the art of the *avant garde* as overdetermined through the structures of perversion, suture, history, and humour.

The different concepts of perversion presented by these analysts and theorists are different in nuance rather than substance, as all are essentially Freudian in their conception of the unconscious as embodied fantasy, and as linked through sexuality to developmental processes that recapitulate infancy in adulthood. These analysts use the genetic and economic axes of Freud's metapsychology as well as the paying attention to the topographic model. The paradigm is qualitatively different from the Lacanian model more familiar to scholars of cultural studies, which emphasizes the structuring function of the signifying systems of the Symbolic order of language. I use the theories of all four analysts as appropriate and refer to their work whenever aware of their influence. However, the writings of many analysts over the past century have passed into a general cultural apprehension of the significance of psychoanalysis as a paradigm for the analysis of visual culture. Whereas the Lacanian discourse is fairly well established, through film theory and literary studies, the other psychoanalytic paradigms that refer to body, affect, genetic and developmental aspects of perversion are less familiar to scholars of visual culture and are thus felt to be more obscure. It is for this reason that I am introducing readers to a range of approaches to understanding the perverse dimension of visual culture through the specific example of a moment in *avant garde* art. These concepts offer a richer and more generative understanding of the relationship between text and unconscious fantasy.

I have chosen to focus on a four-year *duree* in the Parisian painterly *avant garde*, as the artworks in question will be familiar to readers through their frequent reproduction. Although I also discuss works from the decades leading up to this period and from subsequent decades of the 1920s and 1930s, I am particularly foregrounding a transformation that took place between two works by Marcel Duchamp (1887–1968) in which art became redefined from canvas to *objet trouvé*, which constitutes a "transgression" in the terms described by Janine Chasseguet-Smirgel, above. This transgression can be related more specifically to the Freudian concept of fetishism, with its explicit reference to splitting of frames of mind, denial, and the "suspension of disbelief". However, although this chapter explores the perverse elements of the structure of innovation within the modernist idiom of the "new", as a manifestation of an unconscious fantasy of the triumph of the infantile over the paternal—of innovation over tradition—perversion may be a necessary component of all cultural practice. This chapter explores a moment of transgression, a "paradigm shift" or "quantum leap", in the practices of French *avant garde* artists.

The moderns had, for some decades, been challenging the definition of painting by becoming increasingly self-referential, by making art that contained references to the process of its own making, or references to its own materiality. Simultaneously, painting was becoming less "objective" and less realist, recording the relationship between artist and object rather than the object *per se*. The changes in art between Duchamp's unremarkable Cubist painting *Nue Descendant l'Escalier* of 1912 and the urinal exhibited in the 1916 Armoury show in New York, were of a type that made for a qualitative reconceptualization of art, rather than adding to the quantitative increments of painterly subject matter that had characterized the modernism of the preceding decades. This kind of change is sometimes called "thinking outside the box", and it is this metaphor of containment, boundary, or threshold—ambivalently experienced as prohibitive or paternally oedipal—that interests me here. When we use the concept of perversion to understand the mechanisms of feeling and thought that give rise to such transformations of culture, it becomes apparent that what is being enacted is a "pushing" at, or bursting through, boundaries and frames of reference, and an attempt to break through conventions that are experienced as constrictive. This "pushing the envelope" is an activity that depends on conceiving the boundary and frame as a prohibition requiring "transgression" as much as a "container" offering form. In this respect, the concept of the pictorial frame and the conceptual frame of reference have profoundly oedipal significance as well as historical and semiotic meaning. The "language" of art realism in which the canvas is bounded by both frame and artist's signature becomes, in the twentieth century, a principle of outmoded paternal ancestry that is pushed, through repetition, pastiche, and parody, to disintegration. Because the historical and semiotic aspects of framing are already widely discussed in analyses of visual culture (e.g., Adair, 1994; Cannon-Brookes, 1995; Mitchell & Roberts, 2000; Vedrenne, 1997), I will focus more on the psychic and emotional dynamics of the frame as it signifies in the unconscious.

Duchamp's *Nue Descendant l'Escalier*, typical of the Cubist style of fractured, multiple perspectives, was also influenced by the Italian Futurist problematic of depicting movement within painting. The painting explores some of the limits of the canvas and of the conventions of painting the nude. Not only does the vertical, upright female nude seem to move through a series of "freeze-framed" movements that makes the canvas mirror the technological capacities of photography and mechanical reproduction, but she cannot be made to be a supine, immobile object of erotic contemplation for the spectator. Moreover, she is featureless and robotic too. These traits are fairly typical of a great many paintings of this time and indicate the extent to which painting was being used as an idiom of modernity, representing the rapid changes that were taking place in everyday life and in consciousness.

By 1916 the frame, the canvas, and the painting were gone and the art object had moved off the surface of the canvas, through the frame, and straight on to the gallery floor, where only the eye and mind of the spectator could see the art in the industrially produced, shop-bought urinal. The structure of meaning in the piece, *Objet Trouvé* replicates the economic structure of humour as described by Freud in his 'Jokes and their relation to the unconscious' (Freud, 1905c). It functions by bringing to consciousness the repressed aspects of exhibitionism and commodification that underlay the more idealized, conscious aspects of art. Below, I shall explore in more depth the process of transformation of meaning that enabled the frame to be pushed through to disintegration and suggest that, as "the erotic form of hatred", the modernist art of the French *avant garde* has significance as perversion that has not been fully recognized by historians of modern art.

Picture frame

The last quarter of the nineteenth century brought a dynamic confrontation between centre and edge of the painted image. Fragmentation of the centre and recursivity of the edge became evident in the flattening of perspective in Impressionism, and the impasto brushwork of the Post-Impressionists. Photography, with its mechanical framing, had led to dramatic changes in the relationship between edge and centre, offering a syntactic ordering of spatial relationships that made no reference to the classical arrangement of foreground, *repoussoir*, middle, and background. Perspectival structure based on Euclidian geometry was transformed into a more mobile and less monocular system. These were the changes that led to the pictorial innovations of Cubism and Futurism. The point of view of the centred humanist subject was thought, by the twentieth-century modernists, to be as much a figment of social convention as the first person pronoun was a product of mere syntax. The perspectival grid of horizontals and orthogonal lines was conceived as an optical equivalent of the rules of language.

With the deconstruction of the centre and growing self-consciousness came a reformulation of the edge as a boundary that structures the spatial relationships of the representational world of subjectivity. Modernists in art and literature sought representation of the experience that there was nothing inherently unified, or singular, about human subjectivity. The Surrealists' interpretation of Freud's *Interpretation of Dreams* (1900a) convinced them that the human subject was irreconcilably divided between conscious and unconscious. Most modernists allied their work with a scientific project, and even if this comparison was nothing more than fantasy, the painters were internally driven to depict their predicament of being conscious of themselves as observers rather than being able to paint as if viewing the world through a transparent window. The opacity of the canvas and the material presence of the paint became powerful metaphors for consciousness and subjective awareness of the multiplicity of different types of materialism.

Each of the *avant gardes* of Europe gave expression to different types of fragmentation. Robert Goldwater has analysed these as different Primitivisms, from Gaugin's romantic primitivism through the emotional primitivism of the German Expressionists, to the intellectual primitivism of Picasso and Braque. To the Surrealists he attributes the "primitivism of the unconscious" (Goldwater, 1938, pp. 178–216). Of all the Surrealists it was Magritte (1898–1967) who was the most interested in the concept of frame. Possibly because he had made the transition from commercial artist to fine artist, he was deeply conscious of the significance of paint as a material. His paintings repeat images of frames, windows, drapes, and stages. They provide compelling and playful explorations of flatness and illusion in painting. *Ceci n'est pas une pipe* (1929), the series of paintings featuring images of pipes, writing, frames, and internally framed spaces, are his most focused essays on the theme of the pictorial illusion and its opacity. The scripto-visual elements place these paintings into conceptual art in a way that the paintings of Braque and Picasso, which often incorporate visual citations of newspapers, paintings of fragments of paper, or other written texts, do not. Magritte uses writing with the directness and simplicity of a tradesman, but his directness gives the text the significance of being a signifier of a signifier; in other words, a meta-text. This complex statement is made in a visual style of cheerful innocence, reminiscent of the advertisement or shop sign, whereas Picasso's cultivated "quotations" of newspapers locate his paintings within the tradition of the aesthetic illusion.

The frame is a complex metaphor in art. It is analogous to the proscenium arch of theatre, which signifies the transition between two types of reality, the reality of physical presence inhabited by the audience and the reality of the representational world inhabited by actors as characters within the fiction. As such, the frame in art is what marks the canvas as having the status of a bounded reality. The limits of that edge are of particular significance, and Modernist painters, especially, made self-conscious use of edges without boundaries (Degas) in a way that was formally abrupt for spectators. The purpose of the frame is to invite the spectator to willingly "suspend disbelief" and to enter the play of signification that constitutes the pleasure of visual art. The spectator knows that he or she is looking at paint applied by brush but agrees to "overlook" this level of material reality in order to include another level of representational reality. The modernist, such as Magritte, and to some extent Picasso, too, plays with the spectators' gaze being pulled in and out of each of these two forms of "focus". By including the painting of a sentence, Magritte includes a third axis of focus that adds a conceptual triangulation to the gaze. This third term is the inward gaze of introspection and conscious thought. This marks the transformation of the merged subject of illusion into the self-conscious subject of thinking.

Frame as fetish

According to Stoller, the fetish is a "body part (or an intimately related object such as a garment) split off from the whole human object" (Stoller, 1975, p. 14). Greenacre suggests that the fetish functions as a "new body . . . a sublimely economic condensation of the mother's body that provides, especially through vision, the illusory comfort of union with the mother and simultaneous disengagement, detachment, disidentification from her" (Greenacre, 1953, p. 89).

These descriptions enable us to understand the vacillation between being merged and being distinct, which are the two states of mind required of the spectator of realist pictorial illusionism. It is the frame that gives material representation to the interstitial state of mind of spectatorship.

Freud noted that the fetish is not any body part, but is an object that represents the mother's penis, an imaginary organ whose absence causes such anxiety that it is immediately denied, disavowed, and replaced with a fantasy and a symbolic phallic substitute. This relationship is related to, but different from, the way that the phonetic signifier stands in for the absence of the referent and the presence of the signified. The former represents a fantasy of being united with the phallic mother; the latter rests on an acceptance of the absence that makes the presence of the signifier meaningful.

We now understand why the relationship of separation-from and closeness-to a painting needs to be so materially signified and controlled: the body of the painting represents, in the unconscious, the body of the mother, and the spectator is placed as the oedipal child who must find a way of "knowing" his or her relation to this body, without incurring the punishments that such knowledge might entail.

In the years preceding 1916 there were a number of key moments in the history of painting. One of these was Picasso's painting *Les Demoiselles d'Avignon* (1907). Picasso's challenge to the canonical tradition of realism was partly a stylistic one, using Cubism as an antithesis to realism. However, the stylistic form of Cubism did not challenge the frame of painting, simply the content of what was to be depicted within the frame. Picasso's principal challenge was formal and moral rather than conceptual. The *Demoiselles d'Avignon* transgresses the coda by virtue of its representation of whores in the place of eternal nudes, much as Manet's *Olympia* (1865) shocked the salon forty years before him. X-ray photography reveals the different stages of the painting and shows a male figure included in the space of the brothel, in a way that alludes to the spectator's inclusion into the scene, a reference to self-consciousness of the artist and the self-reflexivity of art. In its final form, *Les Demoiselles* does not include the male figure. The women take on particular vulgar significance, denoted through their poses and through the rough brushwork that is a direct confrontation with the nineteenth-century codes of idealization and aestheticism.

Donald Kuspitt suggests that "the rough, battered, quasi-primitive surfaces of many modern fetish objects, suggesting the crudeness of faeces, is the visual equivalent of smelliness" (Kuspitt, 1995, p. 365). The pose of the whore in a frontal squat in the painting's foreground is one example of what Chasseguet-Smirgel interprets as the "anal universe" of perversion, where the difference between the sexes is denied in favour of a cloacal fantasy of anal indifference. The twisted torso of the squatting female creates a torsion in which the visual presence of the vagina is denied, the vagina's genital significance reduced to that of an organ of excretion rather than accepted as an organ of reception and generation. Chasseguet-Smirgel notes that the logic of this disavowal is to recognize only those organs that signify in the world of the infantile body, and to (violently) annihilate adult genitals. This denial is also indicated in the flattened-out space of the painting, indicating an absence of depth and receptivity that has a psychic as well as art historical significance. The replacement of Euclidian space with distorted or two-dimensional space is equated with states of mind that are based on a "voiding" of affect and meaning. The anal sadistic universe is also indicated in the brushwork that is vigorous and visible to the point of becoming a statement of tactility, of the materiality of the softness of paint and the analogy between painting and smearing. The sensual aspects of this are evident in the joyful display of colour and rhythm, while the more malignant forms of regression to infantile aggression are evident in the disconnected limbs and twisted female torsos. These may caricature the aesthetic, idealized distortions of Ingres's Orientalism, in which the location of female nudes in the space designated as a "harem" enabled distance to be fused with intimacy in a potent combination of desire and control. Picasso confronts the moral duplicity of Orientalist fantasy by the double references, within the three other female nude figures, to Iberian sculpture and to African masks, replacing the nineteenth-century colonies of the Middle East with indigenous art and the art of Africa. The moral injunction that Picasso offers the spectator is that there is pleasure in his art but it offers no hiding place from the embarrassment of being caught looking. The wound of the trauma that is sex has not been sutured with, or veiled by, idealizations of beauty, smoothness, delicacy or coyness. Picasso aims to present *sex as sex* in a new realism. It is this unconscious equation of the visual and the sexual that marks the fine art of modernism as an example of fetishism.

The intellectual structure of fetishism is also the structure of a form of thinking that enters into a "suspension of disbelief", which Freud compares to the syntactic form of the statement "I know, but nevertheless". Fetishism is the disavowal of the significance of the moment of sight that brings with it knowledge of the difference between the sexes. The fetish freezes the moment preceding the sight that brings the loss of innocence, and serves as both acknowledgement and denial of this loss, which is why fetishes are usually visual objects and are often shiny. The frame in traditional painting is precisely what demarcates two types of gaze, announces the presence of the unseen, that which is excluded from the gaze of the spectator. Frames are also, traditionally, ornate and covered in gold leaf or gold paint, connoting their "shine". The frame divides the spectator into a knowing gazer and one who can deny or overlook the boundary indicated by the frame.

Fetishism is neither sublimation nor "sex"; it is a defensive manoeuvre to avoid the confrontation with sexual trauma. It disavows what is seen and creates a memorial to the unseen, a form of thinking that enters into a "suspension of disbelief" that Freud compares to the syntactic form of the statement "I know, but nevertheless". In traditional painting it is precisely the frame (often ornate and shiny as many fetish objects are) that announces the presence of an unseen that is excluded from the gaze of the spectator, and the perversity of fine art generally takes on a specifically fetishistic form as the frame or boundary separating spectator from object or illusion becomes pushed and challenged. It is the disintegration of the material representation of this boundary to which we will now turn our attention.

In 1916 at the New York Armoury Show, Duchamp exhibited the famous urinal, the ceramic receptacle without plumbing, often photographed resting on the floor, signed, in black paint, "R. Mutt". The visual presence of the hand in the painted signature is a reference to the "auratic", which is a signifier of irony and an allusion to the convention of intensified authorial significance within the *avant garde* which seeks to identify innovation with a particular individual. The urinal itself is a reference to industrial production and to the everyday, the two realities that underlie the idealized aestheticism of art culture. However, the urinal adds a level of reference to phallic narcissism, the visibility of the male genital as an organ of urethral rather than generative significance. The perverse act seeks to replace adult genitality with infantile pre-genitality, and here the function of the penis is identified with the function it has had since birth rather than the function it acquires in maturity. This is, unconsciously, an abolition of the difference between the generations, an attack on reality. The urethral eroticism of the phallic phase also relates to the visibility of the boy's organ of micturation, and this is an unconscious component of all scopic regimes in culture, of which art is one. Hence, the conventions of seeing and being seen, of voyeurism and exhibitionism, of private and public views, of recognition, celebrity, and obscurity that make up the conventions of knowing and not knowing in art, are based on an unconscious phallic narcissism. A frame of reference is created that confuses seeing and knowing, and that equates visibility with reality.

Duchamp's urinal exhibited in the gallery refers to this hidden component of exhibitionism of the gallery, and it is the abrupt effect of bringing unconscious drives and fantasies into the place of their sublimation that creates the "shock of the new" and the sense of being reduced to a shameful secret or base bodily, animal, and infantile activity. The structure of this release of repressed meaning is also, we noted, the structure of jokes, and this comic dimension of the urinal remains despite the century that has elapsed since its exhibition. A further meaning of the urinal is the unconscious significance of urethral eroticism as a component of ambition. Freud connects "burning" ambition with urethral aggression, and the aggression of wanting to defeat rivals in competition is represented, in unconscious fantasy, by the act of "pissing on them" in contempt and in victory (Freud, 1908b, p. 175). The Duchamp urinal has transformed the competitive world of modernist innovation in art from the unknowable world of talent, work, and mastery into "a piece of piss", where the artist can buy his art in defiant conquest of waiting to "be bought" by the collector (like the whores in Picasso's painting). That this is an oedipal attack is explicit in the addition of the signature R. Mutt in the place of his own patronym, Duchamp. Kuspitt notes the function of the fetish in modern art as a "magic wand to wave away the existence of the father", in this case by reducing the father's name to the signifier of a dog (Kuspitt, 1995, p. 370). The parodic inversion of celebration in the name of the author invokes the presence of a debased and degraded father. The reference to the dog is connoted, and this is also found in the signifying chain that leads from pissing to the attack on the place of the father as historical precedent and master, by the infantile and animal urethral and bodily world. The fantasy of the art world as a world of dogs sniffing each other's trails of urine—an idea that is both comic and aggressive—is thus present in the piece.

This is the point at which the frame is finally lost in favour of a conceptual, internalized frame that is entirely a product of the spectator's attention to the intentionality of the artist's action or gesture. The spectator is implicated in the representational world in a way that no longer indicates a boundary at which disbelief is to become "suspended". In a perverse act of symbolic attack on the space and history of art the modernist *avant garde* inaugurates a new beginning. It is no overstatement to say that all *avant-garde* art since Duchamp has had to acknowledge the significance of this dematerialization of the frame and its relocation in the intentionality of the artist. To be modernist, art must acknowledge its position within the history of art as a site that attributed meaning to objects and artefacts. Subsequent challenges to the space of art were to take the form of locating art outside the constraints of the bourgeois gallery setting and gave rise to the concept of "site specific" installations such as earthworks, performances, temporary installations, and the complete "dematerialization of the art object" (Lippard, 1973).

It is not uncommon for spectators to consider modernist art such as Duchamp's work a trick, a worthless gesture of contempt for the tradition of an art that rests on apprenticeship, talent, genius, and work. It is not unusual for modern art, more generally, to be considered, by some audiences at least, a world of sham and counterfeit. The idea of the sham is certainly significant for fetishism. Chasseguet-Smirgel suggests that it is because the cognitive structure of fetishism rests on the belief that one object can be substituted for another—pre-genital—one, that ideas of trickery circulate:

> ... the fetish is an imitation of the genital penis, and that imitation, in general, is associated with anality. This leads us back once more to the fact that fetishism and perversion are connected with sham, counterfeit, forgery, fraudulence, deceit, trickery and so on, in short with the world of semblance. [Chasseguet-Smirgel, 1985, p. 81]

The fetish is a phallic substitute for the imaginary organ of the mother's penis, according to Freud (1927e), and this is why there is such ambivalence felt for a signifier for which there is no referent. It is a signifier of an absence, an absence so disturbing that it requires the presence of a fantasy to mask it. The modernist works with pastiche, irony, and wit. He or she draws attention in a self-referential way to the "world of semblance" that is the work of art, showing the ambivalence with which culture views the value of illusion and the status of the "real thing".

Duchamp's work also took the form of assuming the transvestite identity of "Rrose Sélavy" (phonetically: "Eros, c'est la vie") a game of performance and punning that both recognizes Freud's concept of libido and also rejects psychoanalytic concepts of oedipality, by asserting the possibility of being both sexes simultaneously. Because of the denial of sexual difference the *avant garde* culture of fetishism and perversion enforced a rather limited place for both psychic femininity and for women as participants in art culture. Femininity was symbolically equated with castration, the sexual, and dependency. The Surrealists depicted the feminine either as the embodiment of the bourgeois parasitism that they sought to overturn with their revolutionary communist *avant garde*, or else as the incarnation of sexuality and desire. British Surrealist Humphrey Jennings, for example, exhibited his wife in the 1931 Surrealist exhibition in London. Painters from Manet on sought to challenge the canonical idealization of the nude in the classical tradition by depictions of the "whore in the brothel", by which they imagined themselves to be liberated from the hypocrisy of conventions of shame, concealment, and euphemism. Not surprisingly, there were not many women allowed the status of pioneers of modern art at this time. It was not repressive certainly, but this is because fetishism is not a neurosis and therefore does not use the defences of repression. Fetishism is, nevertheless, extremely controlling and defends against intolerable castration anxiety through the defensive use of mechanisms of denial, and the assertion of phallic narcissism.

One artist whose work survived this episode of gender constraint is Meret Oppenheim, a sculptor whose two pieces *Le Déjeuner en Fourrure* (1936) and *Ma Gouvernante* (1936) are both of and about their time. The fur teacup and saucer, accompanied by a teaspoon, is a feminist equivalent of Duchamp's *objets trouvés*, but occupies a domestic scale and frame of reference where his is industrial and mechanical. The ceramic container is covered with fur, rendering the symbol of everyday rituals of civility and refinement functionally useless and revealing the cup as an object of fetishistic veneration, like an artefact of primitive religion. The primitive religion in question here is the class system and its ritualistic exhibition of differences of caste. *Prendre le thé* in France has a different meaning from having "a nice cup of tea" in England, since French Anglophilia rests on an idealization of the upper-middle class, the fantasy that this class is the most refined, and the idea that their rituals must be emulated. The title *Fur Breakfast*, although the cup is not a breakfast cup, is a reference to the table manners and conventions of social codes that multiply around the deeply anxiogenic activities of cooking and eating, which, as structuralist anthropologists remind us, are evidence of our profound ambivalence about the proximity of love and aggression in the appetites of hunger. It refers to the *petit déjeuner*, the first meal of the day, which separates sleeping from waking and ritualizes our journey from unconsciousness to consciousness. Oppenheim also refers to the fetishized world of feminine domesticity, which idealizes the display of objects and accessories over the more human aspects of hospitality. Fur, with its tactile, animal associations, becomes the very surface that cannot be touched, that prohibits touching and the animal warmth of mammalian gregariousness and sociability. Human beings, like all mammals, are defined by their ability to give birth to live young and to feed them through feminine lactation. The tea ritual signifies the human transcendence of the animal mammalian heritage by idealizing the rules that demarcate taking tea from mere relief of appetite. The fur also introduces a level of sexual meaning to the ritual, civil repression of the sexual, and this functions like a joke to facilitate the "return of the repressed". It is at once simple and sophisticated.

The other Oppenheim piece, *Ma Gouvernante*, is also simple, but involves four *objets trouvés* assembled together. A pair of high-heeled ladies' court shoes in white kid leather are bound together with string like a *gigot*, or roast leg of lamb. The points of the heels are decorated with the white paper crests that are traditionally used to decorate or hide the end of the leg bone that protrudes from the roast meat. This is presented on a silver platter. The title underlines the meanings that circulate around the paradox of a femininity that is both an unconscious object of oral gratification, the good mother, and an agent of frustration or prohibition, the bad mother. The dish that cannot be consumed is, as Adrian Stokes defines the work of art, "a piece of cake that survives being eaten" (Stokes, 1978). Art visually excites oral appetite and the desire to incorporate and ingest, but remains intact because of the interdiction on touching art. The elements of meaning that are introduced through the trussing of the shoes reminds us that ligature and binding have a sadistic significance, in so far as they cause pain and diminish freedom of movement; hence the sadomasochistic rituals of bondage and hanging that are frequently found in perverse sexual acts. The trussed shoes replicate a trussed roast, but the high-heeled white kid leather shoes refer to the frustration of appetite by placing visually sexualized accessories in the place of oral gratification. This moves the oral to the visual and the infantile to the oedipal. High heels are often described as fetishistic, in so far as the heel is a phallic displacement that associates the female body with the hardness and armoury of the phallus. Finally, the title, *Ma Gouvernante*, refers to the strictures of the maternal relationship that begin as the mother becomes an object of frustration as she takes on the work of socializing her child. This implies a delay in gratification and a constraint of infantile omnipotence. Often split off from the idea of the good mother because of the ambivalence of infantile impulses, the governess is an embodiment of the phallic mother associated with "governing" and being an executive agent of the law, rather than the gratifying mother of narcissistic union. Here the multiple denotations are bound together and served up in a way that demonstrates the unconscious fantasy that underlies the traditional relationship of viewer to art.

Afraid of nothing

Duchamp's "statement" of 1916 that led to the dematerialization of the frame in art initiated a new language of art that continued to identify itself as *avant garde* and modernist. The contemporary descendents of this tradition are the British artists Damien Hirst, Sarah Lucas, and Tracy Emin, whose work has much of the comedy, aggression, perversity, and audacity of the Dada *avant garde*. The postmodern *avant garde* is, however, more ambivalent than the earlier modern movement, and this marks an awareness of its dependence on bourgeois culture. The *avant garde* exists on the edge of the bourgeoisie and because of it, an unwelcome fact for artists who would rather be autonomous and independent.

Does this give us any sense of what sort of anxiety sufficed to generate such a violent transgression of the conventions of nineteenth-century realism by the modernists of the early twentieth century? Were the Russian revolutions of 1907 and 1917 a portent of the end of "easel art" in the West? Was the outbreak of the First World War a sign of the end of the bourgeois stability and optimism that had upheld the art of the nineteenth century? Was the emergence of feminism in modern European cultures a sign of the end of a romantic fantasy of the artist as hero? Was the development of technological revolutions in transport, electricity, photography, and industrialization a signal of the end of the place of painterly realism? Was it the development of science and its dissemination through the mass media that led to the death of God and the distrust of all illusions?

These are all anxieties that were present in the subject matter and formal properties of the many national *avant gardes* of European modern art movements. There can be no doubt that the certainty of the significance and place of the artist in culture and society was disintegrating, and that this presented artists with the threat of something like a symbolic annihilation. That this was experienced, in the unconscious, as castration anxiety is very likely (Ward, 2003). The fragmentation of centred subjectivity seemed to indicate the end of something. If fetishism is a compromise structure that represents an attempt both to merge with and to differentiate from the pre-oedipal mother, this regressive fantasy would serve as a protective measure. Duchamp's aggressive gesture led to a rebirth of the *avant garde* as a form of masculine protest. In so doing it undermined the frame of the "art object" self-reflexively in the artwork itself. Art developed an interiority of thinking that became more important than its function of offering illusion or pleasure. Modernism remains ambivalently attached/detached from culture and bourgeois society, but the signs of its individuation are present in the self-awareness it indicates to the spectator.

The articulation of perverse component drives and their corresponding fantasies are universal and are the foundation of all sublimation. The defensive structure of fetishism enables a fantasy relation of fusion with the body of the phallic mother to protect the subject from awareness of the need to individuate. As Whitebook suggests, the only means for a relocation of perverse union lies in the psychic space of sublimation (Whitebook, 1995, pp. 217–263). The fantasized union must be renounced, given up as lost, accepted, mourned, and internalized, after which time the psychic capacity for symbol formation is strengthened, the internal representational world offers an equivalent to the external world, and the relationship between outer and inner worlds is found in the relation between word and meaning.

Freud noted that artists may have the capacity for perverse, neurotic, and sublimated libido. Although there have been many changes within psychoanalytic thinking over the last century, much of the thinking on fetishism remains fairly constant. The usefulness of psychoanalytic thinking for understanding visual culture is evident. Whether this kind of study can bring anything to psychoanalysis is another question. Although many analysts suggest that their theories are tested, proven, or disproven in the "laboratory" of their clinical practice alone, Freud was more ambitious for his science, and he wrote over half of his work on problems of culture, religion, art, politics, mythology, and society. Adamant that psychoanalysis should extend beyond being another medical specialism or therapy, Freud pointed out that the unconscious is active in all dimensions of human activity and can be found not only in the consulting room, but in all aspects of culture. As Lacan and Granoff point out: "Freud himself recommends the study of fetishism to all who wish to understand the fear of castration and the Oedipus complex" (Lacan & Granoff, 2003, p. 299).

Notes

1. With thanks to Ivan Ward for his comments on and editing of this essay.
2. A notable exception is the work of Donald Kuspitt (Kuspitt, 1995), on which I shall draw in this article.

References

Adair, W. (1994). Picture framing III: The foundation of the International Institute for Frame Study. *Museum Management and Curatorship, 13*: 321–33.
Chasseguet-Smirgel, J. (1985). *Creativity and Perversion*. London: Free Association Books.
Cannon-Brookes, P. (1995). Picture framing: J. M. Whistler's picture frames in the Freer Gallery, Washington, in the light of 1994–5 Whistler exhibitions. *Museum Management and Curatorship, 14*: 206–12.
Freud, S. (1900a). *The Interpretation of Dreams*. S.E., 4–5. London: Hogarth.
Freud, S. (1905c). *Jokes and Their Relation to the Unconscious*. S.E., 8. London: Hogarth.
Freud, S. (1905d). *Three Essays on the Theory of Sexuality*. S.E., 7: 135–243. London: Hogarth.
Freud, S. (1908b). Character and anal eroticism. S.E., 9: 169–175. London: Hogarth.
Freud, S. (1927e). Fetishism. S.E., 21: 152–157. London: Hogarth.
Freud, S. (1940e)[1938]. Splitting of the ego in the process of defence. S.E., 23: 275–278. London: Hogarth.
Goldwater, R. (1938). *Primitivism in Modern Art*. New York: Random House.
Greenacre, P. (1953). Certain relationships between fetishism and faulty development of the body image. *The Psychoanalytic Study of the Child, 8*: 79–98.

Hyatt Williams, A. (1998). *Cruelty, Violence and Murder: Understanding the Criminal Mind*. London: Karnac.

Kuspitt, D. (1995). *Signs of Psyche in Modern and Postmodern Art*. Cambridge: Cambridge University Press.

Lacan, J., & Granoff. W. (2003)[1956]. Fetishism: the Symbolic, the Imaginary and the Real. *Journal for Lacanian Studies*, 1(2): 299–308.

Lippard, L. (1973). *Six Years: The Dematerialisation of the Art Object*. New York: Praeger.

Mitchell, P., & Roberts, L. (2000). Burne-Jones's picture frames. *The Burlington Magazine*, 142(1167): 362–70.

Stokes, A. (1978)[1963]. Painting and the inner world. In: L. Gowing (Ed.), *The Critical Writings of Adrian Stokes*, 3 (pp. 209–219). London: Thames and Hudson.

Stoller, R. (1975). *Perversion: The Erotic Form of Hatred*. New York: Pantheon.

Vedrenne, E. (1997). L'art bien encadré. *Beaux Arts Magazine*, 152: 89–93.

Ward, I. (2003). *Castration*. London: Icon Books.

Whitebook, J. (1995). *Perversion and Utopia: A Study of Psychoanalysis and Critical Theory*. Cambridge, MA: MIT Press.

CHAPTER NINE

The perverse domination of the fascist and the Sadean master

Antonios Vadolas

Introduction

What is the relationship between fascism and perversion? Interwar Fascism, with Nazism as its dominant expression, has been frequently linked to the notion of perversion and its multi-faceted synecdoche. Texts from discourses belonging both to "popular" and "high" culture emblematize this link: cinematography, social theory, political history, and psychoanalysis. The films of three eminent directors—Luchino Visconti (*The Damned/La Caduta Degli Dei*, 1969); Liliana Cavani (*The Night Porter*, 1973); and Pier Paolo Pasolini (*Salò or the 120 Days of Sodom*, 1975)—all illustrate the proximity between fascism and extreme sexual deviation. In the field of socio-political discourse, compelling analyses of fascism have been offered by thinkers in the Frankfurt School (see Horkheimer & Adorno, 1973) and philosopher Hannah Arendt (1958). For more recent accounts, one might turn to works by Slavoj Žižek (1989, 2000) and Juliet Flower MacCannell (1996). Furthermore, psychoanalytic clinicians and theorists, such as Ernest Jones (1974) and Janine Chasseguet-Smirgel (1985), have produced narratives that posit a connection between fascism and perverse

187

sexuality. These texts all share a "macro-structure". They are narratives produced by and dependent upon a dianoetic context enveloping a message that links fascism to perversion in either its sexual or non-sexual conception.

Rather than relying on ready-formed theories of perverse fascism, this chapter will examine the value of Lacanian discourse theory for assessing the proximity between perversion and fascism. Lacanian concepts have been extensively used within the field of psychoanalytically informed ideology critique (Laclau & Mouffe, 1985; Žižek, 1989, 2000). Yet, a main problem of the implementation of psychoanalytic concepts for this purpose is that they can in themselves become a certain ideological narrative rather than the means for dissecting ideology. A Lacanian critique of ideology has to evolve from an extra-ideological position. In this regard, the analysis of the connection between fascism and perversion should elucidate an ideological phenomenon from a psychoanalytic perspective, without using the psychoanalytic theory of perversion as a way to defend and reintegrate either conservative or leftist views. It may be that Žižek ingeniously rearticulates a Marxist–Leninist critique, but is his post-Marxism also post-ideological? It would not be arbitrary to see in Žižek not only new psychoanalytic advances, but also the theoretical basis for a new radical leftism. If the Lacanian corpus serves as the plinth of the Marxist resistance to capitalism, does this lead to an advancement of Lacanian theory or to a revolutionary sentimentality that instrumentalizes theory? Before we combine psychoanalytic insights on perversion with the condition of subjectivity under specific ideological circumstances, such as fascism, we have to answer the question of who benefits from this intersection. Is it psychoanalysis or ideology? With a Marxist–Lacanian or a Marxist–Freudian framework, it is doubtful whether one can actually avoid ideological indoctrination.

The point of demarcation of the present analysis is the disengagement of psychoanalysis from a discursive context that could take the label of a specific ideological orientation. This is not a *critique* of fascism. It is rather a critique of the implementation of psychoanalytic concepts as an unsurpassable bastion for such accounts. In other words, the aim here is not the articulation of a psychoanalytic explanation of the fascist phenomenon, a metanarrative about fascism; the focus is more on the statements enunciated by the narratives, according to which fascism has links with perverse sexuality. These statements are analysed at the level of discourse, but this is the discourse of the unconscious that only psychoanalysis can elucidate as an intellectual tool that goes beyond discursive limits. If we move beyond discourse, where no ideology operates, psychoanalysis can bestow a more comprehensive view of the factors that lead fascism to be associated with perversion. Linking fascism with the category of perversion is inadequate to explicate the fascist phenomenon, not only at the level of ideology, but also at the level of its barbaric practices.

There is a common denominator underlying fascist ideology and its historical atrocities that has to be re-examined; this is the transcendence of a certain limit, an excess that cannot be captured by existing narratives. But what is this excess and what is its status? To interpret it as a deviation from the norm seems to provide hypostasis to the use of the term perversion when referring not only to sexuality, but also politics. In this chapter, I discuss the limits that the pervert and the fascist appear to surpass, challenging the idea of perversion as deviation. The result is an exposure of the impasses found in those narratives. Behind the contradictions lies the Lacanian Real, the kernel of our subjectivity that evades symbolization. Taking the Real into account adds a crucial dimension to the analysis. The Real that underlies symbolic reality obstructs any singular account of historical phenomena and reveals the impossibility of capturing or of rendering positivistic historical "truth".

Psychoanalysis, despite its highly systematic and explanatory insights regarding neurosis and psychosis, has so far failed to provide an unequivocal account of perversion. Moral implications, the lack of a precise clinical picture, and the occurrence of so-called perverse symptoms in non-perverse psychical structures partially account for the complexity of the notion of perversion. One might wonder if "perverse" as a designation in clinical, political, cultural, or even psychoanalytic discourse sometimes serves as a substitute for the Lacanian notion of the Real, the space of impossible truth. The term "perverse" appears as a signifier for any parasitic condition that escapes firm symbolic meaning. But if one considers the fact that the very essence of subjectivity, namely desire, is founded in the lack that cannot be grasped by symbolic signification, then the term "perverse" designates the status of all desiring subjects. And this is actually one of the most acute observations of psychoanalysis: the origins of desire are first placed in infantile *perverse* sexuality. Judith Feher-Gurewich also notes the adjacency between desire and perversion: "In Lacan's view, perversion is akin to desire per se. For him, as for Freud, human desire itself is perverse, insofar as it defies the laws of adaptation and survival found in the animal world" (2004, pp. 191–192).

In its most common conception, perversion as a designation refers to the excessive element of sexuality that escapes the phallic function and that cannot be incorporated by the symbolic reality of coded sexual behaviours that serve normative or reproductive purposes. This excess might have been labelled differently, had not the oedipal organization of desire gained a certain privileged status in modern culture (becoming a master signifier). Psychoanalysis is partially responsible for this, together with the major institutions of society. As a consequence, any act that deviates from this oedipal organizational pattern receives the perverse designation precisely to mark the (however arbitrary) supremacy of the organization and denounce any element that is not part of it. It fails to succumb to repression. One problem with defining perversion as following a strict oedipal logic is that so-called perverse scenarios are found in the fantasies and the speech of all subjects, even if they are not acted out (symbolized).

Power and discourse

Power may be argued to be the fundamental concept in politics and the underlying fantasmatic core of all ideologies, including fascism. By dissecting the logic of ideological modes of power, we can elucidate the unconscious economy of their hegemony and question perversion as an operative category for understanding not only sociological and political conditions, but also the obscurity of the notion of subjectivity. While it seems uncontroversial to state that power may be the crux of political science, this does not mean that the notion escapes ambiguity. While a thorough analysis of the historical, political, philosophical, and sociological meanings of power is an urgent task, it is one that cannot fall within the scope of the present chapter. My intention instead is to shed some light on another dimension of power that moves away from traditional accounts encompassing the psychoanalytic dimension. Psychoanalysis can elucidate the closed circuits that power produces apropos of the divided subject that is enmeshed in those circuits. In the space of the present analysis, a number of remarks about discourses of power aim to point out that power should not be taken as something that is self-evident and approached as an object of empirical investigation.

Too many scholarly works fall into the trap of regarding the concept of power as something given. Early attempts to define the term are found in Aristotle's *Politics* and later, during the Renaissance, in the work of Machiavelli, Hobbes, and Locke. With the decline of the great empires and the emergence of national states, the notion of power acquired a new interest for theorists such as Weber (1962), who drew the distinction between *Herrschaft* (domination) and *Macht* (power). However, analyses of the notion still remained sporadic until the 1960s, when the introduction of Marxist thought in academic circles initiated a fervent scrutiny of power phenomena (see Black, 1976; Lukes, 1986).

For Horkheimer and Adorno, power is a concomitant to the natural force of reason. If power is unfettered from critical reason, as in the case of bourgeois dominance, natural power tarnishes and takes a deviant form such as fascism: "[A]ll the power of nature was reduced to mere indiscriminate resistance to the abstract power of the subject [...] Among the rulers, cunning self-preservation takes the form of struggle for Fascist power" (Horkheimer & Adorno, 1973, pp. 90–91). To perceive power as a natural virtue that becomes feeble under particular socio-economic conditions of bourgeois domination is to fall into a vague generalization that fails to provide a coherent definition of power. Power seems closer to a system of non-reason than to a system based on reason. This is because there is no rationality that justifies the supremacy of the ideals on which power rests. In psychoanalytic terms, the ideals of power constitute the master signifiers that define it.

A glance at Foucault's work displays power as a central feature of his theorization. Foucault emphasizes the origins of power in institutions founded by discourse. Each institution comprises a body of knowledge with which power is inevitably tied. Foucault, then, does not attribute power to a natural source, but he sees it rather as something constructed and supported by institutions having an effect on the subject's body and soul: "Power is the effect and instrument of political anatomy. The soul is the prison of the body" (Foucault, 1977, p. 30). This statement sums up the familiar view of Foucault as a thinker who sees power operating in all relations without distinction between loci of power and non-power. In a reversal of the theological view, it is the soul that dominates the body as the outcome of discourse. The body is subjected to the prevalent discursive doctrine of power. Thus, perversion, for instance, constitutes a category that refers to a deviation from prevalent discourses that determine normative sexual practices. The complex network of human relationships is regulated by power as a mechanism of submission and domination that imbues every aspect of human life that has to do with overcoming any type of resistance. Foucault's viewpoint is different from theories that stress economic factors, but still he disregards the dynamics of intersubjective communication that escape discourse, namely the subject of the unconscious.

So, do perversion and fascism refer to conditions that impurely transform a natural power into a power of domination? Or are they articulated by bodies of knowledge, and therefore empirically accessible? Whether as a natural artefact or a product of institutionalized discourse, power cannot be effectively apprehended unless the discourse of the divided subject of the unconscious is taken into account. Power is a product of discourse, or better, the fantasy that gives consistency to discourse. As Bruce Fink puts it: "the dominant discourse in the world today is no doubt the discourse of power: power as a means to achieve x, y, and z, but ultimately power for power's sake" (Fink, 1998, p. 29). The primary focus here is on the route by which power is brought together with the triadic conception of existence that Lacan has introduced, namely the three registers of the Symbolic, the Imaginary and the Real. And from the three, the dimension of the Real concentrates most of our critical effort.

Power is formative for all types of socio-political relationships (as well as sexual relationships), but it is not seen as a natural force or a force articulated by discourse. Power cannot be personalized and included into a certain frame, because there is always something that escapes from its locus. Power transcends law since it entails an omnipotent position that imposes and abolishes the latter. It is a promise to the subject; a promise to fulfil what the subject cannot succeed in doing on his own. It resides in the two sides of the law, its normative moral side and its obscene (perverse) side. This explains the common view that sees every power mechanism as indistinguishable from its dark side, corruption.[1] This is not just the content of a paranoid idea; it is also a reflection of the actual fantasy that subsists power. As a fantasy, power goes beyond the normative; each institution of power is aware of the other side of the law.

Power seeps through all aspects of our subjectivity, as Foucault argues, but it acquires meaning in so far as there is a locus in the existence of the subject that remains void of symbolic meaning. This is a zone of *ex-sistence*. Power is structured, acquires meaning, around something that does not exist. The place of non-existence is occupied by fantasy—an ideological structure for instance, or a perverse scenario—which produces an image of fascination or identification and puts in motion power relations. The Other is the guarantor of power that founds all actions of subjectivity. It can be God, the Law, and so on; it is the *I* as a signifier that accompanies the image in the mirror. The symbol and the image are the essence of the system of signification.

From a Freudian perspective, the origins of power reside in the subject's desire to recover the omnipotent narcissistic condition of the first year of life, when the infant had its needs satisfied by its mother, with whom it formed an illusory unity. As Whitebook observes, "for Freud, the desideratum is the mastery of omnipotence" (Whitebook, 1995). The desideratum's aim is to master the lack in the subject's early omnipotence. This lack emerges after the first object cathexes, marked by separation and the realization that there is an external world that operates in ways not always responsive to the subject's needs. This desideratum causes power as fantasy to come to the surface. The subject creates fantasmatic scenarios and constantly searches for power to achieve the fulfilment of his scenarios. Fantasy is a *sine qua non* for the subject's existence and the circulation of its desire. Power is the motive force behind desire; this is the desire to be desired. To put it differently, it is my desire to have the power (fantasy) to be desired, or to impose my desire through oppressive means. Even if I am not desired, the imposition of this certainty as the outcome of the exercise of power, and the other's pretence that s/he desires me, are enough to fill me with *jouissance*. Millions of people worship leaders of totalitarian regimes, while at the same time feeling rage against them. One of the most freezing moments in recent history was the famous case of Ceauçescu. While he was hailing the people from his balcony, the wrath of the assembled audience of Romanian citizens suddenly erupted against their leader and eventually led to a mock trial followed swiftly by his execution. The whole procedure lasted only three days. The incident highlights the role of power in disguising the lack of desire. It is the same totalitarian power as that of the primordial father of *Totem and Taboo* (Freud, 1912–1913a), the hubris that led his sons to execute him.

The soil of power is nothing but a fantasy that promises unification. It promises the means to satisfy desire through the cultivation of an image linked to a certain Good. The Good is what the Law secures, so every fantasy of power ensures that pleasure is met and one does not exceed the limits that would lead one to stumble upon *jouissance*. This underlines the narcissistic status of power. It offers a fantasmatic place of identification for the subject that functions as certification for the desire of the Other. If you follow the Good of power, then you meet the desire of the Other—albeit a cultural, knowledgeable Other/other.

Identity plays an important role in power, since the latter is the narcissistic accompaniment of the imaginary consistency of the image as seen by the subject in the mirror. The whole perceived by the subject is the whole that power promises: an integrated, self-actualized individual and society. The subject's identity is an illusory product, a narcissistic misrecognition, which is constantly challenged by the symbolic modes of intersubjectivity. The ego of the subject is the epicentre of the fantasy of power and the ego always wishes to be dominant. The inevitable schism between the imaginary domination of the ego and symbolic difference seems to support ideological schemes of power that promise reconciliation between the two. But the Other of language always remains incomplete, preventing narcissism from finding completeness in an image. None the less, fantasy is always something that resists, since the image is coherent, supporting at the same time an archaic fear, the fear of fragmentation, the mark of which is carried in the *object a*. This closed, fantasmatic circuit, supported by the *object a*, is what I call power.

From a Lacanian perspective, then, we could apprehend power as the underlying fantasy that supports our relationships with reality, the other as *object a*. For is not the idea of the *object a* based on a perverse rationale that eradicates the other's separate autarkic existence? The source of power as fantasy is the bifurcated drive conceived by Freud: sexuality and death. From the energetics of Freud, Lacan moves to a unitary elaboration of the drive in terms of signification. In Lacanese, power-fantasy touches the realm of *jouissance*, but from a safe vantage point. Power's impersonal and omnipresent character is closely linked to the unrepresentable and ubiquitous nature of the drive that maintains all fantasies of power (ideologies). If the desideratum fuels power as fantasy, then it is not difficult to see the relation of power with the Other. If the Other is the barrier to *jouissance*, then the access one has to it defines the degree of power the subject has at his disposal. Power is focused on the lost *jouissance* of the Other; what the other lacks. This is why it aims at recovering the *jouissance* that once belonged to the subject or the nation and that is stolen by the Other. *Jouissance* is the measure of power and, therefore, the seeking of it renders every relationship subject to power. Power ensures a certainty regarding the mode of *jouissance* dictated by the Other via the master signifier. This very certainty builds a safe, pleasurable milieu, where the subject finds himself. Otherwise, the space of *jouissance* is filled up with uncertainty and anxiety, as one approximates the unknown and unrepresentable factor of the Real.

The Lacanian discourse and the fascist discourse

When one approaches fascism as a symbolic category, as a system that organizes the circulation of signifiers in a certain social setting, the question of the operating discourse arises. Fascist principles can mediate social relationships between subjects, influencing their speech and their overall communication. In order to elucidate the blurred picture regarding the meeting of perversion and fascism, when the primary focus is on collective phenomena that shape social bonds, recourse to Lacan's model of the four discourses is indispensable. (For influential accounts, see: Fink, 1998; Verhaeghe, 1997.) The reason for exploring the fascist discourse and discourses of fascism using the tools of psychoanalysis is twofold. Not only does it allow for a better understanding of other discourses, but it also leads to the advancement of psychoanalytic theory by reappraising ideas applied either in the clinic or to social theory.

Lacan did not develop a schema of a distinct perverse discourse. It is a problematic omission that adds to the mystification of perversion, because all we are left with are four discourses that regulate social bonds between neurotic subjects, strictly speaking. If the absence of the perverse discourse constitutes a paradox, it is not the same for psychosis. Since the psychotic subject does not address the other, difference is not acknowledged. The subject is one with the Other, who exists in psychosis. The pervert, by contrast, tries to make the Other exist *through* the other. In our common perception of the term, the pervert acknowledges the lack in the Other, but only to then disavow it.[2] If we reduce fascism, a type of social bond, to a perverse structure, it becomes difficult to match fascism to one of the four discourses, because there is no perverse discourse in the organization of social relations elaborated in the Lacanian corpus. Does such a discourse exist and if it does, what has fascism to do with it? What is the prevalent discourse in fascism?

The significance of the Lacanian theory of discourse lies in the identification of a number of possible symbolic forms through which the unconscious reveals itself in the intersubjective milieu of communication and the formation of social bonds. Language does not involve only one individual, but always entails the presence of another subject with whom there is an exchange of messages through signification. Language is a prerequisite for a discourse, since without introduction to the system of language I do not attempt to communicate. All communication is organized by instinctual behaviours that lack the multiplicity of meanings that language inaugurates. Within the limits of discourse, language makes possible the formation of social relations between speaking subjects. Discourse constitutes the symbolic and imaginary universe of the subject, the borders of which are determined and constantly defied by death, trauma, violence, anxiety, sexual acts, etc. These are the gaps that evince the impossibility of discourse to encompass everything into the signifying function. What these gaps reveal is the dimension of the Real. This is the most important element in the Lacanian discourse, which goes beyond speech to the core of lack, also conceivable as desire, as that which is without words (Lacan, 1969–1970, p. 3). Speech only marks an occasion in discourse; truth continues to operate outside the capacity possessed by speech for shaping relations.

Lacan delineates four discourses: the discourse of the master, the discourse of the university, the discourse of the hysteric, and the discourse of the analyst (see Table 1, below). For each discourse, Lacan develops a corresponding schema, an algorithm. A rotation of a quarter turn determines the structure of each of the other three discourses. There are three fundamental terms operating in each discourse: the signifier, the subject, and the object. But the signifier never has a singular status. By nature the signifier is defined as the difference between two terms, darkness as opposed to light. This means that in the signifier we are dealing with an *a priori* signifying chain of two terms: the master signifier (S_1) and the knowledge (S_2) that originates from the signifier. This is why we have four terms in each discourse. If we proceed to a more detailed account, these four terms—S_1, S_2, the split subject ($\$$) that results from the relation of one (master) signifier to another, and the object a, or the surplus of enjoyment (a)—occupy four different positions that determine the type of the discourse in operation.

The four positions are summarized as follows:

$$\frac{\text{agent}}{\text{truth}} \xrightarrow{\text{impossibility}} \frac{\text{other}}{\text{production/loss}}$$
$$\text{impotence}$$

Table 1. The four discourses

The discourse of the master	The discourse of the hysteric
$\dfrac{S_1 \to S_2}{\$ \ // \ a}$	$\dfrac{\$ \to S_1}{a \ // \ S_2}$
The discourse of the university	The discourse of the analyst
$\dfrac{S_2 \to a}{S_1 \ // \ \$}$	$\dfrac{a \to \$}{S_2 \ // \ S_1}$

These positions, and the names Lacan gave to them, remain fixed for all discourses, only the terms that occupy them are shifted in a quarter turn. Lacan also included two disjunctions in intersubjective communication: impossibility and impotence. Both underline the fact that desire cannot be completely deciphered; communication, as far as it speaks desire, remains incomplete and impossible. The position of the agent is the dominant position. In the position of production we find perhaps the most innovative element of Lacanian discourse, which is *jouissance* bound to the signifier and knowledge. In Seminar XVII, the relationship between *jouissance* and knowledge is articulated for the first time. "Knowledge is the *jouissance* of the Other" says Lacan (1969–1970, p. 14).[3] Jacques-Alain Miller terms this type of *jouissance* "discursive *jouissance*". Discourse is the intersection of the signifier, knowledge and *jouissance* (Miller, 2000, p. 28). The imposition of the signifier introduces the sphere of the Other and at the same time his *jouissance*: "the signifier is the cause of *jouissance*, . . . the signifier is what puts an end to *jouissance*" (Lacan, 1998, p. 27). The knowledge produced by the signifier initiates a repetitive alteration between the three: signifier, Other, knowledge. The return of *jouissance* marks the limit of knowledge and *vice versa*:

> Knowledge is what causes life to stop at a certain limit on the way to *jouissance*. For the path towards death—this is what it is a question of, it's a discourse on masochism—the path towards death is nothing other than what is called *jouissance*. [Lacan, 1969–1970, p. 6]

The previous conception of *jouissance* as the artefact of transgression, exemplified by Sade, is thus theorized on different grounds in Seminar XVII. It is seen as the product of discourse, the bonus of articulation: "a falling into the field of something that is the order of jouissance—a bonus" (*ibid.*).

The first formalized discourse that Lacan introduces in Seminar XVII is the discourse of the master. The dominant position is occupied by the master signifier (S_1), the symbolic prominence of which is totally arbitrary and absurd. In the name of the supremacy of this signifier, the master asks for obedience, without any justification. The power of the master is indisputable and uncompromised and addresses to the other a command for obedience. The other is not just the receiver of the master's decree; s/he is the slave that genuflects before the master. However, en masse, it is the slave that possesses knowledge (S_2). The master is ignorant and indifferent towards this knowledge, as the master's only concern is to be served and obeyed, and for the system to be productive. The knowledge about how the system becomes productive and how this productivity is maintained is wholly on the side of the slave, who works for the master. In the place of production, the surplus element of the discourse, the object (a) of the production of the slave's exertion, appears. The surplus value of the slave's labour is usurped by the master, while the slave is not in a position to enjoy the surplus enjoyment s/he has produced.

The discourse of the master operates behind any given ideology. Lacan develops his theorization of this discourse based on a Marxist theorization of labour as the force that produces a surplus value and is appropriated by the capitalist. The master's commands must convey certainty with regard to the ascendancy of the power represented. It is the ascendancy of the master signifiers that sustain power. Thus, the master signifiers serve the dominance of a fantasy of power that disguises lack. The representative of this indisputable power must appear non-lacking, as if castration has been escaped by the master alone. But, of course, the master is divided by the signifier and subjected to the Other, like any other subject. However, this division is concealed and it occupies the position of Truth.

In any ideological form of power—whether fascism or communism or capitalism—it is the discourse of the master that is prevalent. The master dominates the discourse and is its foundation. The discourse of the master produces the *object a*, which is then confiscated. The master, while enjoying, must take care *to appear* not to enjoy. This is because surplus *jouissance* is the very perverse element of discourse that cannot be incorporated by the social order, since it is a disorganizing and agitating factor that circumscribes lack. Therefore, the subject of obedience never finds the sought-after *jouissance*. The master employs one of three strategies. Either he displaces the surplus factor on to the enemy, whom he charges with stealing this enjoyment; or, second, he disguises it under a negative camouflage (political and moralistic discourses of perversion indicate how surplus *jouissance* is designated as evil); or else, third, he disguises it under a positive camouflage (the endless and evergrowing list of material objects in capitalism that promise the experience of that *jouissance*). But the subject is the one who produces this extra enjoyment; it is the residue of obedience to the master's symbolic Law. The death-coveting element of fascism, which is linked to *jouissance*, is the real production of obedience to a strict law. The obedience to the laws of the master/Führer that demanded the extinction of the Jews opened the floodgate of *jouissance* in the bloodshed that accompanied the Second World War. The character and the extent of the atrocities, which could not be symbolized, gave rise to an unbearable *jouissance*. The same *jouissance* fuelled the collective guilt that followed the atrocities; guilt functions as an alarm bell that notifies the subject that the Law is leaking and that it must either be restored or totally abandoned.

The master/fascist usurped the surplus enjoyment produced by the execution of the fascist commands that led to the atrocities of the Second World War. In the case of Germany, the moment Nazism fell by revealing the arbitrariness of its master signifiers—in other words, the moment the divided status of the master emerged—an actual division of Germany also occurred. The realization of the fallible status of the law of Nazism hystericized the subjects, who demanded a more sufficient master. It was, of course, very difficult to find another one who would not repeat the same mistake as Hitler and represent the ultimate signifier of German potency. The other in the discourse of the master never achieves his *jouissance*, but constantly moves from obedience to hysteria, setting in motion a continuous recycling of masters.

By rotating the previous algebraic structure for a quarter turn, a second discourse is put together with the four symbols rearranged in different positions. A new type of social bond emerges that aims to fill the lack of desire with an object of knowledge; we are, of course, in the exceptional territory of the university, the temple of knowledge. This time the dominant position is taken by the S_2, which replaces the supremacy of the arbitrary master signifier with the supremacy of knowledge. "Knowledge for the sake of knowledge" summarizes best the despotic command of the dominant position. This command is addressed to the surplus value of the object (a). In other words, the focus of knowledge is on the vindication of the surplus *jouissance* produced by the activity of labour.

The agent of the discourse is still in fetters. Knowledge may be dominant but only due to the assurance provided by the master, who lurks in the position of Truth and whom the agent serves. The hidden master is there to supply the subject who knows with the promise that s/he can avoid castration/division by acquiring knowledge. The more one learns, the more one reaches completeness. Alas, it is unfortunate for the subject that s/he actually ends up in the opposite position, by giving in to the infinite empire of knowledge. The more you know, the more signifiers are at your disposal, the more divided by them you become. Therefore, the struggle to fill the gap of desire is doomed to the worst kind of failure: the perpetual multiplication of desire misled by various objects that are supposed to satisfy it. To take an example, we might call to mind the vast amount of research currently being produced within the various branches of psychology, all of which point towards certain practices and techniques (often contradicting each other, depending on the master, the theoretician, or the scholar whose ideas organize the research) that can advance the subject's quality of life. The result is simply that the subject today, perhaps more than at any other time, is split between different identities, roles, and lifestyles without achieving the promised quality. Hence, desire is left unfulfilled in the discourse of the university. The *object a* in the position of the other remains unutterable, because of an absolute structural limitation: it is impossible for the *object a* to be symbolically represented. Thus, the subject encounters his/her importunate division, which s/he continues to resist through the acquisition of more knowledge, without ever identifying the master. Because the relationship between the subject and his/her master signifier is that of impotence, the subject never knows who s/he is and what s/he wants.

Knowledge is a central component also in the discourse of the hysteric, but it is the reverse of the university discourse. However, it is not articulated as a certainty generated by the concealed master signifier(s), but as a demand for knowledge from the master signifier. The dominant position of the discourse is occupied by the divided subject of the conscious and the unconscious, who interrogates the other as master. The hysteric wants the master to justify the supremacy of the nonsensical master signifier, by producing knowledge that can speak about the division of the hysterical subject. Therefore, in the position of production, knowledge as S_2 is found. But since, in the dominant position, the lack of the subject reigns, the knowledge of the master cannot fill this lack, which will always be responsible for the perpetual conflicts and questions of the hysteric about his/her division. In this way, what is, of course, maintained is desire and what remains veiled is the object (*a*) of desire that occupies the position of Truth. The hysteric becomes feverish and excited by provoking the Other. The knowledge—purportedly contained within the answer given and received—constitutes the hysteric's *jouissance*.

If we had to attribute a discursive system to the pervert, what would it be? It seems appropriate to place the pervert in the same discursive structure as the hysteric, rather than in the discourse of the master, where we have placed the fascist. Sadism, masochism, voyeurism, exhibitionism, etc. are considered as "deviations", and to the extent that desire itself is deviant, the position of the *object a*, the object cause of desire, is as important for the pervert as it is for the hysteric. The *object a* occupies the position of truth and is therefore responsible for any deviation from the law of the master. Whatever knowledge the Other provides for the hysteric; whatever scenarios the Other asks the pervert to perform; desire always remains unsatiated. *Object a* is the perverse core of every subject and, to the extent that it resists the master signifier, it always maintains its deviant and excessive character.

Perverse desire, obsessive desire, hysteric desire, are all described by the discourse of the hysteric. The division of the subject in language hystericizes all subjects whose lack is translated into the desire of the Other. The pervert, like the hysteric, wishes to maintain this lack in the Other, because his/her existence depends exactly on this lack. But the lack for the pervert means *jouissance*, whereas for the hysteric it means Law. The perverse ritual is a constant effort to fill up this lack in the Other, the inevitable failure of which leads to a vicious cycle only partially described by the mechanism of disavowal. Disavowal marks two moments in the recycling of the pervert's acknowledgement of the lack of the Other and the failure of this acknowledgement. It does not mean that these two types of knowledge coexist, but more that one triggers the other. The moment that desire returns as an end to the pervert's *jouissance*, another struggle begins to extinguish this return. But this return always equates with the realization and the maintenance of desire as the lack in the Other. The result is the same as for the hysteric. The difference is that the hysteric asks for knowledge in order to locate him/herself with respect to the Law, whereas the pervert asks for knowledge in order to transcend the Law, to relate him/herself to *jouissance*. This difference notwithstanding, they are both faced with the impossibility of fulfilling their desire.

The pervert is dominated by the Other, but no more than any other neurotic subject in terms of desire, since desire is the desire of the Other. The power of a perverse fantasy is derived by simultaneous awareness and evasion of the dominant position of the Other. This is different from fascism, which is based on a totalitarian fantasy of power that seeks the domination of the Other. Fascism is a fantasy of domination, whereas perversion is a fantasy of escape from domination.

Lacan juxtaposes a fourth algebraic formula to the other three discourses: the discourse of the analyst, which is not limited to the analytic experience. According to Lacan:

> If we characterise a discourse by focusing on what is dominant in it, there is the discourse of the analyst, and this is not to be confused with the psychoanalysing discourse, with the discourse effectively engaged in the analytic experience. [Lacan, 1969–1970, p. 35]

The subversive element that opposes the discourse of the analyst to the discourse of the dominant master is that lack/desire, rather than any type of knowledge or master signifier, occupies the dominant position. It suggests a position that questions and provokes knowledge so that the divided status of the subject emerges. The analysis of dreams, lapsus, parapraxes, free associations that comprise the main psychoanalytic armoury, leads to the realization of the splitting of the subject between conscious and unconscious. A new master signifier is the dead end of the other's associations. The analyst has to assist the other to associate the new master signifier with other signifiers in a dialectical manner.

With the exception of the discourse of the analyst, all the discourses are discourses of power, the fantasmatic basis of which is revealed by the strong and autonomous ego that they try to build and maintain. Psychoanalysis, by foregrounding the gap, the lack in the subject, questions and provokes the dominance of the ego and its fantasy of power: "Psychoanalysis deploys the power of the cause of desire, in order to bring about a reconfiguration of the analysand's desire" (Fink, 1998, p. 29)

Of course, Lacan's four discourses do not exhaust all the possible types of relations that form intersubjective ties. According to Fink, Lacan intended to develop a more expanded formalization of discourse on the basis of the fantasy promoted by the speaking subject. As examples, we can think of Lacan's attempts to theorize the structure of fantasy in perversion or phobias (*ibid.*, p. 30). This does not mean, however, that he intended to formulate separate phobic, obsessional, or perverse discourses. In the absence of such discourses, it becomes rather problematic to discuss the intersubjective implications of phenomena related to one of these notions. It is also important to note, however, that perverse fantasy, perverse psychical structure, and perverse discourse do not necessarily coincide. Fantasy is a fundamental aspect of discourse, whereas the psychical structure of the subject does not restrain him in a particular fixed discourse. Under certain conditions the subject can shift from one discourse to another.

Three systems of domination of the master/ Three systems of impossibility

By alluding to Lacan's four discourses, I have shown that perversion cannot be understood as occupying the same discursive canvas as fascism. Unlike the pervert caught up in his ceaseless and repetitive acts and scenarios, the fascist produces a definitive fantasy of domination. In other words, the pervert is dominated by the Other in as much as he serves the Other's *jouissance*, whereas the master seeks to dominate the Other. The master positivizes the lack of the Other around an object (*a*) and makes the slave work in order to extinguish the object and the concomitant lack in the Other. An extreme example is the way in which the fascist master construed the figure of the evil Jew to substantiate lack.

But in order fully to examine perversion in relation to discourse, another point needs to be explicated. This is the dissymmetry between Sadean fantasy and the common understanding of perversion (as deviant sexual acts). Sadean philosophy, as it is revealed in works such as *The 120 Days of Sodom* (1990) is not just a catalogue of all possible perversions. Sadean philosophy must be understood as a utopian system, which has been erroneously reduced to mere perverse actions. Lacan never explicitly associated his ideas about Sade with a formalized theory of perversion. It does injustice to Sade to see his imaginary system as the precursor of fascist atrocities linked to perverse sexuality, as supported in the narrative of Pasolini's *Salo, or The 120 Days of Sodom*.

Instead of repeating platitudinous views on perversion derived from Lacan's *Seminar VII* (1992) and "Kant with Sade" (1989), I find it most valuable to juxtapose Sade's philosophy with two other systems: totalitarianism (fascism, Stalinism) and the oedipal system. Again, the four formalized structures of discourse that Lacan has outlined function as a valuable tool for dissecting the relations that organize these three systems, which should be seen as separate. I identify three systems that have to do with three organizations of the discourse of the master. In the dominant position we find three different ideals about the impossible articulation of desire (representing "the master"). These masters pack *Truth* into a message, which they then address to the other (the one who obeys the system). These three systems are discussed in the light of an understanding that Law and language are the crux that formalizes the relationships within each system. The second factor that provides the consistency for each system is the notion of power that regulates a closed circuit of fantasy and desire. Power, in its general conception, is indistinguishable from fantasy; it is the effect of loss, subject to the Imaginary, which builds the certainty that the lost object can be retrieved. From this perspective, power bestows the fantasmatic support of relationships operating in each system. Such objects as money, knowledge, the whip, etc. are the products of the subjection of loss to the Imaginary, such that possession of them becomes identical with the possession of power.

Loss has already been mentioned as that which leads us to the most rudimentary element of each discursive system: the dimension of the Real. The place of the Real in connection with each system may be understood following Žižek's recent re-elaboration of the notion. According to his reading, the Real can also be seen in a triadic form: as symbolic Real, imaginary Real, and real Real (Žižek, 1991). The symbolic Real is a structure derived from pure material signifiers empty of meaning or significance; the imaginary Real is the inexplicable "something" eschewed in the world of appearances, the void around which the fascination of the image is structured when something of the unsymbolizable sublime comes forth; and the real Real is not just a structure of the Real but the ultimate limit, where one encounters horror, the unbearable, traumatic Thing.

The oedipal system

There is one simple reason why we should begin with the oedipal system: it is the system that reflects the main neurotic organization in liberal democratic or social-democratic countries. Freud developed the theory of Oedipus by studying familial relationships in the context of individualistic western culture. Thus, Freud's conceptualization of social dynamics was a variation of the relationships he observed in the family of his culture. Early family dynamics are formative for the emergence of power as a type of fantasy that mediates familial, and later social, relationships. In the Oedipus paradigm we are presented with the crucial relationship between the father and the son. The father is the first vehicle of power (power to punish–castrate) and the son has to become the successor of this vehicle. The Oedipus complex is a power complex involving prohibition, Law, obedience, punishment; all of which refer to fantasmatic relations regulating the child's position towards the *Thing*. The boy has to repress a certain kind of knowledge/*jouissance* in order to resolve the conflict. Oedipal organization relies on the mechanism of repression and on a superego that says: "enjoy as little as possible". This is the law that keeps the subject at a safe distance from the *Thing*. This is how paternal (not necessary patriarchal) law maintains our subjectivity. The Law not only maintains our fantasies and our desires, but also our neuroticism at the same time. This is why the Real of this circuit marks its presence in the profuse perverse fantasies of most neurotic subjects. Manifest, perhaps, in phenomena such as body piercing and tattooing, the imaginary Real makes versatile fantasmatic apparitions in the subject's life.

In *Totem and Taboo* (1912–1913a), Freud constructs a model of the first social organization around the myth of the murder of the primordial father by his sons. His hypothesis is based on his earlier theory of the Oedipus complex. The myth is well known: motivated by their resentment of him, the brothers of the primal horde kill and devour their father. The primordial father was the despotic and powerful figure that allowed access to the *jouissance* of the Thing—the mother—to no one other than himself. But the mother was not constituted as a desired object until the prohibition on enjoying her had been established by the Father. Before that, this primordial community was a world without difference. After the brothers had committed their crime and given expression to their hatred, their feelings of love for their father turned hatred into remorse and guilt. The totem substituted for the Father as well as for the creation of God, Freud argues. The initial totemic religion is a product of guilt. But what Freud does not say is whether the sons went on to sleep with the mother, the sacred and forbidden feminine figure of the horde that the father had usurped. If they did partake of this previously forbidden *jouissance*, the sons violated the Law of the Thing and satisfied both incestuous and aggressive wishes. But is there any way back towards lack once those primitive wishes are fulfilled?

Freud's myth has certain implications for politics. Whitebook (1995) connects readings of *Totem and Taboo* that focus on the murder of the omnipotent Father with conservative thinking whereas, he argues, the essay bears an alternative reading that focuses on its egalitarian aspect. This reading emphasizes the status of the brothers' pact—the means by which they succeeded in thwarting omnipotence. The political leader replaced the primordial father and also became the religious leader, setting up a patriarchal society. He took away the "sin" from the society, but he needed to represent the lost prohibition and the penalizing power of the father. In other words, paternal power needed to be restored. The leader/master is situated in a position from which he can punish; he can use violence as a medium of his power to preserve the "Good". He castrates, but he presents himself as if he is not castrated. Punishment constitutes the main feature of a system of domination. The master makes the slave work by means of a continual threat of punishment. In this way, the idea of Good is maintained by the existence of another supra-judgmental position—that of God who punishes and expresses his will through the moral law, the master signifiers. As far as social rules and the moral code are concerned, the Law and God are two sides of the same coin. We do not have to look far back in history in order to find examples of political figures being endowed with god-like properties. Authoritarian political leaders have cultivated a god-like image, the main characteristic of which was the power to punish. It was the imposition of a punitive law that made them powerful.

The Totalitarian system

Repression was considered to be the *modus operandi* of the oedipal system and the generator of a series of apparitions of the Real through unutterable images (the sublime of visual arts, for example). This is the imaginary Real that evolves from repression. The latter aims at keeping something at a distance from consciousness, which, in Lacan, corresponds to the safe distance the Law upholds regarding *jouissance*. In "ordinary" repression, *jouissance* covers this distance through imaginary means, but in a case that I would call "over-repression", the circuit of *jouissance* is modified. It is not enough to impose a certain distance from *jouissance*, it is also necessary to block its imaginary passage or to render it emaciated. The only vent left is the Symbolic.[4] Here the Law says: "Enjoy *this* little (*a*) as much as possible", which means that the imaginary element of the Real does not operate any more. Instead the Real accompanies certain empty symbolic codes and practices, like the "Final Solution" of fascism.

It is the symbolic Real that curves the Symbolic or, to put it another way, *perverts* the Symbolic. The supposed perverse maxim "Enjoy!" is limited to specific orders of the Law. One should find his or her unlimited *jouissance* within the terms of obedience to the strictures of the Law. This results in an over-identification with the Law, which entails not only the repression of oedipal knowledge, but also negation of this knowledge. By inventing numerous anonymous euphemistic signifiers (like the "Final Solution"), the Nazis tried to negate the truth of the massacres that were taking place in the concentration camps. This is how the system of totalitarian oppression is organized, which, in the case of fascism, asks for the execution of the Jew as an act promoted by the Law. It is a law that calls for over-identification with the authority that permits the *jouissance* of obedience to the master. Knowledge (S_2) in totalitarianism is denounced, and this is shown by the act of burning books or the attack on critical thought (with psychoanalysis among the movements to have been vilified by both Nazism and Stalinism). Knowledge is seen as the limit to the *jouissance* of the people. Scientists in the Stalinist order were the slaves working for the *jouissance* of the master, the communist party. But this was not an effort to produce knowledge about *jouissance*; rather, it was a way to ensure *jouissance*. The repetition of fascist and Stalinist crimes was driven by the desire to break the limit of knowledge and ensure the master signifiers (respectively: the superiority of the Aryan race or Socialist ideals). Ensuring these signifiers equated with an attempt to meet their end, which, worded otherwise, is an attempt to achieve the impossible aim of satisfying desire.

For the fascist, the fantasy that fuels will to power is the image of the Superman, as the narcissistic image of perfect wholeness with which the German should identify. What fantasy provides for power is the necessary consistency and certainty of the law, which, of course, points to a certain Good. This presents itself as the "right thing" or the "divine thing", and power has to reveal itself in a position of certainty regarding this Good. Knowing what is Good, the subject of power may not show signs of guilt, if guilt is the recognition of something being wrong. The Good, as dictated by the imaginary father, can only be right and this is what power has to promote. If guilt is recognized by power, what is renounced is nothing less than the absolute right value of the Supreme Good. This becomes corruptible since it cannot keep its promise and fulfil desire; something escapes its supremacy.

Narcissistic omnipotence leaves no space for polyphony in desire. Polyphony is something that marks the impossibility of desire as well as the impossibility of totalitarianism. Totalitarianism is, in fact, rooted in this omnipotence, engraved in a fantasy of power (ideology). If totalitarianism inhabits the desire for lost omnipotence, it is a desire for non-difference at the same time. This does not mean that the different forms that totalitarianism takes, depending on its underlying ideology, are disregarded, but that the motive force behind all ideologies of power has to do with a common unknown factor that exceeds all moral and clinical designations. The fantasy of non-difference provides consistency and certainty in a fiction that accompanies fantasies of power. Ideology is this fictional construct. When ideology is fused with the impossible, in other words, with the fantasy that hypostatizes it, totalitarianism becomes the primary political mode.

The Sadean system

As mentioned above, I would argue that the Sadean system comes closer to the idea of utopia than to a perverse system *per se*. As a historical figure (rather than an author function), Sade may be said to fit better with the first (oedipal) system based on repression. Given that his writings are anything but commensurate with the facts of his biography, Sade may be labelled a neurotic, obsessively cataloguing the abundance of his fantasies, devoting his life to deciphering the imaginary Real, and to finding signifiers that describe it. The texts he produced, however, function in a different system to the one in which he produced them. *The 120 Days of Sodom* describes neither a system of repression nor one of oppression. Rather, it approximates the subversive system of the real Real. The dominant position in the discourse of the Sadean master is occupied by signifiers that are not empty, but are over-charged with *jouissance*. In the totalitarian system, the Real is disguised behind meaningless signifiers. In Sade's textual universe, this very meaninglessness is transformed into the unbearable meaning of his master signifiers. This is what makes his system subversive. For example, "dismemberment", "ceaseless tortures", "repetitive death", organize a system of domination that simply cannot exist; it is *de facto* utopian, as it rests on the dimension of the Real. It is a subversive system, sustained by a subversive fantasy of power—the (impossible) fantasy of the Real encompassed in its absolute form by the subject.

The notorious Sadean fantasy of the indestructible body that maintains its beauty forever through perpetual torments does not renounce unity. If the unity of the image is eradicated in Sade's writings, unity as a recycled substance is maintained, and this substance is the *jouissance* of the body as an interconnected mass where the boundaries between the organic and inorganic are blurred. For this reason, the Sadean fantasy is wholly incompatible with totalitarian power, which always reveals itself through an image and a final end (e.g., the "Final Solution"). In Sade there is no end, but eternity. His system is not seeking accumulation of *jouissance*, but rather finding the diffusion of *jouissance*. In this respect, Sade is not concerned with the eradication of differences—described by Chasseguet-Smirgel (1985) as the primary characteristic of perverse fantasy—rather, he deals in the confirmation of differences in an anarchic and fragmented mode.

The fantasy Sade articulated in his writings illustrates power relationships that are not *per se* perverse, but which have been characterized as such by an *a posteriori* moral designation. This retroactive labelling of Sade as perverse is produced from within a system determined by oedipal power, characterized by the fantasy castration of *jouissance* that the master promotes. Ideological narratives are responsible for the designation of Sade's linguistic system as the source of inspiration for the atrocities of Nazism. This ideological scapegoating serves to conceal political responsibility and guilt under the veil of "perversion". It circumscribes the ideological attitude of disguising the real component operating in politics. This is why modern capitalism cannot be seen as a more advanced system than those that preceded it. As Kunkle notes, commenting on Žižek:

> In contemporary conditions with the loss of symbolic prohibitions and the increasing presence of the superego command to enjoy beyond interdiction, we end up with the ultimate paradox of the overlapping of transgression and the norm, and this means perversion is less shocking and subversive. [Kunkle, 2003, p. 233]

If the real Real also characterizes perversion, which of the Reals is responsible for the designation *perverse*? This question draws attention to an unresolvable paradox and to the failure of perversion as a designation. Does the pervert instrumentalize himself for the Other's *jouissance*? Does he really cross the limit of the pleasure principle? The Other's *jouissance* in Lacan's system has a pleasurable connotation, and this is understandable when we imagine the Other as pointing towards a certain Good, the ideal of the master signifier. In the case of the sadism or masochism valued by Sade's heroes, pain takes the form of a Good that is perceived to have a transactional value. If the sadistic ritual serves a Good, desire occupies a waiting list, in the same way that Lacan envisages power's morality declaring: "As far as desires are concerned, come back later. Make them wait" (Lacan, 1992, p. 315).

Freud supports this point, when he argues that aggression is the main expression that power-as-domination gives to the drive. This can only occur in relation to a certain law. Outward expression is given to the death drive, yet pleasure is derived from the expression of the sexual drive. Freud seems to recognize the bond between the outbound expression of the drive and the notion of power:

> The libido has the task of making the destroying instinct innocuous, and it fulfils the task by diverting that instinct to a great extent outwards—soon with the help of a special organic system, the muscular apparatus—towards objects in the external world. The instinct is then called the destructive instinct, the instinct for mastery, or the will to power. [Freud, 1924c, p. 163]

Conclusion

By implementing the logic of the four discourses outlined by Lacan in his Seminar XVII, the goal of this chapter was to identify the type of discourse that best describes totalitarianism and to question its link to perversion at the systematic level. Narratives of fascism, which implicitly or explicitly create discursive conjunctions between fascist ideology and sexual perversion, suggest that the fascist discourse might indeed be translated into a perverse discourse. Put differently, fascism produces a discourse that foregrounds perverse desire.

In order to avoid falling into the trap of accepting the discursive fantasy of proximity produced by such narratives, it was necessary first to identify the positions occupied by the fascist and the pervert in their social bonds, using the Lacanian theory of discourse. Each discourse produces a certain fantasy of power: the power to satisfy desire. At the level of fantasy alone, it is very difficult to distinguish the lines that separate the fantasized power of the fascist from that of the pervert, since they both strive for the same goal: to make the Other appear complete and non-lacking. Power serves desire and desire is always the desire of the Other (both objective and subjective genitive).

None the less, there is at least one factor that makes fascism and perversion incompatible: the crucial role played by domination.

Fascist power is a fantasy of domination. In all its forms there is an inferior other, a slave that has to work for the fascist's *jouissance*. This was elucidated by the discourse of the master. The case of perversion does not map neatly on to an established discourse, but my analysis has shown that it shares many features with the discourse of the hysteric. This suggests intriguing challenges to the accepted distinction between neurosis and perversion.

My discussion of totalitarianism and perversion in this chapter has been in the interests of demonstrating the importance of separating under-theorized concepts within psychoanalysis, such as perversion, from the ideological concepts with which they are too often and too easily conflated in cultural narratives. Psychoanalytic research is best served by operating in the discourse of the analyst, which involves eschewing naturalized ideology in favour of thorough exploration of the lack found in *all* forms of subjectivity.

Notes

1. Perhaps this is what makes the authoritarian male figure dressed in a uniform that connotes institutional power (e.g. the policeman) such a popular pornographic theme. As one obeys the law, one is also called to obey the perverse order suggested by this authoritarian figure. But this does not add an extra element to one's obedience, rather it reveals the obverse side of it; the very enjoyment found in obedience *per se*. Thus, such pornographic images function at the level of the imaginary Real. Power as something beyond representation is fixed to an image of authoritarian phallic power. The fact that it is linked to the phallic signifier disguises its underlying perverse character.
2. The reader can find more information about the standard view of perversion in psychoanalysis and the role of disavowal in perversion in Laplanche & Pontalis (1988, pp. 306–309; pp. 118–121), and in Evans (1996, pp. 138–140; pp. 43–44).
3. There is as yet no official translation of Seminar XVII (Lacan, 1969–1970). However, Russell Grigg is currently preparing a full translation for publication in the near future. For the purposes of this chapter, I have used a draft of Grigg's translation, but all page numbers refer to the original French version.

4. This is how I interpret the mechanism of negation. In negation the subject tries to bring back something of the repressed Real through symbolic means. It is a pure intellectual process, as Freud notes in his paper devoted to the concept of negation (1925h, p. 236). When Eichmann, like other Nazi officers, claimed that he had nothing against the Jews, he embraced through symbolic means the real core of Nazism: the Jew as surplus. As Freud says: "a negative judgement is the intellectual substitute for repression" (*ibid.*). The Real comes back through symbolic means, but at the same time, its repressed status is maintained.

References

Arendt, H. (1958). *The Origins of Totalitarianism*. London: George Allen & Unwin.
Black, M. (Ed.) (1976). *The Social Theories of Talcott Parsons: A Critical Examination*. London: Feffer and Simons.
Chasseguet-Smirgel, J. (1985). *Creativity and Perversion*. London: Free Association.
Evans, D. (1996). *An Introductory Dictionary of Lacanian Psychoanalysis*. London: Routledge.
Feher-Gurewich, J. (2004). A Lacanian approach to the logic of perversion. In: J.-M. Rabaté (Ed.), *The Cambridge Companion to Lacan* (pp. 191–207). Cambridge: Cambridge University Press.
Fink, B. (1998). The master signifier and the four discourses. In: D. Nobus (Ed.) *Key Concepts of Lacanian Psychoanalysis* (pp. 29–47). London: Rebus.
Flower MacCannell, J. (1996). Facing Fascism: A feminine politics of *jouissance*. In: W. Apollon & Richard Feldstein (Eds.), *Lacan, Politics, Aesthetics* (pp. 65–99). Albany, NY: State University of New York Press.
Foucault, M. (1977). *Discipline and Punish: The Birth of the Prison*. A. Sheridan (Trans.). London: Allen Lane.
Freud, S. (1912–13a). Totem and Taboo. *S.E., 13*.
Freud, S. (1924c). The economic problem of masochism. *S.E., 19*: 159–170.
Freud, S. (1925h). Negation. *S.E., 19*: 235–239.
Horkheimer, M., & Adorno, T. W. (1973)[1947]. *Dialectic of Enlightenment*, J. Cumming (Trans.). London: Allen Lane.

Jones, E. (1974). *Psycho-myth, Psycho-history: Essays in Applied Psychoanalysis*, 2. New York: Hillstone.
Kunkle, S. (2003). Žižek's paradox. *Journal for Lacanian Studies*, 1(2): 224–242.
Lacan, J. (1969–1970). *The Seminar, Book XVII, The other side of psychoanalysis*, J.-A. Miller (Ed.), R. Grigg (Trans.), unpublished.
Lacan, J. (1989)[1962]. Kant with Sade. J. B. Swenson (Trans.). *October*, 51: 55–75.
Lacan, J. (1992)[1959–1960]. *The Seminar, Book VII, The Ethics of Psychoanalysis*, J.-A. Miller (Ed.), D. Porter (Trans.). New York: Norton.
Lacan, J. (1998)[1972–1973]. *The Seminar, Book XX, Encore, On Feminine Sexuality, the Limits of Love and Knowledge*, J.-A. Miller (Ed.), B. Fink (Trans.). New York: Norton.
Laclau, E., & Mouffe, C. (1985). *Hegemony and Socialist Strategy: Towards a Radical Democratic Politics*, W. Moore & P. Cammack (Trans.). London: Verso.
Laplanche, J., & Pontalis, J.-B. (1988)[1973]. *The Language of Psychoanalysis*, D. Nicholson-Smith (Trans.). London: Karnac and the Institute of Psycho-Analysis.
Lukes, S. (Ed.) (1986). *Power*. New York: New York University Press.
Miller, J.-A. (2000). Paradigms of *jouissance*. *Lacanian Ink*, 17: 10–47
Sade, D. A. F. de (1990[1785]. *The 120 Days of Sodom and Other Writings*. A. Wainhouse & R. Seaver (Trans.). London: Arrow.
Verhaeghe, P. (1997). Lacan and the discourse of the hysteric. In: *Does the Woman Exist? From Freud's Hysteric to Lacan's Feminine* (pp. 95–118), Marc du Ry (Trans.). London: Rebus Press.
Weber, M. (1962). *Basic Concepts in Sociology*. Trans. and with introduction by H. P. Secher. London: Peter Owen.
Whitebook, J. (1995). *Perversion and Utopia: A Study of Psychoanalysis and Critical Theory*. Cambridge, MA: MIT Press.
Žižek, S. (1989). *The Sublime Object of Ideology*. London: Verso.
Žižek, S. (1991). *For They Know Not What They Do: Enjoyment As A Political Factor*. London: Verso.
Žižek, S. (2000). *The Ticklish Subject: The Absent Centre of Political Ontology*. London: Verso.

CHAPTER TEN

The feminist ethics of lesbian sadomasochism

Mandy Merck

When, in her influential 1980s account of feminism's "sex wars", B. Ruby Rich assigned "political correctness" the role of *casus belli*, she matched it with an equally notorious opponent. "Nowhere", she argued, "has this Manichean struggle between updated bourgeois respectability and its opposite become more attenuated than in the debate over lesbian sadomasochism" (Rich, 1986, p. 529). As Rich herself notes, that sexuality is a rather odd choice for the "bad girl" part in these conflicts. Heterosexual sadomasochism seems a far more prominent practice, and lesbian feminists have been outspoken in its condemnation, seeing in it the inherent condition of all heterosexuality.

Nevertheless, the perception of some intimate connection between feminism and lesbian sadomasochism persists, posed in terms of their successive historical emergence, unacknowledged ideological complicity, or, in the psychodynamics of feminism, as a family romance. Rich, for example, employs all three explanations to describe lesbian sadomasochism as part of a "daughters' revolt" against the sexual legislations of their feminist predecessors, but enacted within understandings of subjectivity, fantasy, and "health" shared by both sides.

In reviewing these arguments, what lesbian sadomasochism *is* becomes less and less clear. If the discussion concurs at all, it is not in the definition of specific sexual acts (in which most commentators seem to have remarkably little interest) but in a range of wider concerns over genders and generations, power and proper conduct. Gilles Deleuze, who regards sadism and masochism as two very different structures, describes sadomasochism as "one of those misbegotten names, a semiological howler" (Deleuze, 1971, p. 115). Perhaps it is best expressed here by the familiar abbreviation "s/m". Like Barthes's *S/Z* (and its feminist successor, the title of the late British journal *m/f*), s/m suggests opposition without fixed content, content which the appropriately termed "slash" both stands in for and cuts out. In the case of lesbian s/m, one interesting question is how feminism has read this opposition—how it has, in effect, read itself into it.

* * *

The question of content is not fortuitous, since I want to begin with a commentary by Parveen Adams, an editor of *m/f* who has written at length on the form/content of masculinity/femininity within psychoanalytic theory (Adams, 1996a). "Of female bondage" (Adams, 1996b) is her continuation of that project, which discovers in lesbian s/m a unique separation of sexuality from gender.

Adams' enquiry begins with the resolution of the Oedipus complex for the girl—a resolution that, she argues, is bound to be unhappy, no matter how it turns out. Following the account of the Lacanian analyst, Catherine Millot (1990), who draws on Freud's 1924–1934 writing on femininity and the Oedipus complex, Adams traces four possible fates for the girl who has discovered the fact of her own castration. Driven from her mother to her father by her desire for the male organ, she takes refuge in the Oedipus complex for much longer than her brother. From there her dissatisfaction with her own genitals may lead her to renounce sexuality altogether; to continue demanding the phallus from the father (and therefore remain under his oedipal sway); to seek a baby instead of a penis (and therefore detach from the father in pursuit of a man who might give her one); or to deny her castration and identify with her father (the masculinity complex, which also allows the subject to emerge from oedipality into desire—often, but not inevitably, homosexual desire).

These outcomes obviously vary in their consequences for the girl's sexuality, but all of them, Millot maintains, are disappointing. The girl leaves the Oedipus complex as she entered it, under the sign of the paternal phallus. If she opts for femininity and a baby, she is subject to her own demand for the love of a father substitute. If she opts for masculinity and identification with the father, she is subject to the demand of others for the phallus. And that, Millot concludes, "leaves no possibility for the woman of a straightforwardly post-oedipal identification with the woman" (Millot, 1990, p. 314). Or as Adams puts it: "the Oedipus complex pathologizes femininity"(1996b, p. 30)—not occasionally, not incipiently, but inherently.

This announcement is just the beginning of Adams' enquiry, which then proceeds in search of a female sexuality that is not oedipally organized. However, it marks the end of Millot's essay, which is largely preoccupied with another theme: Freud's famous claim, in the teeth of what he recognized as feminist objections, "that for women the level of what is ethically normal is different from what it is in men" (Freud, 1925j, p. 257) and that "They show less sense of justice than men" (*ibid.*).

Freud's distinction sets Catherine Millot off on *her* course: to investigate the consequences for the feminine superego of the various oedipal trajectories described above. If I digress in that direction, it is because I believe that the source texts on lesbian s/m (mainly *Coming to Power* (Samois, 1981)) and the feminist debates which they address are similarly preoccupied with ethics.

Millot begins with "Some psychical consequences of the anatomical distinction between the sexes", in which Freud argues that castration for the girl is not a threat but a reality: she enters the Oedipus complex when she discovers that she has nothing left to lose. Unlike the boy, who had a considerable incentive for breaking off his oedipal attachments, the girl lacks a "powerful motive" to do any such thing. She can linger in her oedipal refuge, waiting for the father to give her the phallus/baby, or eventually transfer that demand to another man. Where the boy makes good his deprivation by identifying with and internalizing the parental prohibition in the form of a paternal superego, the girl assuages hers through a demand for love. The boy's superego is installed inside him. The girl's (such as it is) outside—in the place of that Other "in a position to subject her to ultimately limitless requirements" (Millot, 1990, p. 299). The loss she fears is that of love.

The commensurate formation of the superego is the ego ideal, which functions as the positive term (the role model or badge of identity) to the superego's negative. As Millot puts it, the superego is the source of a demand (the paternal prohibition) and the ego ideal is the object of one—the rejected oedipal demand that precipitates the subject from desire to identification.

But the girl's demand for paternal love—or at least its surrogate—need not be rejected, and in so far as it isn't, no compensatory identification will occur. And there she will remain, without the internal mechanisms of criticism and self-love that the superego and the ego ideal provide for the boy.

But if these mechanisms are a consequence of identifying with the father, what happens to the girl who does so? After all, a girl may also convert her demand to the father into an identification with both his negative and positive manifestations, and emerge with a superego and an ego ideal in their paternal form. But the price of this insistence on an "illusory organ" is severe anxiety, Millot argues, since the girl is now vulnerable to a double threat—of castration *and* exposure as an impostor. Her consequent need to keep up appearances may manifest itself in the conspicuous achievements of the professional woman, feats which inevitably call to mind the public eloquence of Joan Riviere's "Masquerade" patient and her fears of paternal retribution for appropriating the phallus (Riviere, 1986, pp. 35–44).

Millot's final option for the girl—and the only one to valorize femininity—occurs first in the subject's chronological development. Until she believes in maternal castration, the girl will not enter the Oedipus complex but will instead address her demands to the mother. This phallic mother is seen as omnipotent, and identification with her is said to produce both a feminine ego ideal and the menacing maternal superego that Melanie Klein attributes to the destructive projections characteristic of this stage of infantile development (Klein, 1950). Of the three prospects under consideration, this pre-oedipal maternal attachment is singled out to corroborate the Lacanian observation with which Millot opens her paper: that women seem no less vulnerable than men to an "obscene and ferocious" superego (Millot, 1990, p. 294).

The question of the pre-oedipal returns us to Adams's enquiry into the vicissitudes of those sexualities organized in a different relation to the phallus—sexualities which are, by definition, perversions. Among them she cites the traditional perversions of fetishism, sadomasochism, and male homosexuality, all of which are said to share the disavowal of maternal castration. Following Deleuze, Adams identifies this strategy of disavowal in the formal devices of masochism. Its fantasy scenarios entail a disavowal of reality. Its emphasis on delay, suspense, "the frozen moment" (itself a fetish of fixed perversion), disavows sexual pleasure. Its demonstrative features solicit the onlooker's complicity in the disavowal of the social order.

Such disavowals give rise to a series of detachments culminating in the possibility that—in the perversions at least—"the form desire takes will be freed from the penile representation of the phallus and freed into a mobility of representations" (Adams, 1996b, p. 41). But if this might be so, it is not in the case of the classic pervert of literature, the heterosexual male masochist. In his compulsion, rigidity, impotence, and castration anxiety, this figure reveals anything but the plasticity of desire. Behind his elaborate disavowal of maternal castration Adams discerns a sneaking devotion to the paternal phallus, and this ordains a heterosexual regard for traditional gender demarcations that serves as a compensation for the non-genital nature of his pleasures. Perverse, pathological, *and* heterosexual, the clinical male masochist defies the oedipal law only to confirm it. As the obverse of the subject who would escape both pathology and the social order, he is the villain of this piece.

For opposition's sake, if no other, the logic of Adams' argument leads to a figure who is neither male, nor heterosexual, nor simply masochistic—a figure unknown to the clinical literature—the lesbian sadomasochist. Like the heterosexual male masochist, she too stages scenarios involving "fetishes, whipping, bondage, all that goes with the factor of fantasy and suspense; the differences are that lesbian sadomasochism appears not to be compulsive, can just as easily be genital or not, and is an affair of women" (Adams, 1996b, p. 45).

Unlike her neurotic sisters, hetero- and homosexual, whose sexuality is still organized around the paternal phallus, the lesbian sadomasochist exercises the pervert's prerogative and constructs a fetish, for whom constraint is often a psychical as well as physical fact: she is said to construct many fetishes, many pleasures, many fantasies, which she tries on "like costumes". For hers is a fetishism freed from all fixed reference, maternal as well as paternal. Here, Adams employs a definition of fetishism that—in principle at least— "recognises that no one has the phallus" (*ibid.*, p. 41). She goes on, "So the difference necessary for sexuality and sanity has to be constructed on some other basis. The axis of this difference will come to be represented by all sorts of other differences" (*ibid.*, p. 41).

Lesbian s/m literature is read to describe a practice of "choice", "mobility", "consent", and "satisfaction": "a play with identity and a play with genitality" (*ibid.*, pp. 46–47). The power of the maternal phallus (along with the ferocious superego described by Millot) is eluded, and the paternal phallus that rules the male masochist functions as the object neither of desire nor of identification. With it, femininity and its discontents are left behind. Hence Adams's conclusion that the lesbian sadomasochist, while undoubtedly perverse, escapes the pathology that besets her sex.

Adams calls this a "new sexuality", for the development of which she can offer no historical or psychical explanation.[1] Indeed, in a previous essay she complains that neither Freud nor his successors attempt to "account for the appearance of this specific perversion in our culture, for this masochism of the bedroom that is such a recent phenomenon". She goes on to say that "reality is underdetermined by the psychical and that reality remains to be theorized" (Adams, 1996a, p. 13). As for sadomasochism in its specifically lesbian form, Adams concludes her observations by proposing the paradox that a sexuality so transgressive of the social order can nevertheless come into existence only through its relation to "some fledgling piece of external reality" (Adams, 1996b, p. 48). What this reality is, or how it might—in her description—"press forward and make possible a change" (*ibid.*), is left to the disciplines of sociology or psychology to explain. But even at this level of abstraction, Adams's allusion to an external order of being that might enable psychical change would seem to refer most obviously to the opposing title of the volume in which her essay appears—feminism.

* * *

"Of female bondage" was originally published in a collection that attempts to rethink the relationship *Between Feminism and Psychoanalysis* (Brennan, 1989). Its thirteen essays represent an effort to breach the impasse in the way this relationship has been theoretically articulated, notably by restoring certain debates to—as Teresa Brennan puts it—"their specific political *or* psychoanalytic contexts" (*ibid.*, p. 1). Despite these intentions, there is relatively little in this collection about specific *feminist* contexts. That is not to say that it isn't concerned with "power relations between women and men" (*ibid.*, p. 15), or how these manifest themselves in various forms of gendered subjectivity. Nor, in a welcome innovation, are the sexual politics of the host institution—the academy—left unexamined. But feminism itself, as a movement, affiliation, "affair of women" (to borrow Adams's phrase)—with its own power relations, its own psychodynamics—is not investigated in anything like the same detail.

Still, the collection makes some moves in this direction that need to be noted. In an essay on psychoanalysis in the university, Alice Jardine characterizes the theoretical dichotomies that the volume repeatedly addresses—"(1) construction vs. deconstruction; (2) the drive to name vs. disarticulation; (3) unity vs. heterogeneity; (4) the Cartesian "I" vs. complex subjectivity; (5) Anglo-American vs. French; and increasingly (6) a return to literary history vs. literary theory" (Jardine, 1989, p. 82)—in terms of a generation gap between the feminist academics trained in the decade 1968–1978 and those who came after them. To their relationship (whose mother–daughter dynamics are contrasted with the father–daughter transferences of Freud's female disciples) Jardine attributes the full complement of affect: desire, dependency, "demands for recognition and love". But most relevant to my purposes are the reproaches hurled between the two generations:

> Accusations fly about on both sides as to who is really feminist or not; who has been recuperated or not; who is just miming the masters (is it the often more history-minded mothers or more theory-minded daughters?); whose fault is it that there is a general perception that feminism has become facile, tamed while, precisely, the humanities are being feminized? [Jardine, 1989, p. 77]

Now, this is more like it. Not only is feminist academic discourse itself submitted to analysis, but its theoretical disputes are revealed to exhibit an intensely moralizing character—"a politics and an ethics", in Jardine's phrase (*ibid.*, p. 82).

In a further contribution to the same collection, Gayatri Spivak warns against "the quick shift" from identification to prescription in feminism, from a recognition of oneself as "woman" to a political programme based on an unproblematic unity posited by that identity. Not only, she cautions, does this elision disenfranchise those women unimagined in that naming, it risks "the kind of ploy that Nietzsche figured out in *The Genealogy of Morals*" (Spivak, 1989, p. 217)—the invocation of a subordinated identity to legitimate personal vengeance. How, then, do feminists construct what Spivak distinguishes from the category "woman"—"a constituency of antisexism"? Her reply returns us to Nietzsche (via the philosopher Thomas Nagel) and the need to investigate political subjectivity "through the history and psychology of morals" (Nagel, 1979, p. xiii, cited in Spivak, 1989, p. 217).

In her introduction to the collection, Teresa Brennan adds a Freudian footnote to this incipient psychology of (feminist) morals. To explain how oppositional thinking is possible in the face of arguments for the effective internalization of patriarchal norms, she postulates an "ego-ideal identification with feminism" (Brennan, 1989, p. 10). This feminist ego ideal is said to work both positively (facilitating identifications with new political values) and negatively (enforcing its prohibitions with the threat of social disapproval). Since such group identifications are necessarily multiple and often contradictory, they are not—in Freud's description—rigidly determining. Instead they offer what Brennan describes as "a non-reductionist account of the relation between psychical and social reality" (*ibid.*, p. 11).

This, of course, is where we left Adams' model of lesbian s/m: as an unexplained example of just that relation. I want to return to this sexuality, bearing in mind Brennan's admonition to consider both its psychoanalytic and its political contexts. Adams' sources are texts which emerged from the USA's women's movement in the early 1980s, a period of fabled conflict over the politics of sexual practice ("the sex wars") signalled by the 1980 National Organization of Women's resolution condemning sadomasochism, pornography, public sex, and pederasty; the 1981 "Sex Issue" of *Heresies*; and the 1982 Barnard conference "Towards a politics of sexuality".

The introduction to one of these texts, *Coming to Power* (Samois, 1981), a combination of fiction, poetry, autobiography, and polemic compiled by a political lesbian sadomasochistic group, notes, "The intense political battle over S/M is increasingly polarizing members of the lesbian–feminist community. Is S/M good or evil? Is it 'feminist'? Anti-feminist? Or should we even be bothering to discuss it at all?" (Davis, 1981, p. 7)

Whether or not we choose to historicise lesbian s/m as a "new" sexuality emerging out of some as yet unidentified conjuncture of the psychical and the social, it seems crucial to remember that its literature was composed in the circumstances (and the terms) indicated above. These discourses are as available for psychoanalytic readings as any other, but they are as unlikely as any other to be transparent representations of that of which they speak.

In her contribution to the s/m debate in the early 1980s, Judith Butler noted a strong resemblance between the lesbian s/m argument and the "moral feminism" it purported to oppose:

> Sm seems to have some fundamental faith in the rightness of desire: Pat Califia says that sexual desire is "impeccably honest". Sm also believes in wrongness of conscience, and seeks the radical inversion of the Judeo-Christian ethic which is renowned for its contempt for desire. They accuse moral feminists of continuing this anti-sex tradition. In turn, moral feminists charge that Sm has merely appropriated patriarchal power relations and brought them into lesbianism in faintly disguised form.
>
> As these two voices work themselves out, it seems increasingly clear to me that they have more in common than it seems. They can each be seen as an attempt to find a legitimate way of relating lesbian theory and practice. [Butler, 1982, p. 171]

This similarity is most vividly apparent in the erotic scenarios of *Coming to Power*, whose conclusions seem remarkably alike—to each other and to their "vanilla" predecessors:

> Then she floated secure and safe in her lover's arms. Both womyn tender and connected. [Weaves, 1981, p. 20]

> I fell asleep in her arms, all problems and decisions placed aside for another time. [Schrim, 1981, p. 124]

I draw her body around mine, she plants soft kisses at my throat, we drift off into free dreaming, soaring. [Drew, 1981, p. 131]

Meg nestled into Carole's shoulder, feeling safe and more secure than she had in months. [Alexander, 1981, p. 242]

These are four different narratives by four different authors. Their similarity may have been pre-ordained by the ethos which governed Samois's selection of manuscripts: "We talked about whether the fiction portrayed S/M lesbians as strong, self-defining women. Was a caring interaction shown between the characters? How was consensuality (covert or implied) shown?" (Davis, 1981, p. 11).

The conscious project of idealization here should alert us to the secondary revisions in Adams's source material. But why should a group so dedicated to speaking the truth about sexuality (indeed to sexuality as a form of truth) revert to a positive-images policy? Why operate within a feminist ethos at all? One explanation is simply circumstantial: lesbian feminism was where many of *Coming to Power*'s contributors first discovered an erotic community, with which most remained involved. Another sees their support for sexual diversity as a return to the movement's initial liberationist premises, a "corrective to the lesbian feminist tendency in recent years to legislate politically correct and incorrect behaviour" (Butler, 1982, p. 171). Butler's own analysis of the moral community of pro- and anti-s/m positions could be extended to note how this legislative drive is both challenged and duplicated in the highly formal *mise en scène* of lesbian sadomasochism (how-to manuals, handkerchief codes, safety rules, as well as its scenarios of "discipline" and "correction").[2]

Lesbian s/m is often described by its proponents in similar terms—as a theatricalization of ordinary lesbian relations, particularly their unacknowledged power plays:

I have never known lesbians to say to each other something like "let's start a relationship and hurt each other a lot, OK? You be needy and demanding and fearful and manipulative, and I'll be cool and tough and withdraw farther from you while meanwhile becoming completely dependent on you. Then you fall in love with someone else and leave me with no warning. We'll both be broken for months by grief and guilt. Sounds like a good time?" [Lucy, 1981, p. 33]

It is equally possible to see this practice (with its groups, demonstrations, and pamphlets) as a blasphemous parody of feminism, a black mass of the women's movement[3]—but its followers resist excommunication.

Indeed, the introduction to *Coming to Power* describes the collection as a call for "re-evaluation of existing lesbian–feminist ethics, saying, "You must own your 'illegitimate' children" (Davis, 1981, p. 13). Again, the moral tenor of this debate is stressed, in a reproach to "you", the (even then) familiar figure of feminism as Symbolic Mother.

* * *

In her comments on the "impassioned confrontations" in feminist theory, Teresa de Lauretis—like Judith Butler before her—argues that both sides of the lesbian s/m debate are bound together by shared values that unite even these antagonists against non-feminists (Lauretis, 1990). The result is that intensity of both identification and aggression, which Freud has described, in 'Civilization and its discontents', as "the narcissism of minor differences" (Freud, 1930a, p. 114). Refusing what she regards as fruitless accusations of essentialism, Lauretis plots these intra-feminist differences as a succession of displacements—with the debate over lesbian s/m, for example, "recasting" an earlier opposition between lesbians in the women's and gay movements.[4]

Beneath these shifting oppositions, Lauretis discerns "two concurrent drives" in feminism's self-representation: "*an erotic, narcissistic* drive that enhances images of feminism as difference, rebellion, daring, excess, subversion, disloyalty, agency, empowerment, pleasure and danger . . . and an ethical drive that works towards community, accountability, entrustment, sisterhood, bonding" (Lauretis, 1990, p. 266). This "twofold pull" of feminist affirmation and critique is attributed to political necessity, most especially in the case of lesbian feminism, "where the erotic is as necessary a condition as the ethical, if not more" (*ibid.*).

How these apparently contradictory, yet closely related, drives might work together is the subject of Julia Creet's enquiry into the function of feminism in the phantasmatic economy of lesbian s/m (Creet, 1991). Like Butler, Creet pursues the disciplinary implications of a community ethic that regulates sexual conduct in the name of politics. She further observes how this regulatory power is displaced on to the previous generation to equate morality with maternity, and both with feminism. In a footnote tracing maternalist psychology (Dinnerstein, Chodorow, Kristeva) back to its precursors in late nineteenth-century social welfarism, Creet's feminist mothers surpass Alice Jardine's. Where the latter were merely "history-minded", Creet's feminist forebears are *history*.

In Creet's account, this principle of maternal authority, like its paternal counterpart, may survive oedipalization in the superego. (Here she cites Freud's description of moral masochism, which acknowledges the residual influence of both parents in the formation of "our individual ethical sense" [Freud, 1924c, p. 168].) In lesbian s/m writing, Creet maintains, it is maternal authority that is consciously transgressed. The Law of the Father "('woman' as lack)" is "distanced" in favour of the Law of the Mother "('woman' as morally superior)" (Creet, 1991, p. 145).

The tension between these jurisdictions, and the institutional primacy of patriarchal authority, are ingeniously deployed to explain s/m lesbians' complaints against feminism. Beneath their objections to its censoriousness, Creet discerns regret that the Symbolic Mother is *not powerful enough*. In its opposition to violence, she argues, feminism manages only to repress the instinctual aggression necessary for self-preservation. The result, according to Freud's 1915 essay on the instincts, is the "turning around" of primary sadism into an (eventually) eroticized desire for self-punishment, masochism. But as "The hustler", Pat Califia's (1988) dystopian evocation of a post-revolutionary feminist society, suggests, the Symbolic Mother will not lay down the law. Creet concludes: "The wish for an unambiguous authority that would relieve the guilt and desire of the s/m fantasy is unfulfilled by the powers that be [. . .] the feminist authorities are cast as unable or unwilling to specify clear laws and unable to enforce them" (Creet, 1991, p. 155).

Restless, reproachful, unsatisfied, Creet's s/m lesbians seem a world away from Adam's playful perverts. Where the former are subject to an authority that fails them, the latter construct their fetishes as pure simulacra, representations of a phallus that is not only disavowed but "detached" from reference altogether. But Creet's account does supply what Adams' both requires and omits: that encounter between history and the unconscious, between the domain of feminism and that of psychoanalysis, out of which "new" sexualities might emerge. Just how, of course, is the question.

Should we concur (as Creet apparently does) with the Samois claim that lesbian s/m is the spurned offspring of feminism, "daughter of the movement"? Or might feminism function more ambivalently, not so much as "a locus of [unenforceable maternal] law" (Creet, 1991, p. 138), but as a critical guide to that of the Father: "initiating the woman into the symbolic order, but transferring a patriarchal system of gender inequities into a realm of difference presided over by women" (Modleski, 1991, pp. 156–157). This is Tania Modleski's description of the role of the "top" in the lesbian s/m scene—a role that she, too, elaborates in terms of a Symbolic Mother who introduces the daughter to the disciplines of patriarchy while providing a critical frame of female reference and affirmation. The function of this maternal dominatrix might be identified with feminism in so far as it challenges the gendered character of the subordination it enacts—not least by replacing the father as the object of the daughter's devotion.

This gives us three psychologies of lesbian s/m: Adams', which absolves it from the inequities of both gender (the paternal phallus) and generation (maternal authority); Creet's, which emphasizes maternal authority as the conscious focus of both desire and disappointment; and Modleski's, which counterposes maternal authority to the gender system it both transmits and contests. In technical terms, Adams' (which owes much to Deleuze) should be described as *formal* in its emphasis on the dramatic elements of fantasy and suspense rather than the moral poles of guilt and punishment or the erotogenic ones of pleasure and pain. Conversely, Creet's, with its Freudian account of guilt produced by the "cultural suppression of instincts" (Freud, 1924c, p. 170) is *moral*.

Modleski's presents a more difficult case for categorization. Unlike both Creet and Adams, she stresses the sadism in both the paraphernalia and the practices of lesbian s/m: "whips, razors and nipple clips" (Creet, 1991, p. 152) and "the infliction of pain and humiliation by one individual on another" (*ibid.*, p. 154). Yet the scene she chooses to illustrate her observations, from a short story in *Coming to Power*, is a narrative of masochism. In Martha Alexander's "Passion play", Meg, "a thirty-eight-year-old professional feminist" (Alexander, 1981, p. 233) just back from delivering a paper to the National Women's Studies Conference, is transported to tearful ecstasy by a woman who fucks her "like a goddamn dog" (*ibid.*, p. 243) after costuming her in garish makeup, a G-string, rhinestones . . . and a dog collar. Modleski focuses on Meg's shock at beholding her travestied image—"real and unreal" (p. 239)—in the mirror. Her ambivalent identification with this figure "it was her and it wasn't her" (p. 239)—is read in terms of woman's disavowal of her own engendered humiliation.[5] This law of gender, Modleski argues, is beaten out of Meg much as the father is said to be beaten out of her heterosexual male counterparts in certain scenarios analysed by Deleuze. In both cases the agent of punishment is a woman vested with an eroticized mastery; in both patriarchal authority is expelled. Such a structure, defined by its equation of the mother with the law and a concomitant dismissal of the father from the Symbolic order, identifies Modleski's account of lesbian s/m with Deleuze's account of *masochism*.

Creet's analysis displays a similar preoccupation (notwithstanding her argument for the reversibility of the instincts) since it is clearly composed as a polemic on behalf of the masochistic daughter: "We are all too familiar with the feminist adage 'Power within not power over', but how does it translate erotically when our first loves were people infinitely more powerful than we?" (Creet, 1991, p. 155). More controversially, perhaps, I would make the same claim for Adams' analysis, despite her best efforts to defend lesbian "*sado*masochism" from any taint of compulsion or rigidity. She herself describes the practice as "indeed masochistic" (Adams, 1996b, p. 45), and the formal elements she adduces—the fetish, suspense, and delay—evoke the patient idealizations of masochism rather than the sadist's sudden destruction (see Deleuze, 1971, pp. 61–70). Where, then, *is* the sadism in these accounts? (One could complain that a good top is as hard to find in the theory as it reputedly is in the practice.[6]) A few cruelties may be alluded to (and then largely in quotations from autobiography and fiction), but the subjectivity that enacts them is never examined. Nor is its philosophy. Nowhere, for example, do Adams, Creet, or Modleski mention Sade.

In part, this exclusion reflects the influence of Deleuze, who assigns sadism and masochism to separate spheres predicated on "the irreducible dissymmetry" of gender:

Sadism stands for the active negation of the mother and the inflation of the father (who is placed above the law); masochism proceeds by a twofold disavowal, a positive, idealizing disavowal of the mother (who is identified with the law) and an invalidating disavowal of the father (who is expelled from the Symbolic order). [Deleuze, 1971, p. 60]

If, as Deleuze maintains, masochism is the realm of female dominion, we should not be surprised to see its contours emerge in an "affair of women". As for the absence of the sadist, in the Deleuzean scene there is room for only a single subject (the masochist in masochism, the sadist in sadism). Hence, the masochist is said to encounter the woman torturer not as his sadistic counterpart, another subject, but as the mere incarnation of "inflicting pain" (*ibid.*, p. 38). With this observation, however, the utility of the Deleuzean model for this analysis is exhausted. For unlike the configurations he describes, which both derive from the "positive" Oedipus complex, lesbian s/m is a homosexual arrangement. To locate anything like a precedent for it in the literature of sadomasochism, we must turn to the strangely neglected Sade and his "Philosophy in the bedroom" (Sade, 1966).

For these "Dialogues intended for the education of young ladies", Sade assembles a cast of four: the sodomitical philosopher Dolmancé, the bisexual débauchée Madame de Saint-Ange, her incestuous brother the Chevalier de Mirvel, and the fifteen-year-old virgin Eugénie de Mistival. The instruction of this young lady is accomplished by the entire group (abetted by Madame de Saint-Ange's hugely endowed gardener Augustin) in a series of *tableaux* that demonstrate far more pleasures than the strictly heterosexual ones described by Deleuze. At the commencement of the Dialogues, Eugénie has already attracted the erotic attentions of Madame de Saint-Ange, who both arranges and participates in her defloration. By their end, this "little monster" as Saint-Ange affectionately describes her, will joyfully join the others in the torture and rape of her own mother.

To be sure, the polysexual Eugénie is more libertine than lesbian—or, as she proudly proclaims (fucking her mother with a giant dildo while being buggered by Dolmancé), "incestuous, adulterous, sodomite, and all that in a girl who only lost her maidenhead today!" (Sade, 1966, p. 359). The philosophy into which she is initiated is founded on a profound hatred of life ("this universe of woe", as Sade writes in his introduction) and the womb that bears it. (Among other things, "Philosophy in the bedroom" is an advanced textbook on contraception.) But this disdain for maternity perversely licenses sex between women. In the case of Madame de Sainte-Ange, that sex is accomplished in seduction, in the case of Madame de Mistival, by attack. Both women are, in their way, mother figures. But it is notable that Eugénie's passage is from the mother as pleasure (the mistress of the rebels Saint-Ange, with her tireless dedication to *jouissance*) to the mother as pain (the imperious Madame de Mistival, whose attempts to repress Eugénie's sexuality are repaid by the utter devastation of her own).

Angela Carter reads this transformation in terms of the daughter's double disappointment with the mother, as first love object and phallicized ego ideal. Like Catherine Millot, she turns to Klein for a description of the ferocity that informs this relationship.

> Eugénie's transgression is an exemplary vengeance upon the very idea of the good, a vengeance upon the primal "good" object, the body of the mother. In the terms of the analysis of Melanie Klein, "good breast" is the prototype of the fountain of all nourishment; the breast that Sade's libertines take such delight in whipping, upon which they take such derisive glee in wiping their arses, is, as Freud says, "the place where love and hunger meet", a moving symbol of the most basic of all human needs. [Carter, 1978, p. 134]

The spectacle of lesbian s/m as an attack of this magnitude on the mother challenges the assumptions of its feminist apologists. Instead of Adams' utopian exchange of consensual acts and disengendered dildos, Creet's defence of the masochistic daughter from the maternal authority she craves, or Modleski's account of the dominatrix who prepares her daughter for the travails of patriarchy, Sade gives us the top girl. The daughter's position (the only position that these feminists, for all their talk of mothers, ever offer us) is suddenly rendered unbearably cruel. And if daughters can take up torture, they might even embrace its sister vocation and become legislators.

* * *

What comes first, sadism or masochism, the law or transgression, mother or daughter? Not only does Freud change his own position on this question, moving from the primacy of sadism to that of masochism as he articulates the death instinct, but his final reflections on these dualisms become positively vertiginous. Thus, we read that "guilt can turn people into criminals" (Freud, 1923b, p. 52) and that children of the most lenient upbringings are often the most conscience-ridden (Freud, 1930a), while civilization is said to perpetuate the very discontent it was founded to repress, an aggression that the superego simply takes over in its sadistic persecution of the ego (*ibid.*).

It is in this spirit that Lacan returns to Kant "avec Sade", to identify the law not with repression but with that which is repressed—desire. In his *Critique of Practical Reason*, Kant considers a concept of the good founded on the pleasure principle, and discards it: "The end itself, the enjoyment we seek, is not a good but only well-being, not a concept of reason but an empirical concept of an object of sensation" (Kant, 1956, p. 64). So relative a concept, it is argued, cannot serve as the basis of a universal moral law. Instead, Kant proposes the reverse: that the law is not founded on the good, but the good is founded on the law.

Lacan asks us to follow this argument into Sade's "Bedroom", where, eight years later, he, too, issues a maxim that makes enjoyment not the foundation but the object of the law:

> I have the right of enjoyment over [le droit de jouir de] your body, anyone can say to me, and I will exercise this right, without any limit stopping me in the capriciousness of the exactions that I might have the taste to satiate. [Lacan, 1989, p. 59][7]

It is threats like this one that, in "Civilization and its discontents", Freud lists among his grounds for doubting the commandment to love one's neighbour as oneself.

> Men are not gentle creatures who want to be loved and who, at the most can defend themselves if they are attacked; they are, on the contrary, creatures among whose instinctual endowments is to be reckoned a powerful share of aggressiveness. As a result, their neighbour is for them not only a potential helper or sexual object, but also someone who tempts them to satisfy their aggressiveness

on him, to exploit his capacity for work without compensation, to use him sexually without his consent, to seize his possessions, to humiliate him, to cause him pain, to torture and kill him. [Freud, 1930a, p. 111]

But, as the vicissitudes of Freud's own argument (in which his neighbour is on one page a villain and on the next a victim) suggest, it is impossible to propose the general aggression of humankind without accusing oneself. Thus, Lacan in his seminar on the ethics of psychoanalysis:

> Every time that Freud stops short in horror at the consequences of the commandment to love one's neighbour, we see evoked the presence of that fundamental evil which dwells within this neighbour. But if that is the case, then it also dwells within me. And what is more of a neighbour to me than this heart within which is that of my jouissance and which I dare not go near? (Lacan, 1992, p. 186]

And why should our *jouissance* defy approach? Because, as Lacan's Sadeian Kant explains, behind it is the law that "makes it possible" (Kant, 1956, p. 66), the castrating prohibition that engenders our desire for its opposite. We confront that law at the peril of our own undoing, for it is powered by nothing less than the self-aggression that Freud discovered at the root of our conscience and our bliss. Suffice it to say, our morals are as difficult to come to terms with as our pleasures, because they *are* our pleasures.

As we have seen, feminism has not remained wholly unaware of the operations of this libidinal economy in its own ethical exchanges. Even Sarah Hoagland, an avowed opponent of lesbian s/m, observes, in regard to the ostracizing of wrongdoers in lesbian communities:

> While we may find we lose respect for a lesbian at a given time as a result of something she's done, we don't have to destroy her. Such desires involve a scenario of one lesbian saying to another "fie on thee foul dyke" and the other saying "hit me again", while the community sits in silent approval. The scenario we would enact is sado-masochism pure and simple. [Hoagland, 1988, p. 270]

Hoagland's solution to this problem (the condemnation of what could very well be lesbian s/m as its own performance) is a better

Lesbian Ethics. Conversely, Wendy Brown, while also deploring the feminist culture of reproach, calls for its replacement by an "amoral political habitat" (Brown, 1991, p. 77). And, in a parallel argument (which appeared in the same issue of *differences*), Joan Cocks argues against conceding "the moral edge" to "subjective feelings of victimization" (Cocks, 1991, p. 155). Deconstructing, in Spivak's phrase, feminism's "onto/epistemo/axiological confusion", they, too, turn to Nietzsche (1967), elaborating his critique of "slave morality", the vengeful negativity of the oppressed. Brown attributes this *ressentiment* to feminist argument that grounds itself in an epistemology of subordination, a reverse hierarchy through which the subject claims superior knowledge (and moral standing) by virtue of her oppressed identity (precisely the "speaking as a lesbian mother" formula that Creet locates in the feminist investment of maternity with morality). Cocks pursues this valorization of the victim in radical feminist analyses of sex, which have enlarged to incorporate more and more practices into a politicizable sphere of abuse. Her central example, "the condemnation of lesbian sadomasochism for being infected with the proclivities of patriarchal desire" (Cocks, 1991, p. 56), returns us to the question at hand.

As a psychical diagnosis, *ressentiment*, in which the sadism of moral accusation clothes itself in the most luxuriant masochism, seems wickedly appropriate for a feminist ethos so deeply implicated in the sadomasochism it condemns. Challenging this morality's ontological claims, insisting that we speak from desire ("what I want for us") rather than identity ("who I am") are among Brown's estimable suggestions for improving the tenor (and temper) of our debates. But her closing recommendation—"For the political making of a feminist future, we may need to loosen our historically feminised attachments to subjectivity and morality" (Brown, 1991, pp. 80–81)—posed politely though it is in the subjunctive rather than the imperative, cannot elude its own logic. A new (if arguably more attractive) morality of "explicitly postulated norms" (*ibid.*, p. 81), simply replaces the old guilt trip. The law can no more be escaped in feminism than it can in the Sadeian bedroom.

There, Eugénie concludes her attack upon her mother by sealing up her fount of life: "Quickly, quickly, fetch me a needle and thread! ... Spread your thighs, Mamma, so I can stitch you together—so that you'll give me no more little brothers and sisters" (Sade, 1966,

p. 363). Doing so, despite her criminal intentions, the teenage libertine upholds the law. For, as Lacan points out with immense satisfaction, she succeeds in closing the very passage forbidden to the oedipal child (Lacan, 1989, p. 75).

That final touch, although suggested by Madame de Saint-Ange, is appropriately authorized by the father—literally by Mistival *père*, as Dolmancé ruthlessly informs his prostrate wife, and by the Dialogues' "leader and instructor" himself. Whether this means that the law is always on the side of the father is another question. (It will shortly become one for Monsieur de Mistival, should he—like Saint-Florent at the climax of Sade's earlier *Justine*—attempt the sadistic pleasures of penetrating an infibulated vulva. For Dolmancé has previously ordered his syphilitic servant to fill Eugénie's mother with his "poison".)

The wayward workings of the law take us back to Freud, and his arch dismissal of feminism and female morality in "Some psychical consequences of the anatomical distinction between the sexes" (1925j). Here, as we have seen, he argues that women's castrated state renders us proof against the oedipal threat, and therefore ethically deficient.

> Character-traits which critics of every epoch have brought up against women—that they show less sense of justice than men, that they are less ready to submit to the great exigencies of life, that they are more often influenced in their judgements by feelings of affection or hostility—all these would be amply accounted for by the modification in the formation of the super-ego which we have inferred above. We must not allow ourselves to be deflected from such conclusions by the denials of feminists, who are anxious to force us to regard the two sexes as completely equal in position and worth ... [*ibid.*, pp. 257–258]

The irony of these accusations lies not only in the vast literature of female morality rehearsed in this essay, but in feminism itself. What is this movement, if not one of those "great exigencies of life" to which women are supposed to be unequal? What does it seek, if not justice? If this is (to agree with Freud) a matter of "submission", of bowing to our obligations, the ambitions of feminism are also more aggressive—"to force us", he complains, "to regard the two sexes as completely equal": to institute (*jouissance* indeed) our own law.

The imposition of women's equality may be an odd fantasy on which to conclude these remarks about lesbian s/m. Or maybe not. The sex wars have taught us the error of attempting to fuse out political and sexual imaginaries, but they have also demonstrated the futility of trying to keep them apart.

Notes

1. This term is reminiscent of Joyce McDougall's description of the perversions as reparative "neo-sexualities" (McDougall, 1985).
2. Similarly, B. Ruby Rich argues that neither the pro- nor the anti-s/m factions "seems to recognize fantasy as a sphere apart, shaped by social and psychological factors but lacking any inherent linear relationship to action itself" (Rich, 1986, p. 533). And Inge Blackman and Kathryn Perry note the similarity between radical feminism and s/m lesbian arguments for a " 'real' sexual being underneath" (Blackman & Perry, 1990, p. 70).
3. My favourite denunciation in this vein is Ti-Grace Atkinson's: "The twisting of c-r into a proving ground for the prevalence of sexual masochism among women, and by implication its acceptability as a static condition, is outrage almost past expression" (Atkinson, 1982, p. 92).
4. On this history of oppositions see also King (1990, pp. 82–101).
5. I read Meg as the lesbian version of Riviere's masquerader, another public speaker who guiltily surrenders the purloined phallus after a display of professional competence. (See Riviere, 1986.)
6. Thus, Pat Califia: "It's a truism in the S/M community that bottoms outnumber tops about ten to one" (1992, p. 17).
7. This is Lacan's paraphrase of the "Sadeian maxim" advanced at length in "Philosophy in the bedroom". *Jouissance* carries the sense of both orgasmic enjoyment and the seigneurial right to enjoy the property of others. These combine in "Philosophy in the bedroom" (Sade, 1966, p. 18). See also Ferguson (1991, pp. 13–14) on Sade and the reformulation of French property rights in the 1780s.

References

Adams, P. (1996a)[1988]. PerOs(cillation). In: *The Emptiness of the Image: Psychoanalysis and Sexual Differences* (pp. 12–26). London: Routledge.

Adams, P. (1996b)[1989]. Of female bondage. In: *The Emptiness of the Image: Psychoanalysis and Sexual Differences* (pp. 27–48). London: Routledge

Alexander, M. (1981). Passion play. In: Samois (Ed.), *Coming to Power* (pp. 228–242). Boston, MA: Alyson.

Atkinson, T.-G. (1982). Why I'm against s/m liberation. In: R. R. Linden, D. R. Pagano, D. E. H. Russell, & S. L. Star (Eds.), *Against Sadomasochism* (pp. 90–92). East Palo Alto, CA: Frogs in the Well.

Blackman, I., & Perry, K. (1990). Skirting the issue. Lesbian fashion for the 1990s. *Feminist Review*, 34: 67–78.

Brennan, T. (Ed.) (1989). *Between Feminism and Psychoanalysis*. London: Routledge.

Brown, W. (1991). Feminist hesitations, postmodern exposures. *differences*, 3(1): 63–83.

Butler, J. (1982). Lesbian S&M: The politics of disillusion. In: R. R. Linden, D. R. Pagano, D. E. H. Russell, & S. L. Star (Eds.), *Against Sadomasochism* (pp. 168–175). East Palo Alto, CA: Frogs in the Well.

Califia, P. (1988). The hustler. In: *Macho Sluts: Erotic Fiction* (pp. 104–141). Boston, MA: Alyson.

Califia, P. (1992). The limits of the s/m relationship. *Outlook*, 15: 16–21.

Carter, A. (1978). *The Sadeian Woman*. New York: Pantheon.

Cocks, J. (1991). Augustine, Nietzsche, and contemporary body politics. *differences*, 3(1): 153–162.

Creet, J. (1991). Daughter of the movement: The psychodynamics of lesbian S/M fantasy. *differences*, 3(2): 135–159.

Davis, K. (1981). Introduction: What we fear we try to keep contained. In: Samois (Ed.), *Coming to Power* (pp. 7–13). Boston, MA: Alyson.

Deleuze, G. (1971)[1967]. *Masochism: An Interpretation of Coldness and Cruelty*. New York: George Braziller.

Drew, H. (1981). The seduction of earth and rain. In: Samois (Ed.), *Coming to Power* (pp. 127–141). Boston, MA: Alyson.

Ferguson, F. (1991). Sade and the pornographic legacy. *Representations*, 36: 1–21.

Freud, S. (1915c). Instincts and their vicissitudes. *S.E.*, 14: 109–140.

Freud, S. (1923b). The ego and the id. *S.E.*, 19: 12–59. London: Hogarth.

Freud, S. (1924c). The economic problem of masochism. *S.E.*, 19: 159–170. London: Hogarth.

Freud, S. (1925j). Some psychical consequences of the anatomical distinction between the sexes. *S.E.*, 19: 248–258. London: Hogarth.

Freud, S. (1930a). Civilization and its discontents. *S.E.*, 21: 64–145. London: Hogarth.

Hoagland, S. (1988). *Lesbian Ethics*. Palo Alto, CA: Institute of Lesbian Studies.
Jardine, A. (1989). Notes for an analysis. In: T. Brennan (Ed.), *Between Feminism and Psychoanalysis* (pp. 75–98). London: Routledge.
Kant, I. (1956)[1788]. *Critique of Practical Reason*. L. W. Beck (Trans.). New York: Macmillan.
King, K. (1990). Producing sex, theory and culture: Gay/straight remappings in contemporary feminism. In: M. Hirsch & E. F. Keller (Eds.), *Conflicts in Feminism* (pp. 82–101). London: Routledge.
Klein, M. (1950)[1933]. The early developments of conscience in the child. In: *Contributions to Psychoanalysis* (pp. 267–277). London: Hogarth.
Lacan, J. (1989)[1962]. Kant with Sade. J. B. Swenson Jr (Trans.). *October, 51*: 55–75.
Lacan, J. (1992)[1959–1960]. *The Seminar, Book VII, The Ethics of Psychoanalysis*, J.-A. Miller (Ed.), D. Porter (Trans.). New York: Norton.
Lauretis, T. de (1990). Upping the anti [*sic*] in feminist theory. In: M. Hirsch & E. F. Keller (Eds.), *Conflicts in Feminism* (pp. 255–270). London: Routledge.
Lucy, J. (1981). If I ask you to tie me up, will you still want to love me? In: Samois (Ed.), *Coming to Power* (pp. 29–40). Boston, MA: Alyson.
McDougall, J. (1985). *Theaters of the Mind*. New York: Basic Books.
Millot, C. (1990)[1985]. The feminine superego. In: P. Adams & E. Cowie (Eds.), *The Woman in Question* (pp. 294–314). Cambridge, MA: MIT Press.
Modleski, T. (1991). *Feminism without Women*. London: Routledge.
Nagel, T. (1979). *Mortal Questions*. Cambridge: Cambridge University Press.
Nietzsche, F. (1967)[1887]. *On the Genealogy of Morals*. W. Kauffman (Trans). New York: Vintage.
Rich, B. R. (1986). Feminism and sexuality in the 1980s. *Feminist Studies, 12*(3): 525–561.
Riviere, J. (1986)[1929]. Womanliness as masquerade. In: V. Burgin, J. Donald, & C. Kaplan (Eds.), *Formations of Fantasy* (pp. 35–44). London: Methuen.
Sade, D.-A.-F. (1966[1795]). Philosophy in the bedroom. In: R. Seaver & A. Wainhouse (Eds.), *The Marquis de Sade* (pp. 128–294). New York: Grove Press.
Samois (1981). *Coming to Power*. Boston, MA: Alyson.
Schrim, J. (1981). Mirel. In: Samois (Ed.), *Coming to Power* (pp. 124–132). Boston, MA: Alyson.

Spivak, G. (1989). Feminism and deconstruction, again: Negotiating with unacknowledged masculinism. In: T. Brennan (Ed.), *Between Feminism and Psychoanalysis* (pp. 206–223). London: Routledge.

Weaves, S. (1981). On the beam. In: Samois (Ed.), *Coming to Power* (pp. 20–28). Boston, MA: Alyson.

CHAPTER ELEVEN

Maternal fetishism

Emily Apter

In proposing maternal fetishism as a "new" perversion with a unique relevance for a broader understanding of motherhood and maternal desire, one must first confront the vexed question of whether the whole notion of perversion is so fundamentally outmoded that it deserves to be discarded as a relic of gender-biased psychoanalysis. Unlike neurosis or psychosis, perversion has not been readily ascribed to women in the history of psychoanalysis. In conformity with class- and culture-bound norms, women were habitually diagnosed as hysterical, maniacal, neurotic, frigid, sapphic, narcissistic, melancholic or psychotic—anything, it would seem, but perverse. Case histories of fetishism, masochism and sadism, from Richard von Krafft-Ebing's sexological work *Psychopathia Sexualis* (1901) to Freud's essay "Fetishism" (1927e), typically featured male analysands. The protagonist of Sacher-Masoch's *Venus im Pelz* (1980) was not Wanda, the dominatrix, but Leopold, the male masochist, who, though whipped and trodden on by a woman, remained empowered in so far as it was he who authorized the conditions of his own bondage and enslavement.

Depending as it does on heterosexually prescriptive distinctions between normal and deviant, the rubric of perversion seems obsolete, particularly in relation to gay and lesbian sexuality. That said, there continue to be circumstances under which "perverse" paradigms remain serviceable: erotic practices traditionally coded as perverse (say, lesbian sadomasochism) may cause the category to signify differently as a counter-discourse to straight sexuality, or as a catch-all referring to mock gender performances (transvestism, strap-on dildos) that release the subject from the confines of repressive gender roles. Within a Lacanian framework, perversion is crucial to understanding the logic of semblance on which subject-formation is based. Fetishism, for example, is treated as an antidote to the *béance* or gaping wound (opening around the splitting of the ego) qualified by Lacan as lack (*manque à être*). Like Clérambault's erotomaniac, who firmly believes that s/he *is* what is lacking in the other, the perverse subject in *being* lack, falls for the ontological illusion of his or her own "lacklessness". It is the credulity of the subject rather than his or her misguided sexual aim that constitutes the "perverse" character of the ego.

In addition to being a theoretical component of the Lacanian logic of subjectivity, perversion has a controversial role to play in redefining motherhood and the bounds of Eros within the family structure. Maternal fetishism—the problematic assayed here—may be drafted iconoclastically in this vein as a female perversion defined by the mother's objectification of the child, or as a form of maternal gratification adjudged perverse by a society rife with anxiety over child abuse. Predicated on fetishism *tout court*, maternal fetishism is conceptually forged from practices of erotic objectification in which animate subjects forge a sexual relation to inanimate objects or live part-objects. According to the Freudian classification, perversions such as paedophilia and necrophilia could be identified by the way in which the clinical subject manipulated another human being as object or instrument of *jouissance*. In the case of fetishism, transvestism and zoophilia, non-human objects, living parts of the body treated as dead, or partial objects substituted for the whole, are "surinvested" (overvalued) to the exclusion of all other targets of desire. In the Lacanian scheme, it is the dismantled, dismembered body (*le corps morcelé*) that is fetishistically preferred to the integral or totalized corpus because it presents, as it were, a body equipped with prosthetic parts (already split or symbolically castrated) rather than a body at risk of phallic loss. Any new theory of maternal fetishism worth the name reverts to the phantasm of a body-in-pieces as support of the supra-phallic mother. The phallic mother herself *is* the supreme fetish, a psychic prosthesis or figure of semblance standing in for what Lacan would call the "object cause of desire" (*das Ding*). Capable of *jouissance*, by turns threatening and controlling, the phallic mother gives "perversion" new traction as a figure of maternal desire, and its offshoot, maternophobia. Maternophobia is compounded within psychoanalysis by the eclipse of the mother's desire by that of the child, and by the murderous cast ascribed to the infant's maternal dis-identification.

Though it remains unclear whether there *should* be a theory of maternal fetishism, such a theory, at least in principle, contributes to the revision of gendered orthodoxies within psychoanalysis and refocuses attention on taboo zones of desire within the family. Though the problem of maternal desire is diffused throughout psychoanalysis, driving monolithic concepts such as the Oedipus complex, maternal narcissism, and melancholia, it remains curiously effaced as an autonomous subject of study. The oedipal narrative hangs portentously over discourses around maternity, sexualizing the child–parent love duet as a prelude to the patriarchal law's neutering of the bond. However, as Parveen Adams noted in her essay "Mothering" (1990), maternal desire has been consistently cordoned off in the psychoanalytical literature on child development, displaced by the notion of infant need elaborated by Donald Winnicott and his followers.[1] Julia Kristeva's important writings on motherhood (particularly "Stabat Mater", 1984 and "Freud and love: treatment and its discontents", 1987) have stressed the role of empathy (*Einfühling*) in pre-oedipal and later transference love; in her words a "psychic osmosis/identification" that "lets one hold onto the joys of chewing, swallowing, nourishing oneself . . . with words" (Kristeva, 1987, p. 27). However, the problem of maternal desire in Kristeva is typically subsumed within the powerful rush of maternal passion (the Passion), or foreclosed by the abjection of the mother's body; its "realness" supplanted by semiosis.[2]

Mired in a Freudian paradigm figuring the child or "little one" as a compensatory object for the absent maternal phallus, maternal desire remains a dark continent. The sexuality of Christ upstages the question of what Mary wants. But surely the time is ripe for a change; and one might begin by acknowledging maternal fetishism as a "perversion" that desublimates the eroticism of the child without, on the one hand, socializing and aestheticizing it into the culture of cuteness, or, on the other, reducing it to the scandal of paedophilia. As alarming cases abound in which parents are had up on criminal charges for photographing their naked children, debate has been increasingly focused on the boundaries of domestic propriety and the censorship of prepubescent nudity. But these sensationalist cases, freighted by moralism, often obscure the murkier issue that lies behind them: that children, like their caregivers, are desiring and desirable subjects, imbricated reciprocally in desire and perversion. To really begin to work through the complexities of these themes, one must begin to de-idealize maternal love, refusing to mark off its separation from the zone of eroticism even while affirming a vigilant opposition to child abuse. While recognizing the psychic damage caused by molestation and paedophilia, one might begin to explore what it would mean to destigmatize discourses of perversion (uncoupling them from normalizing frameworks and challenging the ingrained psychoanalytical assumption that there is no perverse mother because the mother, by definition, has what she wants). One could attempt to re-imagine the mother's body as something other than an exclusive site of castration anxiety and memorial loss. And one might attend more closely to matricidal sub-texts informing psychoanalytic accounts of sublimation and creative thought. In 1980 Monique Plaza sounded the alarm on the depth of "hatred of the Mother in psychoanalysis", tracing the demonization (in paediatric psychology) of the mother who figuratively suffocates her child through to more sophisticated psychoanalytic condemnations of the mother's pathological inability to detach from an object that is at once "same" (a part of her) and "other" (Plaza, 1980). But the truism that there is nothing short of a maternal death-wish embedded in the Oedipus complex—itself dependent on paradigms of the controlling or devouring mother—takes on renewed significance as the central problem posed by maternal fetishism.

Throughout Lacan's seminar on object relations theory (Lacan, 1994), one finds a repeated critique of the Kleinian maternal body, reduced to "mère symbolique", and equated with the field of symbolic negation. This tendency is far from rare in psychoanalysis and in culture: from Freud's elaboration of the punishment of Jocasta and Gertrude; to the discreditation of "the mother who enjoys" (Hélène Deutsch); to the phobic profile of the "bad mother" on which diagnoses of Munchausen Syndrome by Proxy are built, the maternal imago has been consistently denigrated.[3] Elsewhere, the maternal imago is not so much cast under a shadow of suspicion as it is negated. This is seen in the positioning of the Lacanian "Thing" (*das Ding*) in the place of Melanie Klein's mythic body of the mother, or Judith Butler's re-reading of Antigone as agent of a post-oedipal feminine Symbolic who occupies every position except that of mother.[4] Under these circumstances, consideration of maternal fetishism becomes not just a way of re-setting the parameters of perversion, but also a means of linking the absence of a full-dress theory of maternal desire to a disavowed matricidal impulse within psychoanalysis itself.

* * *

As tenuously acculturated subjects of history, women have typically been associated with the pre-oedipal (even by feminist psychoanalysis) and hence implicitly infantilized. Placed in a realm that precedes or falls outside of the Symbolic order, the mother's desire has been equated with that of the child, setting in motion a process in which the mother contracts the pre-oedipal, almost like a contagion, and is drawn, regressively, to becoming child-like. Fetishizing what the child fetishizes, the mother mimics the signs of pre-oedipal sexuality in such acts as "playing house" (treating her home like a doll's house), refusing a grown-up professional vocation, or adopting juvenile fashion (pink track suits, round-toed shoes, pastels and primary colours, animal prints and accessories). Like the child, the "infantile" mother is attached to a transitional object, but in this case, the object *is* the child. Traditionally, object relations theory (as defined by Winnicott) focused on the weaning process in infants and young children, valuating transitional objects in accordance with their function as surrogate objects of maternal nurture. But following Estella Welldon's 1988 study, the transitional object may conceivably be recast as a maternal fetish:

> My clinical observations show that mothers who display perverse tendencies towards their offspring do so within the first two years

of their children's life. In Winnicott's (1953) terms, the "transitional object" is used by the pervert to be invented, manipulated, used and abused, ravaged and discarded, cherished and idealized, symbiotically identified with and deanimated all at once. This is exactly what I believe takes place in the perverse mother's mind and through her manipulations of her baby. In other words, the baby becomes for such a mother her "transitional object", as proposed by Stoller (1968). Granoff and Perrier (1980) make a similar comment on the type of perverse relationship a mother establishes with her baby in which the baby is first identified as her missing phallus, and then becomes her "toy" or "thing"; this they see as "analogous to the "part-object" relationships of fetishistic perverts. [Welldon, 1988, p. 85]

Here, maternal fetishism, though never so named, comes close to child abuse and masochistic violence (in cases where the mother imagines the baby to be a part of herself). "On some days", Welldon writes of an analysand, "she would choose her right arm to be the baby, on others it would be one of her legs. In this way she felt able to master her impulses to beat up her first child" (*ibid.*, p. 73). In the case of another patient, Welldon discusses the mother's transformation of her teenage son into "an ideal partner, or part-object ideally designed for her perverse purposes" (*ibid.*, p. 93). In this instance, object relations theory makes the bridge between incest and maternal fetishism: incest becomes definable as an extreme form of maternal fetishism resulting from the mother's perverse objectification of her son.

The importance of incest in Welldon's analysis harks back to Karen Horney's 1967 account of how a mother's repressed oedipal love is diverted into a secondary (incestuous) desire for her son, only to be displaced again to students and younger men. Of this teacher-analysand, possessed of intellectual accomplishment and high moral standards, Horney writes:

> Her attempts to solve the problem had taken this form in fantasy: "I am not the small child who cannot get the love of my unattainable father, but if I am big then he will be small, then I shall be the mother, and my father will be my son." [Horney, 1967, p. 177]

Though the logic of dual transference and re-scaled family relations is contorted here, resulting in a fantasy of mothering one's father while sleeping with one's son, it underscores incestuous maternal over-attachment at the bedrock of maternal fetishism.

Where Horney and Welldon emphasize the classic mother–son configuration in their adducement of maternal perversion, Julia Kristeva opens up a space for a theory of maternal fetishism there where mother and daughter fight to the death for a phallic identity in a complex characterized as "love–hate with the maternal ab-ject" (Kristeva, 2000, p. 249). In Kristeva's reconstruction of the Kleinian depressive position, the mother purloins her daughter's maternal dis-identification, which, in the secondary stage of Oedipus, takes shape as a rank hatred of the castrated mother. Maternal hatred enables a paternal identification that brings in its train the daughter's investment in the thinking life. In the quest for the phallic power of thought, the mother *qua* maternal fetishist, fetishizes the daughter's sublimation of the negative affect accruing to maternal withdrawal (*ibid.*, pp. 248–249). In appropriating, *au deuxième degré*, the mechanism of reparation for maternal castration, and in depriving her daughter of the symbolic debt that leads to attainment of the phallic signifier (*le Nom du Père*), the Kleinian mother accedes to power at the expense of her daughter's intellectual inheritance, thereby increasing her vulnerability as a target of matricidal revenge.[5] The maternal fetishist of Kristeva–Klein not only perverts the oedipal law (revealing the extent to which, in its predication on filial castration, the law itself is perverse), but she also marks as perverse the matrix of maternocentric and matricidal objects that outline the force-fields of Kleinian object relations theory.[6]

Kristeva's return to Klein allows us to see the aggressive intent (*Destruktionstrieb*) of maternal fetishism as, paradoxically enough, part of a structure of reparation and sublimation that goes back to an original injury committed against the mother. Yet, this may be read more broadly as a move to redress Lacan's injury to the body of Kleinian analysis. For one could argue that Lacan's entire theory of the object was profoundly indebted to Kleinian object relations theory in ways never fully acknowledged by him or his followers. Kristeva suggests that Lacan exhibited "envy and gratitude" *vis-à-vis* Klein's work (*ibid.*, pp. 364–372), while Mary Jacobus goes so far as to assert polemically that "the Lacanian reading brutalizes Klein" (Jacobus, 1995, p. 150). However, Lacan frequently referred to Klein by name, particularly in sections of the *Ecrits* and the *Ethics*.[7] In his 1954 lesson on "discourse analysis and ego analysis", he credited Klein (in the case of Little Dick) with productively assessing how "if, in the human world, objects become variegated, develop, with the luxuriance that makes for its originality, it is to the extent that they make their appearance within a process of expulsion linked to the instinct of primitive destruction" (Lacan, 1988, p. 68). Lacan seems here to recognize the importance of Klein's theory of the "bad object". However, his interpolation of paranoia at the base of the subject's self-misrecognition, and his monumental conception of the "body-in-pieces" (the early subject's "mirror" image of the phantasm of the dismembered maternal body), paid insufficient due, it would seem, to Klein's seminal notion of paranoid structure in the projection of bad internal objects. In Kristeva's estimation, the publication of Klein's *New Directions in Psychoanalysis* (Klein, 1955) provided impetus for Lacan's and Jean Hippolyte's theory of the subject, a theory that refuted Klein's notion of primal object loss. They used the logic of *Verneinung* or "negation of negation" to posit the subjectivizing force of object-lack (Kristeva, 2000, p. 279). Lacan's famous allegation that Klein had no theory of the unconscious and remained a literalist in her interpretation of symbolic objects may well have obscured the extent of his debt to her conceptual lexicon. Working out a concept of object-lack in the mid-fifties, Lacan formulated his concept of "object-cause of desire" (later referred to as *objet-a*), without explicitly referring to object relations theory. Subsequently, in the *Ethics* seminar, the Kleinian maternal body is sublated in Lacan's definition of *das Ding*, which works to block maternal desire:

> Let me suggest then that you reconsider the whole of Kleinian theory with the following key, namely, Kleinian theory depends on its having situated the mythic body of the mother at the central place of *das Ding*.
>
> To begin with, it is in relation to that mythic body that the aggressive, transgressive, and most primordial of instincts is manifested, the primal aggressions and inverted aggressions. Also in that register which currently interests us, namely, the notion of sublimation in the Freudian economy, the Kleinian school is full of interesting ideas [...] In an article that I shall come back to later, entitled "A

Theory Concerning Creation in the Free Arts", after a more or less exhaustive critical examination of Freudian formulations on sublimation and of Kleinian attempts to explain its full meaning, the author, M. Lee, ends up attributing to it a restitutive function. In other words, she finds there more or less of an attempt at symbolic repair of the imaginary lesions that have occurred to the fundamental image of the maternal body.

[. . .] I can tell you right away that the reduction of the notion of sublimation to a restitutive effort of the subject relative to the injured body of the mother is certainly not the best solution to the problem of sublimation, nor to the topological, metapsychological problem itself. There is nevertheless an attempt to approach the relations of the subject to something primordial, its attachment to the fundamental, most archaic of objects, for which my field of *das Ding*, defined operationally, establishes the framework. It allows us to conceive of the conditions that opened onto the blossoming of what one might call the Kleinian myth, allows us also to situate it, and, as far as sublimation is concerned, to re-establish a broader function than that which one necessarily arrives at if one accepts Kleinian categories. [Lacan, 1992, pp. 106–107]

In evidence here is how, in his ethics of object sublimation and perversion, Lacan used Kant to counter Klein, suborning, if you will, Kleinian object relations theory to the philosophy of *das Ding*.

* * *

Challenging the primacy accorded by Klein to the mother's body as archaic object—a site of restitution and engine of sublimation— Lacan used *das Ding* to widen the relational field of object reference (preparing the way, no doubt, for the pre-eminence of the ungendered phallus in his own thought). He wrote: "In analysis the object is a point of imaginary fixation which gives satisfaction to a drive in any register whatsoever" (Lacan, 1992, p. 113). This move to detach the object from the maternal body would be developed further in the section of the *Ethics* entitled "On creation *ex nihilo*". Here, Lacan glosses Klein's reading, in "Infantile anxiety-situations reflected in a work of art and in the creative impulse" (Klein, 1950), of a case she calls "The empty space", in which the wife of a painter fills the "empty space" left by an absent tableau with a remarkably expert likeness of the beautiful mother. Lacan uses this "empty space" as the basis for his theory of the Thing as a representation founded on a "hole" in the real (1992, p. 121). The Lacanian Thing is a roving signifier, dependent on *non*-referentiality to the mother's body. This maternal occultation is a constant in his work, going back, according to Shuli Barzilai, to the erasure of the maternal imago in his construct of the mirror stage, and to his tendency (announced in the 1938 essay "Les complexes familiaux dans la formation de l'individu" ["Family complexes in the formation of the individual"]) "to find in favor of the father in adjudicating between the parents" (Barzilai, 1999, pp. 2 and 43). Lacan would again target Klein by way of the maternal body in his 1958 review essay "Jeunesse de Gide ou la lettre et le désir" ("Gide's youth or the letter and desire") (Lacan, 1966). Here, according to Kristeva's reading, Klein surfaces as the unnamed referent of "la tripière inspirée" (the inspired tripe-seller), Lacan's horrific figure of roiling reproductive organs, frustrated maternity, and masculine disgust toward the female "black hole" (Kristeva, 2000, pp. 371–372). Effacement of the mother recurs in Lacan's theory of fetishism, as propounded in *Seminar X (Angoisse)* of 1962–1963. In answer to the query "What is desired?" Lacan replies,

> Not the little shoe or the breast, nothing that might embody the fetish. Because the fetish is itself the cause of desire, a desire that attaches itself where it can. [. . .] the fetish is not necessarily attached to the mother's body, it is rather the condition that allows desire to sustain itself. [Lacan, 2004, p. 122, my translation]

A privileged sign capable of being affixed to any gender, and no longer the exclusive property of the mother, the Lacanian fetish functions, in his words, as a "libido stopper" (*Libidohaushalt*); a conflation of Freudian "interruption" (*Aushaltung*) and "content" (*Inhalt*) (*ibid.*, p. 123).

Lacan's defenestration of the Kleinian school—his specularization of the maternal body; his refusal of Klein's attribution of an originary oedipal phantasm to the mother; his recourse to *das Ding* as fetish of object-lack and libido-shifter detached from a gendered body—added theoretical heft to the matricidal tendency within psychoanalysis. And it is in this sense that Lacanian *Kleinism* may be interpreted as the butt of psychoanalytic maternophobia in its most intellectually sophisticated form. For a number of critics, laying bare

Lacan's ambivalently avowed debt to Klein is part and parcel of reclaiming the richness of Klein's reflections on the maternal position; ranging from maternal castration fear, to myths of the phallic mother, to womb envy in boys, to her most famous theory of good and bad objects. For Kristeva, Klein's "genius" lay not just in her singular appreciation of the matricidal vengefulness aroused by loss of the maternal body, but in her ability to convert this "death-dealing" negation of the mother into a precondition of subject-formation, love, and accession to thought (Kristeva, 2000, p. 397). While Kristeva does not address the issue of maternal desire as such in Klein's work, she offers up the figure of a Kleinian Medea bent on "ab-jecting" her daughter's object-lack. The mother's desire, perversely marked, yet hardly visible, becomes in Kristeva's reading of Klein, a pathway to the thinking life.

As both a theorist of matricide and the object, herself, of maternophobia in psychoanalysis, Klein acquires enhanced importance in attempts to understand the "perverse" way in which maternal desire has been traditionally assessed or left under-theorized. Though the return to Klein has come accompanied by the fear of what Mary Jacobus calls "theoretical regression" (a fear of Klein's excessive "literalness" repeatedly stigmatized by Lacan as an obstacle to thinking the Symbolic), a revised version of Kleinian object relations, mediated perhaps by Kristeva's notion of transference love, has led, in Jacobus's words, to "reconceptualizing the shadowy so-called pre-oedipal domain . . . the domain that psychoanalytic feminism in search of an alternative to the Freudian Oedipus complex or the Lacanian Law of the Father has often nostalgically invoked" (Jacobus, 1995, pp. 160–161). Even if one believes that the pre-oedipal is and will remain a site of hermeneutic intractability, it invites the imagination of a post-oedipal field of "fetish relations" charting the distribution of affects, drives, and object attachments along the amatory axis of mother and child. The Kleinian space of therapy propels the thematics of object relations, transitional objects, and personal fetishes to centre stage, lodging them in a gendered space pervaded by maternal desire.

This gendered space of maternal desire remains treacherous, however, for it is here that publicly sanctioned private sentiments mingle with potentially compromising secret longings; it is here that incestuous desire camouflages itself in the guise of protective love. Little wonder, then, that portraits of childhood innocence have been used to block off representations of maternal desire. As Jacqueline Rose surmised in *The Case of Peter Pan*:

> Freud is known to have undermined the concept of childhood innocence, but his real challenge is easily lost if we see in the child merely a miniature version of what our sexuality eventually comes to be. The child is sexual, but its sexuality (bisexual, polymorphous, perverse) threatens our own at its very roots. Setting up the child as innocent is not, therefore, repressing its sexuality—it is above all holding off any possible challenge to our own [Rose, 1984, p. 4]

For Rose, the fabrication of the sexless minor, ubiquitous in children's fiction, performs the powerful function of patrolling the boundaries of adult sexuality, warding off temptations to deviate from compulsory heterosexuality and keeping "perversions" such as maternal fetishism at bay. Evidence of the enduring taboo surrounding discussions of infant–parent sexuality may be seen in the scandal provoked by Jeffrey Masson's controversial indictment of Freud's seduction theory, in which he insisted that actual instances of child molesting belie the fantasy or symbolic status accorded to seduction by Freud (see Masson, 1984, and Malcolm, 1984). Normally kept in check by the frozen ego-ideal of the Madonna position, the erotic mother does, however, occasionally shake loose from her haloed outline, showing herself, like one of Julia Margaret Cameron's famous photographs of "Fallen Madonnas", as (to borrow Carol Mavor's words) *"altered* images of Mother, scratched with sexuality and printed with flesh" (Mavor, 1995, p. 44).

* * *

Mary Kelly's art installation *Post-Partum Document*, completed in 1976, offers an interesting example of how maternal desire may be represented without recourse to the Christian iconography of the *pietà* or the oceanic spectacle of the mother's body. In Elizabeth Cowie's description, the work in its exhibition form was:

> organized in six sections each of which has two distinct parts or orders of material: objects and records of the mother–child relationship, framed and hung on the gallery wall; and written

documentation accompanying the exhibition entitled "Footnotes to the *Post-Partum Document*". The material on the gallery wall consists on the one hand of framed titles and diagrams and on the other of a series of composed and framed objects and texts. Each section commences with a framed title, for example "Documentation I: Analyzed Faecal Stains and Feeding Charts", which is followed by a framed diagram on human metabolism in the first year of life, and the section is concluded by a second title "Experimentum Mentis I (Weaning from the Breast)", a second diagram, the Lacanian schema R (a different aspect of which is emphasized in each section) and adaptations of Lacan's algorithm: Subject over little s. [Cowie, 1981, pp. 115–116]

Cowie emphasizes the work's chronological unfolding, serial organization, taxonomic appearance, and material allusions to the psychic positioning of motherhood. Cowie also remarks on the work's ambivalent accessibility. Tergiversating between invitational intimacy and a distancing formal elegance, it seems to reproduce in the viewer the posture of avowed disavowal characteristic of the "classic" Freudian fetishist, alternately repudiating and monumentalizing the trousseau objects of his cult.

Defined as a pathological attachment to surrogate desired objects conditioning love and feeling between mother and child, maternal fetishism in *Post-Partum Document* translates visually into an economy of partial objects that act (in Kelly's words) as "emblems of desire" rather than simple transitional objects. The fetish works to reveal and disavow separation at one and the same time. The infant's quest for the breast that has been withdrawn (itself a prehistorical enactment of the subject's momentous, castrative splitting and entry into language) refracts maternal postpartum rituals. These rituals commemorate the historic severing of pre-oedipal plenitude with images of miniaturized bodies and cherished infant keepsakes. Kelly's museum of infantile detritus privileges women in the role of gender constructors, preservationists, and caretakers. *Post-Partum Document* ironically frames motherhood at a moment of ritual mourning for passing babyhood. Kelly, it would seem, even goes so far as to endorse the manic tendencies of the Freudian melancholic whose collecting expresses a pathological need to incorporate the qualities of the elusive love object. Neutralizing the negative associations surrounding rituals of melancholia, Kelly transforms the maternal reliquary into an art of mnemic traces, revalorizing the genre of sentimentality. Postpartum sentimentality is thus recuperated as a performative feminist practice that breaks down decorous allegories of sanctified maternity.

Post-Partum Document explores the tactic of signifying maternal erotics without exploiting pictures of the "real" baby. Although the surprising tactic of withholding representation of the child itself is somewhat undercut in the book format of the project by a full-page photograph of the artist with her son in her lap, the absence of figuration in the installation continues, like Freud's celebrated navel of the dream that resists analysis, to exert hermeneutic pressure on the work's interpretation. What is perhaps most compelling about Post-Partum Document for my purposes is the way in which it conflates maternal and infantile erotics. Maternal desire is communicated through visually abstract distillations of psychic affect transposed as conceptual stagings of the trace. In Documentation I, excremental smudges, at once calligraphic and monumental, are, on a more primal level, ghostly, sticky reminders of ejaculation and come. The trace of the baby's dejecta thus commingles with the trace of the mother's bodily fluids. Often distantly mimetic of polymorphously perverse genitalia (quasi-penile outlines in images 16, 28, 30, 32, the impress of buttocks in 23, 27, or vaginal/clitoral diagrams in 20 and 31), these photographed nappy liners uncannily resemble bedsheets that have become like brass rubbings of indeterminately sexed beings.

In Documentation III, (the document recording, in Kelly's words, "a kind of splitting of the dyadic mother–child unit which occurs at 27 months"), there is a record of erotic fury in the agonistic, Twombly-esque scrawls of the toddler laid over the diary entries of the mother. The child's lexic rehearsal is thus matched against the lost legibility of the mother's handwriting, making mother and child, in some sense, perfect partners. Kelly devises multiple strategies for easing erotic access between mother and child, while at the same time acknowledging inevitable social and psychic barriers. Pictured here is a "Symbolic, but 'full of holes'". The holes are where desire, momentarily evading the Law, seeps out. In Experimentum Mentis IV: On femininity, the text reads:

When the mother anxiously poses the question "What do you want?(!)" in response to the child's whining, aggressive or clinging complaints, she is essentially asking herself "What does he/she want of me?" The child's demand constitutes the mother as the Other who has the privilege of satisfying his/her needs and at the same time, the whimsical power of depriving him/her of this satisfaction. To a certain extent the mother recognizes the unconditional element of demand as a demand for love. [Kelly, 1983, p. 109]

The mother's desire for the child and the child's desire for the mother are both explicitly spoken in this section of *Post-Partum Document*. And even the knowledge that the child's phrase "I love you" will eventually be transformed by the Symbolic order into "I love the signifier of you", "I am in love with desire . . .", the original utterance remains there as a refrain, coursing through the unconscious, returning in memory, and erupting like some archaic manifestation of the real into the everyday. In marking out a commons of desire, a space shared by mother and child suffused by a "love" striated by lines of anxiety (what Lacan called *sevrage*, a term less phallocentrically marked than castration), Kelly emphasizes the interchangeable currency of desire and destruction in the infant–mother bond.

Throughout *Post-Partum Document* the representation of the "look" of theory, and the "look" of maternal pleasure function dialectically in relation to the rigorous exclusion of "real" images of women and children. The unrepresentability of the object of maternal desire is thereby given tangibility and seductive power. But this—by now rather familiar—technique of visual abstention also alludes analogically to the workings of commodity fetishism in which labour, the means of production, and exchange value are "disappeared", hidden beneath capitalism's "carapace" (to use Laura Mulvey's term), and figured as the sheen of the commodity calling out "come hither" from its display case.

In *Post-Partum Document* the problem of fetishistic value is localized in the mother's body, which, like the child's body, has become an abjected representation, a site visit to "the vanishing", an artefactual hologram in which the shadow-plays of mother–child infatuation shimmer and fade out. In the mid-1970s, this dematerialization of the mother's body facilitated the shift from heteronormative paradigms of infant need and maternal nurture to discursive critiques of pre-oedipal desire, thereby contributing to a defetishization of that monumentalized social construction: "Mother". We seem ready to risk a re-fetishization of the maternal body that might resignify differently, reassembled "perversely", visibly, and desirably.

Though Kelly explicitly seeks out Lacan rather than Klein in providing what is indeed a very rare picture of what maternal fetishism might look like if it were permitted visibility, she establishes an affinity with the Kleinian project in so far as she produces "art" from maternal negation, treating it as an enabling condition of sublimation and what Klein called "the creative impulse". Just as Kelly substitutes a diagram of the maternal position for the figurative representation of the mother's body, so Klein, in her astonishing interpretation of Maurice Ravel's opera *L'Enfant et les sortilèges* (completed in 1925, with libretto written by Colette), abstracts the maternal body, replacing its totality with three fetishistic signs: skirt, apron, hand. Klein recognized immediately how tailor-made Ravel's ballet-opera was to her theory upon reading Eduard Jakob's review in the *Berliner Tageblatt*. In her 1929 essay "Infantile anxiety-situations reflected in a work of art and in the creative impulse" (which could have been subtitled "Attack on the mother's body"!), Klein wrote, "Everything on the stage is shown very large—in order to emphasize the smallness of the child—so all that we see of his mother is a skirt, an apron, a hand" (Klein, 1950, p. 227). Super-scaled and supra-phallic, the giant maternal corpus is broken down into anatomical and sartorial part-objects, each convertible to domestic objects—armchair, cushion, table, chair—that receive the brunt of the child's anger after he is denied his wish to go to the park. Here, Klein advances the argument that "the Oedipus conflict begins under the complete dominance of sadism" (*ibid.*, p. 229). Consigning all symbols of maternal nurture to destruction, the child is duly punished when the injured part-objects return in his dreams to avenge the mother. Klein notes: "The world, transformed into the mother's body, is in hostile array against the child and persecutes him" (*ibid.*, p. 231). Illustrating Freud's domestic uncanny, or a scene of fetishism in which the inanimate thing suddenly comes alive, the maltreated objects "lift up their arms and cry: 'Away with the dirty little creature'" (*ibid.*, p. 228). In this way, maternal fetishes assert their symbolic force, summoning the child to shake off his fit of maternal hatred. By the opera's end, he is reunited with the archaic mother, having expiated his crime with the incantatory word "Mama" (the *Zauberwort* of the opera's German title).

Ravel's opera, Colette's libretto, and Klein's interpretation of them are all utterly "perverse" in the strong sense in which that word functions in association with a *mise-en-scène* of maternal fetishism. What becomes clear in Klein, is that the maternal fetish "bites back", so to speak. First, there is the construct of mother-as-fetish; a body powerfully absent, yet metonymically signified by the verbal fetish "Mama". One might suppose that the enunciation of "Mama" heralds a Symbolic order regulated by the "Name of the Mother" [*le nom de la mère*]. Second, there is the way in which maternal fetishes reveal disturbing erotic valences hidden within household and nursery objects, prompting such questions as: when is a gadget or a toy a transitional object; a loveable prosthesis; an object for "getting off"? Third, and last, Klein, in her reading of *L'Enfant et les sortilèges*, shows how the maternal fetish may be used as a weapon to combat infant sadism and to elicit contrition. The injured maternal fetish is thus ethically conscripted to de-legitimate maternophobia.

As mother and child find their way back into each other's arms at the end of Ravel's ballet-opera, they challenge psychoanalysis to rethink what it means to "have" the object of the drive by imagining the libidinal circuit of pre-oedipal desire and maternal cathexis as something at once "perverse" and other than "perverse". For our immediate challenge may first to be to conceive maternal subjectivity, a subjectivity that has been consistently negated in the history of psychoanalysis, as a desirous subject position capable of fetishism and perversion. Only then can we begin to rethink such terms outside of pathology and to imagine new futures for the desires of both mother and child.

Notes

1. As Adams puts it:

    It is important to note here that this notion of need is neatly and deliberately separated off from any notion of desire, Winnicott going out of his way to give thanks that child therapists increasingly substitute the term "need" for "desire". [Adams, 1990, p. 320]

2. This extract from Kristeva is also cited in Jacobus (1995, p. 146). Jacobus's return to Klein "with Kristevan hindsight' (*ibid.*, p. 50) provides an important precedent for my own moves in this discussion of Kristeva's book on Klein (published after Jacobus's essay).
3. A diagnosis of Munchausen Syndrome by Proxy rests on the clinician's conviction that a mother sadistically subjects her children to painful and unnecessary medical interventions, or conversely wastes the time and money of medical professionals because of her own neediness for attention.
4. As Butler puts it:

> [Antigone's] crime is confounded by the fact that the kinship line from which she descends, and which she transmits, is derived from a paternal position that is already confounded by the manifestly incestuous act that is the condition of her own existence, which makes her brother her father, which begins a narrative in which she occupies, linguistically, every kin position except "mother" and occupies them at the expense of the coherence of kinship and gender. [Butler, 2000, p. 72]

5. On the interpretation of castration as symbolic debt and object-lack as the kernel of the Oedipus complex see Lacan, 1994, p. 37.
6. The Kristevan–Kleinian revision of the Oedipal paradigm, in which the notion of phallic lack forms the basis for a theory of feminine intellectuality, responds to Laura Mulvey's call for a return to the Oedipus myth as a means of re-imagining the feminine Symbolic order. Mulvey discusses how this project informed her watershed film *Riddles of the Sphinx*:

> The film used the Sphinx as an emblem through which to hang a question mark over the Oedipus complex, to investigate the extent to which it represents a riddle for women committed to Freudian theory but still determined to think about psychoanalysis radically or, as I have said before, with poetic license. [...] Both the history of the Oedipus complex and the history of antiquity suggest a movement from an earlier "maternal" stage to a later "paternal" or "patriarchal" order. For me, as someone whose interest in psychoanalytic theory was a direct off-shoot of

fascination with the origins of women's oppression, this dual temporality was exciting. Perhaps there was an original moment in the chronology of our civilization that was repeated in the chronology of each individual consciousness. Leaving aside the temptation to make speculative connections and an analogy between the earlier culture of mother goddesses and the pre-Oedipal, the idea of a founding moment of civilization, repeated in consciousness, suggested that it might be possible to modify or change the terms on which civilization is founded within the psyche and thus challenge the origins of patriarchal power through psychoanalytic politics and theory. [Mulvey, 1989, p. 177]

7. Dany Nobus has pointed out that there are thirty-three explicit references to Klein in Lacan's seminars, which is more than to Heidegger or to Lévi-Strauss (personal correspondence, 7 July 2004). Elisabeth Roudinesco devotes significant space to tracking the impact of Klein and "Kleinism" on Lacanian theory (Roudinesco, 1993).

References

Adams, P. (1990)[1983]. Mothering. In: P. Adams & E. Cowie (Eds.), *The Woman in Question* (pp. 315–327). Cambridge, MA: MIT Press.
Barzilai, S. (1999). *Lacan and the Matter of Origins*. Stanford: Stanford University Press.
Butler, J. (2000). *Antigone's Claim: Kinship Between Life and Death*. New York: Columbia University Press.
Cowie, E. (1981). Introduction to the *Post-Partum Document. m/f*, 5–6: 115–123.
Freud, S. (1927e). Fetishism. *S.E.*, 21: 152–157. London: Hogarth.
Horney, K. (1967). Maternal conflicts. In: *Feminine Psychology* (pp. 175–181). New York: Norton.
Jacobus, M. (1995). "Tea Daddy": Poor Mrs. Klein and the pencil shavings. In: *First Things: The Maternal Imaginary in Literature, Art and Psychoanalysis* (pp. 129–152). London: Routledge.
Kelly, M. (1983). *Post-Partum Document*. London: Routledge.
Klein, M. (1950)[1929]. Infantile anxiety-situations reflected in a work of art and in the creative impulse. In: E. Jones (Ed.). *Contributions to Psycho-analysis 1921–1945* (pp. 227–235). London: Hogarth.
Klein, M. (1955). *New Directions in Psychoanalysis: The Significance of Infant Conflict in the Pattern of Adult Behaviour*. London: Tavistock.

Krafft-Ebing, R. von. (1901)[1886]. *Psychopathia Sexualis*. Translation of 10th German edn., F. J. Rebman (Trans.). London: Rebman.

Kristeva, J. (1984)[1976]. Stabat Mater. In: *Histoires d'amour* (pp. 225–247). Paris: du Seuil.

Kristeva, J. (1987). Freud and love: treatment and its discontents. In: Léon S. Roudiez (Trans.). *Tales of Love* (pp. 21–56). New York: Columbia University Press.

Kristeva, J. (2000). *Melanie Klein: Le génie féminin 2*. Paris: Gallimard.

Lacan, J. (1966)[1958]. Juenesse de Gide our la lettre et le désir. In: *Ecrits* (pp. 759–764). Paris: du Seuil.

Lacan, J. (1988)[1954]. Discourse analysis and ego analysis. In: J.-A. Miller (Ed.), J. Forrester (Trans.), *The Seminar, Book I: Freud's Papers on Technique* (pp. 62–70). London: Norton.

Lacan, J. (1992)[1959–1960]. *The Seminar, Book VII, The Ethics of Psychoanalysis*. J.-A. Miller (Ed.), D. Porter (Trans.). New York: Norton.

Lacan, J. (1994)[1956–1957]. *Le Séminaire. Livre IV: La relation d'objet*. J.-A. Miller (Ed.). Paris: Seuil.

Lacan, J. (2004)[1962–1963]. *Le Seminaire. Livre X: L'Angoisse*, J.-A. Miller (Ed.). Paris: Seuil.

Malcolm, J. (1984). *In the Freud Archives*. New York: Knopf.

Masson, J. M. (1984). *The Assault on Truth: Freud's Suppression of the Seduction Theory*. New York: Farrar, Strauss & Giroux.

Mavor, C. (1995). *Pleasures Taken: Performances of Sexuality and Loss in Victorian Photographs*. Durham, NC: Duke University Press.

Mulvey, L. (1989). The Oedipus myth: Beyond the riddles of the Sphinx. In: *Visual and Other Pleasures* (pp. 177–201). Bloomington, IN: Indiana University Press.

Plaza, M. (1980). La même mère. *Questions féministes*, 7: 71–94.

Rose, J. (1984). *The Case of Peter Pan or the Impossibility of Children's Fiction*. London: Macmillan.

Roudinesco, E. (1993). *Jacques Lacan: Esquisse d'une vie, histoire d'un système de pensée*. Paris: Fayard.

Sacher-Masoch, L. von (1980[1870]. *Venus im Pelz*. Frankfurt: Insel.

Welldon, E. V. (1988). *Mother, Madonna, Whore. The Idealization and Denigration of Motherhood*. London: Free Association.

CHAPTER TWELVE

Lacan meets queer theory

Tim Dean

This chapter envisions a dialogue between Lacan and queer theory, a sort of round table in which various contemporary theorists of sexuality would directly engage Lacan—and he them. But, of course, Lacan died well before queer theory emerged as such; and, as Thomas Yingling observed, queer theorists prepared to grapple with Freud none the less have remained relatively shy of tackling the corpus of speculative work bequeathed by Lacan (Yingling, 1997, p. 191). On the other hand, I discovered to my disappointment at an International Conference on Sexuation (in New York City, April 1997, where I first presented a preliminary version of this paper) that for their part Lacanian analysts proved far less willing to engage queer theory than I, perhaps naively, had anticipated. Yet spurred on by my conviction that psychoanalysis *is* a queer theory, I've persisted with this imaginary encounter, a dialogue between—to invoke Yeats—self and antiself.

In *Encore*, his seminar devoted most directly to the topic of sexuality, Lacan speaks often of homosexuality, but with the crucial qualification that as far as love is concerned, gender is irrelevant: *"quand on aime, il ne s'agit pas de sexe"* (Lacan, 1975, p. 27). What should we make of this idea that the gender of object-choice remains ultimately inconsequential in love? Is Lacan merely voicing liberal tolerance, anticipating by a matter of months his transatlantic counterparts' elimination of homosexuality from the *Diagnostic and Statistical Manual of Mental Disorders* in 1973? (See: Bayer, 1987; Isay, 1996.) Or, more interestingly, could we view Lacan as foreshadowing by a couple of decades the radical move in queer theory to think sexuality outside the terms of gender?[1] Although I consider liberal tolerance far less passé than do most queer theorists, I want to make the case for Lacan as more radical than liberal on the question of homosexuality. I will make this case by explaining how Lacan's account of sexuality reveals desire as determined not by the gender of object-choice, but by the object *a* (*l'objet petit a*), which remains largely independent of gender. By detaching desire from gender, Lacan helps to free desire from normative heterosexuality—that is, from the pervasive assumption that *all* desire, even same-sex attraction, is effectively heterosexual by virtue of its flowing between masculine and feminine subject-positions, regardless of the participants' actual anatomy in any given sexual encounter.

I intend to show how Lacan makes good on certain radical moments in Freud, such as the latter's counter-heterosexist observation that "the sexual instinct is in the first instance independent of its object; nor is its origin likely to be due to its object's attractions" (Freud, 1905d, p. 148). Through his concept of object *a*, Lacan alters what Freud means when he speaks of sexual objects, and I intend to use Lacan *with* queer theory to mount a critique of the Freudian notion of sexual object-choice as such. It is not so much a question of my isolating those moments in psychoanalytic texts that lend support to a progressive sexual politics, nor even of illuminating the faultlines of these texts in order to reinvigorate them, as psychoanalytic readers from Laplanche (1976) to Bersani (1985); Davidson (1987); and Lauretis (1994) have done so brilliantly. Instead, I am concerned to demonstrate how Lacan pursues the logic of Freudian insights about sex to a new destination—and how we may push this logic yet further for contemporary sexual politics. Thus, I shall argue that this radical Freudian tradition discredits the otherwise amazingly durable nineteenth-century notion that homosexual desire expresses "a feminine soul trapped in a masculine body", or vice versa. In so doing, it also discredits the idea that psychoanalysis is a modern technology designed to regulate and normalize sexuality, as some queer theorists, following Foucault, continue to claim.[2] On the contrary, Lacanian psychoanalysis provides a uniquely valuable source of resistance to just such normalization. In what follows, I elaborate on Lacan's antinormative potential and try to account for queer theory's failure to exploit that potential.

Nature/nurture—neither

"To encounter desire is first of all to forget the difference in the sexes"

(Hocquenghem, 1993, p. 130)

Much of the impasse between Lacan and queer theory stems from problems of translation, difficulties that are as much cultural and ideological as linguistic. To begin with there is the problem of Freud's American reception, which, in seeking to make Viennese speculation about sex palatable in the United States, drastically normalized revolutionary psychoanalytic ideas about sexuality. This is by now a fairly well known story, told in broad historical terms by Russell Jacoby (1975, 1986) and elaborated with respect to male homosexuality most notably by Kenneth Lewes (1988) and Henry Abelove (1993).[3] In his pioneering study of the American domestication of psychoanalysis, historian Abelove argues that Freud's position on homosexuality was far more progressive than those held by his transatlantic followers, both sympathetic and hostile, later in the century: "Freud was perfectly consistent on the subject of homosexuality," Abelove claims; "[w]hat he told the American mother in his letter of 1935, that it was neither advantage, crime, illness, nor disgrace, he had long believed and acted on" (Abelove, 1993, p. 384). However, once Freudianism migrated to the United States, American analysts promoted a fantasy of eradicating homosexuality altogether, wilfully disregarding Freud's conclusion, in his *Three Essays on the Theory of Sexuality*, that "all human beings are capable of making a homosexual object-choice and have in fact made one in their unconscious" (Freud, 1905d, p. 145). Considering this emphasis on the unconscious, we can begin to grasp how the efforts of institutionalized psychoanalysis to "cure" homosexuality remain coeval with American psychoanalytic attempts to cure the *unconscious* out of existence. Seen from this vantage point, Lacan's critique of American ego-psychology is readily appropriable for queer theory's critique of institutionalized homophobia.

Freud's view that, at least in the unconscious, *we're all a little queer*, conforms to what Eve Kosofsky Sedgwick calls the "universalizing" conception of homosexuality—as distinguished from the "minoritizing" conception, which views same-sex object-choice as characterizing a specific group of people, a sexual minority whose identity is thence defined in contradistinction to that of the majority (Sedgwick, 1990, pp. 40–41). "Psychoanalytic research is most decidedly opposed to any attempt at separating off homosexuals from the rest of mankind as a group of a special character", insists Freud (1905d, p. 145), explicitly countering the minoritizing conception of sexual inversion propagated in his own time by figures such as Karl Heinrich Ulrichs, Richard von Krafft-Ebing, and Magnus Hirschfeld. Although the idea of a sexual minority enables a form of political campaigning that culminates in civil rights activism, Abelove's account makes clear how a minoritizing view also serves the American mental health establishment's homophobic purposes by confining homosexuality to a single demographic. And so, while I'm persuaded more by the universalizing than by the minoritizing conception of homosexuality, in the end Freud's contention that we've all made a homosexual object-choice (whether we know it or not) doesn't go far enough, because his notion of object-choice remains trapped within the terms of gender. The very possibility of describing object-choice as homosexual or heterosexual takes for granted that the object chosen is gendered and that—no matter how partial or fragmented the object may be—it's somehow identifiable as masculine or feminine. In contrast, Lacan's concept of object *a* radically revises the Freudian notion of object-choice by leaving gender behind, in a move whose far-reaching implications I wish to delineate.

We may approach the ungendered or degendered conception of object-choice by considering a less appreciated dimension of Freud's American reception, one involving the distinction between a psychoanalytic, largely European understanding of sexual difference and a sociological, largely North American understanding of gender. This distinction is raised by Lacan's comment, quoted above, that *"quand on aime, il ne s'agit pas de sexe"*. Although the French word *sexe* roughly conforms to what we mean by gender, this translation elides the specifically psychoanalytic dimension of sex; and so one is forced to confront the conceptual limits of the terms—*sex, gender, sexuality*—available for this discussion.

Conventionally, we distinguish sex from gender according to the coordinates of certain well-rehearsed debates—essentialism versus constructionism, or the longer-standing controversy known as "nature versus nurture". The force of gender as a concept lies in how it denaturalizes sexual difference, making sex a question of social and historical construction rather than of biological essence. And sexuality, or sexual orientation, tends to be discussed within the framework of these same debates.[5] Indeed, the term *sexuality* is regularly understood to involve questions not only of desire but also of identity, so that the issue of one's sexuality tends to be taken as referring not only to the putative gender of one's object-choice but also to one's *own* gender identity, one's masculinity or femininity. However, we can begin to appreciate the danger of keeping sexuality so closely tied to gender by considering how the diagnosis of "Gender identity disorder," in *DSM*, readily takes over the pathologizing role formerly assigned to "homosexuality" (see: *In the Family*, 1997, p. 3).

To free a theory of sexuality from the ideological constraints imposed by gender categories also permits us to divorce sexuality from the straitjacket of identity. Another way of putting this would be to say that psychoanalysis enables us to think sexuality apart from the ego. And, as I've suggested, this way of thinking becomes possible only through some concept equivalent to that of the unconscious: it remains a basic psychoanalytic postulate that while there is always sex, there can be no sexuality without the unconscious. Thus, for Lacan, sexuality is explicable in terms of neither nature *nor* nurture, since the unconscious cannot be considered biological—it isn't part of my body and yet it isn't exactly culturally constructed either. Instead, the unconscious may be grasped as an index of how both biology and culture *fail* to determine subjectivity and sexual desire. Thinking of the unconscious as neither biological nor cultural allows us to distinguish (among other things) a properly psychoanalytic from a merely psychological notion of the unconscious.

In making such distinctions, I consider it important to specify how Lacan's account of sexuality remains unassimilable to the nature–nurture debate, especially since arguments between essentialists and social constructionists have become increasingly polarized in recent years. Yet, I want to emphasize that psychoanalysis does not offer some compromise between these polarities: rather, Lacan furnishes the conceptual means for developing a genuine alternative to them. At the essentialist pole of this debate neuroanatomists and geneticists, such as Simon LeVay and Dean Hamer, search for the biological *cause* of homosexuality in hypothalmic structure or chromosomes.[6] At the social constructionist pole philosophers, such as Judith Butler, meticulously deconstruct the sex–gender distinction in order to argue that the ostensibly pregiven, immutable category in this conceptual couple—that is, biological sex—is just as much a result of historically contingent processes of materialization as is gender (Butler, 1993). The deconstructionist position takes constructionism one step further by arguing that bodies aren't simply the raw material that social processes use to construct gender and sexuality, but rather that corporeal matter itself must be *materialized* through social processes of embodiment. And for this reason the deconstructionist account of sexuality sometimes advertises itself as a critique of and alternative to—rather than simply a refinement of—social constructionism.

But from my point of view the various sides in this debate miss the point of a psychoanalytic critique of sex, gender, and sexuality, since the purpose of such a critique is not (like deconstruction) to devise ever subtler ways of revealing that what seemed natural is in fact cultural or a positive effect of the symbolic order. Thus, although Butler uses Lacan to support her argument, in the end psychoanalysis authorizes the constructionist (or deconstructionist) account of sexuality no more than it authorizes the essentialist one. Hence Freud's insistence that "the nature of inversion is explained neither by the hypothesis that it is innate nor by the alternative hypothesis that it is acquired" (Freud, 1905d, p. 140). And so, while it's possible to identify passages in Freud that appear to support either side of the nature–nurture debate, I prefer to draw out a psychoanalytic logic that remains fundamentally irreducible to this debate's terms, even in their most recent, most advanced form. By describing sexuality in terms of unconscious desire, I wish to separate sexual orientation from questions of identity and of gender roles, practices, and performances, since it is by conceiving sexuality outside the terms of gender *and* identity that we can most thoroughly deheterosexualize desire.

The queer critique of normativity

"Because the logic of the sexual order is so deeply embedded by now in an indescribably wide range of social institutions, and is embedded in the most standard accounts of the world, queer struggles aim not just at toleration or equal status but at challenging those institutions and accounts"

(Warner, 1993, p. xiii)

Having reached this point, we should now acknowledge that the problems entailed in confining sexuality to the terms of identity also ignited queer theory, which emerged as an intellectual and political movement only during the 1990s, in the wake of feminism, gay liberation, and the AIDS epidemic.[7] Although queer theory's newness and heterodoxical configurations make hazardous any attempt at definition, we may nevertheless characterize these new epistemological and ideological configurations in order to distinguish their most salient features (see Berlant & Warner, 1995). Queer theory views with postmodern scepticism the minoritizing conception of sexuality that undergirds gay liberation and women's liberation (and, hence, academically institutionalized gay studies and women's studies too). Building on the civil rights movements of the 1960s, feminism and gay liberation based their claims for political participation and radical equality, whether assimilationist or separatist, on the foundation of *identity*—female, gay, lesbian, and, more recently, bisexual, transsexual, transgendered identities. By contrast, queer theory and politics begin from a critique of identity and of identity politics, inspired primarily by Foucault's analysis of the disciplinary purposes that sexual identities so easily serve. As Butler encapsulates this Foucaultian critique: "identity categories tend to be instruments of regulatory regimes, whether as the normalizing categories of oppressive structures or as the rallying points for a liberatory contestation of that very oppression" (Butler, 1991, pp. 13–14). Or as Foucault himself put it, ventriloquizing Deleuze and Guattari, "Do not demand of politics that it restore the 'rights' of the individual, as philosophy has defined them. The individual is the product of power" (Foucault, 1983, p. xiv). We can see immediately how this blunt admonition flies in the face of Enlightenment postulates of individual liberty and autonomous agency, upon which US society and politics are based. Before discussing the political consequences of this reconceptualization, I'd like to consider further its methodological implications.

Queer theory's Foucaultian suspicion of identity *tout court* leads in two competing directions. On the one hand, it has inspired a cautious return to psychoanalytic epistemologies among some queer theorists, given how Freud's theory of the unconscious introduces a constitutive subjective division that undermines the possibility of any seamless identity, sexual or otherwise. Even critics with a more thoroughgoing mistrust of psychoanalysis as a heterosexist and homophobic institution have been led, practically despite themselves, to invent conceptual categories tantamount to that of the unconscious (see Dean, 1995).

Yet, on the other hand, queer theory's critique of identity as a regulatory norm has also led diametrically away from psychoanalytic epistemologies, encouraged in large part by Foucault's displacement of attention from identities to practices. Thus, although historicism shares with psychoanalysis the view that identities are essentially illusory, historicism resorts to the empiricist solution of investigating discrete social and cultural practices, whereas psychoanalysis focuses on what, though not exactly illusory, nevertheless resists empirical verification, i.e., fantasy. Foucault makes this distinction explicit in a 1982 interview.

> I don't try to write an archaeology of sexual fantasies. I try to make an archaeology of discourse about sexuality, which is really the relationship between what we do, what we are obliged to do, what we are allowed to do, what we are forbidden to do in the field of sexuality, and what we are allowed, forbidden, or obliged to say about our sexual behavior. That's the point. It's not a problem of fantasy; it's a problem of verbalization. [Foucault, 1997a, pp. 125–126]

I'll return to this problematic distinction between fantasy and verbalization at the end of this chapter, but even without Foucault it is easy to see how the concrete reality of sexual practices appears to carry greater political weight than the comparative ephemerality of sexual fantasies, which often seem luxurious and trivial in the face of material oppression. Yet, I shall argue that such a hierarchy of political seriousness may itself betoken heterosexist logic: fantasy remains so phenomenologically and conceptually inextricable from perversion that the characteristic relegation of fantasy to zones of secondariness, irrationality, passivity, and immaturity should give us pause. Furthermore, the strong vein of utopianism in queer theory suggests the importance of fantasy to its simultaneously political and sexual agendas: "almost everything that can be called queer theory has been radically anticipatory, trying to bring a world into being" note two of queer theory's most prominent spokespersons (Berlant & Warner, 1995, p. 344).

But before we can specify what's so queer about fantasy we must grasp more precisely what queerness implies. Far more than a handy moniker covering the rainbow coalition of non-normative sexualities (lesbian, gay, bisexual, transsexual, and so on), "queer" extends the politics of sexuality beyond sex and sexual minorities' civil rights by insisting that "queer" is opposed not simply to "straight", but more broadly to "normal". Defining itself against the normal, queerness exceeds sexuality, sexual practices, sexual identities; indeed, this is how people whose sexual partners are primarily, even exclusively, of the opposite sex get to count as queer. Queer theory depends on identificatory alliances rather than on identities as such, and queer politics thus involves creating alliances between sexual minorities and other social groups whose marginalization or disenfranchisement isn't necessarily a direct consequence of non-normative sexuality. Hence, the centrality accorded ostensibly nonsexual categories—such as race, ethnicity, and nationality—in queer theory, which isn't so much about being inclusive (under the aegis of an ever-expanding liberal tolerance) as it is about connecting one dimension of social exclusion with others. And in the light of this commitment to discerning alliances, I have often wondered why queer theorists have not forged more of an alliance with Lacanian psychoanalysts, given the thoroughgoing antinormative bias in Lacan's work. Yet, though Lacan reads to me like a queer theorist *avant la lettre*, the institutional history of psychoanalysis, particularly in the USA, has forestalled any such alliance. Forging this alliance is a desirable agenda—with the understanding that it might require both parties to renounce some of their most cherished shibboleths.

If *queer* represents more than merely a broader or hipper term for gayness and more than a new form of avant-gardism, then queer theory's principal challenge must be to confront the consequences of defining oneself and one's politics against norms as such.[8] The implications of such a stance are radical indeed, particularly in a society whose ideology of individualism guarantees maximum liberty to pursue one's own version of happiness—on condition only that he or she conform. In view of this ideological double-bind, Michael Warner correctly identifies queer theory's paradoxically antisocial utopianism.

> Organizing a movement around queerness also allows [queer theory] to draw on dissatisfaction with the regime of the normal in general. Following Hannah Arendt, we might even say that queer politics opposes society itself. . . . The social realm, in short, is a cultural form, interwoven with the political form of the administrative state and with the normalizing methodologies of modern social knowledge. Can we not hear in the resonances of queer protest an objection to the normalization of behavior in this broad sense, and thus to the cultural phenomenon of societalization? If queers, incessantly told to alter their "behavior," can be understood as protesting not just the normal behavior of the social but the *idea* of normal behavior, they will bring skepticism to the methodologies founded on that idea. [Warner, 1993, p. xxvii]

The capaciousness and force of queerness stem not simply from its opposing sexual norms—or what, almost two decades ago, Adrienne Rich diagnosed as "compulsory heterosexuality" (Rich, 1983)—but from its resistance to the very idea of the normal as such. Thus, by contrast with most gay journalism about sexual politics, queer theory, in its avowed opposition to "society itself," assumes that those who've been socially excluded don't *want* to "fit in" or conform as social beings.[9] It is sometimes hard to decide whether this assumption betrays an elitist disregard for the self-perceptions and desires of non-heterosexuals outside the university (particularly working-class queers), or whether it signals a greater ideological awareness enabled by academic freedom and, indeed, promotes a laudatory shouldering of the political responsibilities that accompany institutional privilege.

Queer theory assumes not only that queers' early sense of alienation effectively renders social conformity impossible, but also that queer opposition to social norms represents far more than an expression of aggressivity or "acting out" under the guise of political activism. Furthermore, queer theory stakes its utopian claims on the conviction that opposing "society itself" does not necessarily incur the loneliness of psychosis, foreclosed from all social ties, but that, on the contrary, queer political resistance provides access to alternate forms of community and other social ties— perhaps even other *forms* of social tie, different ways of knotting the subject to society and community (see Agamben, 1993). Indeed, more than a decade before queer theory came along, Foucault was already speculating about the radically different kinds of social tie that homosexuals might establish. Distinguishing between homophobic intolerance of gay sex and horror at the possibility of gay sociality, he explained, in a well-publicized interview, that "[i]t is the prospect that gays will create as yet unforseen kinds of relationships that many people cannot tolerate" (Foucault, 1997b, p. 153).[10]

Lacan's critique of normativity

"Strengthening the categories of affective normativity produces disturbing results"

(Lacan, 1992, pp. 133–134)

Rather than directly adjudicating either queer theory's claims or the philosophical presuppositions on which they're based, I want to explore them further by considering how Lacan's account of sexuality harmonizes with queer theory's. In view of its revisionary interventions in social theory, queer politics could be regarded as quintessentially American, as the latest chapter in a long history of native self-invention, utopianism, and experimental communitarianism that characterizes US social politics. Yet, on the other hand, queer theory's antinormative, anti-identitarian, and antiliberal commitments make it appear every bit as "un-American" as some of its detractors charge. From this perspective, it is significant that Lacan also directs his critique of norms—including what he pointedly calls "the delusional 'normality' of the genital relation" (Lacan, 1977a, p. 245)—against the American ideology of individualism, particularly as it finds expression in the normalizing ethos of "adaptation to reality" that ego-psychology promulgates as the goal of psychoanalytic therapy.

Lacan views the conception of therapy in terms of adaptation as a problem not simply because the reality to which one should adapt turns out to be "heteronormative" (in Warner's terms), but more fundamentally because *reality itself is imaginary*. Since we are accustomed to thinking of reality and the imaginary as antithetical, Lacan's paradoxical alignment of the two warrants careful examination. (And even before grasping the full significance of this equation, we can begin to appreciate that what Lacan means by "the real" must be very far from "reality," if reality is imaginary.) It is when one conceives reality in terms of adaptation that it is given over to the imaginary, in that "reality" thus comes to represent a set of norms or ideal forms to which we're supposed to aspire and on the basis of which our egos must be modelled and remodelled. Hence Lacan's objection to the normalizing function of psychology: "Psychology transmits ideals"—to which he adds, "[i]deals are society's slaves" (Lacan, 1995, p. 262).

Lacan maintains that so long as psychoanalysts focus exclusively on the ego or individual, they will remain trapped within an essentially prescriptive discourse of norms and normativity. Since the ego comes into being through projective idealization—by means of misrecognitions of images of the other—the ego is nothing but a precipitate of idealized models. Whatever their content, these models are susceptible to idealization in so far as their form appears totalized, bounded, and complete; these imaginary models provide the subject points of coherence with which to identify within a seamless picture of the world. By means of these imaginary identifications the subject finds a place in reality—and so experiences a measure of jubilation, irrespective of how culturally prized or disprized that place may be.[11] Thus "reality" constitutes the sum of these models and norms, the imaginary ideals to which we're supposed to conform not merely in our behaviour but in our very existence and perceptions. From this we might say that in so far as reality is imaginary, it is also utopic, a pure projection. Queer theory's counter-utopianism makes more sense in this light. And Lacan himself points out that the American ideology of adaptation mystifies reproductive heterosexuality as the norm: "Goodness only knows how obscure such a pretension as the achievement of genital objecthood (*l'objectalité genitale*) remains, along with what is so imprudently linked to it, namely, adjustment to reality" (Lacan, 1992, p. 293).

However, Lacan's response to normativity is not to produce alternative imaginaries, but to elaborate an alternative of a different order—that of the real, a conceptual category intended to designate everything that *resists* adaptation. As he remarks with characteristic irreverence when alluding to normative accounts of psychosexual development, "what has this absurd hymn to the harmony of the genital got to do with the real?" (Lacan, 1977a, p. 245). In so far as the real represents that concept through which Lacan challenges heteronormativity, queer theorist Judith Butler is somewhat mistaken in her claim that the Lacanian real *secures* heteronormativity (Butler, 1993, pp. 187–222). Of course, it could be objected that Lacan's aligning reality with the imaginary over and against the real simply perpetuates a long metaphysical tradition that associates the world of experience and perceptions (so-called reality) with vain appearances, in contradistinction to an ultimate world of essences beyond appearances. Yet, as Lacan conceives it, the real isn't simply *opposed* to reality or the imaginary domain of appearances, since both the imaginary and the real operate only in relation to Lacan's third order, the symbolic (the relation among these three orders—imaginary, symbolic, and real—should be characterized in terms of neither binary opposition nor dialectic). Furthermore, rather than following the metaphysical tradition, Lacan does not align the order of the real with the world of immutable essences in contrast to an imaginary world of appearances and ephemerality: instead, he situates negativity and mutability on the side of the real rather than on that of appearances. Thus, as I shall explain, although the real has no positive content, it has more to do with sex and death than do the imaginary or the symbolic.

This understanding of the real accounts for my objection to critically analysing sex and sexuality in terms of the imaginary and symbolic—that is, in terms of the images and discourses that construct sex, sexuality, and desirability in our culture. Hugely powerful though these images and discourses are, sexuality pertains more to the real than to the imaginary or the symbolic.[12] Put another way, sexuality is comprehended better according to the specific modes of these cultural images' and discourses' failure. I'm suggesting that we should think about sexuality in terms of the limits, rather than the power, of these images and discourses—not simply their limits in representing some objective truth of sexuality but, more precisely, their limits in determining human sexuality. Nevertheless, I'm aware that in the face of the constant media barrage of sexualized imagery, this claim may appear particularly counter-intuitive. Since the specificity of a Lacanian perspective on sexuality rests on this claim, permit me to elaborate further.

Much of the difficulty—but also the usefulness—of Lacan's concept of the real lies in its de-essentializing, despecifying abstractness. In this regard, the real resonates with the notion of *queer* underlying queer theory. And, as a consequence, the Lacanian real, like queerness, is always relational, oppositional in the subversive sense, rather than substantive (there can be no queer without a norm, and vice versa). From this observation we may take another step and note how the Lacanian real functions similarly to the Freudian unconscious in its constantly undermining social and sexual identities. To grasp what Lacan means by this slippery category, whose quotidian connotations remain so hard to dispel, it helps to bear in mind that the real denotes that concept through which, especially in his later work, Lacan implicitly develops certain aspects of Freud's theory of the unconscious. In so doing, Lacan helps to distinguish a psychoanalytic from a more psychological notion of the unconscious as denoting interiority, depth, or the repository of drives and complexes. If we think of the real in light of the *psychoanalytic* unconscious, we will see more clearly how the real is connected with—indeed, remains inseparable from—sexuality.

The paradox of human sexuality, according to Freud, consists in its diphasic emergence: its initial efflorescence in childhood, prior to maturation of the sexual organs, is succeeded by a period of latency before sexuality re-emerges alongside, yet forever out of synch with, organic changes in the body. Freud's claims on behalf of infantile sexuality entail recognizing that sex comes before one is ready for it—either physically or psychically. In the case of children, it seems relatively clear what being physically unprepared for sex means; psychically it means that the human infant encounters sexual impulses—its own as well as other people's—as alien, unmasterable, unassimilable to its fledgling ego, and hence ultimately traumatic. As a consequence of this capacity to disorganize the ego or coherent self, sexuality becomes part of the unconscious, and it is owing to this subjectively traumatic origin that Lacan aligns sex with the order of the real. The real—like trauma—is what resists assimilation to any imaginary or symbolic universe. Another way of putting this would be to say that the premature emergence of sexuality in humans—its original non-coincidence with biology—splits sexuality off from reality and reassigns it to the domain of fantasy. In so doing, human sexuality is constituted as irremediably perverse.[13]

The problem of perversion

Psychoanalysis inherits the category of perversion from nineteenth-century sexology and transforms it almost beyond recognition. Though Freud followed his predecessors in bracketing homosexuality (along with fetishism, sadism, and masochism) under the rubric of perversion, Lacan rarely aligns homosexuality with perversion. In fact, Lacan says little about homosexuality when discussing perversion; instead, he seems to prefer fetishism as his example of a perverse manifestation, and he takes Sade—who hardly qualifies as homosexual—as his exemplary pervert.[14] Lacan makes same-sex desire independent of perversion by conceptualizing the latter in terms of an unconscious structure of desire, rather than in terms of its phenomenological manifestations or overt symptomatology. Thus, for Lacan, perversion is distinguished less from heteronormativity than from neurosis, on the one hand, and psychosis, on the other. In this Lacan follows Freud, for whom neuroses are the negative of perversions (Freud, 1905d, p. 165). Yet, in reconceiving perversion in terms of structure, Lacan departs from Freud—a divergence that, in my view, doesn't necessarily represent an advance, since Lacan's "structures of desire" often have the effect of reinstituting a subjective identity, albeit at the level of the unconscious. In other words, I remain sceptical about how the Lacanian tendency to speak of "the pervert", "the hysteric", and "the psychotic" unwittingly reinscribes a typology of desire and, ultimately, categories of personhood that Freud's account of perversion ostensibly outmoded.[15] Given this scepticism, I am particularly keen to see how theorizing perversion in the light of queer theory might ameliorate this problem.

Having registered that cautionary note, let me now explain how Freud's theory concerning the irremediably perverse constitution of sexuality is fully consistent with contemporary claims on behalf of sexuality as irremediably queer, resistant to normalization. To take a salient example, Sedgwick, attempting to define queerness, writes:

> That's one of the things that 'queer' can refer to: the open mesh of possibilities, gaps, overlaps, dissonances and resonances, lapses and excesses of meaning when the constituent elements of anyone's gender, of anyone's sexuality aren't made (or *can't be* made) to signify monolithically. [Sedgwick, 1993, p. 8]

From this Sedgwick concludes that "[s]exuality in this sense, perhaps, can *only* mean queer sexuality" (*ibid.*, p. 20). Without acknowledging or apparently even realizing it, Sedgwick is directly echoing Freud's contention that we're all potentially queer and that, paradoxically, perversion *is* the norm. As he concludes the first of his *Three Essays*:

> By demonstrating the part played by perverse impulses in the formation of symptoms in the psychoneuroses, we have quite remarkably increased the number of people who might be regarded as perverts. It is not only that neurotics in themselves constitute a very numerous class, but it must also be considered that an unbroken chain bridges the gap between the neuroses in all their manifestations and normality.... Thus the extraordinarily wide dissemination of the perversions forces us to suppose that the disposition to perversions is itself of no great rarity but must form a part of what passes as the normal constitution. [Freud, 1905d, p. 171]

And then, struggling to adjudicate a version of the nature–nurture debate that prevailed in his own time, Freud immediately adds,

> It is, as we have seen, debatable whether the perversions go back to innate determinants or arise ... owing to chance experiences. The conclusion now presents itself to us that there is indeed something innate lying behind the perversions but that it is something innate in *everyone*. [ibid.]

This is what Jonathan Dollimore calls Freud's "deconstructive assault on normality" (Dollimore, 1991, p. 182), his universalizing description of perversion not as distinct from, or opposed to, the norm, but as internal to it.[16] In Freud's theory of sexuality, perversion doesn't represent a detour or falling away from the norm, as it does in the pre-psychoanalytic, theological conception of perversion. Instead, for Freud, the reverse is true: perversion is primary, rather than a secondary deviation. In the form of polymorphous infantile sexuality, perversion *precedes* the norm, and therefore normal sexuality—that is, reproductive genital heterosexuality—represents a deviation or falling away from perversion. To specify this relation more precisely, perhaps we could say that within the Freudian dialectic of sexuality, the norm *sublates* perversion, ostensibly superseding but never actually eliminating it. There is, thus, a sense in which, by focusing sexuality on the genitals and on a single prescribed act, normal sex represents "paradise lost" in the psychoanalytic cosmology. This is in direct contrast to the theological understanding of this matter, which equates perversion with original sin. In *Three Essays*, reproductive heterosexuality paradoxically designates both an ideal goal to be striven for and, simultaneously, the loss of an ideal state—that of polymorphous perversity.

Hence, Freud's ambivalence toward the process of normalization, his vacillation between speaking on its behalf and speaking *sotto voce* against it. When he speaks on behalf of perversion Freud enters contradiction, bumping up against inherited categories of pathology. As a doctor he is supposed to treat the sick and cure the pathological, but, after situating perversion as *internal to* normality, Freud necessarily confronts a fundamental uncertainty about how to determine pathology in the bewildering world of sexual variation. Freud negotiates this uncertainty, which his own theory generates, by identifying pathology with exclusiveness, or what he calls fixation. Thus, he defines the pathology of perversion formally rather than substantively: "the pathological character in a perversion is found to lie not in the *content* of the new sexual aim but in its relation to the normal" (Freud 1905d, p. 161); hence, it is only so long as "a perversion has the characteristics of exclusiveness and fixation [that] we shall usually be justified in regarding it as a pathological symptom" (*ibid.*). According to Freud, in any isolated instance a perverse manifestation tells you nothing about the subject manifesting it; only when accompanied by "exclusiveness and fixation" can perversion be considered pathological.

Despite the progressive implications of Freud's relativizing perversion, there remains something oddly tautological about his claim that it's not the perversion but its fixation that's pathological; indeed, his critique of sexual exclusiveness can be turned against exclusive *hetero*sexuality, as Freud himself recognized:

> from the point of view of psychoanalysis the exclusive sexual interest felt by men for women is also a problem that needs elucidating and is not a self-evident fact based upon an attraction that is ultimately of a chemical nature. [Freud, 1905d, p. 146n.]

But, of course, the pathologization of exclusiveness and fixation has historically been used by the psychoanalytic establishment not to interrogate "the exclusive sexual interest felt by men for women", but to inveigh against any sexual interest felt by men for other men. And, as Michael Ferguson has pointed out in a painstaking critique of American psychoanalysts' use of the term "fixation" to pathologize homosexuality, it is when "fixation" is linked to a notion of adaptation that it becomes so destructively normalizing (Ferguson, 1994).[17]

Rather than simply dismissing the notion of fixation as ineluctably homophobic, I think we may develop it a little more cogently by recognizing how *the process of normalization itself is what's pathological*, since normalization "fixes" desire and generates the exclusiveness of sexual orientation as its symptom. From this perspective, exclusive homosexuality and exclusive heterosexuality are equally problematic, in that both constrain the mobility of desire, orientating it in increasingly limited ways—first towards persons, then towards persons of the opposite sex, then towards specific sexual acts with persons of the opposite sex, and often towards specific acts with a specific person of the opposite sex. Thus, normalization is less a question of inculcating heterosexuality than of coordinating desire with the ego, freezing fragmented and mercurial unconscious effects into the total form of an identity. In the terms that Lacan develops from Jakobson, normalization involves wrenching the metonymy of desire into the metaphor (or substitutive identity) of the ego.

This process of normalization is pathogenic rather than healthy, in so far as its totalizing impulse remains fundamentally inimical to the contingency and ambiguity that characterize desire. And the fragility of this normalizing process partly explains the hostility and imaginary aggression that emerge in response to whatever or whoever derails its trajectory—for example, queers or those who remain sexually ambiguous.[18] Thus, my point here is twofold: first, that normalization itself, by orientating desire towards a stable sexual identity, is potentially pathological irrespective of whether the identity in question is heterosexual, homosexual, or otherwise; and second, more specifically, that homosexuality nevertheless remains a spectre haunting this process, signalling the possibility of normalization's failure, its *dis*orientation.

Although homosexuality has functioned since the end of the nineteenth century as a synecdoche for perversion—that is, as perversion's most visible representative—this doesn't warrant our characterizing homosexuality as unequivocally antinormative or subversive. Quite the contrary: as an orientation or identity, homosexuality is normalizing though not socially normative—a distinction that often gets lost in contemporary arguments over its political implications. But, on the other hand, as a sign of desire's perverse *resistance* to orientation or identity (its unconscious, perpetual mobility), homosexuality may remind us of how desire itself remains potentially antinormative, incompletely assimilable to the ego, and hence inimical to the model of the person, fundamentally impersonal.

This subtle distinction—between what in homosexuality is normalizing and what is antinormative—must be maintained if queer theory is to elude the impasses of identity politics that it was originally designed to outwit. In order to be as clear as possible about my dual claims here concerning homosexuality, I'd like to invoke French philosopher Guy Hocquenghem, whose queer manifesto, *Homosexual Desire*, anticipates much of the present argument. Hocquenghem opens his book with a polemic that resonates strikingly with Freud's critique of sexual exclusivity:

> "Homosexual desire"—the expression is meaningless. There is no subdivision of desire into homosexuality and heterosexuality. Properly speaking, desire is no more homosexual than heterosexual. Desire emerges in a multiple form, whose components are only divisible *a posteriori*, according to how we manipulate it. Just like heterosexual desire, homosexual desire is an arbitrarily frozen frame in an unbroken and polyvocal flux. The exclusively homosexual characterization of desire in its present form is a fallacy of the imaginary; but homosexuality has a specially manifest imagery, and it is possible to undertake a deconstruction of such images. If the homosexual image contains a complex knot of dread and desire, if the homosexual fantasy is more obscene than any other and at the same time more exciting, if it is impossible to appear anywhere as a self-confessed homosexual without upsetting families, causing children to be dragged out of the way and arousing mixed feelings of horror and desire, then the reason must be that for us twentieth-century westerners there is a close relationship between desire and homosexuality. Homosexuality expresses something—some aspect of desire—which appears nowhere else, and that something is not merely the accomplishment of the sexual act with a person of the same sex. [Hocquenghem, 1993, pp. 49–50]

What homosexuality expresses—indirectly and in popular form—is desire's disquieting disregard for gender and for persons. Or perhaps we could point the distinction more precisely by saying that this is what homosexuality *represents*: homosexuality has been historically, not essentially or expressively, associated with what psychoanalysis views as a transhistorical characteristic of desire. Since transhistorical claims tend to be regarded as little short of heresy, let me reiterate that what psychoanalysis considers essential to desire is precisely that it obtains no essential object: *desire's objects remain essentially contingent.*

But when homosexuality becomes the basis for an identity, this contingent relation between desire and its objects vanishes. Hocquenghem frames the conundrum like this:

Homosexual desire is perverse in the Freudian sense, i.e. it is simply an-Oedipal, as long as it expresses the disorganisation of the component drives. It becomes neurotically perverse in the ordinary sense when it relates to a face, when it enters the sphere of the ego and the imaginary. [Hocquenghem, 1993, p. 149]

Distinguishing between two versions of homosexuality and two kinds of perversion (as well as between their respective ideological effects), Hocqenghem raises a question that, even a quarter of a century later, queer theory has barely begun to address, much less to answer. This question concerns how we may conceive of desire as *not* relating "to a face": how can we depersonify or impersonalize desire so as to retain its original perverse force without simply plunging into sexual anarchy? How can we inhibit the prosopopoeia—the face-making trope—that accompanies libidinal investments while still honouring the other's alterity? I think we may profitably engage these questions by considering Hocquenghem's psychoanalytic antecedents and developing the subterranean Freudian logic that guides his argument; in so doing, we'll push both Lacanian psychoanalysis and queer theory on to new ground.

The impersonality of desire

"Relations between human beings are really established before one gets to the domain of consciousness. It is desire which achieves the primitive structuration of the human world, desire as unconscious" (Lacan, 1988, p. 224).

Hocquenghem speaks not of "depersonifying" or "impersonalizing" desire but, more austerely, of its *dehumanization*: "The sexualisation of the world heralded by the gay movement pushes capitalist decoding to the limit and corresponds to the dissolution of the human; from this point of view, the gay movement undertakes the necessary dehumanisation" (Hocquenghem, 1993, p. 145).[19] This promulgation of dehumanization sits very uncomfortably with post-Enlightenment liberal politics, which takes as a point of departure the dignity of the human individual. Civil rights is one logical outcome of this political stance, as is the post-1968 gay movement that Hocquenghem invokes; therefore, his advocating dehumanization by means of sexuality might be viewed as pushing gay radicalism into contradiction with its liberal origins. After all, it's not hard to see how discussing gay sex in terms of dehumanization could inflame, rather than mitigate, homophobia. Yet the reference to "dehumanization" carries more precise resonances—in general, to the tradition of French antihumanism; more specifically, to the work of Deleuze and Guattari; and ultimately, I'll suggest, to the French psychoanalytic tradition of Lacan. Though Hocquenghem follows Deleuze and Guattari to the letter, referring to "capitalist decoding" and suchlike, he follows Lacan in spirit, explicitly developing an account of queer sexuality that remains only implicit in Lacan.

To boil down a complex philosophical tradition to its most elementary coordinates, let us recall that French antihumanism—for which the names Freud, Marx, and Nietzsche can stand just as well as those of Bataille, Lacan, and Foucault—announces the "death of man" as a fully autonomous, self-governing agent who is master of his world because master of himself. Antihumanism extinguishes this conception of the human in favour of one in which language and various social systems precondition or discipline human agency. Rather than manipulating signs and wielding power, man is reconceived as the conduit for and product of non-human forces greater than himself. Thus we might say that man is unmanned in antihumanist philosophy, finding himself no longer master of his world since he is no longer master of himself. The principal name psychoanalysis gives to this loss of mastery or decentring of the human is *the unconscious*. From this it follows that we may nuance the potentially misleading terms "antihumanism" and "dehumanization" by substituting for them *de-ego-ization*, since it is less the death of humanity or of Man *per se* that is at stake than the obsolescence of a particular conception and ideology of the self. Hocquenghem makes this clear when he concludes—in a formulation anticipating Bersani's—that "[h]omosexual desire is neither on the side of death nor on the side of life; it is the killer of civilised egos" (Hocquenghem, 1993, p. 150. See also: Bersani, 1988, pp. 197–222, 1995).

Deleuze and Guattari's contribution to this antihumanist project remains somewhat ambiguous—an ambiguity that requires interpreting if we are to correctly gauge their influence on *Homosexual*

TIM DEAN 283

Desire. Calling their critique of the ideology of the self "schizoanalysis" rather than psychoanalysis, Deleuze and Guattari substitute for the potentially misleading term "antihumanism" the more pointed "anti-Oedipus", thereby intending to discredit at once the ideology of the sovereign self and the Freudian metanarrative they claim bolsters that individualist ideology. In fact, like most readers of Freud, Deleuze and Guattari find in psychoanalysis a duality, whose halves they cast in highly evaluative terms—the "good" and the "bad" Freud, the liberatory and the repressive dimensions of psychoanalysis. Thus they advance their polemic against the "bad" Freud in the service of a "good" Freud that they incorporate and, somewhat disingenuously, claim as their own.

In the Manichaean universe of *Anti-Oedipus*, desire is the hero and Oedipus the villain:

> The great discovery of psychoanalysis was that of the production of desire, of the productions of the unconscious. But once Oedipus entered the picture, this discovery was soon buried beneath a new brand of idealism: a classical theater was substituted for the unconscious as a factory. [Deleuze & Guattari, 1983, p. 24]

Extolling the promiscuous productivity of the primary process, Deleuze and Guattari object to what they see as the repressive structuring of this process by way of the oedipal triangle, which seems to privatize desire, constraining it within nuclear family dynamics. Like Hocquenghem, they view the anthropomorphization of desire—thinking of desire in terms of persons—as hermeneutically erroneous and ideologically repressive, since, as they point out,

> [t]he unconscious is totally unaware of persons as such. Partial objects are not representations of parental figures or of the basic patterns of family relations; they are parts of desiring-machines, having to do with a process and with relations of production that are both irreducible and prior to anything that may be made to conform to the Oedipal figure. [*ibid.*, p. 46]

Thus, like Hocquenghem, Deleuze and Guattari aim to depersonify desire. And apart from the vocabulary of desiring-machines, their contentions in this matter seem to me wholly compatible with

Lacan's theory of desire as unconscious and originating in the object *a*, which is itself "both irreducible and prior to anything that may be made to conform to the Oedipal figure".

However, the problem with Deleuze and Guattari's account appears as soon as they propose liberating desire—conceptually and in reality. Not only do they wish to unleash primary process productivity directly on to the world, without any mediation or regulation whatsoever, but, in their utopianist valorization of schizophrenia, they render social and psychic processes both transparent and naively beneficent:

> We maintain that the social field is immediately invested by desire, that it is the historically determined product of desire, and that libido has no need of any mediation or sublimation, any psychic operation, any transformation, in order to invade and invest the productive forces and the relations of production. *There is only desire and the social, and nothing else.* [Deleuze & Guattari, 1983, p. 29, original italics]

It is claims such as these that prompted the leading historian of French psychoanalysis to characterize *Anti-Oedipus* as a work "whose principal theses are astonishing in their simple-mindedness" (Roudinesco, 1990, p. 495);[20] such claims also have discouraged many other psychoanalytically orientated intellectuals, including me, from seriously engaging this work. Yet, as Elisabeth Roudinesco recognized and, more recently, Jerry Aline Flieger (1997) elaborated, the significance of *Anti-Oedipus* lies less in its simpleminded polemic than in how that polemic effectively resuscitates the vitality of what it attacks. Following Flieger, we may read Deleuze and Guattari against themselves, emphasizing not their direct critique of Freudo–Lacanian theory, but rather their indirect revivification of its most radical insights at a time when those insights were ossifying into orthodoxy.[21]

The repressive hypothesis redux

Deleuze and Guattari make their critique of Lacan's theory of desire explicit with the declaration that "[t]he three errors concerning desire are called lack, law, and signifier" (Deleuze & Guattari, 1983,

p. 111).[22] With respect to Lacan's doctrine of the signifier, we have observed already how Deleuze and Guattari's desire *for* desire permits no room for mediation, allowing no symbolic intervention between desire and the social other than that of repression, which they view as an unnecessary evil: "representation is always a social and psychic repression of desiring-production" (Deleuze & Guattari, 1983, p. 184). Thus, whereas Lacan conceptualizes the imaginary and the symbolic as heterogenous modes of mediating the real, Deleuze and Guattari substitute for these modes of mediation their idea of the machine, which, defined "as a system of interruptions or breaks (*coupures*)" and operating in tripartite mode, serves in displaced form many of the mediating functions performed by the Lacanian symbolic (*ibid.*, pp. 36–41).

Nevertheless, Deleuze and Guattari resist the idea of a symbolic order, since it is through this concept that Lacan rethinks the Oedipus complex. In order to distance their notion of mechanistic interruption from that of symbolic mediation, Deleuze and Guattari insist that "[t]he desiring-machine is not a metaphor" (*ibid.*, p. 41). Thus, although some critics find their critique of representation fruitful for analysing cultural production, Deleuze and Guattari's rejection of representation as inherently repressive pushes them towards accepting the repressive hypothesis and endorsing liberationist psychoanalytic theories, such as those of Wilhelm Reich and Herbert Marcuse, which seem so naïvely implausible in the wake of Foucault's critique of the repressive hypothesis.[24]

But doesn't this outmoded idea that desire resists norms comport with my claims on behalf of both queer theory and Lacan? I've pointed out that Lacan's category of the real designates that which resists adaptation and remains definitively recalcitrant, and by way of Freud's account of the diphasic emergence of human sexuality, I've suggested that, though the real has no predetermined content, Lacan associates it with the traumatic, unassimilable dimension of sex. I've also suggested that queer theory has something to gain from the psychoanalytic alignment of sex with the unconscious, since this makes sexuality refractive, maladaptive, and therefore always to some extent perverse. In this respect, queer theory is right to claim that perverse sexuality is inherently subversive. And when Warner asks rhetorically, "Can we not hear in the resonances of queer protest an objection to the normalization of behavior in this broad sense, and thus to the cultural phenomenon of societalization?", we now can hear resonances with Deleuze and Guattari's valorization of the schizophrenic, who has indeed effectively resisted "societalization" and stands outside all social norms. But given this conception of the oppositional relation between desire and social norms, we must confront the objection that my theses articulating queer theory with Lacan simply restate the repressive hypothesis.

First, however, Freud's situating perversion as internal, rather than opposed, to the normal requires us to rethink the relation between desire and norms. From a psychoanalytic perspective, the queer is not opposed to the normal, but fissures it from within. Thinking of the relation between normal and queer in this way can be sustained only if we retain a distinction between homosexuality as an orientation or identity, on the one hand, and queerness or perversion on the other. Perversion is always relational, an internal division akin to that of the unconscious, rather than being substantive or an external oppositional force. As soon as perversion or queerness becomes ontologized as an identity—whether in the form of "the queer body" invoked by some queer theorists or the figure of "the pervert" invoked by some Lacanians—perversion loses its disruptive potential.[25] And so the definite article that apotropaically unifies perversion into an identity—*the* pervert— should always be barred. If one takes seriously the idea of a subject split by the unconscious, then no structure of desire provides the basis for an identity. *The* pervert does not exist, except as an ideological construction, an imaginary misrecognition that, in the form of queer identities, lesbians and gays appear almost as ready to make as do psychoanalysts.

We escape the framework of the repressive hypothesis when our understanding of desire treats perversion or queerness as relational rather than substantive, a move that Deleuze and Guattari seem unable to make in so far as their account contains too few conceptual elements to formulate relations in this way. By committing themselves to the axiom that "[t]here is only desire and the social, and nothing else", Deleuze and Guattari foreclose categories of mediation that remain necessary if we are to theorize the relation between desire and the social in terms more nuanced than those of repression or liberation. Beyond even an idea of the symbolic order, their model requires some account of the specific mediating function performed by fantasy. But, like Foucault, they eschew a theory of fantasy in favour of concepts denoting that which seems more concrete, literal, and *real* in a positivist sense.

Not only does fantasy fulfil a crucial mediating function, thereby permitting us to complicate the relation between desire and the social, but it does so by keeping perversion alive and in play. Thus, in my view, queer theory cannot afford to accept Foucault's—or Deleuze and Guattari's—dismissal of fantasy as a ruse of idealism. For me the significance of Lacan's inverting his formula for fantasy ($ ◊ a$) to make the formula for perversion ($a ◊ $$) lies in its maintaining fantasy as always potentially perverse, while also guaranteeing perversion a mobility that defers its solidification into an identity (*the* pervert). Hence the full significance of the ◊ sign (*poinçon*—stamp, punch, or lozenge) that links $ and a, and which Lacan says "is created to allow a hundred and one different readings, a multiplicity that is admissible as long as the spoken remains caught in its algebra" (Lacan, 1977b, p. 313). This ◊ sign indicates a set of possible relations between the subject of the unconscious and its object, a veritable repertoire of relationality. To appreciate how this works, we need to clarify the ambiguous status of the object (a), which, designating neither a person nor a thing, occupies a distinctly multivalent position in Lacan's theory of sexuality.

The ideology of lack

Deleuze and Guattari approach a radical conception of the object by repudiating the notion of lack, perhaps the most significant aspect of their critique of psychoanalysis. "Desire does not lack anything", they maintain (Deleuze & Guattari, 1983, p. 26), whereas Lacan insists just the opposite: that "[d]esire is a relation of being to lack" (Lacan, 1988, p. 223). Antithetical though these claims appear, the direction in which they're subsequently elaborated brings Deleuze and Guattari surprisingly close to the Lacanian position: "Desire does not lack anything; it does not lack its object. It is, rather, the *subject* that is missing in desire, or desire that lacks a fixed subject; there is no fixed subject unless there is repression" (*ibid.*, p. 26). Here Deleuze and Guattari displace lack from the object to the subject, who thus is decentred by desire. See how similar this original decentring of the subject by desire sounds to Lacan's version of the matter:

> Desire is a relation of being to lack. This lack is the lack of being properly speaking. It isn't the lack of this or that, but lack of being whereby the being exists. ... The libido, but now no longer as used theoretically as a quantitative quantity, is the name of what animates the deep-seated conflict at the heart of human action. [Lacan, 1988, p. 223]

For Lacan, as for Deleuze and Guattari, the decentring effect of desire is so fundamental that desire cannot be conceived as following from the loss of any particular object. On the contrary, in this conception of desire what is lost is the fixed, self-identical subject.

Despite the possibility of this dialectical movement, which enables us to discern a deeper compatibility beyond apparent incompatibility, the question of conceptualizing desire in terms of lack remains a stubborn problem, not only for Deleuze and Guattari (and Hocquenghem, too), but also more generally for feminism and queer theory. Although the idea that one desires what he or she lacks may be traced back to Plato's *Symposium*, its development in psychoanalysis is especially objectionable to feminists and queer theorists, in part because psychoanalysis tends to explain lack (and hence desire) in terms of castration. Furthermore, institutionalized psychoanalysis exhibits such a poor record of pathologizing homosexuality as lacking, deficient, and developmentally retarded that it is hardly surprising queer theorists consider the very notion of lack to be ideologically suspect. Since the idea of lack has ultimately theological origins (in which it conveys Man's insufficiency in relation to God), we can appreciate queer theorists' scepticism concerning a concept with the potential to resurrect ancient prejudices about same-sex desire as not simply a sin but one of the most abominable. As Dollimore puts it, "[d]esire implies lack, hence imperfection. To be eternal and hence non-mutable is also to be free of desire" (Dollimore, 1998, p. 81).

The crucial issues here concern which master-term—"lack", "loss", "castration", "death", "sexual difference", and so on—we employ to theorize desire; whether that master-term carries positive or negative connotations; and how those connotations imply invidious distinctions or otherwise embed normative ideologies of gender and sexuality. Although, as Dollimore suggests, it is hard to conceive desire in other than negative terms, the alternative view, which queer theory has found more congenial, involves situating desire in relation to *excess* rather than lack. In the paradigm that Deleuze and Guattari develop from the Spinozist tradition that runs through Nietzsche to Bataille, desire is a matter of production rather than of reproduction, consumption, or exchange; and desiring production operates within a calculus of abundance rather than scarcity, multiplicity rather than singularity. Hence their early definition: "Desire is the set of *passive syntheses* that engineer partial objects, flows, and bodies, and that function as units of production" (Deleuze & Guattari, 1983, p. 26). And it is on this basis that, as we have seen, Hocquenghem maintains that "[d]esire emerges in a multiple form, whose components are only divisible *a posteriori*, according to how we manipulate it" (Hocquenghem, 1993, p. 49).

It is by mapping desire in relation to excess rather than lack (or abundance rather than scarcity) that we reach an understanding of desire as multiple—an understanding that makes desire essentially pluralistic, with all the inclusive implications of pluralism. Conceiving desire in terms of multiplicity enables us to avoid the problem of castration as an explanatory framework, since castration seems to imply a single, univocal model of desire, one that threatens to return us to the binary categories of complementarity and homogeneity so inhospitable to non-normative sexualities. It is for reasons approximating these that even queer theorists who remain unpersuaded by Deleuze and Guattari none the less reject the concepts of castration and lack central to Lacan's theory of desire—or at least the version of Lacan with which we're most familiar.[26]

But, in fact, it isn't hard to demonstrate how Lacan's account of desire depends on a notion of excess that also gives rise to an understanding of desire as multiple and thus in some sense pluralistic. From the very beginning of his return to Freud, Lacan theorizes the unconscious in terms of excess—an excess of meaning:

> The discovery of the unconscious, such as it appears at the moment of its historical emergence, with its own dimension, is that the full significance of meaning far surpasses the signs manipulated by the individual. Man is always cultivating a great many more signs than

he thinks. That's what the Freudian discovery is about—a new attitude to man. That's what man after Freud is. [Lacan, 1988, p. 122]

The new perspective on humanity inaugurated by the discovery or invention of the unconscious involves a sense of loss, but this loss is a consequence of excess—that is, a loss of mastery that stems from an excess of signification. Thus, the paradox whereby excess is not so much the alternative to lack as its precondition entails a more specific problem: that the boon of linguistic subjectivity comes at the cost of subjective unity. This excess of meaning called the unconscious generates desire as a multiplicity of possible connections, metonymic links between signifiers that engender subjectivity. Another way of putting this is to point out how linguistic duplicity—the very possibility that language can deceive—produces the perpetual illusion of a secret located beyond language, and it is this enigma that elicits desire. Hence, for Lacan, the subject and desire come into being at the same moment; and he names this constitutive division that founds the subject "object *a*," a term intended to designate the remainder or *excess* that keeps self-identity forever out of reach, thus maintaining desire.

Lacan commonly refers to object *a* as "cause of desire" in order to emphasize that this object is what brings desire into existence. Although the concept of object *a* emerges in his work fairly early, it does not come into its own until the 1960s, the period conventionally designated "late Lacan", which still remains comparatively unfamiliar in cultural studies, feminist theory, and queer theory. As I argued throughout *Beyond Sexuality* (Dean, 2000), the logic of this concept, object *a*, demotes or relativizes that of the phallus: whereas the phallus implies a univocal model of desire (in so far as all desiring positions are mapped in relation to a singular term), object *a* implies multiple, heterogenous possibilities for desire, especially since object *a* bears no discernible relation to gender. Indeed, Deleuze and Guattari acknowledge this crucial distinction within Lacan's account of desire:

Lacan's admirable theory of desire appears to us to have two poles: one related to "the object small *a*" as a desiring-machine, which defines desire in terms of a real production, thus going beyond both any idea of need and any idea of fantasy; and the other related to the "great Other" as a signifier, which reintroduces a certain notion of lack. [Deleuze & Guattari, 1983, p. 27n.]

However, Deleuze and Guattari decline to acknowledge that this "notion of lack" introduced by the excess of signification is nothing other than object *a*! And it is hardly the case that the concept of object *a* invalidates "any idea of fantasy", since Lacan's formula for fantasy ($ ◊ a$) describes precisely the subject's multiple relations to object *a*, which itself takes multiple forms.

Object *a* takes multiple forms as a consequence of the drive's partiality; it represents the concept through which Lacan develops Karl Abraham's notion of the partial object, as well as Winnicott's notion of the transitional object. However, by object *a* Lacan designates something different than what object-relations theorists mean by *the object*, as this critical remark suggests: "any theorisation of analysis organised around the object relation amounts in the end to advocating the recomposition of the subject's imaginary world according to the norms of the analyst's ego" (Lacan, 1988, p. 254)—a criticism implying not only that psychoanalysis shouldn't concern itself primarily with the patient's object-relations (for example, by attempting to modify the patient's sexual orientation), but also that this antinormative conception of analysis depends on a different conception of the object.

In Lacan's theory the object results from an excess of signification that Freud calls the unconscious; more specifically, it is the effect of this excess on the human body that brings desire into being. In his *Three Essays*, Freud describes this phenomenon in terms of polymorphous perversity, emphasizing the infant's capacity for autoerotic pleasure in any number of bodily openings, surfaces, and activities. As is well known, Freud designates these multiple corporeal apertures and surfaces *erogenous zones*, and this inspires Lacan's account of object *a*:

> The very delimitation of the "erogenous zone" that the drive isolates from the metabolism of the function (the act of devouring concerns other organs than the mouth—ask one of Pavlov's dogs) is the result of a cut (*coupure*) expressed in the anatomical mark (*trait*) of a margin or border—lips, "the enclosure of the teeth", the rim of the anus, the tip of the penis, the vagina, the slit formed by the eyelids, even the horn-shaped aperture of the ear.... Observe

that this mark of the cut is no less obviously present in the object described by analytic theory: the mamilla, faeces, the phallus (imaginary object), the urinary flow. (An unthinkable list, if one adds, as I do, the phoneme, the gaze, the voice—the nothing.) [Lacan, 1977b, pp. 314–315]

Erogenous zones—which are always multiple, never singular—come into being as soon as sexuality is separated from organic functions, that is, in the reflexive moment of autoeroticism. Lacan describes this process as "the result of a cut" that occurs at any number of bodily borders. Not only is "this mark of the cut" (which creates objects *a*), multiplied throughout the body, but it is *my own body* on which the symbolic order makes these incisions. Thus, for Lacan, as for Freud, sexual desire originates in autoeroticism.

In arguing thus, I find myself parting company with Lacanian analyst Bruce Fink, who claims that:

> According to Freud, a young boy's masturbatory behavior generally involves fantasies about the boy's mother, which implies that it is already alloerotic—in other words, that it involves another person. I would even go so far as to claim that, beyond an extremely tender age, *there is no such thing as autoeroticism*. Even an infant's masturbatory touching already includes its parents, insofar as they first stimulated certain zones, showed interest in them, paid attention to them, lavished care on them, and so on. The connection to other people—which is evident in the adult's fantasies that invariably accompany "autoerotic behavior"—is so fundamental that there seems to be no *eroticism*, as such, without it. All eroticism is alloeroticism. [Fink, 1997, p. 269n.21; original italics]

This strikes me as a surprisingly commonsensical—that is to say, un-Lacanian—way of thinking about eroticism. While I agree with Fink that there can be no desire (and therefore no eroticism) without the Other, I remain convinced by the Freudian logic that views human sexuality as emerging in the reflexive turning away from functional activities—feeding and suchlike—that involve other people, and the turning around upon itself of the drive, in the direction of fantasy. It is this double movement that Freud designates as autoeroticism. The specificity of Freud's theory, as he develops it in his *Three Essays*, lies in the idea that sexuality originates in this movement that *breaks* the connection to other people rather than establishing connection.

The significance of this logic for our purposes lies in the implication that desire emerges independently of heterosexuality or homosexuality; and hence the gendering involved in "object-choice" must be a secondary process performed on objects that precede gender—as Lacan's example of "the horn-shaped aperture of the ear" clearly demonstrates. This secondary process, which organizes and thus totalizes objects *a* into a gendered object-choice, shows how personification functions as a strategy of normalization. We might even say that the psychoanalytic notion of object-choice is itself a heterosexist invention, one that runs counter to psychoanalysis's own logic of unconscious desire. If within Freudian metapsychology the notion of object-choice could be understood as a sort of conceptual compromise formation, then Lacan's reconception of the object dismantles that compromise and undoes along with it the normalizing implications of gendered object-choice.

Sexuality versus genitality

Perhaps in homage to Augustine's belief that immaculate conception occurred *per auris*, Lacan's example of "the horn-shaped aperture of the ear" points to the double dimension—tactile and auditory—through which the ear becomes an erogenous zone. This example thus indicates especially cogently the function of fantasy in dispersing erotogenicity throughout the body. The ear can become eroticized not merely because its epidermis is sensitive to tactile stimulation, but because sound elicits our desire too. Thus, although the ear is unequivocally distinct from the genital organs—and, unlike the mouth, it rarely if ever approaches direct contact with them—it remains no less erotogenic for all that.

This disposition to erotogenicity may be read in two ways. On the one hand, it suggests that by means of fantasy "any other part of the body can acquire the same susceptibility to stimulation as is possessed by the genitals and can become an erotogenic zone"; in such instances, declares Freud, the parts of the body thus affected "behave exactly like genitals" (Freud, 1905d, pp. 183–184). There is something surreal in this idea that non-genital parts of the body can behave *exactly* like genital organs—as in those pornographic cartoons by Bill Schmeling, a gay artist known as "The Hun," in which the men's nipples are so distended that they become miniature penises. This way of reading the disposition to erotogenicity takes genitalia as the model for which other organs may become hallucinatory analogues.

However, by the third edition of his *Three Essays on the Theory of Sexuality*, Freud's account of this phenomenon has shifted subtly, and he notes that "[a]fter further reflection and after taking other observations into account, I have been led to ascribe the quality of erotogenicity to all parts of the body and to all the internal organs" (Freud, 1905d, p. 184n.1). Part of what has shifted is Freud's distinction between genitality and sexuality; by 1915 the genitals have forfeited their priority as the model for other erogenous zones. From being roughly synonymous in 1905, *genitality* becomes merely a subset of *sexuality* by 1915, so that although the genital is almost always sexual, what Freud means by "sexual" remains fundamentally irreducible to genitality. For example, in an emendation to the third edition of his *Three Essays*, Freud substitutes the word "genital" for "sexual," thereby registering a sharper distinction between the two (*ibid.*, p. 192). And in thus decisively distinguishing sexuality from genitality, Freud also separates sexuality from gender. This irreducibility of sexuality to genitality is one way of describing the mobility of desire, a mobility that makes sexuality all the more difficult to localize. It is, in so far as it remains unlocalizable, that Lacan explains sexuality in terms of the real. This is worth considering because without localization any disciplinary project is doomed to failure—a fact that should make this psychoanalytic account of sexuality attractive to antinormative politics.

Furthermore, Freud's deprivileging of genitality, which follows from his emphasis on the polymorphous perversity of human sexuality, is clearly useful for queer theory's effort to think about desire outside the terms of heterosexuality. We find a similar deprivileging of genitality in Lacan, who comments that

> [t]hese erogenous zones that, until one has achieved a fuller elucidation of Freud's thought, one can consider to be generic, and that are limited to a number of special points, to points that are openings, to a limited number of mouths at the body's surface, are the points where Eros will have to find his source. [Freud, 1905d, p. 93]

Describing erogenous zones as "generic"—that is, as multiple members of a single class—Lacan specifies their genre through the figure of the mouth. Rather than figuring the mouth as a displaced or secondary analogue for more primary orifices or organs—as, for example, Freud does with Dora—Lacan reverses this priority, thereby eliminating any potential gender bias with his implication that genital orifices represent displaced or secondary analogues for the mouth.

This surreal image of multiple mouths at the body's surface is highly resonant. Lacan takes the mouth as his model for erogenous zones owing to the mouth's multi-valence as a site of entry and exit: it is not only food that traverses this border (and not only other parts of the body), but also less tangible objects—words, breath, voice. Thus, in the first instance, the mouth is a model for erogenous zones because it's the most obvious corporeal point at which inside meets outside (and, of course, life itself depends on the continuousness of this meeting and exchange). But, in the second instance, the mouth is Lacan's model for erogenous zones because it's an organ of speech; and desire involves language as well as the body. Or, to be more precise, desire involves symbolic—as well as material and corporeal—phenomena. Thus, although food mainly goes into the mouth and words mainly come out of it, in fact nothing that crosses this border is restricted to unidirectional movement. By following the same trajectory, intangible objects are liable to become confused with tangible ones, to be fantasized as nourishing, poisonous, or otherwise physically stimulating to the body in the way that tangible objects are. This explains why words become libidinally invested and vocalization itself can be eroticized (see Salecl & Žižek, 1996).

But if the mouth remains the most obvious corporeal zone where inside meets outside—where, that is, something within the body is relinquished to the world outside—it is certainly not the only one. Lacan suggests that from a psychoanalytic viewpoint the body is covered in mouths. And though he refers to "a *limited number* of mouths", his catalogue of bodily borders characterized by a "mark of the cut" points to their multiplicity. What if we were to extend this metaphor of mouths to include all those bodily openings where inside meets outside? If, following Lacan's figure, we may think of the anus as a mouth, why not even smaller holes in the body? Why not think of the pores in our skin—which also breathe, absorb, and excrete—as mouths?

Deleuze and Guattari suggest this interpretive possibility in their sequel to *Anti-Oedipus*, in a discussion of the Wolf Man, where they characterize Freud as asserting, in effect, that "it would never occur to a neurotic to grasp the skin erotically as a multiplicity of pores, little spots, little scars or black holes"; but "[t]he psychotic can" (Deleuze & Guattari, 1987, p. 27).[27] Deleuze and Guattari's criticisms notwithstanding, Freud does in fact come very close to conceptualizing integument in this way when he moves from thinking of the genitals as his model for erogenous zones to thinking about skin as the model: "We have already discovered in examining the erotogenic zones that these regions of the skin merely show a special intensification of a kind of susceptibility to stimulus which is possessed in a certain degree by the whole cutaneous surface" (Freud, 1905d, p. 201). Here Freud is struggling to maintain a primarily physiological account of erotogenicity. Yet his inclusion of "all the internal organs" in the repertoire of potential erogenous zones suggests that it is less a susceptibility to physical stimulus that is the key to erotogenicity than it is a susceptibility to fantasmatic investment.

On this question, Deleuze and Guattari's critique of Freud for constantly subordinating multiplicity to unity carries some merit, in that Freud pursues his insight concerning libidinal investments of the skin in terms not of the proliferating possibilities of multiple holes and surface zones, but of the total form of the ego as a libidinal object: "The ego is first and foremost a bodily ego; it is not merely a surface entity, but is itself the projection of a surface" (Freud, 1923b, p. 26). In thus functioning as the surface by means of which the ego is projected, the skin loses its permeability, its porosity, and thence its potential for multiplicity. This is Freud's *imaginary* account of the skin.[28] By contrast, Lacan's account of fantasy shows how the surface of the body is subject to *symbolic* operations too. It is language's effect on the body that gives rise to fantasy and, in the process, decomposes imaginary unities into fragments (*a*), thereby multiplying desire's possibilities. The possibilities for desire proliferate only when one detotalizes the bodily form on which the ego depends. Thus, like the politics advocated here, fantasy involves a strategy of de-ego-ization or impersonalization that needn't entail chaos or schizophrenic fragmentation, since it follows a certain logic.

The queer logic of fantasy

> Tell me where is fancy bred?
> Or in the heart, or in the head?
> How begot, how nourished?
> (Shakespeare, *The Merchant of Venice*,
> Act 3, scene ii, lines 63–65. ["Fancy"
> abbreviates "fantasy"])

In speaking of a *logic* of fantasy, I am alluding to one of Lacan's unpublished seminars (Lacan, 1965–1966) and, more specifically, to the paradox whereby fantasy isn't opposed to the rational and the logical, as it was customarily denigrated as being, but can be shown to have an order and rationality all its own. Long before Freud made it into a psychoanalytic concept, fantasy played a central role in aesthetic theory, in which it was often (though not always) treated as interchangeable with the category of imagination. I mention this elementary fact of intellectual history because Freud inherited from nineteenth-century German idealism a distinction between fantasy and imagination that pertains to my argument here. This distinction concerns the superior synthesizing power that Kant (and Coleridge after him) attributes to the imagination (*die Einbildungskraft*) in contrast to fantasy (*die Phantasie*).[29] Describing imagination as "an active faculty of synthesis", in his *Critique of Pure Reason*, Kant extends this account of imagination's power in *Critique of Judgment*, arguing that aesthetic imagination is unfettered by "the laws of association" that govern cognition, since imagination follows a higher law or logic of its own (see Wodehouse, 1974, pp. 370–377, esp. 374).

The two main points I wish to extract from the myriad scholastic discriminations involved in nineteenth-century aesthetic theory are these: first, that the basis on which philosophers, poets, and aestheticians subordinated fantasy to imagination (or vice versa) concerned a capacity for synthesis that Lacan describes in terms of the imaginary order; second, that no matter which faculty ended up privileged in these debates, it invariably was characterized as adhering to a logic or laws distinct from those of positivist science. These two points enable us to appreciate the full significance of Freud's reformulating the logic of fantasy in terms of the unconscious and his describing laws of substitution, association, and combination that he identified with the primary process. Indeed, these laws are both higher *and* lower than those of ordinary rationality, since the incessant productions of the primary process can seem akin to the faculty of divine creation that aestheticians associated with the primary imagination, whereas, on the other hand, some unconscious effects, such as repetition compulsion and uncanniness, appear positively demonic.

Let me make clear that Freud's theory of fantasy intervenes in longstanding philosophical debates not simply to redescribe the imagination in different terms, but, more substantially, to elaborate a new category or level of determination. Hence, to the distinction between artistic imagination and daydreaming on the one hand, and the distinction between diurnal reveries and nocturnal dreams on the other, Freud adds the dimension of unconscious fantasy, which is not so much opposed to everyday reality (in the mode of illusion) as it is meant to designate a new mode of reality—what he calls *psychical reality*. Given my contention that Lacan's category of the real may be read as a rewriting of some aspects of the Freudian unconscious, we can see how psychical reality may be aligned with the Lacanian real (as Slavoj Žižek often has noted). And given the heteronomous relation between the imaginary and the real, we can begin to grasp how the psychoanalytic understanding of fantasy radically distinguishes it from the imagination. Thus, if the imagination may be coordinated with the Lacanian imaginary as a synthesizing power, then fantasy must be coordinated with the Lacanian real as a disintegrating force, one that ultimately resists all efforts at assimilation and domestication.

However, this unruliness of fantasy is complicated by Freud's insight that psychical reality *mediates* our access to mundane reality, and therefore fantasy can never be separated completely from more material concerns. As Victor Burgin puts it,

> psychoanalysis deconstructs the positivist dichotomy in which fantasy is seen as an inconsequential addendum to "reality". It

reveals the supposedly marginal operations of fantasy to be constitutive of our identity, and to be at the centre of all our perceptions, beliefs and actions. [Burgin, 1992, p. 87]

In supplying this mediation, fantasy offers itself as an indispensable concept for discussing subjectivity and sociality together, without reducing one to the other. And owing to the psychoanalytic insistence on distinguishing the subject of fantasy ($) from the individual who may be characterized as having the fantasy, this concept justifies our speaking of social fantasy or national fantasy, since fantasy, no matter how private it may seem, is not a strictly individual phenomenon. Indeed, Deleuze and Guattari make exactly this point: "fantasy is never individual: it is *group fantasy*—as institutional analysis has successfully demonstrated" (Deleuze & Guattari, 1983, p. 30; original italics). My epistemological point here is that the idea of "social fantasy" isn't merely a metaphor or a result of viewing the collective analogically, as if it were an individual. Rather, the concept of fantasy describes how a dimension of sociality—the Other—inhabits the innermost, ostensibly private zone of the subject.[30]

Not only is the unruliness of fantasy complicated by its crucial mediating function, but it also must be qualified by fantasy's logic—an issue that returns us to the question of fantasy's relation to verbalization (which was raised earlier by Foucault), as well as to that of fantasy's connection with perversion. Freud's key text on the logic of fantasy is "A child is being beaten" his 1919 study of beating fantasies, which he subtitles "A contribution to the study of the origin of sexual perversions". As our consideration of perversion might have encouraged us to expect, Freud's labelling these beating fantasies "perverse" remains equivocal, since he readily concedes that they're so common as to qualify statistically as normal. Examining these fantasies, Freud observes something peculiar about them, namely, that the person having the fantasy is not immediately identifiable as either the child being beaten in the fantasy or the one doing the beating, and, moreover, that "there is no constant relation between the sex of the child producing the phantasy and that of the child being beaten" (Freud, 1919e, p. 185).

In the course of investigating these enigmas, Freud isolates three phases of the fantasy, each with its own distinct locution. The initial phase, which the subject is able to remember (though with some effort), runs: *My father is beating the child (whom I hate)*. However, the locution in which the fantasy is usually expressed goes: *A child is being beaten. (I am watching.)* Between these two phases Freud infers an intermediate one, which remains permanently inaccessible to the subject's consciousness and runs: *I am being beaten by my father*. This intermediate phase permits Freud to argue with respect to the version in which the fantasy is usually expressed—*A child is being beaten. I am watching*—that "only the *form* of this phantasy is sadistic; the satisfaction which is derived from it is masochistic" (*ibid.*, p. 191). Although in the fantasy as it is consciously expressed, the subject occupies merely the role of spectator, unconsciously he or she is in the position of the one being beaten. This shift from sadism to masochism is accomplished grammatically by the transformation from an active to a passive construction: in order for the subject of the fantasy to remain disguised in it, this fantasy must be expressed using the indefinite article and the passive voice—"A child is being beaten".

Freud's attention to the determining role of these grammatical transformations enables us to grasp that fantasy is not antithetical to verbalization, as Foucault claimed; on the contrary, the logic of fantasy *is* that of verbalization—that of the structure and effects of language. In their classic 1964 paper on fantasy, Laplanche and Pontalis reach a similar conclusion:

> In fantasy the subject does not pursue the object or its sign: he appears caught up himself in the sequence of images. . . . the subject, although always present in the fantasy, may be so in a desubjectivized form, that is to say, in the very *syntax* of the sequence in question. [Laplanche & Pontalis, 1986, p. 26, italics added]

From this reference to desubjectivization we may deduce that fantasy *impersonalizes* the subject, decomposing his or her ego in the *mise-en-scène* of desire. Thus, it is owing to the subject's mercurial positioning in a sequence of mutating terms that fantasy permits identifications across a number of socially regulated boundaries—between active and passive, masculine and feminine, gay and straight, black and white, perhaps even the boundary between the living and the dead. In so doing, fantasy undermines the distinctions such categories are intended to uphold, thereby disqualifying these social categories from providing the grounds for anything but *imaginary* identities.[31]

This notion of identification *across* is central to queer theory, since the word "queer" derives etymologically from the Indo-European root *-twerkw*, meaning "athwart" or "across" (see Butler & Martin, 1994, p. 3; Sedgwick, 1993). Although fantasy's potential for subjective mobility carries a broad range of political implications, it has tended to be construed in distinctly utopian terms, in part because fantasmatic identification furnishes an important *raison d'être* for sympathies and allegiances that otherwise might remain unaccountable on the basis of material interests. Hence, utopian fantasy remains indispensable for queer theory's identificatory alliances and its effort to connect queerness with categories of social exclusion that aren't obviously grounded in sexuality. Indeed, it may be in queer theory and politics that the otherwise exhausted tradition of left utopianism finds its greatest vitality.

Furthermore, this celebrated potential for subjective mobility stems from fantasy's exploitation of component or partial drives—those that lend the child its polymorphous perversity—and therefore, according to Freud, this kind of unconscious fantasy must "be regarded as a primary trait of perversion" (Freud, 1919e, p. 181).[32] Lacan indicates the indissoluble link between fantasy and perversion not only by writing his formulae for these concepts as mirror images of each other ($\$ \Diamond a / a \Diamond \$$), but also by requiring the $\Diamond$ sign to figure the multiple transformations and hence subjective mobility that fantasy entails. This inseparability of fantasy and perversion suggests that queer theory's tendency to follow Foucault in dismissing the claims of fantasy in favour of variations in sexual practice is thoroughly misguided. Indeed, the rationale for characterizing fantasy's logic as queer stems from the terms of Lacan's formula ($\$ \Diamond a$), which insists that in fantasy the subject relates not to another subject, but to an "object" generated by the symbolic order's impact on one's own body. Thus this psychoanalytic account of fantasy reveals heterosexuality as utterly secondary to a more primary structure of relationality that remains stunningly oblivious to both persons and gender.

Yet fantasy's potential for subjective mobility is not unlimited. Laplanche and Pontalis's emphasis on the *syntax* of the fantasy sequence—which accords with Freud's on the grammatical transformations that fantasy entails—suggests that subjective mobility in fantasy is constrained by the logic and laws of language. It is to this constraint that Lacan is referring when he inverts Coleridge's hierarchy, in *Biographia Literaria*, and asserts polemically that

> any attempt to reduce [phantasy] to the imagination ... is a permanent misconception, a misconception from which the Kleinian school, which has certainly carried things very far in this field, is not free, largely because it has been incapable of even so much as suspecting the existence of the category of the signifier. [Lacan, 1977a, p. 272]

This distinction between fantasy and imagination clarifies how fantasy involves the imaginary order (the domain of images) only when the latter has been captured and fragmented by the nets of language: "once it is defined as an image set to work in the signifying structure, the notion of unconscious phantasy no longer presents any difficulty" (Lacan, *ibid.*). This sentence makes clear that Lacan's text coincides almost verbatim with Laplanche and Pontalis's later formulations concerning fantasy, as quoted above. Thus, what should be kept in mind, particularly in view of the tendency in cultural studies to discuss formations of fantasy in purely imaginary terms, is that fantasy involves all three orders—imaginary, symbolic, and real—together.

Nevertheless, the final term in Lacan's formula for fantasy, object *a*, does not belong unequivocally to any one of these three orders. In order to reach my concluding thesis, I'd like to look a little harder at the material object Lacan takes as his prototype for object *a*—the turd. Looking unblinkingly at a psychoanalytic theory of excrement offers the benefit of enabling us to gauge just how incidental to Lacan's account of fantasy, sexuality, and desire is the phallus. Perhaps surprisingly, such an examination will also permit us to say something more concerning the place of love in psychoanalytic theory, a topic that was raised by my chapter's opening quotation from *Encore*—"*quand on aime, il ne s'agit pas de sexe*"—but deferred until now.

The triumph of love

"Every love is an exercise in depersonalization"
(Deleuze & Guattari, 1987, p. 35)

In a formulation rebarbative even by his standards, Lacan locates his paradigm of object *a* in scat. Speaking of what happens to the human organism in the process of subjectification—when, that is, language impacts the body—he explains:

> It is important to grasp how the organism is taken up in the dialectic of the subject. The organ of what is incorporeal in the sexuated [*sexué*] being is that part of the organism the subject places when his separation occurs. . . . In this way, the object he naturally loses, excrement, and the props he finds in the Other's desire—the Other's gaze or voice—comes to this place. [Lacan, 1995, p. 276]

Here Lacan's model for subjective loss is not the phallus but faeces, an ungendered object. In the face of *this* object-cause of desire, the controversy over the concept of the phallus pales into insignificance, since whether or not we're all—men as well as women—missing the phallus, certainly we've all lost objects from the anus. And this distinction remains universally true—irrespective of gender, race, class, nation, culture, or history—in that although we never may be completely certain that nobody has the phallus, we can be sure everybody has an anus. Castration isn't Lacan's only rubric for loss. Or, to put it slightly differently, *phallus* isn't his only term for describing what's lost in symbolic castration. Indeed, as Žižek points out, object *a* is in the first instance the anal object (Žižek, 1994, p. 179).[33] The explanatory virtue of turds over the phallus lies not only in the fact that everybody loses them, but also in the fact that their loss is repeated: it's because loss from this part of the body is multiplied over and over that faeces so aptly figure objects *a*. Now this formulation confronts us with the disturbing implication that in fantasy ($ ◊ *a*) we find the subject relating to its shit. Although in one sense this is true, we also must bear in mind that the Lacanian object isn't, in fact, a material object; instead it designates an absence or loss for which material objects function as both the prototype and the imaginary fulfilment.

When Lacan refers to gaze and voice as "the props [the subject] finds in the Other's desire", he implies that anality cannot be considered a presymbolic "stage", because the Other is already present—a point that Freud clarifies by emphasizing the child's use of bowel movements to communicate with its caretakers. In his discussion of anal eroticism, Freud elaborates on this notion of shit as signifier by comparing the anal zone to the mouth, which "is well suited by its position to act as a medium through which sexuality may attach itself to other somatic functions" (Freud, 1905d, p. 185). If Freud considers mouth and anus as analogous or in some sense interchangeable, then Lacan's image for the erogenous zones could be reformulated yet more surreally to suggest that the body exhibits a number of assholes at its surface.

Furthermore, in some highly evocative sentences added to the third edition of his *Three Essays*, Freud makes clear exactly why faeces as object *a* take explanatory priority over the phallus:

> The contents of the bowels, which act as a stimulating mass upon a sexually sensitive portion of mucous membrane, behave like forerunners of another organ, which is destined to come into action after the phase of childhood. But they have other important meanings for the infant. They are clearly treated as a part of the infant's own body and represent his first "gift": by producing them he can express his active compliance with his environment and, by withholding them, his disobedience.... The retention of the faecal mass ... is thus carried out intentionally by the child to begin with, in order to serve, as it were, as a masturbatory stimulus upon the anal zone or to be employed in his relation to the people looking after him. [*ibid.*, pp. 186–187]

To transpose Freudian into Lacanian terms, we can say that by using faeces as both a sexual stimulus and a means of communication the child's relation to shit involves *l'objet petit a* and *le grand Autre*—that is, anality entails both "big" and "little" others, the different modes of alterity that constitute the subject and his or her desire. But let us be more explicit about what Freud is saying here. His initial claim is that faeces, by sexually stimulating the anus, act like "another organ"—presumably the penis. From this we may deduce that the phallus is less a figure for the penis than, more fundamentally, a figure for the turd. Lacanians have been remarkably reticent about this ineluctable implication, perhaps because a theory of sexuality organized around faeces appears even more questionable than one centred on the phallus. Nevertheless, it is to this point that the logic of Lacan's concept of object *a* has brought us.

Perhaps it takes a gay man to observe that the phallus is simply a turd in disguise; though Freud points out that Lou Andreas-Salomé inferred this connection in her paper on anal sexuality (1916), where she argues that "the history of the first prohibition which a child comes across—the prohibition against getting pleasure from anal activity and its products—has a decisive effect on his whole development" (Freud, 1905d, p. 187n.). In this perspective, symbolic prohibition begins with anal sexuality and a form of pleasure easily confused with genital pleasure, since as Freud remarks elsewhere, "The excremental is all too intimately and inseparably bound up with the sexual; the position of the genitals—*inter urinas et faeces*—remains the decisive and unchangeable factor" (Freud, 1912d, p. 189). Having alluded to Augustine (who remarked that we are born between urine and faeces), Freud immediately proceeds to quote Napoleon: "Anatomy is destiny". However, we should note that Freud isn't referring to sexual difference, as is usually supposed when this aphorism is hauled out as an objection to psychoanalysis, but rather to the inseparability of genital and anal that follows, in part, from their anatomical proximity.

Let me make clear that I'm claiming not that sexual difference is inconsequential to this account of sexuality, just that it is secondary. Desire emerges before sexual difference, through the anal object, and therefore there can be no *a priori* gendering of the object-cause of desire. Hence Hocquenghem's much misunderstood assertion that "to encounter desire is first of all to forget the difference in the sexes" and his correlative insistence on focusing on anal erotics. In my view Hocquenghem's *Homosexual Desire* is not so much a critique of Lacanian psychoanalysis (as many readers seem to think) as it is an elaboration of Lacan's most radical ideas in the wake of May 1968 and Stonewall 1969.

Yet this reassessment of Hocquenghem raises the question of why it hasn't been easier to articulate queer politics with psychoanalysis since 1972. Besides the institutional histories, the prejudice and exclusions, I can't help thinking that this failure of articulation may be explained in part by reference to the fact that excrement remains an extraordinarily difficult topic for sustained discourse: the anal object tests the limits of sexual tolerance far more stringently than mere homosexuality or other manifestations of queerness. Indeed, homosexuality's being branded "the love that dare not speak its name" must have been a consequence primarily of its association with anality. Even Freud, whose broad-mindedness still retains the capacity to astonish, deems perversion most unequivocally pathological when it involves sexual contact with shit:

> [I]n some of these perversions the quality of the new sexual aim is of a kind to demand special examination. Certain of them are so far removed from the normal in their content that we cannot avoid pronouncing them "pathological". This is especially so where (as, for instance, in cases of licking excrement or of intercourse with dead bodies) the sexual instinct goes to astonishing lengths in successfully overriding the resistances of shame, disgust, horror or pain. [Freud, 1905d, p. 161]

In the face of this scenario worthy of Sade, Freud makes a quite remarkable observation:

> It is impossible to deny that in their case a piece of mental work has been performed which, in spite of its horrifying result, is the equivalent of an idealization of the instinct. The omnipotence of love is perhaps never more strongly proved than in such of its aberrations as these. [*ibid.*]

According to Freud the triumph of love consists in fucking corpses and eating shit. Or, to put it another way, the triumph of love entails a kind of "mental work" that—by overriding shame, disgust, horror, or pain—could be identified as specifically queer, because this work consists in struggling against the affect-laden social norms regulating sexuality. Queer politics involves not only the negative effort to resist norms, but also the positive work of intense, almost superhuman loving.

By pointing to one extreme outcome of the discontinuity between sexual instinct and sexual object, Freud reminds us that originally the object of desire is not another person, much less a member of the opposite sex, but something rather more abject. Thinking of sexual object-choice in terms of persons entails a kind of sublimation, an idealizing consolidation of the object, rather than the idealization of the instinct manifested in Freud's examples of necrophilia and coprophagy. When we grasp the idea that erotic desire for another person itself depends on some sort of sublimation—rather than sublimation standing as the alternative to interpersonal desire, as is commonly supposed—then we can begin to appreciate just how strange, how distant from the normalizing perspective on love and sex, psychoanalytic theory really is. In its most fundamental formulations psychoanalysis is a queer theory.

Notes

1. This move to think sexuality outside the terms of gender may be traced to Gayle Rubin's pioneering work (Rubin, 1984), which argues that feminist theory remains insufficient for conceptualizing sexuality. For an illuminating meditation on Rubin's work, see her interview with Judith Butler (Butler, 1994). The move to think sexuality outside the terms of gender remains controversial. Biddy Martin, for example, discusses "the potential obfuscation of misogyny by antinormative stances" (Martin, 1994, p. 119); and Elizabeth Weed, whose argument is closer to my own, suggests how queer theory's displacing attention from sexual difference also involves neglecting psychoanalytic ways of thinking (Weed, 1994).
2. Although Foucault maintained an especially vexed relation to psychoanalysis, this misguided notion derives less from his work than from its Anglo-American reception. As with Freud, Foucault's transatlantic dissemination deformed his thought in a way that has consequences for the reception of other Continental thinkers, including Lacan. For an account of the complexities of Foucault's relation to psychoanalysis, see Derrida (1994). Although in this text Derrida focuses primarily on Foucault's *Madness and Civilization* and only secondarily on *The History of Sexuality*, much of his analysis can be extended to Foucault's treatment of Freud on the topic of homosexuality. Noting the resonance of Foucault's complete silence concerning Lacan (*ibid.*, p. 255, n.19), Derrida argues that "Foucault's project belongs too much to 'the age of psychoanalysis' in its possibility for [Foucault], when claiming to thematize psychoanalysis, to do anything other than let psychoanalysis continue to speak obliquely of itself" (*ibid.*, p. 263). The tensions that Derrida identifies in *Madness and Civilization* should encourage us—by

which I mean Lacanians *and* Foucaultians—to read Foucault more carefully.
3. On the most recent chapter of US anti-Freudianism, see Robinson (1993).
4. In his translation of *Encore*, Bruce Fink renders the passage in question thus:

> Last year I played on a slip of the pen I made in a letter addressed to a woman—*tu ne sauras jamais combien je t'ai aimé* ("you will never know how much I loved you")—*é* instead of *ée*. Since then, someone mentioned to me that that could mean that I am a homosexual. But what I articulated quite precisely last year is that when one loves, it has nothing to do with sex.

In this instance, translating *sexe* as *sex* is potentially misleading and so Fink adds this note:

> The past participle, *aimé*, is supposed to agree in gender with the sex of the person designated in the phrase by the direct object, *te* (here *t'*); if the person is male, the participle remains *aimé*, if female, an *e* should be added to the end: *aimée*. [Lacan, 1998, p. 25]

5. See, for example, the classic contributions collected in Stein (1992) and, more recently, Abramson & Pinkerton (1995). The canonical account of "the construction of homosexuality" is given by David Greenberg, in his book of that title (1988), and of heterosexuality in Katz (1995).
6. See especially LeVay (1993) and Hamer & Copeland (1994). With respect to the search for the gay gene, Guy Hocquenghem's comment virtually a quarter of a century earlier still holds good: "The chromosome theory [of homosexuality] appears to be less a biological 'discovery' than an ideological regression" (Hocquenghem, 1993, p. 76). More recently, LeVay (1996) has examined the history and consequences of scientific explanations of sexual orientation, including psychoanalytic ones. As with the overwhelming majority of lesbian and gay people, LeVay favours the conclusion that homosexuality is innate rather than acquired, essential rather than constructed. This conviction about sexual orientation's innateness can be deemed progressive in so far as it discourages a commitment to reorientation therapy, and, furthermore, it discredits the assumption, so common among conservatives, that homosexuals suffer from a febrile will or

poor moral fibre. In other words, the essentialist view of sexual orientation ostensibly makes homosexuality easier to accept—for both queers and straights. On the other hand, scientific evidence of sexual orientation's organic innateness also can support a virulently homophobic politics, in so far as genetic engineering and eugenics permit the fantasy of a world in which there would be no homosexuals whatsoever. From this we can see that what attracts both progressives and reactionaries—whether they're experts or laypersons—to scientific evidence concerning the biological innateness of sexual desire is its reassurance that sexuality confers *identity*. This kind of scientific evidence also calms any sense of subjective division, any nagging personal sense that I, too, could have unconscious conflict about sexual orientation.

7. On the emergence of queer theory and some ramifications of the term itself, see Lauretis (1991). Because the word *queer* is intended to be gender neutral, I hesitate to offer the customary caveat that I'm focusing here primarily on *either* gay men's *or* lesbians' sexuality. Yet, in thus hesitating to specify non-normative sexualities along gender lines, I want also to emphasize that queer women's and queer men's concerns aren't identical, symmetrical, or analogous—and therefore psychoanalysis should take greater care not to treat them as if they were.

8. This represents an enormous project, one that bears on the longstanding dispute between Foucault and Jürgen Habermas concerning the function of social norms and normativity. In her stringent critique of Butler's intervention in the feminist version of this debate, Amanda Anderson elaborates a helpful distinction between evaluative norms and normalizing norms. Evaluative norms, associated with the Habermasian position, provide necessary criteria for evaluating the rightness or wrongness of an action or practice. By contrast, normalizing norms, associated with the Foucaultian position, involve mechanisms of social reproduction and identity formation internal to hegemonic social structures (Anderson, 1998, p. 9). This distinction tends to get lost in queer theory's antinormativity and might also prove useful for assessing the role of psychoanalysis as a normalizing discourse or practice, since the reduction of all normativity to normalization—that is, viewing all evaluative criteria as fundamentally insidious—obscures and therefore naturalizes the operation of evaluative norms within queer theory and queer practices themselves.

9. For recent arguments on behalf of the desirability of lesbian and gay assimilation into the social mainstream, see Bawer (1993) and Sullivan (1995).

10. In what I take to be the most important work of queer theory to date, Leo Bersani provides a useful gloss on Foucault's comment:

    The intolerance of gayness, far from being the displaced expression of the anxieties that nourish misogyny, would be nothing more—by which of course Foucault meant nothing less—than a political anxiety about the subversive, revolutionary rearrangements that gays may be trying out. Indeed, in this scenario there may be no fantasies—in the psychoanalytic sense—on either side, and if there are, they are insignificant in understanding the threat of gayness. [Bersani, 1995, p. 78]

11. See Silverman (1996), for an original psychoanalytic argument on behalf of new political uses of the aesthetic that would enable different modes of idealization—specifically, less violent or exclusionary ways of seeing.
12. The most compelling demonstration of this distinction—that sex is of the order of the real rather than of the imaginary or symbolic—may be found in Joan Copjec's "Sex and the euthanasia of reason" (1994, pp. 201–236), which uses Kant's antinomies of reason to make this argument about sex and the real.
13. In thus characterizing the diphasic emergence of sexuality, I am summarizing Freud's *Three Essays on the Theory of Sexuality* and drawing on Laplanche's reading of Freud (Laplanche, 1976), and his subsequent development of ideas concerning generalized seduction and the enigmatic signifier (Laplanche, 1989). Whereas Lacan describes the traumatically premature emergence of sexuality in terms of the unsymbolizable real, Laplanche describes the same phenomenon in terms of the enigmatic signifier—an account he presents especially cogently in "The theory of seduction and the problem of the Other" (Laplanche, 1997). Although space prevents me from providing even a brief consideration of the relation between Laplanchian and Lacanian theory here, I would like to note the continuing importance of Laplanche's work for Anglophone theorists of non-normative sexuality, such as Leo Bersani, Jonathan Dollimore, John Fletcher, Teresa de Lauretis, and Mandy Merck. A thorough account of Laplanche's debt to Lacan might provide the key for understanding why these theorists find Laplanche so much more useful than they find Lacan.
14. In his contribution to an early psychoanalytic—and profoundly normalizing—symposium on perversion, Lacan offers perhaps the least homophobic account of perversion by avoiding the topic of

homosexuality altogether; (see Lacan & Granoff, 2003). For his account of Sadean perversion, see Lacan (1989).

15. See, for example, Clavreul (1980, pp. 215–233). Clavreul, who was Chair of Lacan's Department of Psychoanalysis at the University of Paris VIII (Vincennes), writes of perversion and homosexuality as if they were virtually synonymous, thus nullifying his own initial distinction between symptom and structure. He also asserts "[t]he danger that the pervert is always bordering on—I must repeat it—is psychosis" (*ibid.*, p. 225), which gives the lie to any tenable *structural* distinction between perversion and psychosis—and thus compromises Lacan's invalidation of "borderline" diagnoses. Clavreul's paper combines wonderful insights with the most blatant homophobia, recirculating stereotypes of gay men that one must credit to the period in which Clavreul concocted this mixture—the mid-1960s.

16. Dollimore's most recent work significantly develops his earlier book's discussion of perversion (Dollimore, 1998, pp. 138–140). There is an important distinction to be made between this sense of generalized perversion—what Jacques-Alain Miller calls "perversion for everyone" (Miller, 1996, p. 314)—and the more restricted clinical structure of perversion. Yet this distinction itself entails a host of conceptual and ideological problems.

17. Laplanche and Pontalis provide a number of useful distinctions concerning fixation (1973, pp. 162–165). Lacan also points to this notion of fixation in order to suggest a critique of the normalizing impulse in Freud's writing on sexuality:

> In *Three Essays on the Theory of Sexuality*, Freud uses two correlative terms concerning the effects of the individual libidinal adventure: *Fixierarbeit* is the fixation that is for us the register of explanation of that which is, in fact, inexplicable. . . . We are caught up in an adventure that has taken a certain direction, a certain contingency, certain stages. Freud didn't finish at a stroke the trail he blazed for us. And it may be that, on account of Freud's detours, we are attached to a certain moment in the development of his thought, without fully realizing its contingent character, like that of every effect of human history. . . . [L]et us remember that psychoanalysis might seem at first to be of an ethical order. It might seem to be the search for a natural ethics—and, my goodness, a certain siren song might well promote a misunderstanding of that kind. And indeed, through a whole side of its action and its doctrine, psychoanalysis effectively

presents itself as such, as tending to simplify some difficulty that is external in origin, that is of the order of a misrecognition or indeed of a misunderstanding, as tending to restore a normative balance with the world—something that the maturation of the instincts would naturally lead to. One sometimes sees such a gospel preached in the form of the genital relation that I have more than once referred to here with a great deal of reservation and even with a pronounced skepticism. [Lacan, 1992, p. 88]

It is in the light of these sentences that Jacques-Alain Miller's comments regarding lesbians and fixation should be read and severely qualified:

This perversion, this turning to the father [père-version], is nowhere more patent or explicit than in the case of female homosexuals, who constantly attest to an intense love for the father, legitimating the use of the Freudian term "fixation"—the paternal fixation of the female homosexual. [Miller, 1996, pp. 308]

Finally, with respect to the Freudian term translated as "fixation", I note that Laplanche and Pontalis give the German word *Fixierung* (1973, p. 162); the original text of Seminar VII gives *Fixierbarkeit* (Lacan, 1986, p. 106); and Dennis Porter's translation gives *Fixierarbeit* (as quoted above).

18. Here I must add that the fragility of normalization also accounts for the hostility many gay people express toward bisexuality—even though bisexuality conceives sexuality in terms of gender rather than beyond gender. On the normalizing implications of "biphobia", see Garber (1995).

19. Compare the French original:

La sexualisation du monde qu'annoncent les mouvements homosexuels correspond à la mise à la limite du décodage capitaliste, à la dissolution de l'humain; de ce point de vue les mouvements homosexuels disent et font brutalement la déhumanisation nécessaire. [Hocquenghem, 1972]

20. Nevertheless, Roudinesco approaches *Anti-Oedipus* in the right spirit:

If one restricts oneself to its theses, *Anti-Oedipe* is a work filled with crude formulations, errors, and gross oversights. But the book should not be reduced to its explicit content. For to do so would be to err on the subject of the book as much as a reader of

A la recherche du temp perdu who would want to transform the Proustian saga into a story of maternal kisses and rosewater. *Anti-Oedipe* is a great book, not through the ideas it conveys but through the form it bestows on them, through its style and tone: in brief, through that febrile syntax in which—with breath held and like a Rimbaldian drunken boat—the forgotten furor of a language of rupture and unreason comes to be couched. Published at a time when the impasse of the structuralist movement was becoming clear, *Anti-Oedipe* anarchically drew to itself all the hopes of an aborted revolution. At the same time, and because it effected a specifically French synthesis of all the ideals of liberation (from Freudo-Marxism to terrorism, and from the quest for a lost paradise to the cult of drugs), it took psychoanalytic conformism as its principal target, noisily designating the degeneration of Lacanianism into a dogma (Roudinesco, 1990, p. 496).

21. Flieger (1997) brilliantly uses Deleuze and Guattari's own theses to show how their work is far more oedipalist than their critique suggests, and that therefore their attack on psychoanalysis should be understood as a mode of disavowal. Flieger argues that, far from discrediting *Anti-Oedipus*, this negative *modus operandi* illuminates psychoanalytic theory in ways that should be of great interest to those who have hitherto dismissed Deleuze and Guattari from serious theoretical consideration. Here it is perhaps worth recalling that the first volume of their magnum opus appeared in 1972, coincident with Hocquenghem's *Homosexual Desire* and Lacan's seminar *Encore*, which, I'm suggesting, separates a theory of sexuality from the terms of both gender and personhood. And in view of the tendency to read *Anti-Oedipus* as an unequivocal denunciation of the Freudo–Lacanian tradition, it is also worth noting that Félix Guattari, who was gay, had been trained by Lacan and remained both a member of his École freudienne de Paris (EFP) and a practising analyst even after the publication of *Anti-Oedipus*. Hocquenghem, too, while composing *Homosexual Desire*, was teaching philosophy at Vincennes, practically next door to Lacan's Department of Psychoanalysis, and therefore effectively he was working in a Lacanian milieu.

22. Having enumerated these three fallacies, Deleuze and Guattari continue:

> It is one and the same error, an idealism that forms a pious conception of the unconscious. And it is futile to interpret these

notions in terms of a combinative apparatus (*une combinatoire*) that makes of lack an empty position and no longer a deprivation, that turns the law into a rule of the game and no longer a commandment, and the signifier into a distributor and no longer a meaning, for these notions cannot be prevented from dragging their theological cortege behind—insufficiency of being, guilt, signification. Structural interpretation challenges all beliefs, rises above all images, and from the realm of the mother and the father retains only functions, defines *the prohibition and the transgression* as structural operations. But what water will cleanse these concepts of their background, their previous existences—religiosity? Scientific knowledge as nonbelief is truly the last refuge of belief, and as Nietzsche put it, there never was but one psychology, that of the priest. [1983, p. 111; original italics]

23. Explaining that "every machine has a sort of code built into it," Deleuze and Guattari acknowledge that "[w]e owe to Jacques Lacan the discovery of this fertile domain of a code of the unconscious" (1983, p. 38).
24. See Foucault (1978). Flieger makes a similar point, noting that "Deleuze and Guattari adopt the repression hypothesis wholesale" (Flieger, 1997, p. 602). This is how their version of it goes:

> From the moment desire is welded again to the law—we needn't point out what is known since time began: that there is no desire without law—the eternal operation of eternal repression recommences, the operation that closes around the unconscious the circle of prohibition and transgression, white mass and black mass; but the sign of desire is never a sign of the law, it is a sign of strength (*puissance*). [Deleuze & Guattari, 1983, p. 111]

For an example of theoretical cultural criticism based on their critique of representation, see Shaviro (1993).

25. Simon Watney gets at this problem when, in a somewhat different context, he argues the following:

> the very notion of a "homosexual body" only exposes the more or less desperate ambition to confine mobile desire in the semblance of a stable object, calibrated by its sexual aim, regarded as a "wrong choice." The "homosexual body" would thus evidence a fictive collectivity of perverse sexual performances, denied any psychic reality and pushed out beyond the furthest margins of the social. This, after all, is what the category

of "the homosexual" (which we *cannot* continue to employ) was invented to do in the first place. [Watney, 1988, p. 79]

26. See, for example, Bersani (1995, p. 133): "A theory of homo-ness in desire ... will lead us to question the Proustian equation of desire with lack"; (see also pp. 149–151). See also Grosz (1995, pp. 175–180). And Miller (1991, p. 37): "homosexuality would be characterized not by a problematics of castration, but on the contrary by an exemption from one".
27. Thanks to Shannon McRae for drawing my attention to this passage.
28. This account has been developed most notably by Didier Anzieu (1989). In Anzieu's model, unlike Freud's, integument retains the crucial attribute of permeability, a distinction that enables Anzieu to draw suggestive comparisons between the skin and the mouth: "the third function [of the Skin Ego]—which the skin shares with the mouth and which it performs at least as often—is as a site and a primary means of communicating with others, of establishing signifying relations" (*ibid.*, p. 40).
29. Extra note. In Anglophone aesthetics, the canonical topos for these distinctions is *Biographia Literaria*, Chapter 13, in which Coleridge elevates imagination above fantasy and then subdivides imagination into primary and secondary forms:

> The primary IMAGINATION I hold to be the living Power and prime Agent of all human Perception, and as a repetition in the finite mind of the eternal act of creation in the infinite I AM. The secondary I consider as an echo of the former, co-existing with conscious will, yet still as identical with the primary in the *kind* of its agency, and differing only in *degree*, and in the *mode* of its operation. It dissolves, diffuses, dissipates, in order to re-create; or where this process is rendered impossible, yet still at all events it struggles to idealize and to unify. [Coleridge, 1983, p. 304]

30. For exemplary critical studies that exploit these implications of the psychoanalytic concept of fantasy, see Berlant (1991); Salecl (1994); Santner (1996); Rose (1996), and the work of Slavoj Žižek.
31. This idea has generated some very insightful work in cultural studies, one particularly fascinating example of which is Constance Penley's study of Kirk/Spock "slash" fandom, a subcultural phenomenon in which the two male leads from *Star Trek* are figured as gay lovers—often pornographically—in fantasy scenarios produced by and for a community of predominantly heterosexual women. See Penley (1992).

32. Hence also Lacan's point that

> [a] drive, insofar as it represents sexuality in the unconscious, is never anything but a partial drive. That is the essential failing [*carence*], namely the absence [*carence*] of anything that could represent in the subject the mode of what is male or female in his being. [Lacan, 1995, p. 276]

This is another way of saying that sexual difference belongs to the order of the Real more than to the Imaginary or Symbolic.

33. Writing very illuminatingly of the object *a*, Žižek continues:

> In Lacanian theory, one usually conceives of the anal object as a signifying element: what effectively matters is the role of shit in the intersubjective economy—does it function as proof to the Other of the child's self-control and discipline, of his complying with the Other's demand, as a gift to the Other . . .? However, prior to this symbolic status of a gift, and so on, the excrement is *objet a* in the precise sense of the non-symbolizable surplus that remains after the body is symbolized, inscribed into the symbolic network: the problem of the anal stage resides precisely in how we are to dispose of this leftover. For that reason, Lacan's thesis that animal became human the moment it confronted the problem of what to do with its excrement is to be taken literally and seriously: in order for this unpleasant surplus to pose a problem, the body must already have been caught up in the symbolic network. [Žižek, 1994, p. 179]

References

Abelove, H. (1993). Freud, male homosexuality, and the Americans. In: H. Abelove, M. A. Barale, & D. M. Halperin (Eds.), *The Lesbian and Gay Studies Reader* (pp. 381–393). New York: Routledge.

Abramson, P. R., & Pinkerton, S. D. (Eds.) (1995). *Sexual Nature, Sexual Culture*. Chicago, IL: University of Chicago Press.

Agamben, G. (1993). *The Coming Community*. M. Hardt (Trans.). Minneapolis, MN: University of Minnesota Press.

Anderson, A. (1998). Debatable performances: Restaging contentious feminisms. *Social Text*, 54: 1–24.

Andreas-Salomé, L. (1916). "Anal" und "Sexual". *Imago*, 4: 249–260.
Anzieu, D. (1989). *The Skin Ego: A Psychoanalytic Approach to the Self*. C. Turner (Trans.). New Haven, CT: Yale University Press.
Bawer, B. (1993). *A Place at the Table: The Gay Individual in American Society*. New York: Poseidon.
Bayer, R. (1987). *Homosexuality and American Psychiatry: The Politics of Diagnosis*, 2nd edn. Princeton, NJ: Princeton University Press.
Berlant, L. (1991). *The Anatomy of National Fantasy: Hawthorne, Utopia, and Everyday Life*. Chicago, IL: University of Chicago Press.
Berlant, L., & Warner, M. (1995). What does queer theory teach us about X? *PMLA*, *110*(3): 343–349.
Bersani, L. (1985). *The Freudian Body: Psychoanalysis and Art*. New York: Columbia University Press.
Bersani, L. (1988). Is the rectum a grave? In: D. Crimp (Ed.), *AIDS: Cultural Analysis/Cultural Activism* (pp. 197–222). Cambridge, MA: MIT Press.
Bersani, L. (1995). *Homos*. Cambridge, MA: Harvard University Press.
Burgin, V. (1992). Fantasy. In: E. Wright (Ed.), *Feminism and Psychoanalysis: A Critical Dictionary* (pp. 84–88). Oxford: Blackwell.
Butler, J. (1991). Imitation and gender insubordination. In: D. Fuss (Ed.), *Inside/Out: Lesbian Theories, Gay Theories* (pp. 13–31). New York: Routledge.
Butler, J. (1993). *Bodies That Matter: On the Discursive Limits of "Sex"*. New York: Routledge.
Butler, J. (1994). Sexual traffic. *differences*, 6 (2–3): 62–99.
Butler, J., & Martin, B. (1994). Cross-identifications. Introduction to a special queer issue of *Diacritics*, 24: 2–3.
Clavreul, J. (1980). The perverse couple. In: S. Schneiderman (Ed. and Trans.), *Returning to Freud: Clinical Psychoanalysis in the School of Lacan* (pp. 215–233). New Haven, CT: Yale University Press.
Coleridge, S. T. (1983). *Collected Works of Samuel Taylor Coleridge*, vol. 7, J. Engell & W. Jackson Bate (Eds). London: Routledge & Kegan Paul.
Copjec, J. (1994). *Read My Desire: Lacan against the Historicists*. Cambridge, MA: MIT Press.
Davidson, A. I. (1987). How to do the history of sexuality: A reading of Freud's *Three Essays on the Theory of Sexuality*. *Critical Inquiry*, *13*(2): 252–277.
Dean, T. (1995). On the eve of a queer future. *Raritan*, *15*(1): 116–134.
Dean, T. (2000). *Beyond Sexuality*. Chicago, IL: Chicago University Press.

Deleuze, G. & Guattari, F. (1983)[1972]. *Anti-Oedipus: Capitalism and Schizophrenia*. R. Hurley, M. Seem, & H. R. Lane (Trans.). Minneapolis, MN: University of Minnesota Press.

Deleuze, G., & Guattari, F. (1987). *A Thousand Plateaus: Capitalism and Schizophrenia*. B. Massumi (Trans.). Minneapolis, MN: University of Minnesota Press.

Derrida, J. (1994). "To do justice to Freud": The history of madness in the age of psychoanalysis. P.-A. Brault & M. Nass (Trans.). *Critical Inquiry*, 20(2): 227–266.

Dollimore, J. (1991). *Sexual Dissidence: Augustine to Wilde, Freud to Foucault*. Oxford: Clarendon.

Dollimore, J. (1998). *Death, Desire and Loss in Western Culture*. Harmondsworth: Penguin.

Ferguson, M. (1994). Fixation and regression in the psychoanalytic theory of homosexuality: a critical evaluation. In: T. F. Murphy (Ed.), *Gay Ethics: Controversies in Outing, Civil Rights, and Sexual Science* (pp. 309–327). New York: Haworth.

Fink, B. (1997). *A Clinical Introduction to Lacanian Psychoanalysis: Theory and Technique*. Cambridge, MA: Harvard University Press.

Flieger, J. A. (1997). Overdetermined Oedipus: Mommy, Daddy, and me as desiring-machine. *South Atlantic Quarterly*, 96(3): 599–620.

Foucault, M. (1978)[1976]. *The History of Sexuality, Vol. 1*. R. Hurley (Trans.). New York: Random House.

Foucault, M. (1983)[1972]. Preface. In: G. Deleuze & F. Guattari (Eds.), R. Hurley, M. Seem, & H. R. Lane (Trans.), *Anti-Oedipus: Capitalism and Schizophrenia* (pp. xi–xiv). Minneapolis: University of Minnesota Press.

Foucault, M. (1997a). An interview with Stephen Riggins. In: P. Rabinow (Ed.), R. Hurley et al. (Trans.), *The Essential Works of Michel Foucault, 1954–1984. Vol. 1, Ethics: Subjectivity and Truth* (pp. 121–133). New York: The New Press.

Foucault, M. (1997b). Sexual choice, sexual act. In: P. Rabinow (Ed.), R. Hurley et al. (Trans.), *The Essential Works of Michel Foucault, 1954–1984. Vol. 1, Ethics: Subjectivity and Truth* (pp. 141–156). New York: The New Press.

Freud, S. (1905d). Three Essays on the Theory of Sexuality. *S.E.*, 7: 135–243. London: Hogarth.

Freud, S. (1912d). On the universal tendency to debasement in the sphere of love. *S.E.*, 11: 179–190. London: Hogarth.

Freud, S. (1919e). A child is being beaten. *S.E.*, 17: 179–204. London: Hogarth.

Freud, S. (1923b). The ego and the id. *S.E., 19*: 12–59. London: Hogarth.
Garber, M. (1995). *Vice Versa: Bisexuality and the Eroticism of Everyday Life*. New York: Simon and Schuster.
Grosz, E. (1995). *Space, Time, and Perversion: Essays on the Politics of Bodies*. New York: Routledge.
Greenberg, D. (1988). *The Construction of Homosexuality*. Chicago, IL: University of Chicago Press.
Hamer, D., & Copeland, P. (1994). *The Science of Desire: The Search for the Gay Gene and the Biology of Behavior*. New York: Simon and Schuster.
Hocquenghem, G. (1972). *Le désir homosexuel*. Paris: Éditions Universitaires.
Hocquenghem, G. (1993)[1972]. *Homosexual Desire*, D. Dangoor (Trans.). Durham, NC: Duke University Press.
In the Family: The Magazine for Gays, Lesbians, Bisexuals, and Their Relations (1997), 3(2): 3.
Isay, R. A. (1996). *Becoming Gay: The Journey to Self-Acceptance*. New York: Pantheon.
Jacoby, R. (1975). *Social Amnesia: A Critique of Conformist Psychology from Adler to Laing*. Boston: Beacon.
Jacoby, R. (1986). *The Repression of Psychoanalysis: Otto Fenichel and the Political Freudians*. Chicago, IL: University of Chicago Press.
Katz, J. N. (1995). *The Invention of Heterosexuality*. New York: Dutton.
Lacan, J. (1965–1966). *Le Séminaire, Livre XIV, La logique du fantasme*, unpublished.
Lacan, J. (1975)[1972–1973]. *Le Séminaire, Livre XX. Encore*. J.-A. Miller (Ed.). Paris: Seuil.
Lacan, J. (1977a)[1958]. The direction of the treatment and the principles of its power. In: A. Sheridan (Trans.), *Ecrits: A Selection* (pp. 226–280). London: Tavistock.
Lacan, J. (1977b)[1960]. The subversion of the subject and the dialectic of desire in the Freudian unconscious. In: A. Sheridan (Trans.), *Ecrits: A Selection* (pp. 292–325). London: Tavistock.
Lacan, J. (1986)[1959–1960]. *Le Séminaire, Livre VII, L'éthique de la psychanalyse*, J.-A. Miller (Ed.). Paris: Seuil.
Lacan, J. (1988)[1955–1956]. *The Seminar, Book II, The Ego in Freud's Theory and in the Technique of Psychoanalysis*, J.-A. Miller (Ed.), S. Tomaselli (Trans.). Cambridge: Cambridge University Press.
Lacan, J. (1989)[1962]. Kant with Sade. J. B. Swenson (Trans.). *October, 51*: 55–75.
Lacan, J. (1992)[1959–1960]. *The Seminar, Book VII, The Ethics of Psychoanalysis*, J.-A. Miller (Ed.), D. Porter (Trans.). New York: Norton.

Lacan, J. (1995)[1964]. Position of the unconscious. In: R. Feldstein, B. Fink, & M. Jaanus (Eds.), B. Fink (Trans.), *Reading Seminar XI: Lacan's Four Fundamental Concepts of Psychoanalysis* (pp. 259–282). Albany, NY: State University of New York Press.

Lacan, J. (1998)[1972–1973]. *The Seminar, Book XX, Encore, On Feminine Sexuality*, J.-A, Miller (Ed.), B. Fink (Trans.). New York: Norton.

Lacan, J., & Granoff, W. (2003)[1956]. Fetishism: The Symbolic, the Imaginary and the Real. *Journal for Lacanian Studies*, 1(2): 299–308.

Laplanche, J. (1976). *Life and Death in Psychoanalysis*. Jeffrey Mehlman (Trans.). Baltimore, MD: Johns Hopkins University Press.

Laplanche, J. (1989). *New Foundations for Psychoanalysis*, D. Macey (Trans.). Oxford: Blackwell.

Laplanche, J. (1997). The theory of seduction and the problem of the Other. L. Thurston (Trans.). *International Journal of Psycho-Analysis*, 78(4): 653–666.

Laplanche, J. & Pontalis, J.-B. (1973). *The Language of Psychoanalysis*. D. Nicholson-Smith (Trans.). New York: Norton.

Laplanche, J. & Pontalis, J.-B. (1986). Fantasy and the origins of sexuality. In: V. Burgin, J. Donald, & C. Kaplan (Eds.), *Formations of Fantasy* (pp. 5–34). London: Methuen.

Lauretis, T. de. (1991). Queer theory: lesbian and gay sexualities—an introduction. *differences*, 3(2): iii–xviii.

Lauretis, T. de. (1994). *The Practice of Love: Lesbian Sexuality and Perverse Desire*. Bloomington, IN: Indiana University Press.

LeVay, S. (1993). *The Sexual Brain*. Cambridge, MA: MIT Press.

LeVay, S. (1996). *Queer Science: The Use and Abuse of Research into Homosexuality*. Cambridge, MA: MIT Press.

Lewes, K. (1988). *The Psychoanalytic Theory of Male Homosexuality*. New York: Simon and Schuster.

Martin, B. (1994). Sexualities without genders and other queer utopias. *Diacritics*, 24(2–3): 104–121.

Miller, D. A. (1991). Anal rope. In: D. Fuss (Ed.), *Inside/Out: Lesbian Theories, Gay Theories* (pp. 119–141). New York: Routledge.

Miller, J.-A. (1996). On perversion. In: R. Feldstein, B. Fink, & M. Jaanus (Eds.), *Reading Seminars I and II: Lacan's Return to Freud* (pp. 306–320). Albany, NY: State University of New York Press.

Penley, C. (1992). Feminism, psychoanalysis, and the study of popular culture. In: L. Grossberg, C. Nelson, & P. A. Treichler (Eds.), *Cultural Studies* (pp. 479–500). New York: Routledge.

Rich, A. (1983). Compulsory heterosexuality and lesbian existence. In: A. Snitow, C. Stansell, & S. Thompson (Eds.), *Desire: The Politics of Sexuality* (pp. 212–241). London: Virago.

Robinson, P. (1993). *Freud and His Critics*. Berkeley, CA: University of California Press.

Rose, J. (1996). *States of Fantasy*. Oxford: Clarendon.

Roudinesco, E. (1990). *Jacques Lacan and Co.: A History of Psychoanalysis in France, 1925–1985*, J. Mehlman (Trans). Chicago: University of Chicago Press.

Rubin, G. (1984). Thinking sex: notes for a radical theory of the politics of sexuality. In: C. S. Vance (Ed.), *Pleasure and Danger: Exploring Female Sexuality* (pp. 267–319). London: Routledge & Kegan Paul.

Salecl, R. (1994). *The Spoils of Freedom: Psychoanalysis and Feminism after the Fall of Socialism*. London: Routledge.

Salecl, R. & Žižek, S. (Eds.) (1996). *Gaze and Voice as Love Objects*. Durham, NC: Duke University Press.

Santner, E. L. (1996). *My Own Private Germany: Daniel Paul Schreber's Secret History of Modernity*. Princeton, NJ: Princeton University Press.

Sedgwick, E. K. (1990). *Epistemology of the Closet*. Berkeley, CA: University of California Press.

Sedgwick, E. K. (1993). *Tendencies*. Durham, NC: Duke University Press.

Shaviro, S. (1993). *The Cinematic Body*. Minneapolis, MN: University of Minnesota Press.

Silverman, K. (1996). *The Threshold of the Visible World*, New York: Routledge.

Stein, E. (Ed.). (1992). *Forms of Desire: Sexual Orientation and the Social Constructionist Controversy*. New York: Routledge.

Sullivan, A. (1995). *Virtually Normal: An Argument about Homosexuality*. New York: Knopf.

Warner, M. (Ed.) (1993). *Fear of a Queer Planet: Queer Politics and Social Theory*. Minneapolis: University of Minnesota Press.

Watney, S. (1988). The spectacle of AIDS. In: D. Crimp (Ed.), *AIDS: Cultural Analysis/Cultural Activism* (pp. 71–86). Cambridge MA: MIT Press.

Weed, E. (1994). The more things change. *differences* 6(2–3): 249–273.

Wodehouse, A. S. P. (1974). Imagination. In: A. Preminger et al. (Eds), *Princeton Encyclopedia of Poetry and Poetics* (pp. 191–198). Princeton, NJ: Princeton University Press.

Yingling, T. E. (1997). Homosexuality and the uncanny: What's fishy in Lacan. In: T. Foster, C. Siegel, & E. E. Berry (Eds.), *The Gay '90s:*

Disciplinary and Interdisciplinary Formations in Queer Studies (pp. 191–198). New York: New York University Press.

Žižek, S. (1994). *The Metastases of Enjoyment: Six Essays on Woman and Causality.* New York: Verso.

CHAPTER THIRTEEN

On sexual perversion and transsensualism

Vernon A. Rosario

As someone trained in the history of medicine as well as a practising child psychiatrist, I have long been concerned with the role that history—particularly the history of sexuality—can, and should, play in clinical practice. For a decade I have been focusing on transgenderism—a relatively new phenomenon in the history of medicine—by drawing upon my historical and theoretical interests in gender and sexuality in order to assist me in psychotherapy with transgendered children, adolescents, and adults. I will start by situating my historical work on "sexual perversion" and then turn to my recent clinical experiences with transgenderism.

Historically, sexual perversion was central to the early development of psychoanalysis at the *fin de siècle*. Sexual inversion or homosexuality remained a vexing challenge to analysts throughout the twentieth century and continues to be a controversial issue at the fringes of the profession due to the work of the National Association for Research and Therapy of Homosexuality (www.narth.com) and the inflexible views of analysts such as Charles Socarides (1995), who continue to insist that homosexuality is a curable perversion. Despite this shameful legacy, psychoanalytic theories can still teach us much about sexual diversity and assist therapists in working with a wide variety of clients struggling with issues of gender and sexuality.

In preparing this essay I struggled to discern a global strategy, a method, a theory that could easily frame my diverse perspectives. I honestly could not find one, but the effort helped bring into focus my disparate approaches: French literary studies, the history of science, medicine, and psychiatry. Above all, the opposition between cultural studies and natural science is difficult to bridge. For years now academics have discussed the "two cultures" schism, at the academic and cultural level (Snow, 1959). For the vast majority of people today, molecular biology and neuroscience are incomprehensible except in their most simplified and distorted mass media representations. Therefore, I regularly have patients coming for a first consultation convinced (by pharmaceutical company direct advertising) that they have a "chemical imbalance" in the brain that they hope I will correct with a pill. Biomedical researchers and clinicians are often so giddy with the rhetoric of numbers and the anonymity of statistics that they become certain of the objectivity of their knowledge and practices. It is here that historical analysis can begin to upset a dangerous scientific confidence or—to put it more positively—that history can offer a different lens for treating scientific myopia.

In the 1970s, the debate on the social construction of science was raging in history of science circles (Hess, 1997). Academics examined the influence of social factors on the methods, knowledge, and progress of science. Given these mediating forces, what is the truth status of a scientific observation or fact? Is scientific objectivity anything other then a micro-social convention? Although the debate was briefly resuscitated by a coterie of conservative scientists in the 1990s with the "science culture wars" (Gross & Levitt, 1994), constructionism has, to some degree, become widely accepted in the history of science.

The same epistemological questions were posed in the 1980s in a new academic discipline: gay and lesbian studies (Allouch, 1998). The opposing camps gathered under the rubrics of "essentialism" versus "constructionism" (Stein, 1992). The issues were: is sexuality, specifically homosexuality, a relatively modern phenomenon—the product of urbanization, industrial capitalism, and the science of psychiatry; or is it a universal phenomenon that can be found in all cultures and throughout history (albeit with a few minor phenomenological variations)? And if homosexuality is a universal and essential phenomenon, is it the result of biological factors, mainly genes and hormones?

Michel Foucault's first volume of the *History of Sexuality* (1990) was the bible for the constructivists. However, Foucault still held biology and other natural sciences in high regard, while being more critical of the social sciences and psychiatry. In the *History of Sexuality*, he tried to establish a dichotomy between good and bad science:

> Throughout the nineteenth century, sex seems to have been incorporated into two very distinct orders of knowledge: a biology of reproduction, which developed continuously according to a general scientific normativity, and a medicine of sex conforming to quite different rules of formation. [...] [T]he one would partake of that immense will to knowledge which has sustained the establishment of scientific discourse in the West, whereas the other would derive from a stubborn will to nonknowledge (Foucault, 1990, pp. 54–55]

David Halperin, one of the most ardent constructivists, who argues for the historicity of sexuality itself, even entertains the possibility of his theories being defeated by biology: "If it turns out that there actually is a gene, say, for homosexuality, my notions about the cultural determination of sexual object-choice will—obviously enough—prove to have been wrong" (Halperin, 1990, p. 49). Halperin's binary perspective—that either constructivism or biology is right—led us to an impasse we had to overcome in the 1990s.

The general American public, including probably the majority of gays and lesbians, is inclined to believe in the genetic essentialism of homosexuality and other behavioural traits (Wishman, 1996). The genetic argument has even been used successfully in courts to press for gay civil rights. However, most thoughtful scientists realize that homosexuality and other human behavioural traits cannot be simply determined by a single gene and that a multitude of organic and environmental factors must have an influence on sexuality. It is equally important to realize that the issue of aetiology, while fascinating, is hardly the sole mystery concerning the immense variety of erotic manifestations—whether the so-called "sexual perversions" or "normal" sexuality. Establishing a genetic aetiology does not help us understand the familial and cultural moulding of an individual's sexuality or guide the therapist in assisting a client with sexual conflicts to adjust socially and psychologically.

Let me return then to the matter of how historical analysis can assist and enrich the psychological approach to patients. Structuralist, poststructuralist, and discursive methods—from Lacan to Foucault to Butler—are invaluable tools in textual analysis. However, in treating a patient, the therapist becomes an accomplice in the evolution or the writing of a text—a text already and always historically and socially intertextual. Therefore, my clinical work teeters between historical and clinical analysis in order to advance the two. The subjects are literature, cultural and professional history, the medical interview, or anamnesis. The method is a reading that is sensitive to the text or the patient's speech and attentive to the cultural, political, familial, and sociological canvas that is its support and medium.

Histories of perversion

The Erotic Imagination: French Histories of Perversity (Rosario, 1997a) is a history of histories. At the most concrete level, it is a history of the nosology of sexual perversion: masturbation, erotomania, fetishism, and sexual inversion. It is also a history of the professional, political, and epistemological development of psychiatry as a discipline that differentiated itself from neurology and alienism (the asylum treatment of the "mentally alienated"). As cultural history, it explores the unusual intellectual and artistic relationship between doctors and writers in France. The literary schools of Naturalism and Realism established ideological and aesthetic connections between novelistic and scientific spheres that were rich and productive to the creative systems of both professions. The most important common link was positivist, Comtian philosophy, which assumed a tight correspondence between the physical, organic, and human sciences based on biological reductionism.

The Erotic Imagination traces the circulation of stories of perversity between patients, doctors, and novelists. The "sexual pervert" recalled his or her family and erotic history to doctors. Doctors then struggled to formulate a sexual identity, an erotic heredity, and a taxonomic linkage with other individuals who shared the patient's erotic predilection. As I have proposed elsewhere, this search for an erotic lineage still remains an aspect of the American obsession with the gay gene (Rosario, 1997b). Doctors listened, collected, and circulated these histories in order to formulate, in turn, their own genealogical and aetiological story—this one stamped with the authority of scientific objectivity.

Unlike physicians today, the nineteenth-century alienist admitted his perplexity, therapeutic impotence, and unrestrained repugnance when confronted by these sexual perverts. He lets them speak at length for want of having a diagnostic label to paste on them. Thus, in the history of sexual perversion we also encounter the evolution of modern medical writing: the role of the clinical interview, the family history, the effort to penetrate and to represent the patient's experience by means of the voice—that of the patient and the doctor. The nineteenth century is a period in the history of medicine when narrative and voice dominate the professional literature. One only has to contrast nineteenth-century medical essays with the vast majority of current medical articles, where numbers, figures, tables, and statistics predominate and the individual is rendered anecdotal and profoundly anonymous behind the curtain of laboratory tests, radiographs, and standardized questionnaires. Lacking these technologies of objectification, alienists searched desperately everywhere for other examples of perversity in order to formulate a theory. They found them in ancient history, in ethnographies of so-called primitives, and in novels. This is the reason for the importance of novelistic characters in sexology and, inversely, the salience of medical cases and scientific theorization in late-nineteenth-century literature. We therefore discover Emile Zola publishing documents on inversion in medical journals and scribbling notes on medical references in the margins of the drafts of his novels.

The Erotic Imagination is above all a history of the individuals who confessed their perversity and struggled to give voice to their sexual desire in order better to understand it. For this reason, I opened each chapter with a character, a case, a voice: Jean Jacques Rousseau the masturbator; Mlle. G*** the erotomaniac; a young invert examined by Jean-Martin Charcot and Valentin Magnan; Marie D*** the cloth fetishist. They are the ones who tell of the complexity of eroticism—a complexity that frightens doctors who, in response, struggle to tame it by means of a general theory relying on biological reductionism. A mechanism of pathologization is certainly in action, but, at the same time, the alienists and, later, the first sexologists, discover that the more they research and analyse perversity in order to distinguish it from the normal, the more the normal appears perverse.

In 1966 George Canguilhem traced the emergence of the concept of the "normal" in nineteenth-century medicine on the basis of statistical representations of populational data (1989). The normal came to be embodied in the statistically "average man", who was a demographic construct rather than any particular person. The "pathological" could therefore be defined as that which statistically deviated from the norm to any arbitrary degree. None the less, the normal man quickly shifted from being a descriptive fiction to a prescriptive reality: individuals were expected to change their behaviour to approximate the presumed salubrious norm. As far as sexuality was concerned, the normal was more of a rhetorical convention than something easily characterizable and measurable. Sexual normality constantly escaped the grasp of doctors. It was perversion, on the contrary, that was far more evident and widespread in the nineteenth century. Each doctor, of course, presented himself as "normal", but never dared confess in what his normality consisted.

It was Freud who pierced this fiction and finally proposed the universality of perversion. In the concluding summary of his *Three Essays on Sexuality* (1905d), he wrote:

> In view of what was now seen to be the wide dissemination of tendencies to perversion we were driven to the conclusion that a disposition to perversions is an original and universal disposition of the human sexual instinct and that normal sexual behavior is developed out of it as a result of organic changes and psychical inhibitions occurring in the course of maturation... [Freud, 1905d, p. 231]

Freud inverted the sexological formulation of the nineteenth century: it is "normal" sexuality that is a perversion of the natural sexual instinct through phylogenetic, historical, and sociocultural forces recapitulated in the psychodynamics of the bourgeois family triad.

I am not asserting that Freud discovered the *truth* of sexuality and perversion, but that he arrived—in that historical moment—at the logical conclusion of a century of sexual research. The sad thing is that, after Freud's death, most of his followers in psychoanalysis minimized or openly negated this conclusion and instead continued to reify perversity, above all homosexuality, as a sexual pathology (Lewes, 1988).

This brings me to my most recent book, *Homosexuality and Science: A Guide to the Debates* (Rosario, 2002). This work analyses the diverse biological and psychiatric approaches to solving the "homosexual problem" in the nineteenth and twentieth centuries. At one point homosexuality was considered the central problem of psychiatry (particularly psychoanalysis) because of the legal, sociological, and theoretical issues it raised. The national media and presidential attention devoted to "gay marriages" in the spring of 2004 indicates that homosexuality remains a crucial social problem in the US. The psychiatric issue in the past two centuries was to understand how people who seemed fairly productive and healthy could be erotically attracted to people of the same sex. The behaviour seemed so "unnatural", so contrary to the presumed reproductive teleology of organisms that, even setting aside unenlightened moral prejudice on the part of physicians, they were sure that some profound biological defect had to be the cause. However, it was not so much the cretins, lunatics, and paranoiacs, nor even debauched aristocrats who really perplexed doctors, but otherwise unremarkable bourgeois men and women with what seemed an erotic monomania. All the reigning theories and methodologies were deployed: hereditary degeneration, endocrinology, teratology, genetics, neurobiology, and, of course, psychoanalysis. But none, even to this day, has solved the great mystery.

Recently, in the USA, the genetic theory dominates on this matter as so many others. Molecular biologist Dean Hamer and his team published two articles that suggest a statistical association between male homosexuality and a locus on the X chromosome (Hamer, Hu, Magnuson, Hu, & Pattatucci, 1993; Hu et al., 1995). Another team of researchers in Toronto later published contradictory results (Rice,

Anderson, Risch, & Ebers, 1999). As of yet, no specific genes have been convincingly shown to explain the familial clustering of homosexuality (Mustanski, Chivers, & Bailey, 2002). Nevertheless, much of the American public, including gays, is convinced that homosexuality is genetic in most cases (Wishman, 1996). Gay civil rights organizations have relied upon the genetic hypothesis to advance the argument that homosexuality, being an unalterable trait, should be protected against discrimination just as physical handicaps and race are. The argument has often been successful despite the warnings of legal analysts such as Janet Halley (1994) that it is weak, in practice and in principle, to base human rights on biological claims. Certainly, a biological basis is not necessary for declaring that religious and political diversity deserve equal protection before the law. Yet, we see repeated the same political rationale of the nineteenth century, when homosexual rights activist Karl Heinrich Ulrichs invoked the enlightenment of science in his combat against social prejudice, Christian morality, and dated laws. Unfortunately, we have not learned the lessons of history: that the biologization of homosexuality was accompanied by its pathologization. Sexual perverts were spared years in prison but condemned to the asylum, or years on the couch. However, I do not want to be taken for a Luddite. Biology can provide us with fascinating information about sexuality. Yet, researchers, as well as the public, must be wary of simplistic hypotheses based on presumptions that have little foundation other than social and historical prejudice.

Encountering transsexualism

I became interested in transsexualism by chance. I met my first transsexual patient in 1993 when I began my clinical rotations after my doctoral hiatus. Mary (not her real name) was a nineteen-year-old woman confined to a locked psychiatric ward. Although she was not assigned as my patient, I saw her every day on the ward and knew a little about her from our regular treatment team rounds. She was solitary, silent, almost autistic. She had short brown hair and boyish clothes that made her look like a tough tomboy. Yet, she hugged a stuffed toy dog as she huddled in a corner of the common room. I began chatting with her one day and she seemed to want to talk. We found a private interview room and after much hesitation, she confessed that her greatest desire was to become a gay man. She knew that this was somewhere noted in her voluminous chart, but no one—including her therapist—wanted to talk about it. Indeed the team, which was in no way homophobic, was uneasy about discussing the issue with her. Some said they knew little about transsexualism and preferred to defer this to an outpatient consultation with an expert. They were also wary of reinforcing what they suspected was a delusion. As one clinician put it: why should she think of herself as a transsexual if she is already interested erotically in men?

Although I had not had any prior experience with transsexuals (in any setting), I was moved by this patient, whose situation resembled so much the psychiatric treatment of homosexuals in the 1950s (or even today in certain places). I met Mary for daily sessions, giving her time to talk about her past and her hopes for the future. I have described her case in detail elsewhere (Rosario, 1996), so I will just point out that by the end of the month her psychotic depression had improved to the point that she was on fewer neuroleptics and she transferred to a half-way house for young adults, where she came out as a female-to-gay-male. Four years later *he* tracked me down, thanks to the Internet, and brought me up to date. He had soon gone on to college where he was passing full time as male, albeit without any hormonal or surgical interventions. He was active in the campus gay student group and was grappling with dating.

Since that experience I became increasingly interested in transsexualism, having discovered the poverty of medical literature on the subject of female to male (FTM) transsexualism. Even twenty years after transsexualism entered the *Diagnostic and Statistical Manual* (American Psychiatric Association, 1980), many transsexuals continue to encounter hostility or rigid models of transsexualism within the medical profession. For decades, since transsexualism first came to medical and world attention in the 1950s, transsexuals were expected to fit rigid models of "normal" gender roles in order to earn medical treatment or even an empathic ear. Transsexual subjects learned early what these diagnostic criteria were and simply parroted back the approved history in order to gain a psychological stamp of approval. In this process the medical model was confirmed, but our knowledge of the phenomenology of transsexualism became reified around a medical fantasy. The *Standards of Care for Gender Identity Disorders* published by the Harry Benjamin International Gender Dysphoria Association (2001) have evolved significantly in the past decade, in part because of input from transsexual activists. This evolution should not be interpreted whiggishly as our gradual arrival at the "right" concept of transsexualism, rather as an indication of the historically dynamic character of the phenomenon of transsexualism and the nosological confusion from which it emerged.

The nosological history of transsexualism

The history of transsexualism *per se* is a relatively brief one, yet the notion and phenomenon of gender atypicality has long been interwoven in the history of sexual perversion, particularly inversion. Briefly, the standard medical history of inversion or psychosexual hermaphroditism begins in Germany in the mid nineteenth century under the names *conträre Sexualempfindung* (contrary sexual sensation) or *Uranismus*. In 1878 the Italian forensic doctor, Arrigo Tamassia rendered the former as *inversione dell'istinto sessuale* (inversion of the sexual instinct). This was translated into French in 1882 by Jean Martin Charcot and his disciple Valentin Magnan as *inversion du sens génital* (inversion of the genital sense). They represented it as one among many diverse manifestations of "perversion of the genital sense". Although Charcot and Magnan likened inversion to erotic fetishism (named five years later by Alfred Binet [1887]), inversion evolved as a distinct entity. The diagnosis, as I noted earlier, became synonymous with homosexuality—also first defined by German experts.

If we now reread these original texts on perversion and inversion, we find that the inverts' symptoms and erotic traces do not fit easily into our current diagnostic boxes. The first invert patient described by Charcot and Magnan made the following confession:

> I love female attire; I love to see a woman well dressed, because I tell myself I would like to be a woman to dress similarly. From the age of seventeen, I dressed as a woman during carnival and

experienced an indescribable pleasure in dragging my skirts through rooms, wearing wigs, and going strapless.

Women are amazed at how well I judge the relative good taste of their toilette and to hear me talk about these things, as if I were a woman myself. [Charcot & Magnan, 1882, p. 56]

The patient recounts a history of female identity, dress, and occupations since an early age, and sexual attraction to boys and men since the age of six. Like Karl Heinrich Ulrichs and many other inverts of the nineteenth century, this individual presents a classificatory problem: was he a homosexual or a transsexual? Of course, the question is technically ahistorical. He was neither, since he emerged before either term was in public or professional use. The subject himself thought he was unique in the world! Yet the question is still an important one for excavating a prehistory of transsexualism.

The diagnostic problem becomes even more acute with the description of cloth fetishists by Clérambault and erotic transvestism by Magnus Hirschfeld, both in the same year, 1910. Hirschfeld was one of the first openly homosexual physicians who fought tirelessly for homosexual civil rights and other liberal causes. He distinguished homosexuality as a sexual attraction from what he called "transvestitism": the erotic drive to cross-dress. Many of the cases he described in his volume on transvestitism were individuals (like the case presented by Charcot and Magnan) who we would likely classify today as transsexuals (Hirschfeld, 1910). Hirschfeld (1923) also coined the word "transsexual"; however, he used it to designate manifestations of hermaphroditism, or what he designated an "intersexual constitution" (Pfäfflin, 1997). Along the lines of the inversion model, Hirschfeld proposed that homosexuality was a result of hermaphroditic biology that could be manifested in a spectrum from full masculinity to full femininity (Steakley, 1997). He, as well as the most conservative faction of German homosexual organizations, wished to distinguish masculine from effeminate homosexuals: a political tactic for making the homosexual decriminalization movement more socially appealing.

So it was under this diagnostic label of "homosexual transvestite" that a colleague of Hirschfeld's, Felix Abraham (1931), operated on two patients referred by Hirschfeld himself. Abraham performed the first documented genital transformation (*Genitalumwandlung*) surgery. He reasoned that the surgery completed in the body the transvestism of the two patients who were already psychologically feminized. Christine Jorgensen, who first brought transsexualism to worldwide public attention, was also treated under the diagnosis of "genuine transvestism" by her Danish doctors (Hamburger, Stürup, & Dahl-Iversen, 1953). It was only in the 1960s, thanks to endocrinologist Harry Benjamin and his International Gender Dysphoria Association, that transsexualism became a legitimate diagnosis independent of homosexuality and transvestism, and that hormonal and surgical treatment began to gain legitimacy. This was also a time when psychiatry in the United States was still dominated by psychoanalysts, who in general did not take kindly to Benjamin's somatic approach to treating transsexualism.

To explain this hostility I need to take a brief detour into the centrality of the homosexual "problem" in psychoanalysis. For a lengthier analysis, see Lewes (1988). Freud's *Three Essays on the Theory of Sexuality* (1905d) begins with a discussion of inversion and ends with suggestions on the prevention of inversion. Nevertheless, Freud had a relatively tolerant stance, for the time, on the position of homosexuals in society and the analytic profession (Freud, 1951a; Spiers & Lynch, 1977). His formulation of the famous judge Paul Schreber case (1911c), however, linked paranoia and the repression of homosexual desire and would be the cornerstone for an enduring psychoanalytic legacy of interpreting all homosexuality as paranoid and all paranoia as a symptom of repressed homosexuality (Brill, 1934).

It was along this line of analysis that David Cauldwell (1949) used the term transsexualism, with its current connotations, when he sought to describe a psychotic manifestation in a patient. Alluding to Krafft-Ebing's famous book (1984, first published in 1886), Cauldwell coined the term *psychopathia transsexualis*. Since then, one of the central functions of the psychological evaluations required for sex reassignment hormones and surgery is to distinguish true transsexualism from a "homosexual complex" (Fringet, 2000; Michel & Mormont, 1997). Until only very recently, in the USA, the psychiatric stamp of approval was reserved for individuals who denied all homosexual attraction or, preferably, were homophobic. Ideally, the patient had to aspire to the most stereotypical gender role at the end of sex reassignment treatment. Transsexuals, of course, had long figured this out and told the gate-keeping doctors exactly what they wanted to hear, thus only reaffirming the medical model (Stone, 1991). Female-to-gay-male and male-to-lesbian transsexuals thus remained almost unheard of in medical circles. This tendency was still in force, albeit subtly, when my patient Mary was met with incredulity and suspicion in 1993.

Terminology: sex and gender, identity and role

Much has changed in the professional and public representation of transsexualism since the 1950s. In addressing these developments, let me review some terminology in historical context. Since the 1960s, thanks to feminism and psychologist John Money, it has become second nature in Anglo-American contexts to make a distinction between "sex" and "gender". The former designates the material and biological traits that distinguish male and female, while "gender" designates the socio-cultural and historical traits distinguishing male, female, neuter, or ambiguity. It is important to remember that before this (and still in many other languages) there is no way to make a clear distinction and indeed, historically, none was made. Femaleness came as a package deal including a vagina, breasts, emotionality, maternal instincts, dresses, attraction to men, etc. Any divergence from biological, behavioural, or psychological sex typicality led to suspicions of "inversion" in the nineteenth century. This is part of the reason homosexuality, transvestism, and transsexualism all emerged from the common diagnosis of inversion.

Money made a further distinction between "gender identity" and "gender role" (Money & Ehrhardt, 1972), the first designating how subjects themselves claim to be men, women, or other. Gender role refers to the public presentation of a person as male, female, androgynous, or other. In the 1990s, "transgender" became a broad umbrella term to include a variety of gender atypical roles and identities: for example, transsexuals who seek full sex reassignment, part-time and full time cross-dressers, "she-males" (biological males who acquire breasts and present a female gender role but retain their penis), non-transitioning transsexuals (those who cross gender roles without any hormonal or surgical interventions). Many of the individuals with these newer transgender identities pursue their gender identity and role in a more fluid fashion in their quotidian life and through their lifespan, contrary to the two models of gender fixity: permanent biological sex or complete transsexual gender reassignment.

The new transgender

I have seen several dozen transgendered clients in my psychiatry practice since I met Mary. I have also encountered many new transgendered communities and support groups around the USA and in Europe. Academic studies of transgenderism have also greatly expanded in the past decade. Thanks to these clinical, professional, and social experiences I have grown to appreciate the immense variability in transgender presentations, as well as developmental histories of gender identity, gender role, and sexuality. Generally speaking, there is a generational gender divide among transgenders. Older adults are more likely to fit the official 1960s mould of transsexualism, whereas those who came out in the past two decades have more variable presentations and sex/gender goals.

An example of the challenges facing the younger generation of transgenders is apparent in a client who consulted me recently. She was a thirty-two-year-old woman who had just started testosterone treatment. Jean had never been a tomboy as a child but always felt different from other children. She recalled being distressed by the feminization of her body during puberty, but she never thought about being or becoming a boy at that time. It was only during college that she began to identify as a lesbian and she sought lesbian lovers and friends in the gay community. Even then she felt ill at ease, especially in sexual relations and erotic uses of her body. It was only at the age of thirty, thanks to a male-to-female transgendered friend, that she began to develop a transgendered identity. Jean decided to begin testosterone treatment and contemplated a mastectomy and later a hysterectomy. However, when she saw me, she remained in a depressed and desperate state because she could not accept never being able to achieve her ideal of a male body—primarily because of the still relatively primitive state of phalloplasties (surgical construction of a penis). She was forced to be content with a body she deemed incomplete, imperfect and between sexes—a body that she instead wished could be strong, muscular, and masculine. This had not stopped her from working out assiduously and pursuing hormonal and surgical interventions. However, her perception of an unachievable corporeal sex led to an inhibition or block in the development of a male identity. She regularly contemplated suicide because of her corporeal dissatisfaction—the impossibility of feeling like a man because she cannot fabricate the masculine body she fantasizes.

I only saw Jean twice as a consultant for her psychiatrist. I suggested to him that he explore with Jean the links she saw between gender identity and sex. Perhaps if she can re-evaluate these and be more flexible about them she could escape her impasse: since she cannot have the perfectly sexed body she wants, she could not imagine being anything other then a sexual monster and, therefore, hopeless. If she could begin to appreciate the sexed imperfections in most (if not all) people and escape her binarized conception of sex and gender, she might begin to find a new accommodation between her sexual being and her body.

Obviously, it is essential to explore patients' histories: the genesis of notions of gender, and the gender roles they and their family play. I try to define with the patient their conception of male and female elements, and their correspondence with the body, its gendered behavior, and family and social roles. It is also important to explore sexual experiences and desires in order to clarify erotic and somatic desiderata.

Instead of proposing a standardized treatment plan, i.e., sex reassignment, I examine with patients the potential hormonal and surgical options and their real and imagined results. Quite importantly, I try to help them understand that sex reassignment requires lifelong maintenance: medications, medical check-ups, and physical manipulation (neophalluses are prone to complications and necrosis, and neovaginas need to be regularly dilated to prevent stenosis). The surgical ideal is the extirpation of disease in order to effect a complete cure; however, hormonal and surgical sex reassignment does not produce a magical transformation. The transformed sex requires far more maintenance than birth sex.

Sexual construction and universal transsensualism

One critical point that Michel Foucault argued persuasively is that sexuality, madness, and deviation—as well as normality—have social and political histories. Another critical tenet is that the social sciences (and I would include the biological and physical sciences) are the result of human activity and therefore are cultural artefacts. This does not obviate the possibility that historical facts and natural truths can be produced by this scientific activity, but these facts retain the traces of social politics and cannot remain truths unless they remain embedded in a vast network of conventions of knowledge and signification.

While Foucault elegantly demonstrated the historical construction of sexuality, he did little to examine the social construction of sex and gender. American feminist scholars have taken up this line of analysis. Judith Butler (1990) advanced a particularly influential radical argument that we do not simply possess a sex, but that everyone is obliged to perform, to reinvent, to repeat sex in every context: at home, at work, in the bathroom, at the beach, etc. This performativity of sex (and not just of gender) is not a matter of conscious or willed manipulation of gender, but a socialized production of sex that is reiterated, involuntary, and obligatory.

Some analysts have interpreted transsexualism as a radical or even ludic manifestation of this sexual performativity. But I believe that this academic formulation is seriously flawed and, worse, trivializes the difficult trajectory of transgendered individuals. Most transsexuals experience a radical unease with the sex–gender system as they experience it in their body (cf. Prosser, 1998; Rubin, 2003). There are some who engage in a critique of that system as a semiotic social network, but many are impelled to pursue some kind of material accommodation (whether vestimentary, hormonal, or surgical) with that system.

Therefore, I would not simply consider transsexualism as transvestism, representation, or radical manipulation of sex. Transgenders do not just amuse themselves with a game of sex–gender, but labour in a construction zone of sex. In an imaginary or material way, their sex is "under construction"—as one of my patients formulated it for me. This is also true, however, for the "normally"-sexed subject. We all live in a sex-construction zone. At all moments we are expected to defend, reinforce, or reconstruct the social edifice of sex.

While I used the terms "gender", "sex", or "sexuality", and while their use is convenient for distinguishing homosexuality (which is a matter of sexual orientation) from transsexuals (where gender identity is questioned), I also have to acknowledge that these terms erect artificial and at times harmful distinctions. Sexuality and gender are intimately intertwined culturally and historically: it was not out of stupidity that Victorian physicians and twentieth-century sexologists imbricated cross-dressing, homosexuality, hermaphroditism, and transsexualism. At certain historical moments and in certain social environments there have been tight associations between the sexual body, sexuality, and gender identity. For the individual subject, any deviation from the perceived or imaginary cultural norm often leads to an almost total confusion between the terms. Examples include a lesbian girl who is worried about appearing too tomboyish—or even that she may be destined to become a transsexual; a young heterosexual male rendered impotent with the fear of being perceived as gay; men worried about the size of their penis, or women who are dissatisfied with the size of their breasts.

We are all struck from time to time with sex-gender neuroses and distress about the normality of sex. However, I do not want to universally pathologize by relying on the notions of neurosis or sexual perversion. I think rather that this sex uncertainty is a productive and transformational moment. Homosexual or heterosexual, women or men, we all have moments or periods in which sex is interrogated and we realize the energy expended in reaffirming our sexual identity. A psychodynamic understanding of an individual's psychosexual development, coupled with a historico-cultural analysis of sexuality can be the most productive approach to sexual diversity (as opposed to sexual perversity). Rather than erecting sturdier walls between the varieties of gender and sexuality—separating the "normal" and the "perverse"—it would be more productive to speak of "transsensualism": an experience of the self that encompasses sex, the genitals, and all the body, erotic fantasy as well as sexual and sexed acts (urinating, walking, self-exhibition, throwing a ball, posture) (cf. Mauss, 1985). We would all be more or less transgendered depending on how rigid and dichotomized sex and gender norms are in a particular historical and cultural context. From this perspective, transgenderism is our common condition and the transsexual is the courageous person who, at this point in time, is in the most anguishing conflict with the scaffolding of our current system of sexual identity.

References

Allouch, J. (1998). Acceuillir les *gay and lesbian studies*. *L'Unbévue*, 11: 145–154.
American Psychiatric Association (1980). *Diagnostic and Statistical Manual of Mental Disorders, Second Edition. (DSM-II)*. Washington, DC: American Psychiatric Press.
Binet, A. (1887). Le fetichisme dans l'amour. *Revue Philosophique*, 24: 143–167, 252–274.
Brill, A. A. (1934). Homoeroticism and paranoia. *American Journal of Psychiatry*, 90: 956–974.
Butler, J. (1990). *Gender Trouble: Feminism and the Subversion of Identity*. New York: Routledge.
Canguilhem, G. (1989)[1966]. *The Normal and the Pathological*. C. Fawcett (Trans.). New York: Zone.
Charcot, J.-M., & Magnan, V. (1882). Inversion du sens génital. *Archives de Neurologie*, 3: 53–60, 296–322.
Cauldwell, D. O. (1949). Psychopathia transexualis. *Sexology*, 16: 274–280.
Clérambault, G. G. de (1910). Passion érotique des étoffes chez la femme. *Archives d'anthropologie criminelle*, 25: 583–589.
Foucault, M. (1990)[1976]. *The History of Sexuality. Volume I: An Introduction*. R. Hurley (Trans.). New York: Vintage.
Freud, S. (1905d). *Three Essays on the Theory of Sexuality*. S.E., 7: 135–243. London: Hogarth.
Freud, S. (1911c). Psychoanalytic notes on an autobiographical account of a case of paranoia (dementia paranoïdes). *S.E.*, 12: 9–79. London: Hogarth.
Freud, S. (1951a)[1935]. A letter from Freud. *American Journal of Psychiatry*, 107: 786–787.
Frignet, H. (2000). *Le transsexualisme*. Paris: Desclée de Brouwer.
Gross, P. R., & Levitt, N. (1994). *Higher Superstition: The Academic Left and Its Quarrels with Science*. Baltimore: Johns Hopkins University Press.

Halley, J. E. (1994). Sexual orientation and the politics of biology: a critique of the argument from immutability. *Stanford Law Review, 46*: 503–568.

Halperin, D. (1990). *One Hundred Years of Homosexuality*. New York: Routledge.

Hamburger, C., Stürup, G. K., & Dahl-Iversen, E. (1953). Transvestism: Hormonal, psychiatric, and surgical treatment. *Journal of the American Medical Association, 152*: 391–396.

Hamer, D., Hu, S., Magnuson, V. L., Hu, N., & Pattatucci, A. (1993). A linkage between DNA markers on the X chromosome and male sexual orientation. *Science, 261*: 321–327.

Harry Benjamin International Gender Dysphoria Association (2001). *Standards of Care for Gender Identity Disorders*, 6th version. www.hbigda.org/socv6.html.

Hess, D. J. (1997). *Science Studies: An Advanced Introduction*. New York: New York University Press.

Hirschfeld, M. (1910). *Die Transvestiten. Eine Untersuchung über den erotischen Verkleidungstrieb mit umfangreichem casuistischem und historischem Material, I-II*. Berlin: Alfred Pulvermacher.

Hirschfeld, M. (1923). Die intersexuelle Konstitution. *Jahrbuch für sexuelle Zwischenstufen, 23*: 3–27.

Hu, S., Pattatucci, A. M., Patterson, C., Li, L., Fulker, D. W., Cherny, S. S., Kruglyak, L., & Hamer, D. H. (1995). Linkage between sexual orientation and chromosome Xq28 in males but not in females. *Nature Genetics, 11*: 248–256.

Krafft-Ebing, R. von (1984)[1886]. *Psychopathia sexualis. Mit besonderer Berücksichtigung der konträre Sexualempfindung*. Reprint of 14th edn. 1912. Alfred Fuchs (Ed.). Munich: Matthes & Seitz.

Lewes, K. (1988). *The Psychoanalytic Theory of Male Homosexuality*. New York: Simon & Schuster.

Mauss, M. (1985)[1936]. Les techniques du corps. In: *Sociologie et anthropologie* (pp. 365–383). Paris: Presses Universitaires de France.

Michel, A., & Mormont, C. (1997). Le Transsexualisme: Considérations générales et prise en charge. *Revue Médicale de Liege, 52*(3): 163–168.

Money, J., & Ehrhardt, A. (1972). *Man & Woman, Boy & Girl*. Baltimore: Johns Hopkins University Press.

Mustanski, B. S., Chivers, M. L., & Bailey, J. M. (2002). A critical review of recent biological research on human sexual orientation. *Annual Review of Sex Research, 13*: 89–140.

Pfäfflin, F. (1997). Sex reassignment, Harry Benjamin, and some European roots. *International Journal of Transsexualism, 1*(2): http://www.symposion.com/ijt/ijtc0202.htm.

Prosser, J. (1998). *Second Skins: The Body Narratives of Transsexuality.* New York: Columbia University Press.

Rice, G., Anderson, C., Risch, N., & Ebers, G. (1999). Male homosexuality: absence of linkage to microsatellite markers at Xq28. *Science 284*: 665–667.

Rosario, V. (1996). Trans [homo] sexuality? Double inversion, psychiatric confusion, and hetero-hegemony. In: B. Beemyn & M. Eliason (Eds), *Queer Studies: A Lesbian, Bisexual, Gay, Transsexual Anthology* (pp. 35–51). New York: New York University Press.

Rosario, V. (1997a). *The Erotic Imagination: French Histories of Perversity.* New York: Oxford University Press.

Rosario, V. (1997b). Homosexual bio-histories: genetic nostalgias and the quest for paternity. In: V. Rosario (Ed.), *Science and Homosexualities* (pp. 1–25). New York: Routledge.

Rosario, V. (2002). *Homosexuality and Science: A Guide to the Debates.* Santa Barbara, CA: ABC-CLIO.

Rubin, H. (2003). *Self-Made Men: Identity and Embodiment among Transsexual Men.* Nashville, TN: Vanderbilt University Press.

Snow, C. P. (1959). *The Two Cultures and the Scientific Revolution: The Rede Lecture.* Cambridge: Cambridge University Press.

Socarides, C. (1995). *Homosexuality: A Freedom Too Far: A Psychoanalyst Answers 1000 Questions About Causes and Cure and the Impact of the Gay Rights Movement on American Society.* Phoenix, AZ: Adam Margrave.

Spiers, H., & Lynch, M. (1977). The gay rights Freud. *Body Politic (Toronto), 33*: 8–10.

Steakley, J. D. (1997). Per scientiam ad justitiam: Magnus Hirschfeld and the sexual politics of innate homosexuality. In: V. Rosario (Ed.), *Science and Homosexualities* (pp. 133–154). New York: Routledge.

Stein, E. (Ed.) (1992). *Forms of Desire: Sexual Orientation and the Social Constructivist Controversy.* New York: Routledge.

Stone, S. (1991). The empire strikes back: A post-transsexual manifesto. In: J. Epstein & K. Straub (Eds.), *Body Guards: The Cultural Politics of Gender Ambiguity* (pp. 280–304). New York: Routledge.

Tamassia, A. (1878). Sull'inversione dell'istinto sessuale. *Rivista sperimentale di freniatria e di medicina legale, 4*: 97–117, 285–291.

Wishman, V. (1996). *Queer by Choice: Lesbians, Gay Men, and the Politics of Identity.* New York: Routledge.

INDEX

Abelove, H., 263–264, 316
Abramson, P. R., 308, 316
Adair, W., 171, 185
Adams, P., 218–219, 221–224, 226, 228–230, 232, 237–238, 243, 257–259
Adorno, T. W., 187, 191, 214
Agamben, G., 271, 316
Alexander, M., 226, 229, 238
Allouch, J., 324, 340
American Psychiatric Association (APA), 10, 16, 26 36, 39, 57, 152, 331, 340
Anderson, A., 309, 316
Anderson, C., 330, 342
Andreas-Salomé, L., 305, 317
Anzieu, D., 315, 317
Appelbaum, A. H., 34, 38
Apter, E., 15–16, 155, 158–159
Arendt, H., 187, 214, 270
Atkinson, T.-G., 237–238

Bailey, J. M., 330, 341
Baker, E. F., 129, 145

Baker, W. L., 145–146
Barzilai, S., 250, 259
Bataille, G., 36–37
Bawer, B., 309, 317
Bayer, R., 262, 317
Beier, K. M., 13, 16
Bercherie, P., 6, 16
Bergman, A., 113, 125
Berlant, L., 267, 269, 315, 317
Bersani, L., 262, 282, 310, 315, 317
Bieber, I., 152, 163
Binet, A., 332, 340
Bion, W. R., 27, 37, 99–102, 104–107
birth, 127, 141–142
bisexuality/bisexual,160, 231, 252, 267, 312
Black, M., 191, 214
Blackman, I., 237–238
Blakley, T. L., 145–146
Braque, G., 173–174
Brennan, T., 223–224, 238
Brill, A. A., 334, 340
Britton, R., 101, 107

343

INDEX

Brown, W., 235, 238
Burgin, V., 298–299, 317
Butler, J., 225–227, 238, 245,
  258–259, 266–268, 273, 301, 307,
  309, 317, 326, 338, 340

Cabanis, P. J. G., 6, 16
Califia, P., 225, 228, 237–238
Canguilhem, G., 328, 340
Cannon-Brookes, P., 171, 185
Caplan, P. J., 13, 16
Carr, A. C., 34, 38
Carter, A., 232, 238
Castanet, H., 15–16
castration complex, 79, 112
Cauldwell, D. O., 334, 340
Charcot, J.-M., 328, 332–333, 340
charity, 59, 62–63, 69, 77
Chasseguet-Smirgel, J., 23–24, 37,
  150, 153, 157, 162, 165, 167–170,
  176, 179–180, 185, 187, 211,
  214
Cherney, S. S., 329, 341
Chivers, M. L., 330, 341
Christoffel, H., 66, 77
Clavreul, J., 311, 317
Cleckley, H., 26, 37
Clérambault, G. G. de, 333, 340
Cocks, J., 235, 238
Coleridge, S. T., 297, 302, 315, 317
Copeland, P., 266, 308, 319
Copjec, J., 310, 317
coprophilia, 22, 26, 151, 307
countertransference, 51–52, 56–57
Cowie, E., 252–253, 259
Creet, J., 227–230, 232, 235, 238
cross-dressing, 45, 52–53, 333, 325,
  339 see also: transvestism
Cubism, 173, 175

Dahl-Iversen, E., 334, 341
Davidson, A., 6, 16, 262, 317
Davis, K., 225–227, 238
De Lauretis, T., 11, 16, 227, 239, 262,
  309–310, 320
Dean, T., 268, 290, 317

death, 86, 90, 94–95, 119–121, 127,
  138–140, 142, 157, 196, 198, 200,
  247, 251, 282, 329
  and sex/sexuality, 195, 273
  drive/instinct, 69, 133, 139–141,
    212, 233
  near-, 104
  of God, 183
  repetitive, 210
  -wish, 244
Degas, E., 174
Deleuze, G., 66, 77, 159, 218, 221,
  229–231, 238, 268, 282–291, 296,
  299, 303, 313–314, 318
Derrida, J., 307, 318
desexualization, 41–42
desire, 4, 27, 32, 44, 62–63, 66–68, 70,
  74–75, 110, 112–119, 121–124,
  133–136, 138, 140–141, 143, 151,
  153–155, 159–161, 167, 176, 180,
  182, 189, 190, 193–194, 198,
  200–206, 209, 211–212, 218–223,
  225, 228–229, 233–235, 242–243,
  248, 250, 254, 256–258, 262–263,
  265, 267, 275–276, 278–280, 296,
  300, 302–307, 309, 313–315,
  330–331, 3343, 337
  maternal, 241–246, 248, 251–258
  see also: maternal fetishism
Deutsch, H., 13, 16, 72, 77, 245
Dicks, H. V., 28, 37
Dollimore, J., 11, 13, 17, 277,
  288–289, 310–311, 318
Downing, L., 15, 17
Drew, H., 226, 238
Duchamp, M., 75, 166, 168, 170–171,
  177–181, 183–184

Ebers, G., 330, 342
Ehrhardt, A., 335, 341
erogenous zone(s), 91–93, 131, 291,
  293–296, 304
erotic, 3, 36, 73
  capability, 36
  control, 93
  desire, 307, 337

excitement/ecstasy/pleasure, 24, 36, 68
experience, 36, 66
fantasy, 339
fetishism, 332–333
"form of hatred", 10, 168, 172
history, 326–329, 332
in connection with lesbian feminism, 160, 225–227
infantile fantasies, 34
literary imagination, 14–15, 157 see also: Sade, von Sacher-Masoch
manifestations, 325
mother, 252, 254
narcissistic drive, 227
object/objectification, 172, 242, 257
transvestism, 333, 336
eroticism, 3, 20, 28, 36, 60, 292, 328
anal, 135, 304–305
and aggression, 21–22, 25–26
auto-, 20, 160, 291–292
of the child, 244, 254, 291 see also: maternal fetishism
skin, 134–135
urethral, 167, 178
Evans, D., 213–214

faeces, 24, 31, 176, 292, 303–305 see also: shit
father–child relationsbip, 42
Feher-Gurewich, J., 190, 214
feminism/feminist(s), 13, 72, 157–158, 160, 181, 183, 217, 219, 222–227, 229–230, 232, 234–237, 245, 251, 254, 267, 288, 290, 307, 309, 335, 338
Ferenczi, S., 138, 144–145
Ferguson, F., 237–238
Ferguson, M., 278, 318
fetishism/fetishist, 43, 60, 62, 70–71, 79, 84, 95–96, 101–102, 109–110, 118–119, 121–122, 127, 138, 145, 150, 155–156, 158, 165–168, 170, 176–177, 179–182, 184–185, 221–222, 228, 230, 241–242, 246, 250–251, 253, 255–257, 275, 326, 328, 332–333
frame as, 174–185
Fine, B. D., 40, 58
Fink, B., 192, 196, 204, 214, 292, 308, 318
Flieger, J. A., 284, 313–314, 318
Flower McCannell, J., 187, 214
Foster, D. A., 156, 163
Foucault, M., 152–154, 159, 161–162, 191–193, 214, 263, 267–269, 271, 282, 285, 287, 299–301, 307–310, 314, 318, 325–326, 338, 340
Freud, S., 6–9, 12–14, 17, 20, 23, 36–37, 40–41, 43, 58, 60, 69–72, 77–82, 84, 86–89, 95–97, 101, 107, 109–112, 118, 124–125, 128–130, 133, 136, 139–141, 144–145, 150–151, 153, 158, 160, 162, 167–168, 170, 172–173, 175, 177–178, 180, 184–185, 190, 193–195, 206–207, 212, 214, 218–219, 222–224, 227–229, 232–234, 236, 238, 241, 243, 245, 252, 254, 256, 259, 261–264, 266, 268, 274–278, 280, 282–283, 285–286, 289–302, 304–307, 310–311, 315, 318–319, 328–329, 334, 340
Frignet, H., 340
Fulker, D. W., 329, 341
Futurism, 173

Galedary, G., 12, 18
Gamman, L., 13, 17
Garber, M., 312, 319
gerontophilia, 4
Gold, R., 152, 163
Goldberg, A., 42–43, 58
Goldwater, R., 173, 185
Gosselin, C., 62, 78
Graham-Dixon, A., 102, 107
Granoff, W., 184–186, 246, 311, 320
Green, R., 152, 163
Greenacre, P., 165, 174–175, 185

Greenberg, D., 308, 319
Grof, S., 142, 145
Gross, P. R., 324, 340
Grosz, E., 315, 319
Guattari, F., 268, 282–291, 296, 299, 303, 313–314, 318

Haag, A., 12, 18
Halley, J. E., 330, 341
Halperin, D., 325, 341
Hamburger, G., 334, 341
Hamer, D., 266, 309, 319, 329, 341
Hare, R., 26, 37
Harpur, T., 26, 37
Harry Benjamin International Gender Dysphoria Association, 334, 341
Hart, L., 127, 145
Hart, S., 26, 37
Hauch, M., 12, 18
Hess, D. J., 324, 341
Hirschfeld, M., 333, 341
Hoagland, S., 234, 239
Hocquenghem, G., 263, 280–283, 289, 305, 308, 312–313, 319
homosexual/homosexuality, 11, 13, 20, 34, 54–55, 60–61, 65, 71, 92, 129–132, 136, 152, 160, 219, 221, 231, 261–266, 271, 275, 278–282, 288, 293, 306–308, 311–312, 314–315
Horkheimer, M., 187, 191, 214
Horney, K., 246–257, 259
Hu, N., 329, 341
Hu, S., 329, 341
Hyatt Williams, A., 165–166, 186

Isay, R. A., 262, 319

Jacobus, M., 247, 251, 258–259
Jacoby, R., 263, 319
Jadin, J.-M., 15, 17
Jardine, A., 223–224, 228–239
Jennings, H., 180
Jones, E., 187, 215

Joseph, B., 99, 101, 104, 106
Jouhandeau, M., 121, 124–125

Kant, I., 233–234, 239, 249, 297, 310
Kaplan, L. J., 13, 17, 158, 162
Karpman, B., 7, 17
Katz, J. N., 308, 319
Kelly, M., 13, 17, 252–256, 259
Kernberg, O. F., 20–24, 26, 28–29, 34, 37–38, 40, 58
Khan, M. M. R., 62, 78, 150, 162
King, K., 237, 239
Klein, M., 220, 232, 239, 245, 247–251, 256, 257–259
Koenigsberg, H. W., 34, 38
Kohut, H., 43, 48, 58
Krafft-Ebing, R. von, 6–7, 15, 17, 151, 162, 241, 260, 264, 341
Kristeva, J., 243, 247–248, 250–251, 258, 260
Kruglyak, L., 329, 341
Kunkle, S., 211, 215
Kuspitt, D., 176, 179, 185–186

Lacan, J., 71, 75–76, 78, 83–84, 89, 97, 112–116, 119, 121, 123, 125, 159, 184–186, 190, 192, 195–199, 203–205, 208, 211–213, 215, 233–234, 236–237, 239, 242–244, 247–251, 253, 255–256, 258–316, 319–320, 326
Laclau, E., 188, 215
Lamacz, M., 12, 17
Lantéri-Laura, G., 5, 17, 59, 78
Laplanche, J., 130, 145, 213, 215, 262, 300, 302, 310–312, 320
Le Brun, A., 119–122, 125
LeVay, S., 266, 308, 320
Levinas, E., 161–162
Levitt, N., 324, 340
Lewes, K., 13, 17, 263, 320, 329, 334, 341
Li, L., 329, 341
Limentani, A., 136, 145
Lippard, L., 179, 186
Lohse, H., 12, 18

Lowen, A., 129–130, 146
Lucy, J., 226, 239
Lukes, S., 191, 215
Lussier, A., 22–23, 38
Lynch, M., 334, 342

Magnan, V., 328, 332–333, 340
Magnusen, V. L., 329, 341
Magritte, R., 173–174
Mahler, M. S., 113, 125
Makinen, M., 13, 17
Malcolm, J., 252, 260
Manet, E., 175, 180
Marmor, J., 152, 163
Martin, B., 301, 307, 320
Masson, J. M., 86, 88, 97, 252. 260
masturbation, 20, 27, 42, 54–55, 72, 110, 120, 132, 292, 304, 326, 327
maternal fetishism, 159, 241–259
Mauss, M., 339, 341
Mavor, C., 252, 260
McDougall, J., 10–11, 17, 152, 163, 237, 239
Meltzer, D., 24, 27, 38
Michel, A., 334, 341
Miller, D., 315, 320
Miller, J.-A., 198, 215, 311–312, 320
Millot, C., 218–222, 232, 239
Mitchell, P., 171, 186
modernism/modernist, 166–167, 170–174, 177–180, 183–184
Modleski, T., 229–230, 232, 239
Money, J., 4, 9, 12, 17, 59, 78, 335, 341
Montherlant, H. de, 117–118, 125
Moore, B. E., 40, 58
Moreau de Tours, P., 6, 17
Mormont, C., 334, 341
mother–child relationship, 252, 254–255
mother–child–phallus, 115, 117
Mouffe, C., 188, 215
Mulvey, L., 155, 163, 255, 258–260
Mustanski, B. S., 330, 341

Nagel, T., 224, 239
necrophilia, 22, 151, 242, 307
"neo-sexualities", 11, 237
Nietzsche, F., 224, 235, 239, 282, 289, 314
normophilia, 4, 10, 59

object relations/relationship, 13, 21–22, 24–25, 28–30, 36, 113, 244, 246–249, 251, 291
oedipal, 11, 21, 32, 45, 57, 64, 94, 104, 110–112, 171, 190, 208, 218–221, 236, 243, 246
  attack, 179
  child, 175, 236
  conflict(s), 21, 23, 25, 45, 256
    genital, 23
  couple, 32
  fantasy, 169
  father, 34
  law, 247
  mother, 30, 184
  phantasm, 250
  post-, 219, 245, 251
  pre-, 21, 23, 25, 94, 166, 169, 182, 220–221, 243, 245, 251, 253, 256–257, 259, 281, 283–284
  aggression, 23, 25, 32
  mother, 34
  sexuality, 169
  system, 205–206, 208, 210–211
  wishes, 23
Oedipus complex, 23, 63, 65, 110, 116–117, 185, 206–207, 218–220, 231, 244, 247, 251, 258, 285
  Anti-, 283–284, 296, 312–313
Oosterhuis, H., 6, 17
orgasm/orgasmic, 5, 9, 21–22, 25, 31–32, 63, 106–107, 127, 135–145, 237
  anxiety, 139–140

paedophilia, 8, 22, 26, 35, 117–118, 242, 244
paraphilia(s), 4, 9–10, 19, 39, 59, 128, 150

Pattatucci, A., 329, 341
Patterson, C., 329, 341
penis, 13, 24, 33, 62–64, 66–67,
  71–72, 95, 101–102, 112–113,
  116, 118, 132, 178, 180, 218, 291,
  294, 304, 336–337, 339
Penley, C., 315, 320
Perrier, F., 246
Perry, B. D., 145–146
Perry, K., 237–238
perverse femininity, 71–74
Pfäfflin, F., 333, 341
phallus, 65, 71, 73, 79, 93–94, 110,
  112–120, 122–124, 182, 218–222,
  228–229, 237, 243, 246, 249, 290,
  292, 302–308, 337
Picasso, P., 166, 173–177, 179
Pine, F., 113, 125
Pinkerton, S. D., 308, 316
piss *see*: urine
Plaza, M., 244, 260
Pollard, R. A., 145–146
Pontalis, J. B., 130, 145, 213, 215,
  300, 302, 311–312, 320
primitivism, 173
Prosser, J., 338, 342

queer theory, 154, 159, 261–264,
  266–272, 274, 276, 279, 281,
  285–290, 294, 301, 307, 309–310

Rank, O., 141–142, 146
Réage, P., 68, 78
Reich, W., 128–131, 133–142,
  144–146, 285
Rey-Flaud, H., 12, 17
Rice, G., 330, 342
Rich, A., 270, 321
Rich, B. R., 217, 237, 239
Risch, N., 330, 342
Riviere, J., 220, 237, 239
Roberts, L., 171, 186
Robinson, P., 308, 321
Rosario, V. A., 15, 18, 155, 159–160,
  162, 326–327, 329, 331, 342
Rose, J., 252, 260, 315, 321

Rosenfeld, H., 27, 38
Rothenberg, M. A., 156, 163
Roudinesco, E., 259–260, 284,
  312–313, 321
Rubin, G., 152, 163, 307, 321, 338,
  342

Sacher-Masoch, L. von, 241, 260
Sade, D. A. F. de/Sadean, 15, 95, 97,
  119–123, 125, 153, 187, 198,
  204–205, 210–211, 215, 230–237,
  239, 275, 306, 311
sadomasochism
  (s/m)/sadomasochistic, 22, 26,
  142, 182, 224, 235
  lesbian, 217–218, 225, 237, 242
Salecl, R., 295, 321
Samois, 219, 225–226, 229, 239
Santner, E. L., 315, 321
Schorsch, E., 12, 18
Schrim, J., 225, 239
Sedgwick, E. K., 160, 163, 264, 276,
  301, 321
Seltzer, M. A., 34, 38
sexual, 6, 12–14, 19, 133, 153, 180,
  294, 305
  "abnormality", 5, 7
  aggression/aggressive, 166
  aim/object, 7–9, 242, 278, 306, 314
  and the visual, 177
  areas, 24 *see also*: zonal confusion
  behaviour(s), 5, 7, 20–23, 25, 34,
    42–43, 46, 51, 59, 94, 99,
    143–144, 150–151, 190, 268
  child, 252
  deviance, 12
  deviation and fascism, 187–189,
    212
  difference/differentiation, 65, 79,
    158, 169, 180, 264–265, 288, 305,
    307, 316
  diversity, 162, 226, 301, 324
  dysfunctions, 5
  encounter/interaction/
    intercourse/activity, 21, 23, 33,
    35, 63, 137, 143, 262

enjoyment/excitement/
    pleasure/experience, 20–22,
    65, 104, 143, 161, 166,
    221
eroto-, 10
exclusiveness, 278, 280
exhibitionism, 22, 66–67
experimentation, 8
fantasy/phantasy, 5, 20–22, 27,
    29–30, 103–104, 149, 165–166,
    268–269
fetishism, 22, 70–71
transvestism, 22
freedom, 28
identity, 5, 27, 160, 267–269, 274,
    279
inhibition, 25, 28, 32, 36
instinct/drive, 6–8, 212, 262, 275,
    306
  anomalies of:
    anaesthesia, 6
    hyperaesthesia, 6
    paradoxia, 6
  masochism, 22, 67–69, 104–107,
    135–136, 138, 142, 182, 237
    see also: sadomasochism
    feminine, see: perverse
    femininity
minorities, 269
murderers/serial killers, 26
normality, 9–10, 19, 128, 149, 165,
    192, 270
object, 21, 24, 30, 152, 233, 262,
    306, 325
orientation, 5, 157, 265, 267,
    278–279, 291, 308–309
paraesthesia, 6
pathology, 15, 26, 51, 277
perversion(s), 27–35, 39, 41–43,
    45–46, 50–52, 54–55, 57,
    59–63, 129, 153, 204–205,
    299, 314, 323, 326 see also:
    paraphilia
    and jealousy, 63–65
politics, 223, 262, 269–270
power, 11

repression/frustration, 139–140,
    182
sadism, 22, 67–70, 138, 142, 182
    see also: sadomasochism
scenario, 24, 42, 138
    pregenital, 23
science, 161
trauma, 145, 177
voyeurism, 22, 66–67
Shaviro, S., 314, 321
shit/turd, 301–302, 305–306, 316
    see also: faeces
Silverman, K., 310, 321
Snow, C. P., 324, 342,
Socarides, C. W., 136, 146, 152–153,
    163, 323, 342
Spiers, H., 334, 342
Spitzer, R. L., 152, 163
Spivak, G., 224, 235, 240
Steakley, J. D., 333, 342
Stein, E., 308, 321, 324
Steiner, J., 101–102, 107
Stekel, W., 5, 18
Stokes, A., 182, 186
Stoller, R. J., 10, 18, 21–22, 38, 45, 58,
    62, 65, 78, 127, 137, 145–146,
    150–152, 158, 163, 168, 174, 186,
    246
Stone, M. H., 26, 38
Stone, S., 335, 342
Stürup, C. K., 334, 341
Sullivan, A., 309, 321
Surrealism/Surrealist, 173, 180

Tamassia, A., 332, 342
Totton, N., 128, 133, 146
transference, 41–42, 45, 47–51,
    53–54, 56–57
    dual, 47–51, 56, 246
    father–daughter, 223
    love, 251
transgendered, 159, 267, 323,
    335–336, 338–340
transsexual, 267, 269, 330–336,
    338–340
Tsang, D. C., 12, 18

urine, 178–179, 305
urophilia, 22

vagina/vaginal, 24, 71–72, 176, 254, 291, 335
Valas, P., 6, 18
"vanilla" intercourse, 160, 225
Vedrenne, E., 171, 186
Verhaeghe, P., 75, 78, 196, 215
Vigilante, D., 145–146

Ward, I., 183, 185–186
Warner, M., 267, 269–270, 272, 285, 317, 321
Watney, S., 314–315, 321
Weaves, S., 225, 240

Weber, M., 191, 215
Weed, E., 307, 321
Welldon, E. V., 245–247, 260
Whitebook, J., 156, 163, 169, 184, 186, 193, 207, 215
Wilson, G., 62, 78
Wishman, V., 325, 330, 342
Wodehouse, A. S. P., 297, 321

Yingling, T. E., 261, 321

Žižek, S., 156, 163, 187–188, 205, 211, 215, 295, 298, 303, 315–316, 321–322
zoophilia, 22, 242